Great Britons of Stage and Screen

Great Britons of Stage and Screen

In Conversation

Barbara Roisman Cooper

ROWMAN & LITTLEFIELD
Lanham • Boulder • New York • London

Published by Rowman & Littlefield
A wholly owned subsidary of The Rowman & Littlefield Publishing Group, Inc.
4501 Forbes Boulevard, Suite 200, Lanham, Maryland 20706
www.rowman.com

Unit A, Whitacre Mews, 26-34 Stannary Street, London SE11 4AB

British Library Cataloguing in Publication Information Available

Library of Congress Cataloging-in-Publication Data

Roisman Cooper, Barbara, 1941–
  Great Britons of stage and screen : in conversation / Barbara Roisman Cooper.
    pages cm
  Includes bibliographical references and index.
  ISBN 978-1-4422-4620-1 (hardback : alk. paper) — ISBN 978-1-4422-4621-8 (ebook)
1. Actors—Great Britain—Interviews. 2. Actresses—Great Britain—Interviews. 3.
Motion picture actors and actresses—Great Britain—Interviews. I. Title.
  PN2597.R65 2015
  792.02'8—dc23
                                                                        2015012649

♾™ The paper used in this publication meets the minimum requirements of
American National Standard for Information Sciences—Permanence of Paper
for Printed Library Materials, ANSI/NISO Z39.48-1992.

Printed in the United States of America

For my husband, Martin,
and
my parents,
Helen and Isadore Roisman

Contents

~

Foreword

Few, if any, can hold a candle to Barbara Roisman Cooper, the author of this fascinating book, *Great Britons of Stage and Screen: In Conversation*, when it comes to asking the kind of questions you'd want to pursue if you were spending thirty minutes or three hours visiting over several cups of tea with Dame Angela Lansbury, Simon Callow, or Jeremy Irons, who are but three of twenty-two Brits she has interviewed at length for this impressive volume.

One of the many things that makes Cooper such a consummate interviewer is her passion for her subjects. Although California born, she is the personification of a dedicated Anglophile, having made some seventy-two visits to England since 1965, her interest in all things British initially triggered by Sherlock Holmes, although as she has said, "Once on British soil, I fell in love with the museums, the theatre, the stately homes and castles, and, especially, the people." Indeed, that initial love for Sherlock still lingers: she has been attending the events of the Baker Street Irregulars for more than twenty years and was officially invested as a BSI in 2008; she also belongs to and attends the events of the Sherlock Holmes Society of London.

The love she has for England extends to the British theatre and film and the constellation of actors who inhabit those institutions. It's the high regard she has for these magical worlds that has triggered this engaging book.

You'll immediately discover it is no ordinary work. Her interviews (*conversations* is actually the better word for what she has mastered) are fresh, thoughtful, and illuminating, and bring forth compelling observations from her subjects, which invariably elicit engaging revelations.

It is obvious that those being interviewed trust her. I did, from the first time I met her, and that was some forty years ago, and I fully understand why her latest interview subjects would feel the same. You may have already noted the incredible lineup of achievers she profiles in this volume, which is, hopefully, the first of several by Cooper that will feature a wide variety of professionals, from those known to those equally talented artists and crafts-people who contribute behind the curtain and camera.

This time her focus is aimed, with a sure hand, on such British stage lumi-naries as Sir Derek Jacobi, Dame Eileen Atkins, Stephen Greif, and Stephen Fry, along with many best known for their film and/or television work: Jean Simmons, Michael York, Peggy Cummins, and Dame Joan Collins.

Included in the formidable group are many who are celebrated worldwide for their work on stage *and* screen, among them Sir Ben Kingsley, David Suchet, Alfred Molina, Richard Todd, Felicity Kendal, Isla Blair, Dame Eileen Atkins, and Julian Glover, plus, of course, the aforementioned Dame Angela and Messrs. Callow and Irons.

What comes out of this kind of information only surfaces when trust is accompanied by truth, along with the confidence that discretion will be used if any revelations might accidentally slip out. Cooper, bless her, is not out to shock or embarrass in that irritating way that seems to be the norm in our twenty-first-century world. She's a pro, here for the long run and here to entertain, yes, but more importantly to further bringing to life the backgrounds, attitudes, private thoughts, and reminiscences of these extraor-dinary individuals.

Bravo, Barbara.

—Robert Osborne
Host, Turner Classic Movies

~

Preface

Laurence Olivier made me do it!

In 2007, I attended the unveiling of sculptor Angela Conner's statue of Laurence Olivier as Hamlet in the forecourt of the Royal National Theatre on London's South Bank. The bronze sculpture of the great actor commemorates both the centennial of his birth and his role as the National's founding director.

I had a chance meeting at the event with actor Stephen Greif, who, I discovered, has had a career of more than four decades and continues to be active in theatre, film, television, and radio. I realized that I had seen him on the London stage in *Fallen Angels* with Felicity Kendal and in an episode of the iconic *Dr. Who*. Who knew?

Wouldn't it be interesting to interview him for a theatre- or film-related publication? Shouldn't he be recognized for his body of work? There must be others whose names aren't in the forefront of the theatre-going public but whose names appear further down in film credits. They certainly have untold stories which deserve recounting.

And so began the journey to tell their stories.

After an extensive discussion about the possible project, Greif referred me to colleagues, who then generously referred me to their associates; others responded to my written requests for interview.

Interview venues took me to backstage greenrooms and dressing rooms, homes, private clubs, film studios, and restaurants. I ventured to towns and villages across the United Kingdom: Waltham Cross, Amersham, Norwich,

Pluckley, Grantham, and Sevenoaks, as well as New York and Los Angeles. There was a walk in a bluebell-blooming garden, a drive through the flowering countryside, and a luncheon at a high-volume bistro.

This project includes some of the names on theatre marquees and above-the-title in films. Without exception, these professionals were gracious, generously giving of their time, and candidly offering previously untold anecdotes about their careers and colleagues.

Sadly, several of those I interviewed have taken a final curtain call, but their words and work are still in the spotlight.

They are all truly Great Britons.

So thank you, The Right Honourable The Lord Olivier, OM.

And thank you, Stephen Greif.

~

Acknowledgments

My initial acknowledgments must go to the actors whom I interviewed for this project. Their time and interest were more than I could have expected.

Theatre archivists, librarians, agents, grammar school and university archivists, personal assistants, press officers, photographers, business associates, and friends, both in the United States and the United Kingdom—to them, bravos, bravas, bows, and curtsies: Alexandra Aslett, Librarian and Archivist, St. Paul's School; John Bacon, Director, Planned Giving, New York Public Library; Samantha Bain, Administration and Events Manager, New Wimbledon Theatre; Justin Bickersteth, Registrar, Highgate Cemetery; Anne Bradley, Archivist, Bristol Grammar School; Angela Bray, Personal Assistant to David Suchet; British Film National Archive: Vic Pratt, Fiction Film Curator; Laura Butler, Press and PR Officer, Yvonne Arnaud Theatre, Guildford, and Dan McWilliam, Head of Sales and Marketing; Caroline Brown, Archive Services, University of Dundee; California Rail Road Museum: Cara Randall, Librarian, and Kathryn Santos, Archivist; Daryl Cameron, Chief of Staff, British Consulate General, Los Angeles; Alan Capper; CART Founder-Director Peggy Webber and Allen Eckhouse, Public Relations; David Chadderton, Editor, British Theatre Guide; Caitlin Collins, Deliberate PR; Giles Conisbee, Head of Marketing, Pitlochry Festival Theatre; Catherine Cooke, Senior Business Systems Analyst, Information Services, Marylebone Library; Anne Cooper, Farnham Theatre Association, Ltd.; Rebecca Crigler, Lucille Lortel Foundation; Jo Crocker, PA to Stephen Fry; Logan Culwell, Playbill Vault; Billie Curran, PA to Felicity Kendal; Kathryn

Darling, Corporate Communications Officer, University of London; Dori Dalton, Information Specialist, Santa Fe, New Mexico, Chamber of Commerce; Mairéad Delaney, Archivist, Abbey Theatre; Christine De Poortere, Peter Pan Director, Great Ormond Street Hospital Children's Charity; Judith Devereaux, PA to the late Richard Todd; Marc Di Sotto, Enquiries Assistant, Reference Services, National Library of Scotland; Darren Dalglish and Bona Ruocco, editors, LondonTheatre.co.uk, whose brilliant website kept me up to date on productions, casting, and more; Nick Davison, Press Officer, University of Greenwich; Jane Dore, Information Librarian, Worthing Public Library; Lesley Dye, Marketing and Communications Officer, University of Hull; Roni Ellis, Salford Arts Theatre; A. Nicholas Fargnoli, PhD, President, James Joyce Society, Professor of Theology and English Literature, Molloy College, Rockville Centre, New York; Hannah Falvey, Administrator and Assistant to the Artistic Director, Regent's Park Open Air Theatre; Karen Fisher, Associate Producer, Theatre Royal Stratford East; Dena Flekman, Corymore Corp.; Sir Christopher Frayling, former Rector, Royal College of Art; Erik Garcia, Marketing Associate, International City Theatre, Long Beach, California; Martin Gostanian, Visitor Services Supervisor/Senior Researcher, Paley Center for Media, Los Angeles; Duncan Gilmour, Director, Corporate Affairs and Company Secretary, James Finlay, Ltd.; Derek Graham, Memberships Manager, Nottingham Playhouse; Andrew Granath, Latymer School; Tracy Granger; Hampstead Theatre: Charlie Griffiths, Press Assistant, and Becky Paris, Marketing Manager; Daniel Handler (a.k.a. Lemony Snicket); Juliet Handley, Development Manager, Wellington School; Janice Headland, former Archivist, BFI Library; John W. Henderson, Henderson's Film Industries; Patrick Hoffman, Director, Theatre, Film and Tape Archive, New York Public Library for the Performing Arts; Billy Rose Theatre Division: Thomas Lisanti, Manager, Permissions and Reproduction Services; Jeremy Megraw, Photograph Librarian; Doug Reside, Curator; Jessica Hogg, Archives Researcher, BBC Written Archives Center; Dr. Jan-Christopher Horak, Director, UCLA Film and Television Archive; David Howells, Curator, RSC Collection; Jason Joiner, Showmasters, Ltd.; Roison Iremonger, PA to Managing Director, Gaiety Theatre, Dublin; Phil Jackson, Theatre Manager, Minack Theatre, Cornwall; Shaunagh Kirby, Head of Communications, University of Aberdeen; Leslie S. Klinger; Doris Koplik, Director, Media Relations, Long Beach (California) Opera; Dr. Christopher Lee, Program Leader, Film Studies, School of Arts and Media, University of Salford; Bryan Lewis, Operations Manager, Aldwych Theatre; Diane Lyle, Chair, Friends of Ludlow Arts Festival.

Also Max Miller Appreciation Society; Rachel Marriner, Customer Services, West Yorkshire Playhouse; Aoife McGrane, Office Administrator, Gate Theatre, Dublin; Tanya McKee, BBC Audience Services; Claire Mckendrick, Chief Library Assistant, Special Collections, University of Glasgow Library; John Minoprio; Maria Morris, History Assistant, Oxfordshire History Centre; Royal National Theatre: Lucinda Morrison, Head of Press; Laura Hough, Assistant to Directors; Erin Lee, Archive Manager; Gavin Clarke, Archivist; Elena Carter, Claire Brunnen, and Georgia Butler, Archive Assistants; Katy McGahan, Curator Nonfiction, Curatorial Unit, BFI; Rosie Money-Coutts, PA to Paul Lyon-Maris, Independent Talent; Nick Munagian, Library Assistant, McCormick Library of Special Collections, Northwestern University, Evanston, Illinois; Ellen Murphy, Senior Archivist, Dublin City Archives; Mike Park, University Photographer, Marketing and Communications, University of Hull; Debbie Plentie, Press and Public Relations Manager, CFT; Mandy Pover, Archives Assistant, City Central Library, Stoke-on-Trent; Colleen Quigley, Manuscripts Librarian, Performing Arts Collection, Queen Elizabeth II Library, Memorial University, Newfoundland, Canada; Mandy Rees, Voice and Speech Trainers Association; Christina Rice, Senior Librarian, Photo Collection, Los Angeles Public Library; Caroline Richardson, General Manager, Norwich Playhouse; Beccy Rimmer, Marketing Manager, Soho Theatre; Brian Robinson, BFI Communications Manager, Archive and Heritage; Mary-Louise Rowland, Deputy Archivist, Hurstpierpoint College; Silke Ronneburgh, Deutsche Kinemathek, Museum für Film und Fernsehen, Berlin; Rosy Runciman, Archivist, Cameron Mackintosh, Ltd., and Delfont Mackintosh Theatres, Ltd.; Ellie Samuels, *Spotlight*; Stephanie D. Savage, Grants and Programs Coordinator, the Lyndon Baines Johnson Foundation, Austin, Texas; Nadiah Scamell, Press Officer, Queen's Theatre, Hornchurch; Adrian Shindler, Humanities Reference Service, the British Library; David F. Silver, President, International Photographic Historical Organization; Ed Stratmann, Associate Curator, Motion Picture Collection, George Eastman House; Michael Sweeney, Deputy Chairman, Oscar Wilde Society; Theatre Royal Bath: Christine Bayliss, Archivist; Emma McDermott, Press Officer; Graeme Savage, Marketing Officer; Sherborne School: John Harden, Secretary, Old Shirburnian Society, and Rachel Hassall, School Archivist; Fiona Tait, Archivist, Library of Birmingham; Hilary Thomas, Registrar and Director, National Film and Television School, UK; Simon Thompson, Press Manager, Lyric Hammersmith; Peter Thorley, Corporate News Officer, University of Leicester; James Thornton, Library Manager, RADA; Peter Thorley, Corporate News Officer, University of Leicester; Lynne Truss; Emma Tugman, Theatre Administrator,

Harrogate Theatre; Alice Udale-Smith, Editor, *Varsity,* Cambridge University; University of Bristol Theatre Collection: Laura Gardner, Keeper, Theatre Archives; Jill Sullivan, Archive Assistant.

As well as Simon Vaughan, Archivist, Alexandra Palace Television Society; Fiona Wilkins, PA to Simon Callow; Kathy Williams, US West Coast Liaison, Noël Coward Society; A. B. Wilman, St. Michael's Players.

Some institutions and individuals deserve separate bows and kudos: Linda Harris Mehr, Director, Academy of Motion Picture Arts and Sciences' Margaret Herrick Library, and her staff, with special appreciation to Sandra Archer, Head of Reference Services; Stacey Behlmer, Coordinator of Special Projects and Research Assistance; Jenny Romero, Research Archivist; Lucia Schultz, Authority Control Librarian; and Libby Wertin, Reference Librarian; the executive staff at the Hyatt Regency London—The Churchill, especially, Michael Gray, General Manager, Area Director United Kingdom and Ireland; Jorge De Jesus, former Executive Assistant Manager, Rooms; and Hamdi Banoha, Head Concierge. A special tribute to Rob Wilton Theatricalia, who always had time to fact-check theatrical names, dates, and theatres from his enormous theatre program collection and patiently answered innumerable questions about productions; Robert Osborne, TCM host, a personal friend, whose passion for, and knowledge of, film is unparalleled; Kevin Brownlow, Photoplay Productions, for his dedication to preserving and restoring silent films and for his generous offer of time, advice, and interest in this project, not to mention his incomparable knowledge of early film.

And to Stephen Greif: had I not fortuitously met him, there would be no *Great Britons*. His unstinting belief in the project is most appreciated.

Abbreviations

AD	assistant director
ARP	Air Raid Precautions
ASM	assistant stage manager
BAFTA	British Academy of Film and Television Arts
BAM	Brooklyn Academy of Music, Harvey Theatre, New York
BBC	British Broadcasting Company
BFI	British Film Institute
CBE	Commander of the Order of the British Empire
CFT	Chichester Festival Theatre
DBE	Dame Commander of the Most Excellent Order of the British Empire
ENSA	Entertainments National Service Association
HUAC	House Un-American Activities Committee
ITV	Independent Television (now Channel 3)
KBE	Knight Commander of the Most Excellent Order of the British Empire
LAMDA	London Academy of Music and Dramatic Art
MBE	Most Excellent Order of the British Empire
NT	National Theatre, London
OBE	Officer of the Order of the British Empire
RADA	Royal Academy of Dramatic Art
RAF	Royal Air Force
ROH	Royal Opera House
RSC	Royal Shakespeare Company

RST   Royal Shakespeare Theatre, Stratford
SAG   Screen Actors Guild
SMT   Shakespeare Memorial Theatre

CHAPTER ONE

∼

Dame Eileen Atkins, CBE

It's astonishing how often people buy tickets not having a clue what they're going to see.

Dame Eileen arrived early at the Hyatt Regency London—The Churchill for the interview. The lounge is abuzz with conversation and clinking glasses. A bit too cocktail-boisterous for an intimate discussion, and, at the suggestion of the concierge, we relocate to a conference room large enough for the cast of a Shakespearean play. She orders a Bloody Mary.

In her midseventies, the actress is whippet-thin. She is dressed in jeans and blue turtleneck sweater, and her blue eyes have a haunting tinge of green. Her voice is that of a trained actress, resonant and melodious.

Born in East London in 1934 to working-class parents, her father was an under-chauffeur and gas meter reader; her mother, a seamstress and barmaid. The young Eileen's early education took place at Latymer's Grammar School. She later received a scholarship to the Guildhall School of Music and Drama. From dancing in a gentlemen's club to performing with the most celebrated theatrical companies, Dame Eileen has been there and done that.

She can grimace about some of her work, but she also smiles with delight at recalling other work. Her catalog of theatre performances rivals any actor working today. Her inspiration and muse, Virginia Woolf—whom she resembles in an astonishing way—is legendary, as is her outspokenness on a variety of topics, from acting and directing colleagues to writing and developing two iconic television series.

～

What about your yesterdays? Was there a teacher who directed you toward a career in acting?

Yes, there was teacher at my grammar school, Rev. Michael Burton [some sources say Ernest L. Burton], who taught English, drama, and divinity, and who I thought—at the age of twelve—was a very, very old man, probably all of thirty-two. He was fabulous. He saw that I was going absolutely mad at school. He stopped me from marrying a boy who I was crazy about when I was fifteen. Years later, that boy—now grown—came with his wife to see one of my plays at the Old Vic. He was then a bank

Photo by Alison Jackson

manager, and she was a headmistress. I asked him, "Why didn't you keep taking me out?"

He told me that the instructor took him aside and told him, "Leave that girl alone. She's going to be something other than a banker's wife."

I should be thankful to both of them forever.

You attended Guildhall School of Music and Drama with a teaching credential curriculum, not drama.

The man who saved my life, that teacher, said to my parents, "She has to go to drama school." They thought because I wanted to be in the theatre that I was going to be a chorus girl. They didn't understand plays at all. This teacher told them, "We're going to put her in for a scholarship at RADA. If she doesn't get in, then let her do a teaching course at the Guildhall."

On the day of my sister's wedding, the telegram came from RADA that I didn't get in. I ruined the wedding with my screaming and shouting. I can be very badly behaved.

I went to Guildhall for the teaching course, knowing that I was *never* going to teach. *Never!* I was only sixteen, and today I wouldn't be allowed to start at that age. I quickly sussed that if I didn't say anything, I could do the drama course as well. I used to attend classes for both teaching and drama curriculum, and I would be there from nine in the morning to nine at night and get home to Tottenham sometime after ten. I failed the first round of my teaching course. I put in for it again and finally did pass, and I have my degree. But there was never any question in my mind that I would teach.

What about your attempts to get acting jobs?

At first I couldn't get anything. I remember my ex-mother-in-law[1] saying, "Darling, can't you even get a game show?"

A lot of that had to do with the fact that I didn't know how to present myself. I used to be called "the plain one" or "the intellectual one" by casting directors. It was simply that I didn't know how to do my hair, what makeup to put on, what to wear. I had no money for any of those things anyway. I couldn't believe how much money people spent on presenting themselves. I remember how Vanessa Redgrave could present herself and how I couldn't. I thought Vanessa was a big, plain girl. I didn't think she was very good. Now I think she's sometimes miraculous.

One day, she showed me a movie magazine with pictures of Sophia Loren, Brigitte Bardot, and Jeanne Moreau, tore them out, and stuck them on the wall. She asked, "Why aren't we film stars?" She began to transform herself. She said, "I've studied my face. I've looked at it. Carefully. I'm going to lose two stone. Then I'll have my hairline taken back with electrolysis. I'm going to grow my hair very long and have it dyed blonde." She even thought of having two ribs removed. Nine months later, I met her in the street and didn't recognize her. I went on holiday with Vanessa when she was playing very nice parts at the RSC as early as a production of 1959 in *All's Well*. I was a walk-on in Stratford. She is the only woman I ever shared a bed with because we could only get this little council house to stay in. I was so terrified that I put a bolster down the middle of the bed.

You've maintained a personal relationship with her.

We've been friends for a long while. I'm intrigued by her. She's so extraordinary because she's either marvelous . . . or dreadful. She's nothing in between. She has a very good effect on me. I've learnt a lot from her. She's so wild. There's something enormously to be admired about Vanessa.[2]

Returning to your early days, what happened when you finally arrived at Stratford?

I couldn't get into Stratford through the ordinary audition process although I had auditioned, and the report was very good. I was about twenty-three and married to Julian Glover. I had told him very bluntly, "You should try for Stratford this year because they've got Michael Redgrave, and he's very tall for Hamlet. They'll want a lot of tall men, and you're over six feet two inches." I was dead right. They heard a few lines from him, and he was in.

I went up to Stratford with him and got a job as an usherette at the theatre. Then I moved up to selling postcards in the foyer. Then to the box office. There were some funny incidents when I was working front of house. People smoked in the theatre in those days, and there was a slit in the wall that said, "Ashes." I remember an American asked me, "Are those Shakespeare's ashes?"

I approached director Toby Robertson, who seemed the poshest member of the company, and told him, "I need a winter coat, and I can't afford it. I've seen one for £10 in town. Will you lend me the money? I'll pay you back a pound a week." He lent me the £10. He's been my friend for life.

Loads of people left the company in 1957; one person got a movie; Brian Bedford broke his nose. I was such a pain in the ass at home that Julian—whom I'm still friendly with even though we divorced in 1966—said, "I think they're going to have to take some extra people on." And he very sweetly went to RSC director Glen Byam Shaw and asked, "Would you take my wife into the company?"

Glen said, "We don't take wives. She'll never play anything; she'll just fill up the stage." He was very ratty then and enjoyed playing the angry man.

About two months later, Stephanie Bidmead, who was playing Audrey in *As You Like It*, went into hospital. The understudy was also taken ill. I thought,

"I'm going to learn the role." I stayed up all night and learnt the role, arrived at the theatre the next day, and asked, "So who's going to play Audrey?" No response.

"I know it. I've played it," I lied. I was on. Dame Peggy Ashcroft played Rosalind in the production.

From then on, darling Patrick Wymark, who played Touchstone, kept pushing me forward with things. I occasionally got a few lines. I played a small role as Lady in Redgrave's *Hamlet* in 1958.

And Byam Shaw's reaction?

He asked me back for another year. At one point, I was understudying Dorothy Tutin about 1961 in Peter Hall's *Twelfth Night*. I thought maybe I wasn't as good as I thought, but one or two of the company members said some nice things about me.

Not long ago, I attended a party, and two people who had been associated with the company at that time were there. The wife, who hadn't even been in the company then but had crept in to see her actor-husband in the run-through, said to me, "You know, you were the most amazing Viola. When anybody asks me now what's the best Shakespeare I've seen, I say, 'Eileen Atkins when she was understudying Dorothy Tutin.'" That was music to my ears.

You moved into television very soon thereafter.

Again, it was Patrick Wymark, whom I shall love forever, who spoke to a television friend of his who was doing *Hilda Lessways* in 1959 in Birmingham for the BBC. He told his friend, "You have to use this girl." I played Maggie Clayhanger to Judi Dench's Hilda. It was her first television, too. We played sisters. She and I came together again in *Cranford* almost fifty years later. It was very sweet. My part as Deborah Jenkyns was so small, just two episodes of the series, and I'm dead at the end of the second. Even though I was working with Imelda Staunton in *Came a Gypsy Riding* at the Almeida at the same time, I couldn't resist working with Judi, and I knew it would be fun. The shoot was wonderful for me. I didn't do my bits all at once. I was in and out all summer. There's nothing more wonderful than working with a phalanx of fabulous actresses. They were all so good. I say "actresses" very distinctly because the village in *Cranford* is mainly a female village. Along with Maggie Smith, we're now just three old dames.[3]

Besides acting, you also created one of the iconic television series, *Upstairs, Downstairs*, with your colleague, Jean Marsh. What was the origin of that series, which ran from 1971 to 1975, and what is the status of the revival?

It was an amazing piece of luck on our part. Jean and I used to watch *The Forsyte Saga* in the midsixties and say, "Very well for them, but what's happening downstairs?"

Everybody was saying, "Wasn't it wonderful in those days?"

It wasn't wonderful for either Jean or me. We both knew that downstairs wasn't quite so much fun as upstairs. Her mother and my father were in service. As under-chauffeur, my father had to clean the car and keep the chauffeur awake while his master, the Portuguese ambassador to England, went to Edward VII's parties. He got in the car one day to teach himself how to drive and nearly got sacked.

Jean and I have known each other for so long that to this day we don't know who had what thought. But we came up with the title *Below Stairs*.[4] Jean made the original contact with producer John Hawkesworth, and there is a story that he came up with the title. While I was doing *Cranford*, one of the writers, Heidi Thomas, came to me and said, "I terribly want to go on with *Upstairs, Downstairs*."

I thought, "Nobody'll take it."

At the same time, someone came to us and said he could make a film of it. He could get us into Pathé. We didn't think it was a particularly good idea; on the other hand, we didn't want to say no. We gave the movie people at Pathé the rights for two years. I was very honest with Heidi and told her about our agreement with Pathé, but a year in, there was no script. It was all very awkward. The contract for the revival has been confirmed. And in the new contract, it says the title belongs to Jean and me. Hopefully with two initial episodes and a further six, it will be my pension.[5]

What was your thought about *Upstairs, Downstairs* as a series rather than a film?

As far as I was concerned, it's much more correct that *Upstairs, Downstairs* should be a television series, not a movie. I keep saying at the meetings, "Let's all try and concentrate on what series have been successful as movies." Of course, it's been one in a million. For example, *The Avengers* [1998] was dire. Neither Ralph Fiennes nor Uma Thurman had my idea of camp. I wanted to be in it because I wanted to be camp, but it didn't work. I think the *Star Trek* series works, but it's very rare that it does.

That series was followed by *The House of Eliott*, which you and Jean Marsh put together.

I had an idea for a situation comedy. When I presented it to the producers, they said, "Yes, but we really want another series like *Upstairs, Downstairs*. That would suit us very well."

"Oh," I said, "it just so happens that I've got one." Of course, I didn't.

"What can I come up with?" I thought. I asked myself, "Why did people watch *Dallas*?" The answer: pretty women, clothes, period stuff. People will still like that. I stayed up all night writing the treatment and called Jean in Los Angeles. It was the early eighties, and she was there doing the television series *Nine to Five*.

I said, "I've done this treatment, and I think it's better if it goes with both our names. Do you want your name on it?" By then, people had linked our names together.

When she said yes, I asked, "Can I have the bigger percentage of royalties this time?" She'd got the larger percentage on *Upstairs, Downstairs*. We're talking about *minute* royalties. She agreed. The series ran for three seasons.

Besides acting and developing two distinguished television series, you're adept at adapting other writers' works, especially those of Virginia Woolf.

When it comes to writing, I love doing adaptations. I'm really messing about with other people's words. I'm most proud of my award for my script of Virginia Woolf's *Mrs. Dalloway* because if there is an afterlife—which I don't believe there is—I don't think she'd be waiting for me with a rolling pin. I would tell her, "I've made a better entertainment out of *Mrs. Dalloway* than you would ever have done. You're the genius, but I know how to take that genius and make it better."

How did you become interested in Virginia Woolf and become a devotee?

I didn't even read her work until I was thirty-five. When I was twenty-eight, somebody sent me a script about her just when I was just getting to be noticed. This was around the time of my first theatrical hit, *Exit the King*. I thought, "This woman is interesting." The writer never got the Woolf thing off the ground. A few years later, somebody gave me a copy of *The Waves*, and I was terribly put off by it. I thought, "I can't read this." Then I started reading her diaries, then the letters. I came to her through her diaries, essays, and letters. Then I was ready for the novels. I don't find her difficult at all now, and I don't understand why anyone finds her difficult. I'm bright. I'm intelligent, but I'm *not* an intellectual in any way. Her work doesn't need an intellectual mind. I'm not in love with her; that would be silly. But she's like my talisman. I go back and read a bit of her diaries if I'm feeling down or I want my brain perked up. I just go into her mind.

How did the idea of portraying Woolf in a one-woman show begin?

I had decided that I never wanted to do a one-woman show. But I got letters from people asking for poetry readings, and I was endlessly asked to do charity stuff. The first was *A Room of One's Own*.[6] I thought, "Instead of endlessly reading poetry, I could do the letters of Virginia Woolf." That began with the Vita Sackville-West and Woolf letters and became *Vita and*

Virginia. I did them first at a Sunday evening reading. It was like Topsy: it grew and grew. I did the readings with different actresses. Then I tried it at Chichester in 1992, with Penelope Wilton, a fabulous actress, and then went with it to the Ambassadors Theatre in '93.

For my sins, I did a rehearsed reading in 2009 of Virginia's only comedy, *Freshwater*, directed by Jonathan Musby, which she wrote in 1923 and then completely revised in 1935. It's ghastly. A bad, bad play. We performed it at the Charleston Festival. Timothy West was Tennyson, and Sam West played G. F. Watts. I was Julia Margaret Cameron. Lynne Truss adapted it from the various versions.[7]

How did Vanessa Redgrave become associated with the *Vita and Virginia* project?

We had a little disaster at Chichester. Producer Robert Fox loved our project and said he would take it straightaway into London. Playwright David Hare came down to take Penelope to lunch on the day of opening night and said to her, "You've got to be in my movie, *The Secret Rapture* [1993]." She didn't particularly want to do it. Maybe he'd got wind of something interesting with *Vita and Virginia* and realized she'd want to transfer with it to the West End. But he did get an absolute promise from Penelope to appear in the film. Penelope, whom I adore, made me promise that I wouldn't do *Vita and Virginia* without her. We waited a year after Chichester. By then she had promised to do *The Deep Blue Sea* for television.

I remember Robert saying, "We're losing what we had at Chichester by waiting." When we finally opened at the Ambassadors Theatre, we had lost everything. We had nice reviews but did no business. Then an American producer, Julian Schlossberg, said he'd seen it, went to Robert, and said it would do well in America. When he and I spoke, he said he was willing to have a go at it in America, but Penelope didn't want to go to America. He asked, "Would you do it with Vanessa?" I told him she was one of the first people I sent it to when I was just trying it out, but she never answered.

Anyway, Vanessa and I did it. I was jolly grateful she did, and we had a big hit in 1994 at the Union Square Theatre in New York. Zoe Caldwell directed.

Playing opposite Michael Gambon in Yasmina Reza's *The Unexpected Man* must have been a challenge. He has the reputation of being difficult.

That is one of my favorite plays, I have to say. I know it's nobody else's. I first did it with darling Mike. He was so naughty on some occasions. As we walked into the theatre for a matinee, he'd say, "I'm not bothering this afternoon. Fuck 'em."

I would say, "Well, Michael, you know me. I shall be acting this afternoon."

What I like about him is his extreme danger. He's the most dangerous actor I know, but he gets bored very easily. He can be both angry and sentimental. He'd come on stage—it was the same with Larry Olivier—and you get the feeling from them that they didn't give a shit.

I saw Mike lose his temper once. I don't remember the specifics; it was with the wardrobe mistress, and she was being very, very, very stupid. I could see his fury at the stupidity. It was truly terrifying. He didn't say much. He didn't fling anything. I do remember gasping and thinking to myself, "Gosh, Eileen, you've got a temper but nothing like that."

I worked with him beautifully, apart from him saying he didn't want to act at the matinee, and then he always did. I had no trouble with him.

We were supposed to tour, but we couldn't because of Mark Thompson's amazing set: a railway car compartment with chairs on a glass floor through which we can see rail track. The set is another actor in this play. Matthew Warchus, the director, called up and said, "We can't get the set in the theatres they've given us." We ended up not touring. I did the play with dear, dear Alan Bates off Broadway at the Promenade Theatre in 2000.

There are stories about actors "corpsing"[8] during a performance. Under what circumstances has it happened to you?

I am very suspicious of actors who say they've *never* "corpsed." In America, the phrase is "never going up." If any actor says to me, "I've never corpsed in my life," I don't think they're very good. There's something about being right on the edge when you're acting. You are right out there with every filament of your being; you're drawing things up from you that you don't know from where. If, in the middle of all that, somebody is supposed to enter with a crown and scepter and trips—it's funny. And you're brought back with a smack to the ludicrousness of the situation. Here we're on the stage pretending to be someone who everyone knows we're not. Most of us are nowhere near the person we're playing, but the audience suspends belief for a couple of hours to join with us in imagining that we're this other person.

I've had a couple of monstrous instances of corpsing. I was in a very good production of *Heartbreak House* in 1975, directed by John Schlesinger at the Old Vic with Colin Blakely—wonderful actor, now sadly dead. Also with Anna Massey, also now sadly gone, and a wonderful American actress, Kate Nelligan. In the last scene, Graham Crowden was sitting in a deck chair. It collapsed, and he couldn't get out of it because he was so fat. The audience could see it. Anna and I were nearly hysterical; tears were rolling down our faces. He, of course, couldn't see the funny side of it. Somehow he got out of the chair, and we got back into it. In the end, the audience gave us a round of applause.

What about stopping a show? Either when you make your entrance or because of some piece of business?

I always thought I'd stop a show at the end of my career. Of course, now that I'm in my seventies, I don't think it will happen. Just by stepping in the middle of the stage and saying, "You all know I'm Eileen Atkins and not the Queen of Sheba. This is a ridiculous farce we're putting on here, so shall we just stop and go home?"

I did get angry with the audience at the National's Cottesloe when I was doing Joanna Murray-Smith's *Honour* with Corin Redgrave. It was an enormous success. He would stop the show and address the audience because mobile phones were ringing. I let that go and was able to get over it. However, once there was a flash from a camera. It was terrible. I stopped and admonished the audience for their behavior.

There's a story about a performance of the production of *Suzanna Andler*, directed by Howard Sackler in 1973 at the Wimbledon Theatre, in which you, literally, stopped the show. Is it true?

Yes, I stopped the show . . . completely. There'd been endless rows about the production because I'd agreed to take the play in one form, and two weeks before we were about to go into rehearsal, the playwright, Marguerite Duras, sent the script that she'd rewritten. In between the two versions, she'd become a Marxist. The original was a brilliant love story, and then she'd put in a whole Marxist tract. I refused to do that version, so we had a horrendous time.

When I wasn't asked to go to New York with *Vivat! Vivat Regina!* I said I would do *Suzanna Andler*. The producers of *Vivat!* had gone to Katharine Hepburn and Bette Davis and someone else. They'd all turned down the role of Queen Elizabeth. The producers realized they were stuck, and they had to come to me. I said, "I'm awfully sorry, but I've accepted another play." I didn't particularly want to go to New York at that time anyway. I'd had enough of *Vivat!* I'd been playing it forever. But then, Binkie Beaumont, a loathsome man, said to me, "I will put *Suzanna Andler* on for you in the West End when you come back from New York."

I thought, "To hell with it," and I went to New York and had a wonderful time.

Because *Suzanna* was such a difficult play to sell, Binkie promised me he wouldn't put me on a long tour. I've never minded touring. At most, he said, it would be Oxford and Cambridge, university towns, and then bring it into a small West End theatre. I found, though, he'd done a complete reversal. I read about it when I was on holiday in Spain with the director I was living with at the time while I was waiting to start rehearsals for *Suzanna* with director Howard Sackler. Binkie booked me on a twelve-week tour in places like Hull and Aberstwyth. I flew back to London, but there was nothing I could do about it. That was Binkie. He had no belief in our *Suzanna*. That was his way of fulfilling his pledge. If something is on tour for three months, he could say it didn't work, and then he could back out of the West End production.

We opened in Cambridge, and the play there was a smash hit, mainly because we had John Stride playing opposite me. He'd just been in a big television series, *The Main Chance*. We were an absolute knockout hit, where we hadn't been in some of the smaller theatres. Suddenly, Binkie realized he'd got this hit on his hands, and he could bring it in, but he didn't have a theatre. By this time, I was in a rage. We got to Wimbledon, which is a huge barn of a theatre, and usually has musicals on, and we were doing a delicate little French play.

Now to stopping the show. I remember it was a matinee. I could hear noises in the audience talking, unwrapping sweets. At the interval, I said to someone, "This is pure hell. Only a bastard like Binkie would put us on in this theatre."

At the beginning of the second act, I have a telephone conversation, and the audience has to imagine what my husband is saying on the other end. One of my lines is, "Actually, I'd like to kill myself."

Somebody in the audience shouted out, "Yes, why don't you!"

My next line is: "I'm a little bit drunk."

Somebody else shouted out, "I should say so. That's what it seems like."

I suddenly broke. I put the phone down and moved forward to the audience. I said, "I didn't want to play this play for you, and you don't want to see it. Why don't you all leave now? I will pay back everyone's money out of my own bank account because I'd rather that than all of us being miserable. Good afternoon." I walked off stage.

The manager said, "Go back on stage."

I said, "No, not until I've paid everyone who's having a miserable time has left."

Of course, these old age pensioners in the audience hadn't had this much fun for years. Nobody had ever stopped and talked to them from the stage.

I told the manager, "If there are people still in the audience, I'll go back." I walked on stage and said, "We have to go from the top again. You understand that. We're not starting in the middle of a scene."

Some had left, and the management refunded their money. At the end there were ovations. It's astonishing how often people buy tickets not having a clue what they're going to see.

And the move to the West End?

At the end of the tour, Trevor Nunn asked me to play Rosalind in *As You Like It* at Stratford.

"Trevor," I said, "I'd love to, but the bit is between my teeth now with *Suzanna Andler*. It's had some success on tour, and I'm determined to show Binkie up by bringing it into London because he's behaved so atrociously."

Trevor told me, "I have a disaster on at the Aldwych at the moment, *The Island of the Mighty* by John Arden [directed by David Hugh Jones, which opened December 5, 1972]. Would you like the theatre for *Suzanna?*"

After we opened with Dinsdale Landen replacing John Stride, reviewers wrote how brave Binkie was to bring it to the West End. I was so angry. Binkie came to my dressing room after a performance and exclaimed, "We did it." I went absolutely potty.

"Get out of my dressing room," I shouted.

He died that night, March 22, 1973. Apparently, he fell over and hit his head. I now always think, "I killed Binkie Beaumont."

A happier production was the film version of *The Dresser*, with the screenplay by Ronald Harwood based on his play about stage actors, and here was a group of stage actors acting in a film.

Here we were, a load of theatre actors who suddenly struck it lucky and were in a film. Albert Finney as Sir and Tom Courtenay as Norman—divine, both of them. They have a wonderful sparring relationship in the story, gently sending each other up. They're both lovely people. I know Albert—who introduced me to vodka—a bit better than I know Tom, who is wonderfully droll, which I didn't know before we started. He looks so serious. I thought he wouldn't stand a chance against Albert because he seemed so bland. Peter Yates, the director, is a wonderful, lovely, lovely man.

I love Ronnie Harwood to bits. He's adorable and such fun, and he wrote a splendid screenplay. He was on the set all the time, and I remember him saying some very nice things about the rushes. He probably did that with everyone because he's a very kind man. Ronnie has endlessly offered me plays, but for some reason or another I've not been able to accept. The timing probably. I upset him once by turning down a part in his play, *Another Time*, because I wasn't Jewish. He said, "Since when do you get the idea you have to be Jewish to play the part?"

I said, "I'm sorry, but I really do think you need a Jewish woman." Janet Suzman played Belle Lands.

At a screening at BAFTA of *The Diving Bell and the Butterfly*, which Ronnie wrote, I was asked to introduce it, and I hadn't even seen it. I had to do the chat with the audience. Thank God, when I watched it, it was a great movie, and Ronnie had done a great script, so everything I'd said was true before we even started.

A great admirer of yours said, "I am a devotee of Eileen Atkins. I saw her as Elizabeth in the *Vivat! Vivat Regina!* She was marvelous. Claire Bloom played Mary." Do you know who that is?

That was Charles Jarrott. He was so wonderful. He was raging with fury that he wasn't allowed to use me as Elizabeth in his film *Mary, Queen of Scots*. It's always satisfying that anyone notices the work someone has done.

Another of your admirers is Sir Richard Eyre, who directed you in Tennessee Williams's *Night of the Iguana* and Ibsen's *John Gabriel Bjorkman*. What do you expect from directors generally?

I expect directors to tell me what to do. As an actor, I'm very directable; that I do know. I take a part, and then it goes through me, and I'm able—I hope desperately—to serve the writer, giving what the writer has said to the audience because they need someone like me to facilitate it. Absolutely, I'm a facilitator. Someone's going to help me get it right. And that's the director. I don't see myself as the creator of anything. I don't like not being directed. I come to rehearsals with as few ideas as possible. I don't like being left alone as some actors do—no names—who don't like being directed. They think they know best. But the weird thing is that anyone outside you knows more than you do.

I nearly turned down playing Hannah in *Iguana* with Richard. I don't like playing Americans; maybe it's because I've been there so much. I know more about Americans than a lot of the people who daily do American accents and say they're playing Americans. Once I'd been to America, I'd say I'm not playing Americans because we don't really know about playing them any more than they do about playing us. It's such a big leap. I love America, but I don't like Los Angeles.

Anyway, Richard persuaded me to take the role. He told me that Hannah comes from Nantucket and has been all over the world. I thought she would be a very different American. Richard drew me into it. He kept saying, "Eileen, it's a wonderful part. . . ." And it was!

Your husband, who isn't associated with the theatre, assisted you in a directorial way when you were having difficulty. How did that happen?

My second husband, Bill Shepherd, had only been to the theatre twice in his life when I married him. He thought I was a painter. Soon after we were married, I was in a play, *The Lady's Not for Burning*. The director, George Baker, is a darling man, but he's not a director. I love him so much, and it was really awkward. I wasn't getting any help from him, and I got other directors into previews to help me. They told me, "We can't help you. It's a mess."

Dame Eileen Atkins as Elizabeth I, in the 1972 Broadway production of *Vivat! Vivat Regina!*, directed by Peter Dews. *Photo by Friedman-Abeles/© Billy Rose Theatre Division, the New York Public Library for the Performing Arts*

I said to Bill, "I've got to open in this play, and I don't know what to do."

He sat up with me all night, and we went through the play line by line. In one place, he said, "You're supposed to arrive as if you've been running through the streets; you think you're going to be hung, drawn, and quartered, I don't quite get that when you come on stage."

"And what else?" I asked.

All he'd say was, "I believe that" or "I don't believe that."

By the time we got through the night, I knew what I was doing.

Your career has spanned theatre, film, and television. What is the difference in acting in those media?

You have to project for the theatre. A lot of people don't learn to project. It's perfectly easy thing to learn. I tried to teach Josephine Hart, Lady Saatchi, who did a chat at the Donmar during the T. S. Eliot Festival. She just could not do it. I loathe body microphones. When actors wear one, it looks like they're from another planet. I don't like the theatre being miked. It's utterly disgraceful that actors use them. I like the pure voice.

It always amuses me when people say filming is so much more real than theatre work. It's absolutely bollocks. Forgive me; my language is disgusting. There was actually a makeup woman in Los Angeles who refused to make me up because I used the "f" word. It's surprising that a few words should so offend people. About filming, I also have to think, "Did I hit my mark? Oh, yes, my foot is on the mark."

It's rubbish to say filming is "more real." Someone might say, "We're really in a house." It can be just as real on stage. You're *playing* something. It isn't real—ever! It's *never* real. To me, filming is the least real. I dislike filming for that reason.

Recently, someone who worked at the BBC went to the archives and got me a copy of *Electra*, which I'd done on the BBC *Play of the Month* on October 24, 1974. In those days, it wasn't live; we could only see it the night it played. I'd not seen it then except for the first few minutes because I was with a man who was rude about the production. He'd wanted to direct it and didn't get it, so I'd turned it off.

Apart from the fact that I popped my eyes a bit too much and I could see the whites all the way 'round, I was remarkably happy with the portrayal of Electra. I think everybody in it [Rosalie Crutchley, Julian Glover, Martin Shaw] was terribly good. I remember that the director, Michael Lindsay-Hogg, stopped the tape only four times in an hour and a half. We had five cameras. What he got was quite extraordinary. It was wonderful seeing the production so many years later. Bill had tears streaming down his face when everybody dies.

I gave the tape to a drama student who told me that it's better than anything he sees on television today.

You received a DBE, having previously been awarded a CBE. What was the process for receiving the highest honor?

MBE is the lowest, mostly given to people who've done charity work. Then comes the OBE; then CBE. Then—maybe or maybe not—a damehood, a DBE. Usually, the CBE comes first, and then apparently, you're checked out after ten years to see what you've done or if you've remained stagnant.

Typical of what happens to me, the letter offering the DBE got lost in the post, so I never received it. I got a phone call asking why I hadn't replied. When they told me, I said that I'd have to think about it. The woman on the other end said, "Oh, do say yes."

You're not supposed to tell anyone. Anyone! I didn't even tell my husband. What made me finally decide to accept was that if I hadn't, every time there'd be a discussion amongst actors—which is often—about who might be damed or knighted, I would say, "I was offered it, but I turned it down." Did I really want to say that every time? I said to myself, "Stop being so damned silly and accept it." I called back and accepted. I still didn't tell anyone. Three days before it was going to be announced, I told my husband. He said, "That's wonderful."

I thought it was going to put something between us, and it would be the beginning of trouble. It didn't. Once it was announced, I was deluged with letters. I felt terrific, and I've never stopped feeling terrific about it.

What about the ceremony?

Her Majesty Queen Elizabeth II had given me my CBE. I received the DBE at Buckingham Palace from Prince Charles. After I curtsied and stood up, he said, "That was a wonderful curtsy." He's lovely. Then we were ushered into a side room, and someone removed what he'd put on because it wasn't the real thing. We're told we'd get the real thing in a few weeks' time.

I sailed out of Buckingham Palace on a cloud toward the exit. There were two exits, one read, "Press," the other, "Photographs," which is where you stopped if you wanted a photo of yourself as a memento. I went toward the press exit. Press? There was one photographer who was taking a photo of Patrick Stewart. I greeted Patrick, who had received an OBE. He couldn't have been sweeter; he threw his arms around me, and the photographer said, "Patrick, could you tell your friend to step aside?"

It's all so camp. I feel sorry for the Royals because they must have the strangest conversations at the ceremony and other events. They have to go to the most boring things and sit through them.

I met Prince Charles at a do a little while after that. He's very interested in acting. He asked me, quite earnestly, "How do you cry?" I said something completely untrue, and to this day, I don't know why this came out of my mouth. I said, "I just imagine all my cats being crucified." He moved away very quickly. It's very weird what you say when you're with royalty.

Your great friend, Vanessa Redgrave, was offered a DBE. What was your advice to her?

It was awkward because Vanessa was offered a DBE the year before. She called me up. She shouldn't have. She said, "You'll never guess what I've been offered."

I told her, "You can't accept it. Your politics . . ." I put down the phone and thought, "I think she wants it." I called her back and said, "You're doing a lot of very good charity work these days. It might be very useful because if you're in Africa or somewhere and they see *Dame* Vanessa Redgrave. You might get into places you wouldn't have done."

But she refused. Corin, her brother, put an absolute kibosh on it, and she does what her brother says.[9]

⌒

Selected Credits

Theatre

Love's Labour's Lost, Regent's Park Open Air Theatre (1953; Robert Akins); *Cymbeline*, SMT, Stratford (1956–1957; Peter Hall); *The Tempest*, SMT, Stratford (1957; Peter Brook); *Pericles*, SMT, Stratford (1958; Tony Richardson); *The Tempest*, Old Vic (1962; Oliver Neville); *Semi-Detached*, Saville (1962; Tony Richardson); *Exit the King*, Edinburgh Festival, Royal Court (1964; George Devine); *The Killing of Sister George*, Duke of York's; Belasco, New York (1965–1967; Val May); *The Promise*, Henry Miller's, New York (1967; Frank Hauser); *The Cocktail Party*, CFT; Wyndham's (1968; Alec Guinness); *Vivat! Vivat Regina!* CFT, Piccadilly; Broadhurst, New York (1972; Peter Dews); *As You Like It*, RST (1973; Buzz Goodbody); *Saint Joan*, Prospect Theatre Company at the Liverpool Playhouse; Old Vic (1978; Toby Robertson); *Sergeant Musgrave's Dance*, Old Vic (1984; Albert Finney); *Medea*, Young Vic (1986; Toby Robertson); *The Winter's Tale*, NT, Olivier (1988; Peter Hall); *Mountain Language*, NT, Lyttelton (1988; Harold Pinter); *Exclusive*, Strand [now Novello] (1989; Michael Rudman); *The Night of the Iguana*, NT, Olivier (1992; Richard Eyre); *Vita and Virginia*, CFT; Ambassadors (1992–1993; Patrick Garland); Union Square Theatre (1994; Zoe Caldwell); *John Gabriel Borkman*, NT, Lyttelton (1996; Richard Eyre); *The Unexpected Man*, RSC at the Pit; Duchess; Promenade, New York (1998, 2000; Matthew Warchus); *The Retreat from Moscow*, Booth, New York (2004; Daniel Sullivan); *Doubt*, Walter Kerr (2006; Doug Hughes);

There Came a Gypsy Riding, Almeida (2007; Michael Attenborough); *Harold Pinter: A Celebration*, NT, Olivier (2009; Ian Rickson); *All That Fall*, Jermyn Street; 59E59, New York (2012; Trevor Nunn); *The Witch of Edmonton*, RSC, Swan (2014; Gregory Doran)

Film
Inadmissible Evidence (1968); *Sharon's Baby* [a.k.a. *The Devil within Her*] (1975); *Equus* (1977); *Wolf* (1994); *Gosford Park* (2001); *Cold Mountain* (2003); *Last Chance Harvey* (2008); *Robin Hood* (2010); *Beautiful Creatures* (2013); *Magic in the Moonlight* (2014); *Suite française* (2014); *ChickLit* (2015)

Television
The Wednesday Play, "Fable" (1965); *Major Barbara* (1966); *W. Somerset Maugham*, "The Letter" (1969); *BBC2 Playhouse of the Week*, "She Fell among Thieves" (1978); *BBC Television Shakespeare*, "Titus Andronicus" (1985); *PBS Masterpiece Theatre*, "A Room of One's Own" (1991); *Screen Two: Language of Lost Cranes* (1992); *Bertie and Elizabeth* (2002); *Agatha Christie's Poirot*, "Murder on the Orient Express" (2010); *Upstairs, Downstairs*, three episodes (2010); *Doc Martin*, fifteen episodes (2011); *Valentine's Kiss* (2015)

Writer/Creator
Upstairs, Downstairs (1971–1975), associate series creator with Jean Marsh (also three episodes based on original series, 2010); *House of Eliott* (1991–1994), creator/writer/series deviser with Jean Marsh; *Mrs. Dalloway* (1997), screenplay

Awards and Nominations

Exit the King, 1964, Clarence Derwent Award, Best Female in a Supporting Role, winner; *The Killing of Sister George*, 1965, *Evening Standard*, Best Actress, winner; also, 1967, Tony, Best Actress in a Play, nominee; *Vivat! Vivat Regina!* 1972, Tony, Best Actress in a Play, nominee; also, Drama Desk, Outstanding Actress in a Play, winner; *The Night of the Tribades*, 1978, Drama Desk, Outstanding Featured Actress in a Play, winner; *The Dresser*, 1983, BAFTA, Best Supporting Actress, Film, winner; *Cymbeline, The Winter's Tale, Mountain Language*, 1988, Olivier, Best Supporting Performance, winner; *A Room of One's Own*, 1991, Drama Desk, Outstanding Solo Performance, winner; *Night of the Iguana*, 1992, Olivier, Best Actress in a Play, nominee; also, London Critics' Circle Theatre Award, Best Actress, winner;

Indiscretions, 1995, Tony, Best Actress in a Play, nominee; *Vita and Virginia*, 1995, Obie, shared with Vanessa Redgrave, winner; *A Delicate Balance*, 1997, *Evening Standard*, Best Actress, winner; *Mrs. Dalloway*, 1999, *Evening Standard*, Best Screenplay, winner; *The Unexpected Man*, 1999, Olivier, Best Actress in a Play, winner; *The Retreat from Moscow*, 2004, Tony, Best Actress in a Play, nominee; *Honour*, 2004, Olivier, Best Actress in a Play, winner; *Cranford*, 2008, BAFTA TV Award, Best Actress, winner; also, Emmy, Best Supporting Actress, Miniseries or TV Movie, winner

Honors

CBE, 1990; DBE, 2001; Doctor of Letters, *honoris causa*, 2010, Oxford University

Notes

1. During her marriage to actor Julian Glover, whom she met when they were appearing at Butlin's Holiday Camp in Skegness, Lincolnshire, in the mid-1950s.

2. When Vanessa Redgrave accepted her BAFTA Fellowship on February 21, 2010, she said, "I've always been jealous to this day of Dame Eileen Atkins because she actually did get to be a member of Terry's Juveniles, and I never did. I'm really sad about that."

3. Dench received her DBE in 1988; Smith received hers in 1990.

4. The book *Below Stairs: The Classic Kitchen Maid's Memoir* by Margaret Powell is credited as being the inspiration for the both the original television series *Upstairs, Downstairs* and *Downton Abbey*.

5. In August 2011, BBC News wrote that Atkins, who played Maud, Lady Holland, in the revival, left the show because she was reportedly "unhappy with the direction the new scripts are taking."

6. Adapted from Woolf's lecture at Girton College, Cambridge.

7. According to Ms. Truss, "It was a very successful evening."

8. British theatrical slang for an actor who unintentionally breaks character by laughing or making another actor laugh.

9. Corin Redgrave died in 2010 at age seventy.

CHAPTER TWO

~

Isla Blair

As an actor, I am very lucky. I brush bits of people's lives that many people wouldn't ordinarily get to do.

Isla Blair is standing on the front step of her home in the London suburb of Barnes, waving goodbye to Julian Glover, her actor-husband of forty years, who is off to the airport where he is flying to Malta for a few days' filming. The farewell wave to him becomes a welcoming greeting to the visitor. Since it's raining, she quickly ushers the visitor into the house. To ward off the chill, the actress, whose deep-fringed copper-colored hair gleams in waning light, prepares tea in the kitchen.

The home, which she describes as "an absolute haven," stands on what were originally acres of orchards. The ready-to-bloom pear tree just outside the kitchen window is the highlight of the lush garden. "It's over a hundred years old and still bears lovely eating pears," boasts the actress.

The front room is lined with framed flyers from the formidable catalog of plays in which they have appeared. They also collect biographies of theatre personalities, including those of Laurence Olivier, David Niven, and John Gielgud.

Along with the pot of tea, she places a selection of biscuits on the lace-covered dining table, and she begins her personal and professional reminiscences.

~

Like so many theatrical colleagues of your generation, you were not born in the UK. In your case, it was India. Then, as with others, you were sent "home" for schooling. What is your story?

My grandparents went out to India from Scotland in the early twentieth century as pioneer tea planters for James Finlay Limited, a Scottish company. My father, Ian Blair Hill, was born there. At the age of three, he was sent back to Scotland for schooling and didn't see his parents until he was twenty-one!

I was born on September 29, 1944, in Bangalore rather than the hill station in South India where my father worked on the tea plantation. He was in the RAF Transport Command and stationed in Bangalore. We later moved back up to the hill station in a beautiful place called Kerala, which is the only democratically elected communist state in the world. Like all the British children, I had an *ayah* [nanny], who was terribly important to me.

As was the custom, we went "home" when I was five and a half. Air travel was fiendishly expensive, so my sister, Fiona, who is three and a half years older, and my parents, who came with us, traveled by ship, the RMS *Orion*.

Photo courtesy of the author

During the voyage, the man in charge of the ship's entertainment asked, "Is there someone who would like to sing for us?"

I volunteered right away and sang "The Girl That I Marry," much to the consternation—and delight—of my parents. I was about to launch into another song when my father told me, "That's enough, Isla."

We went to Scotland to visit relatives, and then Fiona and I were enrolled in St. Maray's School in Kilbryde Castle in Dunblane. I next saw my mum again when I was eight. I didn't see my father again until I was eleven. Those long gaps were just part of the life we led. The odd thing was getting to know my parents the wrong way 'round inasmuch as I didn't know them very well as a child, but when I was sixteen, they came back to England for good. It was then that I started to get to know them. Most children at that age are getting ready to leave home, but I was just getting to know my parents. I became very, very close to them. It was a strange thing.

What sort of theatre did you attend when you were young?

I returned to India a few years ago and again met some of whom I call "the children of the Raj." We agreed that ours had been a blessed childhood, one that we took for granted at the time. We didn't know how special it was until we left it behind.

I wrote an article about it for the Finlay's publication. There is a photograph of my sister and me in some sort of production, captioned "Pixies Dance." I can't have been more than three. Even at that young age, I must have been interested in performing if that photograph is any judge. I remember that when my parents first came home, they took me to see Kiss Me, Kate [1951] with Patricia Morison at the Coliseum. I remember the experience very clearly. I sat absolutely transfixed. I was so overwhelmed by the occasion. I asked if I could please go and see it again. We didn't.

As a special treat at school, we were taken to the circus. I hated the circus, and I hated pantomimes. What I wanted to see were what I call "proper plays."

When my parents were away, I used to stay with people who had sort of a holiday home for children whose parents were abroad. As a teenager, I stayed in Surrey, and I'd see plays at the Leatherhead Theatre in the early sixties. They did comedies like The Amorous Prawn by Anthony Kimmins. They were awful. I wanted to see Shakespeare or Shaw. I was a snobby girl in terms of what I wanted to see.

I also remember seeing a few productions at the Royal Court. I saw John Osborne's Look Back in Anger there, about 1956, with Kenneth Haigh as Jimmy Porter, directed by Tony Richardson. I was quite young and didn't understand it. I hadn't seen anything like it before, and it left a great impression on me. At the Old Vic, I remember seeing Saint Joan with Barbara Jefford

[1960], and I saw one or two Shakespeare plays there before the company moved to the South Bank.

Did you participate in theatrical productions at school?

I was in all the school plays. I was the leading light, actually. I won the acting cup every year. I played a lot of men's roles: Brutus in *Julius Caesar* and Edmund in *King Lear*. I also played Hermia in *Midsummer Night's Dream*.

Those early roles obviously inspired you.

I knew very early on that this was something I *had* to do. I just had to do it. I absolutely loved acting and was very passionate about it. I bought plays just to read. It seems an odd thing for a child to have done that. I found plays so interesting, sometimes more interesting than the novels my friends were reading, like Kathleen Winsor's *Forever Amber* and other "bodice rippers." I was reading Wilde and Shaw. Very peculiar.

Once you decided on acting as a career, what was the trajectory?

My parents thought I was too young to try for drama school and wanted me to go to university and read English or drama. I made an agreement with them that I could try for drama school and see what happened. I thought about RADA, LAMDA, and Guildhall, but my parents said, "RADA's the one. You'll have to get into that. If not, then you'll do what we've asked and go to university first." RADA was the only one they'd heard of, and if I was accepted there, they would agree to my attending.

Thinking about it now, to be honest, my parents were right. It would probably have been the more sensible to go to university first. I shouldn't have gone to drama school so young. I was younger than anybody by far—just sixteen—and I'd come from a girls' private boarding school and had really never been with boys before.

What were your audition pieces for RADA?

I did a poem, *The Destruction of Sennacherib* by Byron: "The Assyrian came down like the wolf on the fold/And his cohorts were gleaming in purple and gold . . ." [Decades later, Blair can still recite the entire poem.] A poem is the *last* thing anyone should do in an audition. I did a bit of Rosalind from *As You Like It*, and I did a bit of an American play, *Street Scene* by Elmer Rice, with an American accent. Why I chose those pieces I don't know. How embarrassing that must have been! I get all hot and cold when I think of it now.

And the RADA audition?

I remember coming out of the RADA audition, and my mother and sister came to meet me. I was desolate. I said, "I've blown it." I was amazed when I was accepted. I had my seventeenth birthday about nine days after I arrived at RADA.

In fact, I got an Arts Council grant. What happened was this: I auditioned at RADA, but my parents couldn't pay the fees. I had to try out for a grant from the West Sussex County Council. I *had* to get the grant. So there was another audition to see if I'd qualify. I went to Chichester, I remember, and auditioned for all these Arts Council men in suits. I did various pieces for them, and they judged whether I was worthy. I got the grant, which paid my fees and a £5-a-week subsistence. That's what was done then.

What recollections do you have about the classes at RADA?

Everyone was so much older than I was, and I was intimidated. I almost couldn't move in my classes because I felt so shy and frightened. I thought I was hopeless; indeed, I was by comparison to some of these people, including Anthony Hopkins.

There was a man there called Christopher Fettes, who later founded the Drama Centre, whose method I strongly disapprove of. That "method" is a form of bullying. Acting, for me, in many ways is about confidence. He, along with Yat Malmgren, taught the Laban theory.[1] I didn't know what they were talking about. Christopher was just horrible to me. He was the first person I'd seen wearing black leather trousers! I remember overhearing him saying to Nell Carter, the elderly woman who was teaching Shakespeare, "What on earth are they doing allowing this child to come in? I don't even know if she's got any talent, but she's far too young to be here."

I remember thinking, "He's absolutely right!"

What thoughts did you have about wanting to leave RADA after that first term?

I told my parents, "I've made a mistake. I'm no good. I'm hopeless. I'm the least good in the class, and I don't know what they're talking about half the time. I'm frightened and nervous all the time. I can't go back."

My father, a slow-speaking Scot, listened to me, and when I finished, he sat me down and said, "I'm very disappointed in you, Isla, because I never thought you were a quitter. If you leave now, you will never know if you're good or not because you will never have given yourself the chance. Of course, it's tough. I'll bet you half the other students are just as frightened and nervous as you are. They just hide it." He said, "Go back for the next term. If you still hate it after you've been there three terms, then maybe you're right, and it's not for you."

Fortunately, when I returned, I moved into another group of students, and I started to flower.

Was there someone at the school who was supportive of you?

Although I don't think I was particularly good, I was very lucky inasmuch as the principal, John Fernald, gave me very showy parts in my last term. I was in one production of *Prison without Bars* by Frank Keiller, not a good play but a showy part, then *The Codocil* from Kafka's book, and a musical, *Two Bouquets* by Eleanor and Herbert Farjeon, slight and frothy and great fun, and I was able to sing. Those roles made a great difference in my life because I was seen by a lot of agents, which was, again, lucky.

Were you then able to complete your studies at RADA?

Yes, I finished the two-year course, and I received my certificate. Today, the course is three years. It's a very different process now than it was in my day. I now sit on the audition panel at RADA. We advise students *not* to do a poem, but to do a monologue from a play. The students are required to do a classical piece, Shakespeare or Marlowe and the like, and something from a modern play written after 1960. They actually go through four auditions. I see an early group. There are now just under four thousand applicants for some twenty-eight places.

"Oh, God," I think, "I'm sitting in judgment of somebody's life."

With the RADA certificate in hand, what was next?

I got an agent! Julian Belfrage, one of the great agents, had seen me in one of those RADA productions. Now my son, Jamie, also an actor, is with that agency.

Julian was very young, about thirty, but he was like an uncle to me. He instructed me that whenever I went on an audition, I had to have enough money to immediately go a phone box and tell him how I got on. That was his rule. He almost immediately set me up for an audition in 1963 for the musical *The Boys from Syracuse* at the Drury Lane Theatre. After the audition, as required, I called him.

He said, "I want you to go straightaway to the Strand Theatre [now the Novello]. The producers of *The Boys from Syracuse* have rung and said they think you are too young for that part, but they think you are right for a part in *A Funny Thing Happened on the Way to the Forum*."

Off I went, and on the same day, I auditioned for *Forum*. Afterwards, I called Julian again. He said, "They want to see you again in a couple of days' time. But I want you to meet me at Jules' Bar on Jermyn Street."

When I met him, I must have obviously looked a bit of a scruff because he told me, "Go and buy a nice dress and get your hair cut. I want you to look good. Here are £10."

What happened at the second audition?

That audition was for the understudy for Philia, a smallish part. And I got it! At £10 a week. At the same time, I was offered a season at the Bristol Old Vic, playing small roles. I kind of wanted to do *that* more than *Forum*.

Julian had some serious career advice about the options: "I think you should do six months as the understudy. I'll also make sure that you get a lot of television work and some radio. You won't be bored, I promise you. And you'll make a lot of very good contacts."

Did you take his advice? And the result?

Yes, I trusted Julian. I took the understudy role. The actress playing Philia, Sally Smith, arrived about four days into rehearsals. It then transpired that Sally was no longer playing the part. I was never told what happened. I was just nineteen when I took over the role and had to deal with some of the greatest icons of the theatre: George Abbott, the legendary, scary director; Larry Gelbart and Burt Shevelove, who wrote the book; and lyricist Stephen Sondheim. In the press, there was the headline "Understudy Takes Over Role." There was a lot of publicity, lots of interviews. I was photographed for the *Tatler* magazine.

I stayed in the role for nearly the whole run—at £40 a week—and at the same time, I did a lot of Sunday night television programs, including *Arms and the Man* and *Henry V*. Of course, I had to get permission from the producers of *Forum* because I'd rehearse for television during the day, play *Forum* at night—eight shows a week—and then we'd film the television program on Sunday, when there was no theatre performance. Julian kept his word, and I was very busy. It was fantastic.

Your costars in *Forum* were three of the great British comics. How competitive were they with each other?

These legendary comics, Frankie Howerd, Kenneth Connor, and "Monsewer" Eddie Gray, didn't get on well with each other. That has to be said. They would sabotage each other any way they could, but they were incredibly kind to me because I was the straight woman to their antics. I was not a threat to them.

Any regrets about not going to the Bristol Old Vic?

None. What was good about my not going was that when I did get there, I went to play leading parts. In my first season there, I played Desdemona in *Othello*; Dotty in Tom Stoppard's *Jumpers*; and Mary, Queen of Scots in *Vivat! Vivat Regina!* by Robert Bolt. We'd rehearse one while playing another in the evening. It was quite tough but an extraordinary experience. I learned so much.

You also became associated with the Prospect Theatre Company in the midsixties, where you met the second of two Julians who have played important roles in your personal and professional life.

I was just twenty-one. Again, this opportunity came through Julian, my agent. At the same time I was asked to join Prospect in *Boswell's Life of Johnson*, I was asked to play Hermia in *Midsummer Night's Dream* in Regent's Park.

Julian said, "You can play Hermia another time." Again, good advice.

For me, the best thing about being part of the Prospect Company was that I met Julian Glover. I played Fanny Burney, an amazing woman, and doubled as one of Boswell's paramours. The company at the time included Timothy West and Sylvia Syms. Besides meeting Julian, who became my husband and is so romantic [she says with a twinkle in her eyes], I was able to play all the parts I dreamed about with the company. Among others, I played Viola in *Twelfth Night* to Derek Jacobi's Andrew Aguecheek. We toured around the Middle East with that.

At about the same time, you were making a name for yourself in the Hammer horror films. Your recollections?

By the time I made *Taste the Blood of Dracula*, I had already been in a segment of the film called *Dr. Terror's House of Horrors*. With *Dracula*, in which I turn into a vampire, I became known as the "Scream Queen." With Hammer it was all gore and sex. All the girls had their bosoms pushed up to their necks.

I remember going to a dentist in Hampstead for a fang fitting. They were fitted to my own teeth like crowns. I looked at them in the mirror and said, "Oh, yesh, they're very nish." I wish I'd kept them. They'd probably be worth a fortune. Sometimes I'd get very giggly when I had my fangs in, and I had to say to Martin Jarvis, who was playing my lover, "Kish me!" I couldn't say it without giggling.

Christopher Lee, as Dracula, became furious if anybody laughed. Quite rightly he said, "If you don't take this seriously, the audience won't. You've got to absolutely believe in it."

The film was quite gory. At one point, I had to kill my on-screen father, Peter Sallis, by putting a stake through *his* heart because he was trying to kill *me*. At lunchtime, there he was, sitting in the Elstree canteen with this stake coming out of his side. It was *very* funny.

I also remember that we filmed at Highgate Cemetery. That was quite spooky. We had to run around all these tombs.

There is a scene where I'm inside the coffin. It was not a particularly pleasant experience having the coffin lid lowered down over me. Everyone talked to me constantly to keep me calm. I was wearing false eyelashes, and

I remember opening my eyes when the lid was closed, and my eyelashes brushed against the top of the coffin. It was a bit scary.

In one scene I had to be thrown into a pond and Anthony Higgins, as my brother, had to fish me out. It was a terribly cold November day when we filmed it. I was given ice cubes so that my breath wouldn't show, but they couldn't stop my body from steaming. I had to be doused with cold water, which was not comfortable.

My son, Jamie, was just a baby then, and the worst thing was having to leave him. I was desperate to get home after filming each day. I'd get into my car, one of those tiny mini-cars, still with the bite makeup on my neck. I remember being at a traffic light and seeing people do double takes.

So many memories, some funny, some not so.

As an aside: It was lovely being part of that company, so many good people in it. I still get sent photographs from the film to sign, and I get stopped at stage doors by people asking me to sign things related to the film. When we were doing it, we had no idea it was going to be a cult film.

You have worked with a variety of directors who have diverse directorial methods. What do you expect from a director?

It's a joint enterprise between the director and actor. We all want to serve the playwright and decide the best way to do that. I expect an overall plan of what the director wants the production to be like. I think it's the director's job—in the theatre, anyway—to create an atmosphere which allows the actor to be creative and not feel frightened that he or she is going to make a fool of themselves. The actor should be prepared to jump off a diving board and make a terrible belly flop and say, "It doesn't matter."

I should feel supported and encouraged by the director and be given notes saying, "I understand what you're trying to do, but it's not working" and maybe give me an idea about how to make it work.

The worst way a director can direct an actor is to get up and do the line. That's so destructive because I wouldn't be able to see the way into the role myself. The director could say, "I think you're slightly mis-inflecting that line because if you underline *that* word, it offers a different meaning."

For example, a short line, "*Mum's* dead" versus "Mum's *dead*."

But for the director to demonstrate would be the worst.

You have played roles written by two of the great contemporary playwrights, David Hare and Ronald Harwood. What challenges you in their work—and words—as an actor?

I played at the National in David's *Stuff Happens*, about the run-up to the Iraq War. All of us—and there were twenty-two characters on stage—were ciphers, who had to get information across to the audience. I played three roles: Laura Bush, New Labour Politician, and Bereaved Mother. It was incredibly frightening because there was no single character to hold on to. It was like giving a lecture, so all of us—not just me—were really nervous. Every night we were all terrified that we were going to dry because instinct didn't come into it. We were simply there to give a piece of information. I admire David's writing tremendously, and I admire his research in his plays, but his style of writing was hard to learn.

Ronald Harwood, on the other hand, writes warm, funny dialogue and was easier to learn than David's. I played Pauline Strauss, wife of composer Richard Strauss, a battle-ax, a terrifying woman, in *Collaboration*. I adored the character; she was probably a nightmare to live with, and, apparently, Hitler really was terrified of her, which was good. She clearly adored her husband, and she was fierce in defense of him.

With all good playwrights, if you change a word or even a comma, you do so at your peril. It changes the rhythm. That's true of both Ronnie's and David's work but particularly Ronnie's work. If you do it absolutely the way he's written it, it works. I admire his work because he writes very human characters; there's a vulnerability about them.

In film, there is always a chance that the role will, either in part or as a whole, end up on the proverbial cutting room floor. Perhaps your unkindest cut of all was in the Beatles' film A Hard Day's Night in 1964. What is the story?

I had met the Beatles at various nightclubs just to say hello. I was a fan, but not a screaming fan. I wasn't falling over in a faint because I met them.

I was still doing *Forum* when Julian got me this film. I had two days in a scene with Paul McCartney in which I was supposed to be a young actress rehearsing a scene from Shakespeare, and he comes in and says, "You're doing it all wrong," or something like that.

I was told that on the days we were shooting that I mustn't give away the location of the shooting. I arrived at the Shepherd's Bush tube station near the studio at seven o'clock in the morning. On the soundstage, there was Paul; Dick Lester, the director; me; and just a few crew members.

Paul was absolutely charming. He talked a lot about his mother's death, which had been very recent, and he was very sad. We talked about all sorts of things: why I wanted to be an actor, the strain of his dealing with fans. I have pictures of a cake that was brought in with candles and Paul and me blowing them out. I don't quite know what that was all about. There's a great picture of Paul and me laughing.

At the end of the first day's shooting, he asked how I got to the studio. I told him I'd come on the tube and that I had to go back to the theatre where I was still playing. He said, "I'll give you a lift." I accepted.

I don't know how they found out, but when we walked out of the studio, there were crowds of screaming girls waiting for him. Because I was with him, they kind of attacked me, too, and pulled my hair. We jumped in his car and sped away. It was horrible, really quite frightening.

The next day when he asked, "Would you like a lift?" I said, "Thank you very much, but I'll take the tube."

There I was turning down a lift from Paul McCartney. In the end, my entire scene was cut from the film.

When I performed a revival of *Forum* at the National, playing Domina, or as we call the part, "the old bag," Paul came backstage to see me. He also came to see me in *The History Boys* at Wyndham's, and we met afterwards. He said some of the lines that were cut from *Hard Day's Night*. I asked him how on earth he remembered them. He said, "I just do!" He's a very, very nice man, actually. The next day, I got a huge bouquet of white flowers from him. I went up in the cast's estimation.

In *The Battle of Britain,* you were also cut, but you still have a small bit.

I played Mrs. Andy, wife of the Ian McShane character. The decision was made not to dwell so much on people killed in the Blitz, which is what my scenes were about. The emphasis was more on the pilots, which I think was understandable. We can't imagine what those Canadian, Polish, American, and British pilots went through during the Battle of Britain. Those airmen were just fantastic.

Incidentally, Julian did a fifteen-minute short film called *Battle for Britain.* He plays a 101-year-old Polish airman. I'm in it, but if you blink you'll miss me, but it was lovely to be part of it. It was shown at the Riverside Studios in Hammersmith. First was *Battle of Britain*, then Julian's short, then a Q and A.

You made an interesting decision in a four-part television series, *Final Cut,* which caused quite a stir. And it wasn't cut!

In the series I play Claire Carlsen—not a very nice character—private secretary to Francis Urquhart, played by Ian Richardson, the second handsomest man in England, Julian being the *most* handsome. In the role, I have an affair with Paul Freeman as Tom Makepeace, the foreign secretary. I did two nude scenes with Paul. Initially, I wasn't very keen to do it; after all, I was fifty years old, but I was attracted to the part by the dialogue by Andrew Davies.

People said, "How embarrassed your son and husband must be."

I was nonplussed, but Julian encouraged me, saying it was a fantastic part. In fact, both Julian and Jamie were supportive. Once I accepted, I was at the gym every day. I wanted to be as fit as possible. That was vanity. The first nude scene was in the first episode and the second was in the third of the four episodes. We filmed each scene twice: once for showing in the UK, where I was actually nude; the second time was for airing in the US, in which I was wearing a petticoat and bra! The scenes were choreographed, much as a dance would be. It turned out to be the longest exposure of a woman's body on UK television at the time.

I was surprised at the backlash I had from women. One, an actress who shall remain nameless, wrote a rather scathing piece in the press about me, that I had obviously done it to revive a flagging career. I thought that was a little bit mean. But never mind . . . Almost fifteen years before, I'd had a nude scene with Antony Sher in *The History Man*, but I was much younger.

You shared the stage with Richard Harris, who had the reputation as being difficult. How true is it?

One of the flyers I recently acquired was the one for Pirandello's *Henry IV*, with Richard. I was terribly fond of him. Actually, he was a darling, despite his hell-raising reputation. We became good friends, and I even gave an address at his memorial.[2]

We did *Henry IV* at Wyndham's, but Richard had been on tour with it before that. Even before the tour, he went through five directors. It was a matter of Richard saying, "Either they go or I do." Val May finally took the challenge. Richard even got rid of his leading lady, Sarah Miles, as well as the designers.

I arrived for rehearsal in York and then went to London for an additional two weeks' preparation before we opened, all without Richard. He never sent a card or phoned to welcome me.

Julian was furious: "How can you put up with this? It's outrageous."

There was something in me that made me think, "Richard wants me to react strongly."

I'd heard from the stage manager that the play was the one Richard had seen as a boy in Dublin, and it made him want to be an actor, so it was hugely important to him. I, in my stupid, potted psychology, thought, "Maybe he doesn't really want to open in London because he might fail."

I just ignored that and rehearsed with the understudy. The technical rehearsal was with a new set and new costumes. But not with Richard. He didn't turn up at the dress rehearsal either. He didn't turn up at the first preview because he said his back was bothering him. Things were getting worse and worse.

The first time I met him? Literally, it was when I popped into his dressing room before we went on stage for the second preview.

Something happened at the fourth preview during his long monologue. I have no words in the scene at all; I just look at him. Suddenly, out of the blue, Richard said, "What are you staring at?"

That line isn't in the play. Although I was terribly nervous, a strange calm came over me. Julian, Jamie, and I had often talked about lines from Shakespeare that could be said to cover any eventuality on stage. I thought of a line at that moment, not from Shakespeare, but from Marlowe's *Tamburlaine the Great*, and ad-libbed, saying, "Is it not passing brave to be a king,/And ride in triumph through Persepolis?" I did a huge curtsy and walked off stage. The curtain came down. It was the end of the act.

Richard came into my dressing room at the interval and went down on his knees, laughed, and said, "I'll never do that to you again!" The next day when I went into my dressing room, it was filled with flowers from him. I think because I appeared quite calm, he knew—even though I hadn't rehearsed with him—that I wouldn't put up with anything on stage. He subsequently called me "Matron" or "The Diva." Thereafter, our relationship was very close, but it was a bit of a hairy beginning. Richard very sweetly, very generously told that story himself.

You've said of Derek Jacobi with whom you had a long working relationship in the two-hander *Mad, Bad, and Dangerous to Know*, "He makes acting exciting."

He does. He really does. I'm a huge admirer of him. He's just adorable. He's an actor who is never absolutely the same at every performance. He'll end up in the same place, but he gets there in a slightly different way, which meant that I had to respond in a different way each time. That made it exciting. I love that rather than being completely the same every night.

The name of the play is taken from Lady Caroline Lamb's description of Byron. Derek played Byron, and I played all the women in his life. We went all 'round the world doing *Dangerous*. We toured to Israel, New York, and Los Angeles. We did one-off performances for charities as well.

I remember him as Malvolio in *Twelfth Night* [2008]. He was so nervous about playing that role. "Oh, all these people who've played it before me!" he said. But he was fantastic. He and his partner, Richard Clifford, are close friends of ours. We visit them in their house in France. They're just such nice people.

In *The Company Man,* you took on a challenging role. How did you approach it?

It's a new play by Torben Betts, a very dark play about a dysfunctional family. It's strong and upsetting but also very funny. My character, Jane, has motor neuron disease.[3] It's a terrible disease that affects the voice; it paralyzes the tongue [Blair demonstrates the sound], so you can't speak properly. It makes your voice come from the back of your throat, and actors are trained to have the voice come from the front. My voice became very hoarse, but it had to be in order to get the right sound.

The story takes place in one day, and there are flashbacks to when Jane is twenty years younger and didn't have the disease. I go from a wheelchair-bound invalid to the woman I was. Back and forth. The play focuses on the decisions which she made throughout her life: If she'd done that then, would that or this have happened? At the end, she decides to end her life with her daughter's help.

I did a great deal of research into the disease and worked closely with a woman who has the disease and was supported by the MND Association. David Niven had MND and I again read his books *Bring on the Empty Horses* and *The Moon's a Balloon*, but his condition is not mentioned in either, but they gave me some insight into the character. I also read *My Better Half and Me* by Joss Ackland's wife, Rosemary. She had the disease and chronicled her day-to-day events most articulately.

We played at the Orange Tree, Richmond, for five weeks. We had interesting responses from the audience: they either loved it or hated it; they mostly loved it, but those who hated it still got something out of it. The weird thing is that no critic from a major paper came to review it. They didn't bother to come even though they had reviewed Betts's other work at other theatres. It's insulting to the playwright. The audience there likes their Shaw and Pinero and the like, so the critics don't equate the Orange Tree with *new* writing. But we *want* the critics to come, even if they come and hate it! We all said that if this play had been on at the Donmar or the Royal Court or the Almeida, they'd have been there. So many good critics, like Michael Billington of the *Guardian*, who champion new writing . . . where was he?

How do you keep your performance fresh doing eight shows a week?

First, the instinct part of being an actor helps. Most actors say, "I'm always nervous before a performance," and people say, "But you've been doing it for weeks."

That's true, I know. But I can't help it. There's a little flutter before I go on stage. I wish there wasn't because it's not very comfortable. For *Company*

Man, for example, it was quite frightening every night. That particular part is very emotional and very raw. I was having a great difficulty sleeping; I couldn't turn it off. It had happened before when I did *The Verge*, also at the Orange Tree, which was written in 1921, about a brilliant botanist who was going through a nervous breakdown.

I was talking about this in the bar at the theatre after a performance of Betts's play, and a woman overheard what I was saying. She came up to me and said, "I'm a doctor, and I'm doing a paper on actors. I'm interested to hear you talk about this. Can I explain to you why you're not sleeping?"

I said, "Well, I guess it's because I can't turn my brain off."

"No," she said, "I can see the real tears and the feelings that you're going through. But your body doesn't know that you're acting, so your body is being pumped with adrenaline and all sorts of other hormones and chemicals. That's why, at the end of the performance, you can't 'come down.' It takes time to 'come down.'" She also asked, "When you finish a play, do you get a bit depressed?"

I told her, "I miss my colleagues but also the part I'm playing."

"It's the adrenaline you miss," she told me.

What she said was so obvious, and I hadn't thought of it until then. Now it doesn't bother me that I'm not sleeping. It's annoying, though.

Is there a play that is particularly memorable . . . because it was fun?

Noises Off by Michael Frayn was one of the most joyous experiences I've ever had. It was like going to a party every night. I took over the role of Dotty in 2001 from Lynn Redgrave—darling Lynn.

At the beginning of the play, I have a line where I ask the director, "Is that what I do now?" I remember hearing about an audience member asking for his money back at the interval. He was upset, I was told, and said to the box office manager, "The actors don't know what they're supposed to be doing." [Blair squeals with laughter at the recollection.]

I did the play for about six months at the Piccadilly. It was one of those plays I absolutely adored.[4]

What acting advice did you receive that has been helpful?

Anthony Quayle, a wonderful actor, a wonderful man, said something to me that has hung with me absolutely forever. I was going through a phase where a dear friend of mine was getting all the parts I went up for. It was very difficult on our friendship because I couldn't help being envious, being jealous. Anthony said to me, "You must never envy anybody anything because you never know what they're going through."

That particular friend, I knew, was desperate to have a child and couldn't, and I'd had a child. His words put my feet back on the ground and made me sort out my feelings about this friend. I took her out to lunch and said, "I like you so much, and I have these awful feelings about you." She told me that I had just got a part *she* wanted. Because it was out in the open, it wasn't a problem again. I am very grateful to Anthony for his advice.

With a decades-long career as an actor, what are your thoughts about acting as an art or craft?

Gosh. I think for me, it's more of an art. You learn basic techniques in drama school, such as projection and movement, which is the craft side of acting, but you learn later the part that makes an audience want to be with you, to go, as it were, on the journey with you in the story you're part of, and that comes from deep inside. That part is the art, and it's terribly hard to put into words.

Sometimes when we're acting—and it doesn't happen with every performance—something comes from *outside*. We have a family expression: "It makes you fly."

I'm more of an instinctive actor, I suppose, rather than I am an intellectual one. I go through thought processes and what things mean and about the subtext.

The director, Adam Barnard, has a system of breaking down the script into each individual thought, which, for me, is sort of stifling. And he knows this. If I can't find the part for myself, I feel it will never belong to me, that it was prescribed by someone else, and I would never feel it. It may sound silly, but I have to come to the part from the inside.

I remember talking to Judi Dench about that, and she said, "Oh, I just do it, however it comes."

I wouldn't put myself anywhere near Judi, but I have a similar feeling. I know my best work comes when I haven't even necessarily thought about it. That's what makes the audience want to watch, to be with me rather than when everything is clinically worked out.

As an actor, I get to do and learn so many bits and pieces of life that I wouldn't probably know if I weren't an actor. I learnt to ride sidesaddle for the role of Lady Caroline in a television series, *When the Boat Comes In*. I learnt how to crochet and cross-pollinate a flower. For this current role, I learnt about motor neuron disease. We're so lucky as actors because we brush bits of people's lives that most people don't get to do.

Selected Credits

Theatre

A Funny Thing Happened on the Way to the Forum, Strand (1963; George Abbott); *Boswell's Life of Dr. Johnson*, Assembly Hall, Edinburgh (1966; Toby Robertson); *The Man of Mode*, RSC, Stratford (1971; Terry Hands); *Miss Julie*, RSC at the Place (1971; Robin Phillips); *Subject to Fits*, the Place (1971; A. J. Antoon); *Popkiss*, Arts, Cambridge; Globe (1972; Richard Cottrell); *The Grand Tour*, Old Vic (1972; Toby Robertson); *Twelfth Night*, Prospect Theatre Company at the Round House (1973; Toby Robertson); *Vivat! Vivat Regina!*, Bristol Old Vic (1973; David Phethean); *Jumpers*, Bristol Old Vic (1973–1974; John David); *Othello*, Bristol Old Vic (1973–1974; Val May); *Hobson's Choice*, Bristol Old Vic (1973–1974; David Phethean); *Blues Whites and Reds*, Birmingham Rep (1974; John Burgess); *The Rivals*, Prospect Theatre Company at the Old Vic (1978; Anthony Quayle, Ian Judge); *King Lear*, Old Vic (1978; Toby Robertson); *Miss in Her Teens*, Old Vic (1979; John Dove); *Padlock*, Old Vic (1979; Toby Robertson); *Hay Fever*, Yvonne Arnaud, Guildford (1980; Michael Blakemore); *Mad, Bad, and Dangerous to Know*, RSC Swan; Ambassadors; US tour; (1981, 1992; Jane McCulloch); *Henry IV* (Pirandello), Wyndham's (1990; Val May); *What the Butler Saw*, NT, Lyttelton (1995; Phyllida Lloyd); *Hamlet*, Norwich Playhouse (1996; Julian Glover); *The Verge*, Orange Tree, Richmond (1996; Auriol Smith); *Tartuffe*, Theatre Royal Bath (1997; Michael Grandage); *Noises Off*, Piccadilly (2001; Jeremy Sams); *In Praise of Love*, Theatre Royal Bath (2001; Deborah Bruce); *Mrs. Warren's Profession*, Bristol Old Vic (2002–2003; Deborah Bruce); *A Funny Thing Happened . . .* , NT, Olivier (2004; Edward Hall); *Stuff Happens*, NT, Olivier (2004; Nicholas Hytner); *The History Boys*, NT, UK tour (2006–2007; Nicholas Hytner); *Collaboration*, CFT (2008; Philip Frank); *The Company Man*, Orange Tree, Richmond (2010; Adam Barnard); *The Breath of Life*, Lyceum, Sheffield (2011; Peter Gill); *Steel Magnolias*, UK tour (2012; David Gilmore); *The Lyons*, Menier Chocolate Factory (2013; Mark Brokaw); *Made in Dagenham*, Adelphi (2014; Rupert Goold); *Damsel in Distress*, CFT (2015; Rob Ashford)

Film

A Hard Day's Night, scenes deleted (1964); *Dr. Terror's House of Horrors*, "Disembodied Hand" (1965); *Battle of Britain* (1969); *Taste the Blood of Dracula* (1970); *Valmont* (1989); *The Match* (1999); *Mrs. Caldicott's Cabbage War* (2000); *Afterlife* (2003); *Johnny English Reborn* (2011)

Television

The Liars, four episodes (1966); *The Dickie Henderson Show*, twelve episodes (1968); *The Saint*, "The Ex-King of Diamonds" (1969); *When the Boat Comes In*, four episodes (1976–1977); *Blake's 7*, "Duel" (1978); *Dr. Who*, "The King's Demon, Parts I and II" (1983); *The Beggar's Opera* (1983); *Hammer House of Mystery and Suspense*, "Tennis Court" (1984); *The History Man* (1991); *Inspector Morse*, "Cherubim and Seraphim" (1993); *The Final Cut*, four episodes (1995); *A Touch of Frost*, "Fun Times for Swingers" (1996), "True Confessions" (1997), "No Other Love" (1997); *Heaven on Earth* (1998); *The Mrs. Bradley Mysteries*, "The Worsted Viper" (2000); *Midsomer Murders*, "Death and Dreams" (2003); *Law & Order: UK*, "ID," "Broken" (2010); *Single Father*, four episodes (2010); *Johnny English Reborn* (2011); *Quick Cuts* (2013); *Grantchester* (2014)

Publications

A Tiger's Wedding: My Life in Exile (2011)

Notes

1. A theory developed by Rudolf Laban that analyzes movement; it is used by actors, dancers, choreographers, and directors.

2. Harris died in 2002 at age seventy-two.

3. Also called amyotropic lateral sclerosis (ALS, Lou Gehrig's disease)

4. Blair's son, actor Jamie Glover, appeared in the same play a decade later as Garry LeJeune (2012; Lindsay Posner) at the Novello.

CHAPTER THREE

Simon Callow, CBE

Learning to play a character is like learning to speak a foreign language.

The "street" leading to the Brydges Club is adjacent to the Coliseum, home of the English National Opera. Brydges Street is so narrow that two people cannot pass each other. The doorway to the club is nondescript and easily missed. Inside, Simon Callow is seated with friends at a table on the restaurant level and waves. "I'll be there in a few minutes. Just going to buy a wok!" he announces.

The room where the interview takes place is up a winding, narrow staircase. The decoration is eclectic: four volumes of Harmsworth's 1906 Self-Educator; a painting of an Arab on a camel in a broken frame; a still of a cowboy on a palomino from an unidentified film; several pictures of oceangoing vessels. A candlestick props open the window.

Born in Streatham, London, sixty-five-year-old Callow is not just an actor; he directs, writes—more than a dozen books, so far—and is a theatre historian of note. Having made his purchase, Callow, enters, divests himself of his scarf and jacket. The sleeves of his rumpled shirt are rolled to the elbow. He orders tea. His energy is palpable; his words tumble out in torrents with hardly a breath between thoughts. His hands constantly thread through his curly silver hair as he speaks.

There were people in your early life who set you on the path as an actor. Who were they?

There are two grandmothers, "both alike in dignity" [he laughs at his reference to a line from *Romeo and Juliet*]. Completely different people. My paternal grandmother had a great impact on me at an early age. She actually saved my life, I'd say. Toto, my father's French mother, did everything she could to encourage me to lead a disciplined and culturally enriched life. She was the one who, whenever I went to visit her, required that I spend the first half hour of my visit doing handwriting. I had to do calligraphy, italics, copperplate, and something called Marian Richardson [an educator who developed a method of penmanship]. I'm very grateful to her now, but I hated it at the time. Then we'd go to the theatre, not because she loved the theatre but because it was something that one should do.

Whereas my other grandmother was the pleasure principle incarnate, and I never went to the theatre with that grandmother. She *was* the theatre. The theatre was redundant. She had been a chorus girl at one point, and she was very flamboyant and expansive. She and I used to dress up and play games and improvise plays. It was wonderful.

But we mustn't leave my mother out of this. She was much more like Toto. She believed that everything you did had to be earned. For example, if you went to the theatre or to see a film, then you couldn't watch the television that night because you'd had enough pleasure. Everything was rationed. She was very strict in many ways. The concept of lolling about and doing nothing was absolutely intolerable to her. She used to break into my room to ask what I was doing. I'd say, "I'm reading a book."

She'd say, "Then you can come and do the washing up." Or, "There's a floor that needs to be scrubbed." Unless I was doing my homework, that was the only justification for my being on my own. Reading a book didn't count *at all*!

I understand her reason for that, and I don't criticize her for that. She believed that her life and that of her generation had been wasted because of the Depression. She left school when she was fifteen. She had no qualifications. She was determined that I would have qualifications and wanted to instill in me the work principle.

I now feel unspeakable guilt if any day passes without having achieved something. That's the only remnant of my Catholicism. I feel guilt about it, really as if I've committed a sin of some kind by not having *done* something, not having anything to show for the day.

Your father went out to Africa, and your mother took a job as secretary at a school in Goring-on-Thames when they separated. After some shuttling

Photo courtesy of Riverside Studios

**back and forth between the UK and Africa when they attempted reconcili-
ation, you attended a variety of schools. Besides some theatrical work in
school, how did you begin your education as an actor?**

I went to the theatre with my grandmother, as I mentioned. Then as a
teen, I went to the opera and read voraciously about theatre. Visits to the
National at the Old Vic became compulsive so much so that I wrote a letter
to Laurence Olivier, and he wrote back and invited me to work in the box
office at the theatre.

That was really the beginning of my education as an actor. I watched all
the plays and talked to the actors and decided that I wanted to see if I could
do it, which by no means was certain in my mind. I had no reason to know
that I could do it. I'd never done a play except in my infant school. Then I
decided to go to university. I thought if I was going to try to be an actor, I
thought I could go to drama school—but I felt I was too old; I was nineteen.
I sort of knew that drama school wouldn't be a good idea for me. Then I
thought I could go to university; I'd heard that people like Ian McKellen and
Alan Howard and other actors had not had drama school training but had
been to university. That's how *they* learnt.

At Queen's in Belfast, I joined the drama society, and I did my very first acting there. I played a barrister in a Danish play called *The Political Tinker* by Ludvig Holberg. It was nothing but a bit of fun. Then I was cast as Trigorin in Chekhov's *The Seagull*. I suddenly realized how very, very, *very* far from being an actor I was. But Queen's was just a chapter along the way. I left after nine months and never got my degree. I decided to leave university and go to drama school, but I went back to work again in box offices at the Aldwych when the RSC was there and also the Mermaid Theatre.

You chose the unconventional Drama Centre in Chalk Farm, rather than a more conservative one. What was the attraction?

It was founded in 1963 by a trio of teachers who left the Central School— Christopher Fettes, John Blatchley, and Yat Malmgren—and was radically different from RADA, LAMDA, and the other drama schools of the time. It's now integrated into Central St. Martins School of Art and Design. These teachers were extraordinary, towering figures, who probably wouldn't be allowed to run a drama school now because they were entirely original. Everybody who went there said it changed their lives, for better or for ill. Some couldn't deal with it.

I didn't enroll until I was twenty-one, emerging at twenty-four, so I was older than many of the other students. For me, those three years just answered everything I needed. Had the school not been so stimulating, I would have not been engaged by it.

What it was really like, I realize in retrospect, was like having Zen training where the whole point of the master is not to teach you anything but to wake you up [he slaps his hands together] to your own thoughts and wake you up to live in the now rather than dreaming or being nostalgic or whatever. That was what they were about. One of the most famous things they used to say was, "Leave yourself alone," meaning don't try to impose things on your performance. What you're trying to do is to connect with the inner life of the character, which is your own inner life, rather than putting on a face, putting on a mask, a voice. It was incomprehensible to us because we didn't know where this inner life was supposed to come from.

Now I understand what they were talking about, and I understand a lot more about acting. The most important perception I've had about it is that acting is thinking the thoughts, penetrating into the mind of the character. One of the principal tools of the Drama Centre was how helpful improvisation can be to get you to that pitch: to awaken you to the minute-by-minute playing, the line of the scene, the action of the scene.

The kind of improvisation I'm talking about is when you have such a connection with the character's thoughts that you can actually speak in their
words, more or less in the way the author would have done it. You can actually improvise Shakespeare, just as you should be able to improvise Samuel
Beckett—God help us! [He peers over his glasses.] It would be terrible Beckett, but it would be Beckett, nonetheless.

Learning to play a character is like learning to speak a foreign language.
If you're always translating in your head in a foreign language, you're not
speaking. It's only when you start to actually think in, say, French that you're
speaking French. [He stops, looks astonished, and says] I've never thought or
said that before.

The basis of the Centre's curriculum was Stanislavski, wasn't it?

Absolutely. The evolving Stanislavski, along with Rudolf Laban and Carl
Jung—although the teacher who made a huge difference in my life, Doreen
Cannon, was a pupil of Uta Hagen, who was, in turn, a pupil of Stella Adler,
which goes right back to the Group Theatre and Lee Strasberg. Strasberg
really vulgarized and ossified Stanislavski's insights. I also think that Stanislavski was, naturally, like any great teacher in that a lot of what he wrote
came from self-reflection and self-observation. He was an unusual kind of an
actor: he was intensely self-conscious in front of the public.

Many of us feel quite the opposite. He feared what he called "the great
black abyss" of the auditorium; many of us love that great abyss. He was also,
it is said, dyslexic, so he used to paraphrase plays all the time to the rage of
Vladimir Danchenko, his codirector at the Moscow Art Theatre, who was
a playwright. It was a perfect combination because they each had what the
other lacked, even though they stopped speaking to each other in the end.

Those three years at the Centre were the happiest years of my life.

From there, your career had a remarkable upward trajectory.

It was an exemplary trajectory. I was "discovered" by Peter Farago, went
straight to his company, the Young Lyceum, in Edinburgh, in absolutely minor parts, including as the front end of a horse in Georg Büchner's *Woyzeck*,
then into rep[ertory], which was utterly liberating and thrilling and exactly
everything I needed. I only did it for four months, but it was enough to get
the hang of it. But repertory is all gone now.

Back to Edinburgh again to work at the Lyceum. I then had the great good
luck to be in the same city as Mike Ockrent, who was running the Traverse
Theatre. When I joined him, I had an extraordinarily fulfilling time including getting a part which every young actor dreams about: the Crown Prince
in *Schippel*, directed by Mike. Charles Marowitz booked it for his and Thelma
Holt's Open Space Theatre in London, but it was Mike's production.

It's a play about a male voice quartet, highly bourgeoisie. When a replacement is needed, the only person who has an adequate voice in the town as a replacement is the plumber. The members of the quartet are disgusted at the idea of this new tenor, but the Crown Prince just happens to drop by at that moment, and they have to sing for him. The prince says to the group, "You're wonderful, especially the tenor." The tenor falls in love with the sister of the leader of the quartet and so does the Crown Prince.

I was originally cast in the quartet, but because of my problem with not having very good pitch and having to sing all those harmonies, it was really, really hard for me. Acting the Crown Prince was James Snell, very handsome, upper class, perfect casting for the prince but bored to death playing parts like that. When I told him I was going to have to give up the part of the plumber, he told me we could exchange roles. I took on the part of the prince even though I wasn't anything like James. I wasn't handsome or upper class, so I invented a different kind of prince. It bore no relation to the original German play at all. It was a bespoke part, sort of run up for me by the playwright. It was gorgeous. Indeed, I think I was very funny in the part. People liked it, and I got exceptionally good reviews.

There was a happy accident at the Open Space. My mustache wouldn't stay on. The theatre was small and very hot, and everybody could see this thing flapping. In the great love scene, I said, "My darling," and threw the mustache away, "I love you." That gesture endeared me to the critics.

Harry Secombe came to see it and decided he wanted to do it in the West End. That production, with Harry, went on to the West End in 1975 as *The Plumber's Progress*, at the Prince of Wales Theatre, with Harry as the plumber. That was a completely new production, new set; some of us from the original production stayed on with Harry.

What do you recall about Harry Secombe, one of the original members of *The Goon Show*?

Harry was, on the one hand, part three of that great comic team; Spike Milligan and Peter Sellers were the other two. On the other hand, he was a singer of some distinction; he had a huge voice. He was a professional Welshman, and used to front a program on television called *Songs of Praise*. He was absolutely a national figure. The one thing he couldn't do at all was act, not at all, *at all*. The role of the plumber was basically an acting part with a few songs thrown in. He tried desperately hard . . . and failed. He did everything he could to stop gooning around and not do comic stuff and just play the part properly, but he felt a great responsibility about it all. He was the kindest, sweetest man. Whenever he felt a bit down, he'd send a bottle of champagne to everybody in the cast. I think he drank most of his during performances.

When Spike Milligan came to see the play, he said, "Mike, what are you doing? You're killing his natural talent. Let him do what he wants to do."

In the end, Harry got pneumonia. What happened was so typical and interesting: Harry's understudy, the actor who originally played the part, the distinguished actor Roy Marsden, also became ill. There was no understudy for the understudy. We stumbled on a bit with Roy, and then we stopped altogether. It wasn't a success. It ran for maybe four months in 1975, '76.

But my name was in lights above the Prince of Wales Theatre.

Despite your protestations about not being musical, you appeared as Count Fosco in *The Woman in White*, and you have directed a number of operas. How did you overcome that self-described weakness?

I have a rather unreliable ear, so it's all a bit difficult, but I'm very much in love with music. I know a lot about it, and a lot of my friends are musicians. It's rather like driving, which I don't do anymore because I have to be perpetually vigilant. It's exhausting for me to be in a musical because I have to keep thinking about everything all the time.

Among the operas I directed was *Die Zauberflöte*. Oh, my God, how difficult that was. I even conducted an orchestra in a film called *Victory* in which I play a character called Zangiacomo, conductor of an all-female orchestra. The women came from the Munich Philharmonic, and I told them, "I apologize in advance for my beat."

"Oh," they replied [Callow does a German accent], "it is a model in comparison to Maestro Celibidache," who was their conductor.

You went completely the opposite direction for your next role.

I did a fringe play. Here is where luck comes in. Roy was about to go into a one-act play, *The Soul of the White Ant* by Snoo Wilson. But Roy was desperately in love with a woman in Edinburgh.

I asked about the play, and he said, "You do it!"

I thought, "It's set in Africa. I grew up in Africa. I can do a very good South African accent." I went to do the play at the Soho Poly Theatre, a lunchtime theatre. It was a huge hit, mad and glorious and funny beyond belief. We did an expanded version and transferred to the Bush Theatre.

David Hare saw the play at the Soho Poly and suggested that I join his Joint Stock Company in *Devil's Island*, a new play by Tony Bicât that he was directing. It was a great success . . . until we came to London, where it was a disaster at the Royal Court. It was offbeat in the wrong way. It wasn't fashionably offbeat. And unfashionably offbeat doesn't work.

Speaking of David Hare, you've said that the English have produced no auteur-directors. Isn't he an example?

I wonder what sort of person I had in mind when I said that. An auteur-director is something you'd normally apply to film rather than the stage. Harold Pinter was sort of an auteur-director, although he didn't necessarily do the best production of his own plays.

But, yes, David is an an example of an auteur. He's remarkable; he's a very uncommon figure altogether. Steven Berkoff might be considered an auteur, as he has created a language, a vocabulary of theatre all his own. David hasn't quite done that. That hasn't been his purpose, his intention.

Didn't Pinter often see himself as an actor?

Yes, when he wanted to be. Let me rephrase that: sometimes he was wonderful . . . sometimes. He was fantastic in his play *The Hothouse*, one of the most brilliant comedies I ever saw in my life. He directed the original in 1980 at the Hampstead Playhouse; in 1995, he played the lead in Chichester, later transferring to the Comedy Theatre [now named the Pinter]. I wrote him a card saying that he should have won the *Evening Standard* Comedy Performance of the Year.

He wrote back, "I felt happier getting your card than the day [cricketer] Len Hutton scored a century," which was completely incomprehensible to me. I have no idea about cricket.

Returning to the upward course of your career: As a very young actor, you played Titus Andronicus. Was that another "accident"?

Yes, another happy and wonderful accident. I was sitting in my kitchen with Gillian Barge, a wonderful actress, now sadly gone, who I'd worked with in Joint Stock. She said she had just been in Bristol where they were casting *Titus Andronicus*, with Adrian Noble directing. They were having trouble because the excellent actor Morgan Sheppard had had to pull out, and they didn't know who could play it.

She said, "You should play it."

"But," I protested, "I've never done Shakespeare." That was true. The Drama Centre eschewed Shakespeare in favor of other Elizabethan playwrights.

She phoned Adrian, who I'd gone to drama school with, and he asked me, "Would you consider doing it?"

"I'm supposed to be doing Snoo Wilson's play *The Glad Hand* at the Royal Court," I told him.

"Simon, this is *Titus Andronicus* that I'm offering you."

"All right. I'll do it."

I had to tell Snoo, who said, "But he is dead." He thought it was a necrophiliac jag of mine doing a play by a dead writer.

It was my first experience with Shakespeare, although I had always been immersed in Shakespeare. I'd read it and seen Shakespeare plays until they were coming out of my ears. But not *Titus Andronicus*, which was very rarely done in those days. All I had to go on were the reviews of Laurence Olivier's performance in Peter Brook's legendary 1955 production in Stratford. And that was a bit daunting.

The main thing I had to discover about it was how to use myself physically. Adrian and I had no idea what we were doing in that regard. We had a long technical rehearsal; we had the dress rehearsal at midnight and another dress rehearsal at three o'clock the following afternoon and then went on to do the play. I was rumbling around, and by the end of the play, I literally had no voice at all. I was sent back to London to get some injections. I had to remain silent for three weeks. I wasn't allowed to speak at all, except when I was performing. It was a very interesting Trappist period of my life.

How much has luck played in your career?

"Luck," somebody said, "is readiness plus opportunity."

Because of *Titus Andronicus*, some weird and wonderful accidents happened, all in the first part of my career and almost never in the second. Almost everything in the second part has been work made by me. I've created my own work. I've noticed the same thing but altogether different in both ends of the scale in Orson Welles's life in that Orson's luck ran out. He had the luckiest twenty-five years that anybody could have and then the luck ran out.

But opportunity is the crucial bit here. As an example, somebody had obviously seen me in something and was told John Dexter was in town at the Savoy. He was thinking of doing *The Beastly Beatitudes of Balthazar B* by J. P. Donleavy. My agent told me Dexter would pay my fare to go up to town and meet with him for breakfast. He promised I'd be back in Bristol by 10 a.m. for a performance of *Titus Andronicus*.

John was a famous monster, but utterly charming and funny and brilliant. We got on immensely well. But after the meeting, I didn't hear from him. A year later, he phoned me up and said, "Peter Shaffer has just written a new play about Mozart, and you'll be playing Mozart."

That came to pass all because I met him earlier about a play that never happened. In the end, John Dexter didn't direct the play, much to his disgust. Peter Hall directed. Peter had never seen my work any more than John

Simon Callow, CBE ⌒ 47

had or that Peter Shaffer had. I never read for it. They just gave me the part. The slot where John would have directed *Amadeus*, he directed *As You Like It*. I played Orlando for him, my second Shakespeare part. It wasn't a success for any of us. My Orlando wasn't liked; Sara Kestleman's Rosalind wasn't liked; John's production wasn't liked. I kind of stand by it. It was rather wonderful; austere, but rather wonderful.

Looking back, how do you assess Paul Scofield's role as Salieri in that premier production of *Amadeus*?

I was terrified because of his reputation and his work that I'd seen. But he was so sweet, funny, modest, easy and relaxed and generous, not difficult at all. Not a man for small talk, though. We didn't discuss what we were going to do; we just got on with it. He was an actor of such powerful integrity, such force, and such strange poetry within his own personality, so unlike Larry Olivier, who was sort of a pentathlete of an actor, transforming himself into extraordinary shapes, in a rather extrovert kind of way. Paul was always about an inner transformation. I thought he'd be a bit monk-like, but he wasn't at all. He played the old Salieri as a bit of a camp old clout. He was under great pressure because Shaffer kept on rewriting the play as we were rehearsing. Oh, God, yes. Every day. It was driving Paul mad because his process was absolutely about absorbing the words and letting them sink in deeper and deeper. But they were changed every day. I was full of disgusting energy, insatiable energy, bumping and jumping around him.

The most extraordinary thing of all happened when we finally hit the stage: Paul absolutely, literally opened out, and I could see him getting huge in front of me, just towering. He filled the space with his inner energy.

At the first preview, the whole audience just sucked him in. I'd never seen it before and not very often since. [Callow sucks in another huge breath.] It was absolutely physical, a palpable thing. He was like a huge magnet in the auditorium, him giving them what they wanted. He was doing something with the audience that I couldn't quite figure out. He was the character, but *we* didn't seem to have any great relationship. I tried to drag him back to me, and he slapped me down every time. I would sort of trample on his lines or something. He would just look at me and say the line again clearly.

There was this huge copulation going on between Paul and the audience. How it happened I don't know, but I decided, "I'm going to try that, too." I started to get a relationship with the audience, and Paul instantly relaxed. We were then playing the right game: there was suddenly a ménage à trois, which he adored. From then on, I adored working with him.

In the great scene when Salieri welcomes Mozart to the court with a little march, after the court's all gone, they have a chat. Mozart says, "You know that little bit? I love it," and he plays it, and then says, "If you just did this and this," and turns it into "Non più andrai" from *Figaro*. I spent the whole rehearsal period every day having piano lessons with a member of the music staff. I had to know exactly where my hands should be and exactly what the physical movement should be.

But Paul just sat at the piano and nobody would have thought that he wasn't playing the piano because it was irrelevant. The actual physical action was nothing. You couldn't see our fingers on the keyboard because of the way the piano was positioned on the stage. His hands were up in the air when the music was playing. Nobody cared. He didn't trade in realism of that kind. He traded in an inner life.

There's a great story about Scofield in *Lear*, directed by Peter Brook. Paul was just thirty-nine when he played Lear at the RSC. Peter said, "Paul, you've got to pay some attention to the physical life of Lear. He's got to be old."

Paul said, "It will come." Almost imperceptibly, day by day, he was getting older and older. The finished portrayal didn't have anything to do with makeup; it was in the eyes; it was in difficulty of movement. It was absolutely to do with imagination, letting it happen inside his brain, just as he let words fill with meaning.

Paul didn't tour because he didn't like to be away from home. Home was his absolute refuge; it was the source of everything. What he did at home, who knew? He didn't dissipate himself on anything else. He got onto the train down to Balcombe in Sussex for some supper, a glass of whiskey; he smoked a couple of pipes, read. Nothing that you could analyze.

Alec Guinness did the same in a very different way. Alec *was* interested in physical manifestations, and he would slave for weeks to get a tiny, tiny little piece of business exactly right. In one instance, when Alec played Shylock at Chichester, and in order to prepare, he took a plane to Jerusalem and stood in front of the Wailing Wall for a day. Then he came back and played Shylock. When he walked on stage, he brought on stage with him the whole of Jewish history.

You probably think that's the most pretentious thing you've heard, and how could I possibly know, but if you'd seen it, you'd think, "This man's bones are filled with oppression and grief." It was incredible.

When Olivier played Shylock in Jonathan Miller's production at the Old Vic, he did more spectacular physical things. Everything was masterly. The inner life came to him in a different way.

How did you approach the role of Toby Belch in *Twelfth Night*, a role that has a long history?

People say, "Oh, Toby Belch—he's just another drunk, isn't he?" They say he's very nasty. Well, he is very nasty, but there's a bigger story than that. Any time you try to reduce Shakespeare's stories to a single, simple proposition, you're traducing it.

The thing that is extraordinary about Shakespeare is the degree to which he plunges into the heart of every aspect of human experience. He's incapable of writing a stereotype. He writes archetypes, which are fantastically hard to do, to release, embrace and to realize on stage. Only the very, very greatest actors do it. In the end, the job is to learn how to think the thoughts of this character.

Once I've learnt to think the thoughts of Toby Belch, then I'll be playing Toby Belch. It was fine. He reminds me rather alarmingly of my father, and that's going to be, I hope, a fairly profound line of investigation for me. My father was a disappointed hedonist. He was a man who never wanted the party to end, but it had ended years before I was born. He was of the war generation, and they knew how to party. They really did because they might be dead tomorrow. Everybody of his generation—my mother, my aunt, my grandmother, his cousins and family and friends—many of them in their nineties now, were, of course, all defined by the war. The war was their time, and, God, they lived.

I think Toby is in a situation like that where it's gone away from him, and he can't quite understand why, and it makes him crazy. When he sees someone like Malvolio, it's like a red rag to a bull. He's everything that has spoiled Toby's life as far as Toby's concerned. It's not true because Toby has spoiled his own life, just as my father spoiled his life.

At the moment, I don't see how I'm ever going to be able to play the part at all. I find it incredibly difficult. It seems impossible. I read a play, and I think, "I'll have to stand on the stage and say these lines."

The same thing happened when I was going to play Pozzo in *Waiting for Godot*. I thought I could play Pozzo easily. Everybody said that I was born to play Pozzo. I started rehearsing, and I didn't even know where to begin with this character. He looks as if he's just a kind of ringmaster, a raging tyrant. If you genuinely look at every single word in the part, you realize that he comprehends universes. He's human history; he's the man who enslaves another man. That's human history, isn't it? I finally did find a way into it.

What, then, is the actor's responsibility, the job, as it were?

The job is: you have to be able to read what's there. Not many actors are very good at reading, either aloud or just reading. It takes us quite a long time to be penetrated by what has been written. Many of us spend quite a lot of our lives doing work, which doesn't have any secret to yield or any depth in it at all, so we struggle to make the surface attractive.

If you have the extraordinary experience of working in a play by Shakespeare or Eugene O'Neill or David Hare, you've got something of substance, something which you have to be humble enough to say, "What's here? What is it that I'm not seeing, that's not quite apparent yet?"

Samuel Johnson said about actors: "The Drama's laws the Drama's Patrons give/For we, who live to please, must please to live." How correct was he evaluating what actors do and that responsibility?

Up to a point. "Pleasing" is not all what we're about. You mustn't forget the sacerdotal aspect of acting. We're priests as well. We're vagabonds and jugglers and entertainers and priests. We have it within us to summon up some of the energies of the universe and profoundly resonate with our fellow human beings. It's enormously satisfying when it happens; there's nothing like it, nothing on earth like it.

At the end of the day, is acting an art or craft?

It's both, of course. There's no such thing as art without craft. There is certainly the opposite. It depends on how you do it. Art is only craft taken to a pitch where it becomes creative. If you're a skilled craftsman, you can start to do interesting things.

To put it another way, a more fanciful way, is to say that craft is a kind of sanity, is logic, is comprehension, and all the rest of it. Art is a kind of madness. It has to be. Art is the anarchic element, the bit that you can't completely control or understand. Craft makes coherent an expression of art. Art is intuition, imagination, fantasy, sinking into the bowels and dwelling in the id.

You moved to the other side of the footlights to direct. Having been an actor, what do you expect your role as a director should be? Do you have to divorce yourself from being an actor to direct?

There's a fear on the part of actors, sometimes, that I'm going to make them act the roles the way I would act them, which couldn't be further from the truth. My job, it seems to me, after the initial, preliminary task of making sure everybody knows what the play is about and to get to know the play *together* . . . and once that process is achieved, and I've heard about what they're all feeling about what they want to do, then my task is—the task of all directors always is—to harness the play and their feelings about the play so that it's a coherent, or at least a convincing world or expression on the stage.

What I like is the process of exploration. I like to get to the point where actors are bursting to get to their feet and push even a little bit further. It's terribly important that everybody is listening to the play. A play is just mere surface; it's just the words. There's a subterranean kingdom of the play that we need to have dwelt in before we can start rehearsing. My whole hope is to be like Max Reinhardt, who had this sort of weird seventh sense: he could pick up from what the actor wanted to do and then bring it out and give him exactly the shape needed to let that happen.

What do you expect the actor to come to you with?

A lot. I would be very pleased if they haven't made final choices about what they want to do physically on the stage. But I hope they will have absolutely immersed themselves in the play and the part and run it through their brains many, many times.

I don't find it very satisfactory to find someone who's come in as a blank sheet of paper. Actors have got a little conditioned to do that because directors have such arrogant and settled views about what a play or a part should be that actors ask themselves, "What's the point of doing anything until I find out what he's got to say?"

By that point, it's almost too late. I was always pleased that Peter Hall said to everybody, "Could you have the lines learned by the first day?" It means that the actors have engaged with the play.

There's a wonderful guy who, when we were at drama school and working on a Feydeau farce, used to start every day's rehearsal by everybody telling the plot. Everybody would miss something. It would be your turn today, and you'd start and no [he smacks his hands together], you've left something out. By the time we actually got onto the stage, we were thinking about plot.

You also directed a film, just one, *The Ballad of Sad Café* with a screenplay by Edward Albee, with Rod Steiger, who was known to be difficult. Your recollections?

I was fond of Rod, but he really was a monster, a childish monster. He sort of knew it was a game. That was all right; it's when they don't know it's a game that's really tough. There was a great moment when he makes a speech about love, one of the great prose passages in the whole of twentieth-century American writing—about the lover and the beloved.

He was a very sentimental actor, and I had to guard against that. When I gave a note to Rod, I had to come in to him with a chair and a whip.

He said, "Oh, my God," and he called his wife over.

"Paula, how long have we been together?" he asked her.

"Twenty-five years," she said.

"In all that time," he asked, "have you ever known me to take a note from a director?"

She said, "No, Rod."

"I did today. The shame of it," he said.

Any thoughts about directing more films?

It's not my passion. What I'd really like to do is write screenplays. I love writing screenplays. I have written a number of them, but nobody has had the intelligence to film them. Some of them are genuinely rather good. It's a lovely medium. I would direct a film again, but it would have to be intensely personal. *Ballad* wasn't. It was just given to me by Ismail Merchant. What a ball breaker for a first venture!

Have you sorted out whether you are an Oxfordian or Stratfordian or even a Baconian relative to the authorship of Shakespeare?

It's very clear which flag I wave: Shakespeare was Shakespeare. I don't think there's anything to the other ideas at all. The only thing I think about it is—the most famous instance is the very interesting life that is the parallel between Oxford's life and that of Hamlet. There's absolutely no reason why Shakespeare wouldn't have known about that. London was a very small and intense community. He could pick up pretty well anything he wanted to know. Shakespeare, like any other writer, would seize on a morsel of something and think, "My God, there's a play in that."

I can't be bothered to go beyond the point of the 1623 folio, only seven years after Shakespeare died. Ben Jonson calls him, "Sweet swan of Avon."

I'm not aware of Bacon or the Earl of Oxford coming anywhere near the Avon. Then Jonson goes into some detail about what a wonderful guy he was, and he was easy to work with. And, if you want to know what he looked like, here's a picture of him at the front of the First Folio, says Jonson. Why would Ben Jonson, who was Shakespeare's rival, say all of that? He showers him with the most exalted praise on this man he knew, this man from Stratford.

Why wouldn't somebody have exposed it at the time? London was full of malicious and malevolent people who were longing for an opportunity to trounce the recently departed dramatist. It's just all preposterous, as far as I'm concerned.

I think sometimes, oddly enough, the Oxfordians in their weird passion to promote their man do draw attention to aspects of the plays that we might not even be thinking about. I do think there's some value to all of that.

Two of my acting colleagues take other views: Derek Jacobi is a fervent Oxfordian; Mark Rylance is a passionate Baconian.

You have created your own work, including your one-man show *The Man from Stratford* by Jonathan Bate.

That is a journey through Shakespeare's life and times, but perhaps more important is that going through his life is the journey through life itself. We take the Seven Ages of Man as the spine of the piece. I have to say, when we finally sorted the play out and got it to where it should be as a play, the last third of the play just numbs the audience into an awed recognition of the great and terrible things that happen to us as we get older.

The idea is to look at the Seven Ages of Man and ask, "What was it like to be an Elizabethan baby?" and "What was it like to be an Elizabethan schoolboy?" or a soldier or whatever. We also asked, "What was the law in Shakespeare's time?" and "What did that mean?" And out of that springs the characters who speak of these matters.

Your touring schedule for those one-man productions is monumental. How do you accommodate yourself to the various venues and audiences? How different is it each time you step onto a different stage?

I can't emphasize how utterly, absolutely that is the case. I like it. It keeps me constantly alive, constantly working on creating a relationship with the audience, but it's true that a first performance in any new venue is a little bit of a car crash. I think, "Ah, why is that light suddenly there? And the acoustics are so different." But it's amazing how quickly I get used to it. Sometimes in the UK, I had a couple of split weeks, but normally, I have three days here, three days there. I like going to different places and playing to different audiences.

In a one-man play particularly I've got the physical environment around me. The lighting plot is sort of my choreography, and then I've got the relationship to the audience. All those things change because sometimes we play in theatres like that [he spreads his arms wide]; sometimes we're playing in theatres like that [he closes in his arms]; sometimes a theatre without any proscenium arch at all; sometimes the lights will come in from there [he points up to the right], sometimes from there [pointing to the opposite corner]—everything changes.

One of the recent Shakespeare gigs was in Trieste in the Teatro Stabile di Trieste, 1,500 seats, a hu-u-u-uge auditorium. There are not many 1,500-seat theatres on the road in England. It was very much an amphitheatre feel. I didn't know how I was going to get through it, but the acoustics were wonderful. Within a day or two I was able to find a way of relating to the audience. It was fantastic. The Italians adored it.

The more people you play to, the more places you go to, each of them tells you something different, and the hope is you can hang on to that and absorb it into the whole.

That's one of the glories of a one-person play. You can change the text, the moves, or the light very easily. One's striving all the time to kind of make it richer and fulfill it more and more.

What about the loss of camaraderie when playing with other actors when you're doing a one-person production?

I don't feel that. I have the camaraderie of the audience. The beauty of a one-man show is that if you realize that it needs to go faster, then you make it go faster; whereas, if you're with other actors, you have to sort of negotiate with them, and they may not feel that way. There will be this interesting but quite tense relationship. It's a great joy to play with others, but I don't miss it when it's not there. There are certain actors I've had fantastic relationships with on stage. It can be complicated with other actors.

How much does your research for the one-man shows play in your defining the character, whether Shakespeare, Wilde, or Dickens?

When I have time, I read the standard biographies or letters. But research is not the main thing. It's that business of thinking, "Oh, I see. He's that kind of guy. He's the kind of person who could do that. What does that tell us about him?"

I've played about twenty-five real characters. With a character in a play, all you have are the words on the page, which is a lot, a great deal. Real characters always fascinate me because there's always so much to go on. With Paul-Marie Verlaine in Christopher Hampton's *Total Eclipse*, I listened to his poetry, and I listened to the music he loved. I was interested in the basic thread of Verlaine, which is that he was on the strange axis between sentimentality and violence, which is part of the alcoholic community. That's what I wanted to find. He wrote the most ineffably tender poetry in the French language, lovely, lyrical, exquisite. Then he thumps his pregnant wife. What kind of man is that? I got images of him, wonderful cartoons. Tony Sher always draws his characters and, from those drawings, he can reveal sort of the inner life of the character. I don't have the capacity to do that, though.

For *The Importance of Being Oscar*, I actually ran my fingers through Oscar Wilde's hair. Merlin Holland has all the stuff of his grandfather's, including this great lock of Oscar's hair. It's in perfect condition, with just a fleck of gray.

Actors have said, "Every job that I finish feels like the last job I'll ever do." Is that what you believe?

Absolutely. It's been that way through the centuries. It's because there's something fairly deep in that. It's not just because of unemployment or because of insecurity. It's because every part is utterly different from every other part and must be. You're trying to tell an entirely different story, one that's never been told. You must believe that.

You can't say, "Oh, I'm going to do Toby Belch again. I know how to do that. I've seen it on the stage multiple times. It's going to be easy."

I think you have to approach every play as if it has been delivered to the printer the morning before. We've just got to find out what's in it. It's not ever all that clear.

You've taken up a pen to great acclaim, writing biographies of Charles Laughton and Orson Welles, a rather disparate pair.

They are indeed. Orson's book started because I wanted to write about his theatre work, which wasn't so terribly well known and had inspired me. As a young actor, I'd read John Houseman's book, *Run Through*, and he gives the most wonderful account of the Mercury Theatre. I thought, "That's what theatre should be like."

I started writing about the theatre and did it very thoroughly. Everybody I interviewed asked, "Why are you just doing about the theatre? Why don't you write about his full life? We haven't recognized the Orson Welles we knew in anything anybody's written."

I did my first interview in 1989. The first book was about thirty-five years of his life. The second volume is five hundred pages and is about five years of his life. Now I'm on the third volume.

I wrote about Laughton because he was a great actor. I think he is the greatest English movie actor we ever produced. He didn't do much on stage, relative to film, although he had a brilliant theatre career. My unfavorite of all his films is *Hobson's Choice*. I find him so clumsy in the comedy, and director David Lean has no humor.

Laughton's outstanding performances are in *Les Misérables* as a wonderful Javert in 1935; *Rembrandt* in 1936; *The Hunchback of Notre Dame* in 1939; and *Witness for the Prosecution* in 1957, a gorgeous kind of English character comedy. When I spoke to Billy Wilder about *Witness for the Prosecution*, he said, "After we finished principal photography, we had to shoot the court scene reaction shots. The first AD was going to stand in. Laughton happened to come back to the lot, and he asked me, 'Would it help if I were to stand in?'" Laughton played every part; he played Marlene Dietrich; he played Ty

Power. He was just in love with acting. He was a bit fed up by the end of his career and exhausted by the reading tours he did.

And other writing ventures?

If I ever write another book about theatre, it would be the book that Kathleen Tynan, widow of theatre critic Ken Tynan, who, on her deathbed, begged me to write about Ken and Larry Olivier. That would be wonderful. I would love to write those, but it's just the time it takes. I might try fiction, which may even take longer, but it's in my control; it doesn't involve me unendingly reading ninety-seven books.

⌇

Callow concludes the interview by announcing he has an appointment with his laryngologist on Harley Street; he slides into his jacket, throws his scarf around his neck, and strides out.

Selected Credits

Theatre

Ane Satyre of the Three Estates, Assembly Hall, Edinburgh (1973); *Woyzeck*, Assembly Hall, Edinburgh (1973; Radu Penciulescu); *Hefetz*, Traverse, Edinburgh (1974; David Mouchtar-Samorai); *Schippel*, Traverse, Edinburgh; Open Space (as *The Plumber's Progress*), Prince of Wales (1974; Mike Ockrent); *The Doctor's Dilemma*, Mermaid (1975; Robert Chetwyn); *The Soul of the White Ant*, Soho Poly, Bush (1976–1977; Dusty Hughes); *Epsom Downs*, Joint Stock Company, Round House (1977; Max Stafford-Clark); *Flying Blind*, Royal Court (1978; Chris Bond); *Mary Barnes*, Birmingham Rep (1978; Peter Farago); *Amadeus*, NT, Olivier (1979; Peter Hall); *As You Like It*, NT, Olivier (1979; John Dexter); *Sisterly Feelings*, NT, Olivier (1980; Alan Ayckbourn, Christopher Morahan); *The Beastly Beatitudes of Balthazar B*, Duke of York's (1981; Ron Daniels); *Total Eclipse*, Lyric Hammersmith (1982; David Hare); *Faust, Parts One and Two*, Lyric Hammersmith (1989; David Freeman); *The Alchemist*, NT, Olivier; Birmingham Rep (1996; Bill Alexander); *Importance of Being Oscar*, Savoy (1997; Patrick Garland); *Chimes at Midnight*, CFT (1998; Patrick Garland); *The Mystery of Charles Dickens*, Belasco, New York (2002; Patrick Garland); *The Woman in White*, Palace (2005; Trevor Nunn); *Present Laughter*, Theatre Royal Bath (2006; Michael Rudman); *Equus*, Theatre Royal Bath (2008; Thea Sharrock); *Waiting for Godot*, Theatre Royal Haymarket (2009; Sean Mathias); *Twelfth Night*, NT, Cottesloe [now Dorfman] (2011; Peter Hall); *Being Shakespeare*,

Trafalgar Studios (2012); BAM, New York (2014); Harold Pinter (2012; Tom Cairns); *The Man Jesus*, Lyric, Belfast (2013; Joseph Alford); *Chin Chin*, Theatre Royal Bath; UK tour (2013; Michael Rudman); *Inside Wagner's Head*, Linbury Studio, ROH (2013; Simon Stokes)

Opera and Theatre Director
The Infernal Machine (1986, Lyric Hammersmith); *Die Fledermaus* (1988, Theatre Royal, Glasgow); *Shirley Valentine* (1988, Vaudeville; 1989, Booth, New York); *Single Spies* (1988, Queen's; NT, Lyttelton); *Carmen Jones* (1991, Old Vic); *Shades* (1992, Albery); *Il turco in Italia* (1997, Broomhill Opera); *H.R.H.* (1997, Playhouse); *The Pajama Game* (1999, Birmingham Rep); *Die Zauberflöte* (2008, Opera Holland Park)

Film
Amadeus (1984); *The Good Father* (1986); *Four Weddings and a Funeral* (1994); *Ace Ventura: When Nature Calls* (1995); *England, My England* (1995); *Victory* (1996); *Shakespeare in Love* (1998); *Creditors* (2015)

Television
Inspector Morse, "The Wolvercote Tongue" (1987); *The Crucifer of Blood* (1991); *The Woman in White* (1997); *Dr. Who*, "The Unquiet Dead" (2005), "The Wedding River Song" (2011); *Inspector Lewis*, "Counter Culture Blues" (2009); *Being Shakespeare* (2011); *Agatha Christie's Poirot*, "The Labours of Hercules" (2013)

Awards and Nominations

Room with a View, 1985, BAFTA, Best Actor in a Supporting Role, nominee; *Shirley Valentine*, 1989, Drama Desk, Outstanding Director of a Play, nominee; *Carmen Jones*, 1992, Olivier, Best Director of a Musical, winner

Honors

CBE, 1999

Publications

Being an Actor (1984); *Orson Welles*. Vol. 1, *The Road to Xanadu* (1996); *Charles Laughton: A Difficult Actor* (1997); *Orson Welles*. Vol. 2, *Hello Americans* (2006); *My Life in Pieces: An Alternative Autobiography* (2010)

CHAPTER FOUR

~

Dame Joan Collins, OBE

*Being an actress is like being a book in a lending library; someone "borrows"
you, and then you're put back on the shelf until someone else "borrows" you.*

Dame Joan Collins, actress, producer, and prolific author, and her fifth husband,
Percy Gibson,[1] to whom she's been married since 2002, have a spectacular view of
Los Angeles from their twenty-fifth-floor West Hollywood condominium. The late fall
sunshine floods into the living room where white orchids shimmer and a silver bowl
filled with lemons sparkles. Andy Warhol's portrait of the actress is hung on a prominent wall. The living space is modern and comfortable. The couple also maintains
residences in London's fashionable Belgravia neighborhood and in the South of France
near St.-Tropez.

Born in 1933 in a London suburb, the still-stunning Dame Joan, now in her
eighth decade, is slim and chic in a nautically themed ensemble: white linen pants
and a blue-and-white-striped sweater. A curl of her lush black hair peeks out from
beneath her sailor cap. She wears her signature bright red lipstick with flair.

During the interview, she offers a frank appraisal of her sixty-year career, her
colleagues, and her credits. She is intelligent and articulate and has a sense of humor
about her life, which has seen triumphs and tragedies.

In the words of her costar, Richard Todd, "She's a classic survivor and has
worked darn hard for her success. She's always cheerful and an amusing companion, [and] very witty."

~

58

Photofest

Your father was a theatrical agent in association with Lew Grade, booking talent for music hall and variety shows. Your mother had been a dancer, and your grandfather and aunts in show business as performers. You come by performing honestly.

Yes, it's in the genes. It's something that I wanted to do.

My father, Joe Collins, was partner in a theatrical agency with Lew Grade called Collins and Grade. His father was also a theatrical agent. He didn't want me to be in "the business." He wanted me to be a secretary, settle down, find a good man, and be a good wife and mother. He was strict and authoritarian. My mother was wonderful, adorable, kind, and loving.

My paternal grandmother, who had been a singer and dancer, was the family member who encouraged my theatrical ambitions. I got my first good review at the age of three in a children's play about fairies, which read, "Joan Collins makes a very believable fairy." When I was nine, I played Ivan—a boy—in Ibsen's *Ghosts* at the Arts Theatre, directed by John Fernald, who went on to become principal of RADA.

I must be one of the few actresses who can say that she had a happy childhood. There was a dashing around from place to place during the war, but, basically, I was happy.

You were a fan of a number of actors during your early years. Who were some of them?

My favorite was Jean Simmons, whom I've often been compared to. She was my favorite movie star. I loved her, and I had a scrapbook of her. Much later, I got the role as the English girl when they couldn't get her.

But I also admired Gene Kelly; Danny Kaye; Maxwell Reed, who I married [she pauses, and then adds] unfortunately; Anthony Newley, who I also subsequently married; Cary Grant and Lana Turner and Frank Sinatra.

I got to meet them all when I arrived in Hollywood in 1955 for *Land of the Pharaohs* at the end of the Golden Era, when the gilt was just beginning to wear off. It was the end of that fantastic period of movies that, I think, started in the late thirties and finished in the fifties.

How young were you when you began taking lessons?

There were dancing lessons at the age of three.

Eventually you attended drama school.

I attended the Cone-Ripman School and then RADA.

Do you recall your audition pieces for RADA?

I did a scene from Shaw's *Caesar and Cleopatra* and a piece as Emily from Thornton Wilder's *Our Town*.

You left RADA after about a year. The reason?

I had been "discovered" by a modeling agency while studying to be a serious actress, and from that I was again "discovered" by Bill Watts, who became my first agent.[2]

I began moonlighting in film and taking time out from classes at RADA without telling anyone. I did a bit in *Lady Godiva Rides Again* and *A Woman's Angle*, in 1951, '52. Then I tested for *I Believe in You* at Ealing; that film and *Judgment Deferred* are movies that nobody's ever heard of.

I was finally told by the people at RADA, "Oh, you can't do film. Those people can't act. You have to make a choice: finish your course here, or you can go and do that movie." I was seventeen.

When I got the part, at £30 a week, my choice was to leave RADA. Ironically, I am now honorary president of the RADA Associates and give lectures there.

You had the opportunity to work in rep as well.

Yes, and, unfortunately, it really doesn't exist anymore. I was an AASM—an assistant assistant stage manager—and assistant props master. I understudied all the small parts, especially maids, and learned the strangulated verbs of Swedish and French and Mancunian, the Manchester accent. This was during the summer holidays at a theatre in Maidstone, Kent. I learned from the bottom up and learned a lot from watching the actors.

The leading lady was so grand. [Collins laughs, throwing an arm out and gesturing in a theatrical manner.] I thought, "Is this how actresses are supposed to act?" They all thought they were Larry Olivier and Vivien Leigh, and here we were in a tiny little rep in Kent.

With almost no repertory companies today, what do young actors do?

They have to go into daytime television. There are still dramatic schools, but apparently in England, you have to get a university degree and be twenty-one before you can go to dramatic school. I'm sorry to say, but today, there's such an emphasis on youth, that they really need to be available to go into movies if they're eighteen, nineteen, or twenty.

What about some of your other work in the early fifties? You were just a teen then.

Good Lord, some of it was so long ago. I'm not too good at going down memory lane. I was eighteen, and I was working with these unbelievably famous actors, Robertson Hare, who had been a legend in the theatre since the 1920s; Kenneth More; George Cole, who is still with us at eighty-eight, I'm happy to say.

That was the time when I was playing tarts and delinquents. I remember Our Girl Friday in 1953, directed by Noel Langley, who was scary. In that film, I was the first girl to wear a bikini on-screen, even before Brigitte Bardot. It was quite, quite shocking. Loads of pinup pictures of me were published. A lot of them were retouched because navels were not allowed to be shown in those days. No belly buttons! I have stills of myself in the bikini that I wore—I wore bikinis all the time—with the navel painted over like a Barbie doll! There was even a flower discreetly placed in my cleavage. No navels; no cleavage.

That wasn't the only time that I had my navel covered up. In Land of the Pharaohs, I had to wear a ruby in my navel. Because we were shooting in Italy, and I kept eating spaghetti, which I love, I put on weight, and the ruby kept popping out, infuriating the director, Howard Hawks.

The last film you made in the UK prior to going to Hollywood was The Good Die Young, directed by Lewis Gilbert.

Ah, lovely Lewis. Adorable. I had made Cosh Boy with him the year before The Good Die Young. Whenever I see him now, he greets me with, "Joanie, darling. I'm so happy to see you." He is a wonderful, kind person, and he taught me a lot, and a lovely director. And he's still with us at ninety-four.

The part of Mary Halsey in the second film was difficult; I was playing Richard Basehart's wife, and, again, I was a teenager, nineteen, and Richard was, what, forty? That was a huge age difference. Lewis helped me through everything.

Just recently, I was switching channels at my home in London and watched the film. I saw Richard; Stanley Baker; Gloria Graham; Margaret Leighton; Freda Jackson, who played my mother; and Laurence Harvey, whom I already knew then because I'd worked with him in *I Believe in You*. He had become quite a good friend.

As I was watching, I thought, "That's me. All the rest of them are dead!" It was truly terrifying.

I don't think I had more than three words with Freda Jackson off the set. She scared me to bits and kept to herself. She didn't want to share her off-the-set time with little old me!

I enjoyed doing that movie. I used to sit and watch those wonderful actors; they were marvelous. We didn't have videos or DVDs then, so if we wanted to watch actors work, we went to the theatre or the cinema. Young actors today don't realize how lucky they are. They can watch Marlon Brando or Robert De Niro over and over again.

How much of a culture shock going from the UK to 20th Century Fox?

It actually wasn't a culture shock. It was a good shock. A fabulous shock. It was glamorous and wonderful and exciting. I loved it even though it was the midfifties and the tarnished end of the Golden Era in Hollywood.

I think the main difference is that there is hot and cold running food all day in the US; in the UK, there are breaks throughout the day for tea. Other than that, a set is a set; technicians are technicians. All the technicians I've ever worked with have been immensely professional. And the hours they work! They've all been wonderful, and I have great respect for them in both the States and the UK.

My huge regret is that every time I went back to 20th I never took a camera and went onto the back lot to photograph those Indian villages, those Normandy castles, and New York streets. And now it's the Century City shopping mall and a residential area with high-rise buildings.

***The Land of the Pharaohs* was your first film in Hollywood. Recollections?**

I was amazed I was cast in the role of Princess Nellifer. I was *so* wrong for it. I was, what, nineteen or twenty? Director Howard Hawks liked his women with deep, husky voices. [She lowers her voice to demonstrate.] He also liked his women tall and skinny. I was five foot five inches, with a round face, and I certainly didn't have the requisite husky voice.

It's astonishing that everybody seems to love that film. It's extraordinary. Even my daughter Katy called me after she saw it and said, "I've just seen this wonderful movie of yours, *Land of the Something*."

"You mean *Land of the Pharaohs*? You really liked it?" I asked in amazement.

Hawks had made wonderful films in the thirties, *Dawn Patrol* and *Scarface*, and in the forties, *His Girl Friday* and *Ball of Fire*. *Land of the Pharaohs* is certainly not one of his greatest films.

Besides *Land of the Pharaohs*, what other Hollywood film was a disappointment?

Island in the Sun is a terrible film. Percy ran it the other day. I thought that there would be something good about it, but there wasn't anything that I could see, except maybe the locations in Barbados and Grenada. It was a hackneyed story. And the love story between Harry Belafonte and Joan Fontaine was without any conflict. Talk about a mismatched couple!

Imagine Diana Wynyard as my mother and James Mason as my brother; in real life, we were only three years apart. How could my mother and my brother be the same age! I had great respect for Diana. Besides James Mason, so many of the cast were much older than I was; there was Joan Fontaine and Basil Sydney as my father.

The best thing about *Island in the Sun* was working with Stephen Boyd and the British crew. We all got along so well. We played poker and stayed up late and drank rum punches and did our scenes and finished early enough to get to the beach.

What about Robert Rosson as a director?

He was not a kind director. He was brusque and didn't have much time for any of us. One day he called, "Action," and Patricia Owens and I hadn't even got our gloves on. Everybody wore white gloves then as members of this ex-pat family living on the island in the 1950s. I don't know who *he* hung out with.

Your second film in Hollywood was *The Virgin Queen*, in which you played Lady Beth Throgmorton. In the second volume of his autobiography *In Camera*, Richard Todd, who played Sir Walter Raleigh, wrote, "When I heard about the casting [of Joan], she was not at all my idea of a demure English rose . . . [but] she was splendid . . . and excellent in the role."

Oh, my God. That is so sweet. I also worked with him later in another film, *Subterfuge*, and again in the mideighties in a play, *Murder in Mind* by Terence Feely, with Moira Redmond and Geoffrey Davis for producer Duncan Weldon.

I had a terrible accident at the Yvonne Arnaud Theatre in Guildford during the dress rehearsal for that play: I fell and broke my elbow. The doctor said I couldn't go on, but I was told I *had* to go on because there was no understudy! The first night I was in agony. I wasn't allowed to take painkillers. There I was running around on stage, jumping into cupboards and boxes. For the next two weeks, Richard had to put up with me playing with my arm in a cast.

What do you recall about working with Bette Davis as Queen Elizabeth I in *The Virgin Queen*?

She was horrible to work with. She didn't like any of us who played her ladies-in-waiting: Marjorie Hellen, who later changed her name to Leslie Parrish; Lisa Daniels; and Lisa Davis. It was on this film that I first worked with anybody of my own age. The four of us had giggles and fun and lots of yoiks off and on the set, and we hung out together during the shooting. But as one goes through life, one's friends change, especially in Hollywood.

Anyway, in one scene, I had to kneel down and lace up one of Bette Davis's satin shoes. She kept wiggling her foot, making it very difficult for me. She wiggled and wiggled. Finally, she kicked me clear across the set.

Joan Collins as Lady Beth Throgmorton kneels at the feet of Bette Davis as Elizabeth I in *The Virgin Queen* (1955). *20th Century Fox/Photofest © 20th Century Fox*

The director, Henry Koster, was furious with *me* and blamed *me* for it.

"Vat is wrong mit you? [Collins assumes a German accent.] You're years younger than her. Kneel down, and do vat the old bag vants!" he said.

I knelt down and, being young and strong and healthy, I grabbed her foot between my knees and yelped my line. She didn't mess with me after that.

Years later, I met her when I was doing *The Night of 100 Stars* [March 8, 1982]. It was at the height of *Dynasty*. I was wearing this silver lamé dress, which was cut very low in both front and back, and I had huge hair. I was sharing a dressing room with Davis, Jane Russell, and one or two others. Bette was sitting in a chair, smoking, looking me up and down with those eyes. She said, "You almost have that dress on, my dear."

Not one to take a comment like that lightly, I said, "Yes, Bette, dear. It actually needs a little bit of adjusting. Would you mind pulling the skirt down?"

Glaring at me, she knelt and pulled down the dress at the hem.

The next day she called costume designer Nolan Miller. I heard that she'd asked him, "How could you allow that Collins girl to wear that outrageously revealing dress?"

His reply: "If you've got it, flaunt it!"

Is it true that you replaced Marilyn Monroe in *The Girl in the Red Velvet Swing*?

Marilyn, who I had met, was going to do *The Girl in the Red Velvet Swing*, but the studio decided she was too old. [Monroe was twenty-nine years old in 1955; Collins was twenty-two.] She went to New York to study at the Actors Studio, so I took on the role as Evelyn Nesbit replacing Marilyn.

Many of the directors you worked with in Hollywood were already legendary. They must have seemed very old.

All of the directors I worked with were terribly old; at least they seemed old to me at the time. Hawks was at least in his sixties; Noel Langley was, I think, forty-two; Henry King was in his seventies; Robert Rosson was in his early fifties; and Leo McCarey was sixty-two. I worked with loads of directors who seemed to be on their last legs.

I worked with the three legendary Henrys: Koster, King, and Hathaway.

Would it be an accurate assessment that you were often intimidated by your directors, either because of their history or because you were so young?

Yes, I was always quite intimidated by my directors, beginning with Basil Dearden in *I Believe in You*. I called all my directors "Mister." I never called my directors by their first name. It was always Mr. Hawks, Mr. Dearden, or Mr. King.

I was always the youngest person wherever I worked. I had been brought up to have a healthy respect for my elders and betters and also policemen, doctors—anybody in command. I was basically from the generation that said, "Children should be seen and not heard." For me to be chucked into the British film industry at the age of seventeen was intimidating.

Some of these people whom I worked with were basically Victorians, so they had a different mind-set from my generation, people who were born in the thirties and after. These were people of my father's generation—he was born in 1906 or '07—and had set ways about women. Many of these men were from that generation, many of them born in the teens and twenties— and even before. Because my father was of that generation, I knew that kind of man. They were men whom I could respect, but still found a bit intimidating. People had lots of respect for their elders in those days because that's how they were brought up. Everybody of my generation was the same way.

Which has now completely changed. [She laughs at the thought.]

Even working with John Forsythe on *Dynasty* was—I hate to say "chauvinistic" because that sounds mean, but I think he was somewhat put out when I came into the series, and suddenly the show shot up in the ratings. People were saying, "It's because of Joan." I think he didn't like that.

You mentioned your first agent, Bill Watts. Most actors see them as a necessary evil. Are they?

Most agents do very little, most of them. The one I have now, Peter Charlesworth, is very good because he's a brilliant negotiator. He's been in the business for a very long time, and I would say he has been my best agent.

I have had some really bad agents, business managers, financial advisers . . . and husbands.

You had always wanted to play Amanda in Noël Coward's *Private Lives* on stage. You finally had the opportunity in 1990 in London at the Aldwych, toured the UK, then transferred to Broadway in 1992. Where did it all begin?

I met producer-manager Binkie Beaumont when I was nineteen or twenty. He told me that when I was older and more sophisticated I would be able to play Amanda. He was right. He was possibly there when Gertie Lawrence and Noël Coward played in the original run in 1930, and they were in their midthirties. That role was my Broadway debut. I remember the director in London, Tim Luscombe, always wore jeans with a hole in the crotch.

What about the role of Amanda was so appealing?

I liked the sophistication, the charm of the character. I liked the fact that it was written in a time when women didn't have much of a voice. Women were wallpaper or arm candy. Amanda is a very strong, opinionated, and witty woman. I like that.

Do you have first-night nerves?

First nights in the theatre aren't any scarier than any other first night. I don't suffer tremendously from first-night nerves, but I have a certain amount of trepidation. I figure if I know my lines and know my marks and know my business and my character, the only things that can go wrong are that the lights fail or that some audience member's telephone goes off. I never expect to get good reviews because I've never been the critics' darling. Many of them have always hated me in whatever I did. I did get some good ones, however, in *Private Lives*.

I'll never forget—was it Houston or Denver?—that a very fat female critic criticized me for having a tummy.

I thought, "Isn't that rather like the pot calling the kettle black?" People like to find fault with actors.

The London production of *Over the Moon* by Ken Ludwig occurred at one of the most tragic times in history, especially for Americans. How did that affect the production?

It was a very sad time because 9/11 had just happened. The play opened in mid-October and was scheduled to run for thirteen weeks. But it closed December 15, 2001, just after seven weeks.

Everybody was consumed by the tragic events, particularly Ken Ludwig, who is American, and Frank Langella, also an American. All Frank wanted to do was get back to New York. He was finally let go and replaced by Michael Cochrane. The rest of the cast and I didn't get along terribly well with Frank. He's a wonderful actor, and, as he told me many times, he is the best actor of his generation.

You've worked with some interesting theatre directors, one of whom was Nigel Patrick, originally an actor, who appeared in *The Executioner* with you. Does a former actor make a good director?

Nigel directed me in *The Last of Mrs. Cheyney* by Frederick Lonsdale at the Cambridge Theatre with Simon Williams and Elspeth March in March 1980, just before *Dynasty*. Patrick was absolutely brilliant. He was opinionated but a wonderful director. I don't care how opinionated a director is if he's really good. I've worked with some pretty mediocre directors.

I'd say to him, "I can't get a laugh here. What can I do?"

In one instance, he suggested: "What you should do is walk upstage, you look away, turn back, then turn and look behind you. You'll get the laugh."

And it worked!

In one of the best reviews I ever had, the critic wrote about this role, "Joan Collins is an actress [who is] always better than her material."

As you said, you've worked with some good directors and mediocre directors. What do you expect from a director?

I expect him to give me something original. I'm usually told just to do what I *want* to do. I rarely get a director who has already conceived ideas of what must happen with my character. I expect the best. I expect them to be there to help, to be a psychiatrist, a father, a mentor, all of those.

It sounds like many directors don't do their "homework."

Particularly in television.

You worked with another Patrick, an actor who became a director, Patrick Garland, in *Full Circle* by Alan Melville.

He is lovely. I love Patrick Garland. He was the father figure and a mentor, as a director should be. Every time I see him, he says, "We must work together again."[3] I enjoyed working with some very good actors, including Nikolas Grace.

That production was just a piece of froth, but fun. It was an excuse to go on tour and make some money!

We very seldom make friends—well, you do make friends during a production, but not friends that last. Nick and I—Nicko is his nickname—became really good friends on this production. I just spoke with him yesterday. John Quayle was also in the cast and is a wonderful actor.

You've been associated with some of the legends of theatre and film during your career. Your recollection of these actors?
Nigel Hawthorne:

I loved him to bits, absolutely adored "Nige." He was a good friend. When I think about him, I remember the savaging the critics heaped upon him when he did *King Lear* in 1999; they were frightful and nasty. The *Evening Standard* took all the reviews and compiled them and put them on page 3. He cried for weeks. We did a film together, *The Clandestine Marriage*, the same year. He played Lord Ogleby to my Mrs. Heidelberg. He and I were associate producers on that production. I miss him. Lovely person. [Collins is overcome with emotion as she recalls their association and has to stop to compose herself.]
Esmé Percy:

He was very, very old, about seventy in 1957, when he directed *Praying Mantis*, one of my first plays. He was very nice to me. He said all sorts of encouraging things to me, and told me I had huge potential. I was quite good in that.

Orson Welles:

Not a lovely person! Another gorgon, a terrifying man. I worked with him in the television version of the Buzz Kulik–directed *The Man Who Came to Dinner*. Lee Remick played Maggie Cutler, and I was Lorraine Sheldon. We used to cower in the corner and giggle as we watched him scream and yell and intimidate everybody. He never could remember his lines; he had two students holding up cue cards with his lines. And he drank red wine out of a teacup.

Gene Kelly:

Loved him. He was wonderful to me. Of course, he was one of my favorite movie stars, and he'd sent me an autographed picture when I wrote to him when I was young. I went to Hollywood and became part of his set, as it were: Adolph Greene, Betty Comden, Sidney Chaplin, George Axelrod, Harry Kurnitz, all of these great people. He kind of took me under his wing and told me that I should never do any stunts because I'd be putting a stuntwoman out of work. When I was executive producing *Sins* [directed by Douglas Hickox] in 1986 a few years later, I cast him in it. I went to the Crillon Hotel in Paris to interview him. Here I was interviewing Gene Kelly.

"Would you play my older husband?" I asked. "I would love you to do it." He agreed, and he was the best and fun to work with.

What was the advice John Gielgud gave you about actors?

He told me that actors are victims of their own physicality. For instance, I had a script in which I wanted him to play a gardener. I was going to play a ballet teacher.

He said, in that luxurious voice of his, "Darling, I couldn't play a gardener. Look at these hands. Are these the hands of a gardener?" And he added, "You could never play an unattractive woman unless they put prosthetics on your face."

I understand that. It's true, except with an actress like Meryl Streep who can do anything!

Besides film, theatre, and television, you moved into working on a series of commercials for Cinzano. Were they as funny to shoot as they are to watch?

The commercials were made over a five-year period beginning in 1978 with comedian Leonard Rossiter.[4] He made me laugh all the time. He was so hysterically funny that we'd have to stop after the rehearsals so that I could scream with laughter. He was so naturally talented as a comedian. He referred to me as "The Prop." I don't think he was a terribly happy man, though. Very few comedians are.

In each spot, the premise was that at one point Leonard would spill Cinzano vermouth over me. I had six or seven outfits for each shoot.

No one ever had any idea those television spots were going to be so successful. The first one was directed by Hugh Hudson, who went on to direct *Chariots of Fire*, and the second one by Alan Parker, who directed *Midnight Express*.

I was only supposed to do two. Then they were going to use someone else. But they liked me so much that they wanted me to do them all. I did about ten.

There were also some advertisements for British Air, which you didn't get paid for. How did that happen?

Instead of receiving residuals, I flew free for years. The head of British Airways said to me, "When we gave you this job, we didn't realize you would be taking a British Airways flight once a week to various destinations and six times a year from Los Angeles to London!"

It actually worked out really well for me because I was living in Los Angeles doing *Dynasty*, and I could go back and see my children, who were living in London. It was perfect. The arrangement was much, much better than receiving residuals.

You've been photographed by two of the top stills photographers: George Hurrell and Cornel Lucas. What was their difference in styles?

I spent hours with Corny in the Pinewood stills gallery, posing for those early pinup pictures. He was adamant about the position I was in. He'd say, "Move your left arm a bit to the right. Move your head up. Move your head down. Turn sideways." It drove me crazy. Then he would take masses of pictures.

But Hurrell, who photographed me for some dozen pages in the December 1983 issue of *Playboy*, would pose me and then take *one* frame. Just one. I have the outtakes from the *Playboy* session in a bank vault. There were about eight of them. I did have very little on! It was the first time I'd done anything like that. George Hurrell was *the* genius behind the camera.

You changed the course of nighttime television drama with your role in *Dynasty*. You first appeared in the final episode of the first season and continued as Alexis for the next eight seasons, appearing in just over two hundred episodes. Actors talk about the perils of typecasting. When were you approached for the role, and how did that role affect you and your career?

It was while we were on holiday before touring with *Murder in Mind* that I was approached by Aaron Spelling about the role of Alexis. I immediately flew out to Hollywood. I'm afraid the producers of the play were not happy with my decision to leave the production. They were, however, able to replace me with Nyree Dawn Porter for the remainder of the tour.

Over the course of the series, the producers found that the audience loved to hate me; columns were filled with loads of stories about me. Things came out about me that were complete fabrications, complete lies. But it added to the myth that I was this bitch. If I was so hateful, why did everybody love me so much?

The typecasting thing is still there. I don't look dissimilar now to the way I looked then, so I get recognized all the time.

We were recently in a shop buying sports clothes for the grandkids. I was wearing no makeup, my hair was covered with a baseball cap, and I was in jeans. People never think I go out like that, but I do. This young guy asks, "Are you Joan Collins?"

"Yes," I said. "How did you know?"

"Oh, I recognized your voice."

I find it extraordinary. I'll be in the supermarket and say to Percy, "Shall we buy these tomatoes?" and suddenly three people turn around.

If I have such a recognizable voice, I'm very surprised that I've *never* been asked to voice a character in an animated film. It's one of my great regrets.

In one episode of *Dynasty*, I even got to sing "See What the Boys in the Back Room Will Have," which Marlene Dietrich sang in *Destry Rides Again* in 1939. I wore leather trousers and a jacket with fringe.

I had some fine directors on the series: Gabrielle Beaumont, Don Medford, Irving Moore, Nancy Malone. They were the good ones, particularly Irving, who became a good friend. And Nancy was excellent.

What's the most surprising aspect about being an actor?

I don't like being called an "actor." I'm an actress.

I once asked Vanessa Redgrave, "What do you call yourself?"

"An actress, of course," she said.

I think that I'm rather like a book in a lending library. I sit waiting for people to borrow me, and then I'm put back on the shelf again until the next time.

What's left to do?

Many things. Many things. I'm writing. I'm doing a little independent movie called *Fetish*. I have my one-woman show, and I'll hopefully get a lot more gigs. There's talk about maybe doing another play. Whenever I talk about doing something, it never happens. There was going to be a movie last year, and it was cancelled the week before it was supposed to begin shooting.

I'm going to New York next week to do a fashion layout for the jeweler Alexis Bittar. Then I'm off to London to see my children. I had a glamour show in London on ITV, *Joan Does Glamour*, which did very well.

But there are things in the pipeline, and I am very busy.

～

Selected Credits

Theatre
A Doll's House, Arts Theatre, (1946; n/a); *Jassy*, Queen's (1952; Peter Dearing);*The Seventh Veil*, Q Theatre, Kew (1952; Peter Dearing); *The Praying Mantis*, UK tour (1953; Esmé Percy); *Claudia*, Q Theatre, Kew (1953; Jack Minster); *The Skin of Our Teeth*, Q Theatre, Kew (1954; Peter Dearing); *The Last of Mrs. Cheyney*, CFT, Cambridge (1980; Patrick Lau, Nigel Patrick); *Murder in Mind*, Yvonne Arnaud, Guildford (1981; Anthony Sharp); *Private Lives*, Theatre Royal Bath; Aldwych (1990–1991; Tim Luscombe); Broadhurst, New York (1992; Arvin Brown); *Over the Moon* [a.k.a. *Moon over Buffalo*], Yvonne Arnaud, Guildford; Theatre Royal Bath; Old Vic (2001–2002; Ray Cooney); *Full Circle*, Theatre Royal Newcastle; Churchill Theatre, Bromley; tour (2004; Patrick Garland); *One Night with Joan Collins*, US tour (2009); New York (2012); UK tour (2013; Percy Gibson); *Dick Whittington*, Birmingham Hippodrome (2010–2011; Jonathan Kiley)

Film
Lady Godiva Rides Again [a.k.a. *Bikini Baby*] (1951); *A Woman's Angle* (1952); *I Believe in You* (1952); *Turn the Key Softly* (1953); *The Slasher* [UK title: *Cosh Boy*] (1953); *Decameron Nights* (1953); *The Square Ring* (1953); *Our Girl Friday* [a.k.a. *The Adventures of Sadie*] (1953); *The Good Die Young* (1954); *Land of the Pharaohs* (1955); *Stopover Tokyo* (1957); *Island in the Sun* (1957); *The Bravados* (1958); *Rally 'round the Flag, Boys* (1958); *Subterfuge* (1968); *The Executioner* (1970); *Sharon's Baby* [a.k.a. *The Devil within Her*] (1975); *The Big Sleep* (1978); *Decadence* (1994); *A Midwinter's Tale* [UK title: *In the Bleak Midwinter*] (1995); *Molly Moon: The Incredible Hypnotist* (2014); *The Time of Their Lives* (2014)

Television
Academy Awards, 1959, "It's Bully Not to Be Nominated," performed with Dana Wynter and Angela Lansbury; *Fallen Angels* (1972); *Hallmark Hall of Fame*, "The Man Who Came to Dinner" (1972); *Great Mysteries*, "The Din-

ner Party" (1974); *The Adventures of Ellery Queen*, "The Adventure of Auld Lang Syne" (1975); *Tales of the Unexpected*, "Neck" (1979); *Fantasy Island*, "My Fair Pharaoh/The Power" (1980); *Dynasty*, 204 episodes (1981–1989); *The Making of a Male Model* (1983); *Roseanne*, "First Cousin, Twice Removed (1993); *Will & Grace*, "My Best Friend's Tush" (2000); *These Old Broads* (2001); *Rules of Engagement*, "Les-bro" (2010); *Benidorm* (2014); *The Royals* (2015)

Awards and Nominations

Dynasty, 1984, Primetime Emmy, Outstanding Lead Actress in a Drama Series, nominee; also, 1982, 1984, 1985, 1986, 1987, Golden Globe, Best Performance by an Actress in a TV Series, Drama, nominee

Honors

Hollywood Walk of Fame star, 1983, 6901 Hollywood Blvd., Hollywood; OBE, 1997; DBE, 2014

Publications

Nonfiction: *Past Imperfect* (1978); *Second Act* (1997); *Passion for Life: An Autobiography* (2013); Fiction: *Prime Time* (1988); *Love & Desire & Hate* (1991); *Misfortune's Daughters* (2006)

Notes

1. Gibson is thirty-two years her junior. When she's asked about the age difference, she jokes, "Well, if he dies, he dies!"

2. In her autobiography, *Past Imperfect*, Collins remembers that Watts "is without a doubt the one who not only believed in my ability, but went out on a limb to tell everyone how much potential I had" (22).

3. Garland died April 19, 2013, at age seventy-eight.

4. Rossiter died in 1984 at age fifty-seven.

CHAPTER FIVE

~

Peggy Cummins

Out of the films you make, you're lucky to get one or two that are worthwhile.

Peggy Cummins, the cult film favorite, is easily identifiable at the Barons Court Underground station: sunglasses with red frames that match her signature bright red lipstick and platinum hair falling in slightly tousled shoulder-length waves, à la Veronica Lake. The actress, a stylish eighty-eight years young, is dressed in a cream sweater open at the neck, showing a strand of pearls, and dark trousers. She moves and speaks as if she were decades younger. She acknowledges that she has taken Pilates and yoga twice a week for some time, accounting for her sprightly walk and slim figure.

Cummins has walked to the Underground station from her flat that overlooks the famed Queen's Club tennis courts on Palliser Road, which is just around the corner. She previously lived in Herstmonceux, East Sussex, on a multi-acre estate with her late husband, Derek Dunnett.

Cummins regularly organizes luncheons and dinner parties for her great friend, Oscar-winning costume designer Julie Harris, at her flat in Kensington. Former colleagues join together and share stories. Among those who have been included are director Lewis Gilbert, actress Muriel Pavlow, and playwright Hugh Whitemore.

On the dining room table, Cummins has laid out a stack of albums with photographs and clippings chronicling her career. She laments that she has lent out some of her memorabilia and has yet to have anything returned. As she riffles the pages, her younger self stares back, and she returns to those days and reminisces about the time, the people, and her career.

⌒

Where did it all start?

I was born in 1925 in Prestatyn, Denbighshire, in North Wales, but I'm Irish. My mother was Irish and so was my father. My full name is Augusta Margaret Diana Fuller. And what am I called? Peggy. All old horses are called Peggy. But I'm glad to be Peggy because now I *am* an old horse!

As a child in Dublin, I attended the Abbey School of Ballet, which was run by Muriel Kelly, who had been associated with Dame Ninette Valois, founder of the Royal Ballet, when she was head of the school.

How did you choose your stage name?

My mother's name was Margaret Cummins. I took her maiden name in homage to her.

Photo courtesy of the author

Was she interested in acting?

She was very good at the piano and loved singing, but she wasn't an actress herself. By the time I left America in 1950 to return to England to be married, she had appeared in two films under the name Margaret Tracy.[1] That was the extent of her acting.

There was art in the family through my brother Harry, who was a painter. However, my other brother, William, was in the RAF, and my father is what would today be called a financial adviser.

There is a story from various sources that say Patrick Brock, an actor with the Gate Theatre, discovered you at a Dublin tram stop.

That's absolutely nonsense. It's possible someone from the Gate Theatre came to the dancing school and saw me, and that's how I became associated with that theatre. But to say he "discovered" me is not true!

Your earliest roles were, oddly, as boys.

Yes, I played many boys beginning at the age of twelve. My first performance, if you can call it that, was in 1937 at the Gate in *The Duchess of Malfi*, a very gruesome play by John Webster. I played one of the children, only seen in silhouette because they had been murdered—thank you very much. That was my start in the theatre. Again at the Gate, I played Kolya, in *A Month in the Country*. I even managed to appear in Shakespeare as Macduff's son, Fleance, in *Macbeth*. That was in October 1937. The great Micheál MacLiammóir ran the theatre with his partner, director Hilton Edwards, who designed the costumes.

I have a review where the critic wrote [she refers to the clipping] that I was "a gifted child actress"!

Even at the age of twelve, I was still playing boys: Prince Albert Edward in *Victoria Regina* and, at the Abbey, *On Baile's Strand* with Cyril Cusack. In that I played a servant boy in just six performances for some special event.

I also appeared in November 1938, at the Gate as a girl in *Women without Men*. In the review [which is pasted into an album], the reviewer in the *Leader* wrote, "Little Peggie [sic] Cummins . . . has a wonderful personality and a beautiful voice, and showed a rare intelligence in her acting. . . . [The play] was worth coming to, if only to see and hear [her]."

Just before I left for London, there was a lovely play at the Gate called *Marrowbone Lane* by Robert Collis. I played Maggie, and I remember scrubbing the floor in that play.

And then to London?

After those productions in Dublin and before the war, I went to London in 1938, just after I celebrated my thirteenth birthday. I appeared as Maryann in *Let's Pretend* at the St. James's Theatre. It was my London debut. It was called a "children's revue for grown-ups." And a reviewer kindly referred to me as a "delightfully assured little colleen."

I was so young that I couldn't work more than a few hours a night, and even though my mother was usually with me, there always was somebody standing outside the theatre at ten o'clock or ten thirty to see that I left the theatre on time.

Laurence Olivier and Vivien Leigh performed at that theatre years earlier,[2] and when the theatre was about to be demolished in 1957, they led a protest—to no avail. The theatre was pulled down and replaced with an office block.

By 1940, you were cast in your first film, *Dr. O'Dowd*. Did you know that it is now considered a "lost film"?

Oh, what a terrible shame that it's lost. Maybe it's in some vault somewhere. I hope so.

I only recently realized that I had a contract with Warner Bros.–First National for that film. It starred a *very* famous English music hall performer, Shaun Glenville.

I recall we were shooting in Lake Windermere, and I tripped and cut myself. I still have the scar on my leg. [She pulls up a pant leg and shows the scar on her left calf.] In fact, I have so many scars from falls from bicycling and horseback riding that it's amazing I'm still alive at all!

We finished the film just two days before the beginning of the war. There is a promotional photograph of me filling sandbags at the studio when we returned from location. We were helping to protect the studio from German bombs.

Shooting that film, as with my work in the theatre, I was limited to the number of hours I could work because of my age.

At Warners, were you acquainted with Doc Salomon, who ran the studio?

Yes, lovely man. He thought I was the best thing since sliced bread. He was terribly particular that everything was, as he said, "all right for Peggy." He became a great friend to my mother. Tragically, he was killed when a flying bomb hit the studio in a night bombing raid in July 1944.

When did you finally step out of theatrical trouser roles?

That would be in 1941. I was given the opportunity in *Ah! Wilderness* by Eugene O'Neill. I played opposite a very young Richard Attenborough, now Lord Attenborough. It was his first play, and I played Muriel McComber, who is in love with him. The production ran at the Intimate Theatre in Palmers Green.

Your first starring role on stage was in *Junior Miss* as Fuffy. How did that come about?

I really don't remember how it happened. I was probably just in the right place at the right time. It was most likely my agent, the American Al Parker, who negotiated that role for me. I was in that production for a year, beginning in March 1943, at the Saville Theatre on Shaftesbury Avenue, a huge theatre seating more than a thousand. It was a lovely play and a great success. It's now an Odeon cinema.

American GIs who came to London during the war saw both *Junior Miss* and *My Sister Eileen*, which was playing at the Savoy with Coral Browne and Sally Gray, directed by Marcel Varnel.

What was it like to be on stage during the war?

The damage to the West End was due to the doodlebugs, which were flying bombs. In some way they were even worse than the Blitz bombing [September 7, 1940, to May 10, 1941]. They were horrible. We could hear them coming in when we were on stage, but it was when the sound stopped—and there was silence just before it hit the ground—that we had to worry because we didn't know whether it would explode on us or had crashed further away and would explode there. We just held our breath. We were trying to act even though we heard this sound coming over. But we carried on.

The production finally left London and toured for the armed forces with the production for ENSA.

By Christmas in 1944, you were playing Alice in *Alice in Wonderland*.

Yes, things began to happen very quickly during this period of my career. *Alice* was definitely not a panto[mime]. It was a marvelous play with music by Richard Addinsell, a very upper-class version of the Lewis Carroll story. We played at the Palace Theatre, a beautiful venue. It was an unusual production, in that as the Queen of Hearts and White Queen, Sybil Thorndike played the roles at a midmorning performance, and in the afternoon, Margaret Rutherford took the roles.

Do you recall what you were paid?

It was an enormous sum: £75 a week!

Was Dame Sybil the grand person she seemed to be on stage?

No, not really; actually, not at all. Very down to earth.

Your subsequent stage role was in *Temporary Ladies*. What recollections do you have about that role?

We played at the Q Theatre in Chiswick, where I did a number of plays. Sadly, it, too, was demolished in the late fifties. It was a very funny play, directed by Beryl Alcorn. I had a marvelous part of 2nd Sub Gough, ATS [Auxiliary Territorial Service]. I think I was meant to be a comedienne. I don't know what I became!

Another production at that theatre that I recall was *The Moon in the Yellow River*, directed by Esmé Percy.

Did you have an agent at the time?

Oh, yes. My first agent was Christopher Mann and his associate, Aubrey Blackburn, a charming gentleman. Al Parker, who I mentioned, was my next agent and was also Dickie Attenborough's agent. Parker was an American and had been an actor, then a director. One of the films he directed was *The Black Pirate* with Douglas Fairbanks Sr. When he came to England, he set up a theatrical agency, Al Parker, Ltd.

In those days, agents came 'round to theatres to see the plays, and I think that the play Parker came to see was probably *Temporary Ladies* at the Q, and he must have somehow convinced me to sign with him. He had a reputation of chasing his female clients around his dinner table, but he never chased me. And I never got a part by going on my back.

He sent me for the role in *Junior Miss*, even though I was really hoping to get another part, one in *My Sister Eileen* because I wanted to play a grown-up part, but it didn't happen.

Who offered you a contract at 20th Century Fox?

It was probably Frances Harley, Fox's London representative, who most likely saw me in *Junior Miss*. Although it is also possible that Darryl Zanuck might have been in London just as the war was finishing and saw the production. It was Al Parker who negotiated my contract with the studio.[3]

With a Hollywood contract in hand, how did you travel from the UK to New York in 1945?

Since it was just after the war, transport of any kind was not easy. But the studio knew how to organize the transportation for my mother and me. The studio wanted me in Los Angeles immediately, so we weren't able to take a ship. We flew on a seaplane from Galway. The aircraft was an armed forces plane. We were the only civilians on board; everyone else seemed to be high-ranking officers. It took two or three days, hopping from one landing strip to another until we finally landed in the Hudson River!

We arrived in New York—appropriately—in July 1945 and stayed at the Sherry-Netherland Hotel on Fifth Avenue. The studio president, Spyros Skouras, had come to New York to meet me, but we had been delayed, and so the poor man had to return to Los Angeles. It wasn't until much later that I finally met him.

From New York, how did you travel to Hollywood?

It was a long, *long* train journey to California. If I remember rightly, we took the train from New York to Chicago, and from there we took the Atchison, Topeka, and Santa Fe *Super Chief* to Pasadena. The first things I remember about arriving in California were the orange trees and the smell of the blossoms. Wonderful!

What had the studio arranged for you?

I tested for the role of Jennifer Jones's sister in *Cluny Brown*, but I was pulled out of that and tested for Amber in *Forever Amber*. I was cast in that high-profile role, and production began in early 1946. And then . . .[4]

Therein lies a tale of revolving doors, not only of directors, but also actors, including you. From your perspective, what happened?

I had three directors on the film. First there was John Stahl, hired then fired. Then Howard Hawks, who said he would do the picture with *me*. I was sorry he didn't direct. Finally, there was Otto Preminger.

It was a merry-go-round! Not only were directors replaced, but also several actors. Richard Greene replaced Vincent Price. I think Vincent was glad to leave. Fortunately, I worked with Vincent later in *Moss Rose*. Sara Allgood replaced Ethel Griffies. George Sanders replaced Reginald Gardiner. I stayed on after so many actors were released. And the script by Ring Lardner Jr. and Philip Dunne was being revised on a daily basis, which was not conducive to a smooth-running production.

There were rumors that I became ill on the set. I don't think I was ill, but I'd come from England, and everything was happening terribly quickly: a screen test, costume fittings, interviews, just a whirlwind of activities. I just didn't know where I was. I started to lose weight.

To this day, I truthfully do not remember how or when I came off of *Forever Amber*. It was such a shock that I can't reenact or think about it even after all these years. It was such a long time ago.

What was your salary on *Forever Amber*?

It was about £250 per week, which was quite a bit for the time and far from the £75 a week I had earned on *Alice*.

Once you stepped into the costumes, they had to be remade for your figure.

Ha! That wonderful designer René Hubert, who had designed costumes for a more voluptuous figure than mine and had to remake them for me. Even though I didn't get to wear his creations in this film, I was later fortunate to have him design costumes for me in *Moss Rose*.

How did you learn that you had been released from the picture?

After not too many days of filming,[5] I really don't know what happened or who told me. It wasn't my agent. I think it may have been a studio executive. I don't know if anybody knows exactly who decided. Was it money? Was it blamed on the fact that I wasn't sexy enough? If it was that, I thought it was unkind because I was sexy enough in *Gun Crazy*, just a few years later.

Maybe I wasn't the right kind of sexy in *Amber*. Maybe I was too young. Maybe I wasn't voluptuous enough. I still have a number of photographs in the costumes and hairstyles I was dressed in. I do think that the cameraman, Leon Shamroy—who I adored—knew what was going on, but he never said. I don't know if there's even anybody alive today who knows the real story. If I had begun in Hollywood with *Cluny Brown*, I think my career would have been very different.

You must have had exceptional strength of character to move ahead after that setback.

I think I must have. I was just a piece of meat. There were an awful lot of people who were getting information through somebody else. I was unaware of that, really. I wasn't getting any information. I didn't know *what* was going on. That was Hollywood.

But the press were all wonderful to me, both before and after the *Amber* debacle. I never had anything against the press. Fox had given me a big buildup, a big splash when I arrived in America. I was interviewed by some of the biggest names in Hollywood press circles: Louella Parsons, Sheila Graham, and Walter Winchell. I especially remember Walter Winchell, who had very kind words about me on his Sunday night program. He spoke like he was spitting out machine gun bullets—tat-tat-tat-tat-tat. He had a negative reputation, but he didn't blast me about *Amber*. I think he blamed the studio more than me.

Your first Hollywood movie, then, was *The Late George Apley*.

Yes, that film marked my debut in America. All those wonderful British actors who came to Hollywood by way of Broadway were in that cast: Ronald Colman, Edna Best, Richard Haydn. A year after the film, most of the cast appeared in a live thirty-minute radio broadcast of the screenplay on the *Screen Guild Theatre* program [March 8, 1948], including Colman, Best, and even Charles Russell, who played my boyfriend in the film.

What do you recall about working with Ronald Colman?

He was a lovely actor, but I remember he never looked at me during our scenes together. He always talked *to* the camera although he was talking to me. But that was Colman; he liked the camera. His costars came in a distant second.

Once under contract to a studio, they could require you to accept any role. You turned down a role in *Thunder in the Valley*, though. Why?

I turned down that film, which I was sorry I did. It was a story about horses. I went on suspension, so I didn't get any salary. I probably wasn't thinking correctly at the time after all the hullabaloo about *Amber*. Another Peggy, Peggy Ann Garner, took the role. I realize now that I should have done it.

The studio kept you busy with other films, however.

Yes, some interesting ones. Among the more interesting was *Moss Rose*,[6] directed by Gregory Ratoff, my first picture with him; I worked with him twice more on *If This Be Sin* [1949] and *Operation X* [1950]. Ratoff was originally an actor. Even when he was directing, he was still acting! He had a tremendous personality. And that Russian accent!

I remember when we were shooting *Moss Rose*, and one day, I was sitting on the set with Ethel Barrymore, Vincent Price, and Victor Mature. A dialogue coach had been brought in to teach us various accents. I had to do a Cockney in the first part of the film, and then a much more upper-class one in the remainder of the picture, which takes place in a country house. I didn't think I was good at that accent; I could have done an Irish one better.

Ethel Barrymore asked in that famous voice of hers, "Who is *that* man over *there?*"

None of us wanted to explain why he was there, but Ratoff piped up and said, "Oh, he's here to teach *me* English." The coach was, in reality, to work with Victor and me on accents.[7]

No one was going to tell Ethel Barrymore, "We have a dialogue coach here to help *you*."

In the credits for that picture, the studio billed *me* above Barrymore! I didn't think that was right.

Interestingly, in *Gun Crazy*, to cover the slight British accent I had, I have a line that explains it: "My father owned a shooting range in Brighton."

The studio then assigned you to *Escape* in 1948.

That was with Rex Harrison. He may have been called "Sexy Rexy," but he was a good actor. I think he was quite keen on this film, but it didn't come off very well even though the cast was superb: William Hartnell, Jill Esmond, and Cyril Cusack. I knew Rex's wife, Lilli Palmer, quite well. We went together on the same ship, the *Queen Elizabeth*, when we all returned to England.

At last, there was the role of Annie Laurie Starr in *Gun Crazy*, the role that established you as a sexy actress and a cult figure.

Until *Gun Crazy*, I'd played pretty blonde types, so I loved the idea of this character and that I was able to play against that type. This was a meaty part I'd been hoping for. I had always wanted to play Bette Davis–type roles, and this was a chance to get close to them.[8]

Your costar John Dall had recently completed *Rope*, directed by Alfred Hitchcock. What was your working relationship with Dall?

We were both stage actors, so that was an important connection between us. We both felt very strongly about the story and liked it. John and I gave reasonable performances in the film. John was so good that he made me look good, but we were dependent on so many people: the writer, director, the cameraman and operator, the costume designer, Norma Koch—all of them. It wasn't me. It wasn't John. We all made the film.

It was tragic that John died so young at age fifty-two [in 1971].

What are your thoughts about director Joseph H. Lewis, who brought the film to fruition?

He had the vision, along with the producers, the King brothers, to cast me in the film. I have the greatest respect for them for giving me the chance.

After we finished the film, it was years before I saw him again. About 1986 he came to England for a screening of the film at the BFI, and I saw him again. He was a great director who had the qualities of Eddie Goulding and Howard Hawks. He was never given due credit.

I received a letter from his daughter after his death in August 2000. In it she wrote that she wanted me to know that "Pop [had] great affection for you. He always talked about you with such love. . . . He would go to talk to different groups . . . [when] *Gun Crazy* was shown, and . . . he would address the groups after the film. . . . He would never take credit for his great directorial job. He always said [to the audience], 'Peggy made the picture. She should have won the Academy Award for that performance.'"

There are some exceptional scenes in that film. Among them is the bank robbery scene.

The screenplay was written by Dalton Trumbo, who was blacklisted at the time. Screen credits went to MacKinlay Kantor, who wrote the original story, and Millard Kaufman, who acted as "fronts."

Joe gave us the idea of what that scene was about. All I was told was, "You'll both be in the car. You'll be driving, Peggy. Cameraman Joseph Harlan and soundman Tom Lambert will be in the car behind you."

The part that terrified me was that I would be driving. I've never been a good driver.

Our dialogue was absolutely ad-libbed. Since we weren't supposed to be a particularly articulate pair, we overlap dialogue in several instances. I was playing it cool, but I was shaking inside.

We were on location in Montrose, a small town east of Los Angeles. I don't remember rehearsing the scene. And I'm sure that three-and-a-half-minute shot—which seemed like a half an hour—was only done in one take. I don't think John and I could have done it a second time, considering the parking space, the other cars on the main street, and so on. For that scene Joe left it up to John and me, and we managed it in a single take.

You returned to England and appeared in *Street Corner*, directed by Muriel Box. Is there a different directorial process between a male and female director?

No, nothing really different. She was very gentle in her way and very sympathetic. Forgive me for saying this, but it is true—men are a bit tougher. I also appeared in her film, *Cash on Delivery*. I was very fond of her.[9]

You took on another sexually charged role in the gritty *Hell Drivers*.

[Cummins laughs at the reference.] I was billed third on that film after Stanley Baker and Herbert Lom. Way down in the credits list is Sean Connery. I have a photograph [she extracts it from her album] of the scene at the town dance. The caption reads, "An abbreviated dress with well-spaced lace." When I walked on the set, the crew raised their collective eyebrows. For those days, it was a very risqué costume.

Cy Endfield, the director, was named a Communist by the HUAC and also blacklisted like Trumbo, and he came to England from the States where he directed several pictures. On *Hell Drivers*, he used the pseudonym C. Raker Endfield.

Also in England, there was *In the Doghouse*, 1961.

It was about a vet. It wasn't a great film, but I played opposite handsome Leslie Phillips. Another of my costars was Rosie, the monkey. Oh, she was lovely, just gorgeous. The only trouble was that she wouldn't let any of the male actors come near her. She only wanted to be with me, so when Leslie came in, she'd bare her teeth. And I played opposite a lion, but it had no teeth.

Not only did I have those animals to deal with, but I was also expecting my daughter, but nobody knew. I remember Leslie saying to me, "Hmmmm. You've got a lot on top!"

Peggy Cummins as Peter Pan in the 1955 La Scala Theatre production, directed by John Fernald. *Photo courtesy of Great Ormond Street Hospital Children's Charity, Christine De Poortere*, Peter Pan *Director*

Prior to that you returned to the theatre in the early fifties in an interesting, albeit disappointing, production of *Cupid and Psyche*.

It was a frightfully intellectual and very strange play by Benn Levy, who also directed the production. Levy's wife, the American-born Constance Cummings, a hell of a better actress than I ever was, was in it. Patrick McGoohan was in the cast, one of his early roles. I later worked with him on *Hell Drivers*.

We began the tour at the King's Theatre, Edinburgh, and then went to Newcastle and the Royal Court Theatre, Liverpool. We went into London at the Lyric Hammersmith with the intention of going on to the West End. It didn't happen.[10]

In 1955, you slipped into the green tunic of the boy who didn't want to grow up, Peter Pan.

A great many well-known actresses had played the role [Anna Neagle, Ann Todd, Glynis Johns, and Margaret Lockwood, among them]. I had been asked to play the role several years earlier but declined, but I accepted when the Daniel Mayer Company asked. My husband had misgivings because I would have to cut my hair, and he liked it long! But he knew how important this role was to me.

If I recall, the costume was created from a fabric called Viyella.

The wonderful Frank Thring played both Mr. Darling and Captain Hook.

Our production played at the Scala Theatre off Tottenham Court Road. It, too, has been pulled down, and there's a block of flats there now. So many wonderful theatres are lost.

In your film roles, you didn't seem to use much makeup.

With a great cameraman—and I worked with some of the best—they know how to light the face, so I really didn't need much makeup, just mascara, a wash of pancake, and lipstick, always as red as possible.

After you married, you owned a sheep farm in East Sussex. That is a far cry from the stages of Shepperton and 20th Century Fox.

We owned about fifty acres and ran sheep. We did our own lambing, which meant that sometimes we were outside at one o'clock in the morning waiting for the ewes to give birth.

Although you have retired, you are not forgotten. You still receive an enormous number of fan letters each month. After all these years, it must be most gratifying to look back on your career.

I get maybe ten a week, especially about *Gun Crazy* and *Night of the Demon*. It just astounds me.

Even though I never attended a proper drama school, I learned from those actors during early days at the Gate and the Abbey. How lucky I was to work with such wonderful actors as Edward G. Robinson, Ronald Colman, Vincent Price, David Niven, and so many more.

When I read the amazing press notices of this young girl, I think, "Who is this person they're writing about?" It *is* me, but I don't recognize this person. It was another life.

～

Selected Credits

Theatre
Gate Theatre, Dublin: *The Duchess of Malfi* (c.1930; Hilton Edwards); *Judgment Day* (1937; Reginald Jarman); *Macbeth* (1937; Hilton Edwards); *A Month in the Country* (1937; Hilton Edwards); *Saint Joan* (c.1937; Hilton Edwards); *Women without Men* (1938; Hilton Edwards); *Marrowbone Lane* (1939; n/a). **Other:** *On Baile's Strand*, Abbey Theatre, Dublin (1938; Hugh Hunt); *Let's Pretend*, St. James's Theatre (1938; Steve Geray); *Ah! Wilderness*, Palmers Green Theatre [a.k.a. Intimate Theatre] (1941; n/a); *Junior Miss*, Saville; tour, including Royal Court, Liverpool (1943; Marcel Varnel); *Alice in Wonderland* and *Through the Looking Glass*, Palace Theatre (1944; Esmé Church); *Temporary Ladies*, Q Theatre (1945; Beryl Alcorn); *Cupid and Psyche*, King's Theatre, Edinburgh; Newcastle; Royal Court Liverpool; Bromley Little Theatre; Lyric Hammersmith (c. 1952–1955; Robert Stanton); *Peter Pan*, Scala Theatre, tour (1955; John Fernald)

Film
Dr. O'Dowd (1940); *Old Mother Riley Detective* (1943); *English without Tears* [a.k.a. *Her Man Gilbey*] (1944); *The Late George Apley* (1947); *Moss Rose* (1947); *Escape* (1948); *Green Grass of Wyoming* (1948); *If This Be Sin* [a.k.a. *That Dangerous Age*] (1949); *Gun Crazy* [a.k.a. *Deadly Is the Female*] (1950); *The Passionate Sentry* (1952); *Street Corner* [US title: *Both Sides of the Law*] (1953); *Meet Mr. Lucifer* (1953) *Always a Bride* (1953); *Cash on Delivery* (1954); *The Love Lottery* (1954); *The Ship Was Loaded* [a.k.a. *Carry On, Admiral*] (1957); *Hell Drivers* (1957); *Curse of the Demon* [a.k.a. *Night of the Demon*] (1957; Jacques Tourneur); *Dentist in the Chair* (1960); *Your Money or Your Wife* (1960); *In the Doghouse* (1961)

Television

Picture Page, BBC, interview (March 2, 1939); *Coffee Stall*, BBC, singing "Spring Song" (March, 15, 1939); *The World Our Stage*, "The Man on a Balcony" (November 2, 1957, "celebrating the twenty-first anniversary of BBC television"); *The Human Jungle*, "Dual Control" (1964)

Honors

Look Magazine, "Most Promising Actress," 1946; First Honorary Commander, 582nd Air Supply Squadron, RAF Molesworth, 1954

Other

Night of the Hundred Stars, Palladium, July 18, 1960; Cinema Museum, London, April 2, 2011, guest, in conversation with Jo Botting; TCM Classic Film Festival, Los Angeles, 2012, guest, in conversation with Robert Osborne; Film Noir Foundation, San Francisco, 2013, guest; Festival Lumière, "Art of Noir," Lyon, France, 2013, guest

Notes

1. *Smart Woman* and *Sign of the Ram*, both in 1948.
2. *Caesar and Cleopatra* and *Antony and Cleopatra* (1951).
3. It is possible that Zanuck could have seen Cummins in the play as he was in Europe at the time as a commissioned colonel in the American Signal Corps Reserve.
4. According to TCM host Robert Osborne in an e-mail to the author on September 19, 2011, "It was announced in the trades even before she was tested that she was to play the role of Bette Cream in *Cluny Brown*, the character who has the romance with Peter Lawford. It would have been a wonderful first American movie for Peggy, a delightful role in an Ernst Lubitsch comedy with two major stars, Charles Boyer and Jennifer Jones. Probably the only reason she was pulled from the film was when the negotiations with MGM to borrow Lana Turner to play the title role in *Forever Amber* broke down, and 20th realized they had a likely bet for the role of Amber right under their noses."
5. Some sources say six to ten days, others say thirty-nine days; filming was halted on August 4, 1946.
6. In an interview promoting his role as Alfred Hitchcock in the film *Hitchcock* in 2012, Anthony Hopkins was asked about his most frightening cinematic moment as a youngster. He referred to a scene in *Moss Rose* in which Peggy Cummins goes through a country house calling, "Audrey. Audrey." Cummins, he recalls, walks into a room lit by a fireplace. There is a close-up of Cummins; she screams, and there is a

cut to Audrey, played by Patricia Medina, dead, eyes open and staring straight ahead. Said Hopkins, "It was the most terrifying moment of my young life."

7. According to the *New York Herald Tribune* issue of September 23, 1951, Mature was originally supposed to be Sir Alexander Sterling, an Englishman. Since he had difficulty with the accent, his character's name was changed to Michael Drego, and the character became a Canadian. Previously shot scenes were dubbed by the actor.

8. In 1998, *Gun Crazy* was placed on the Library of Congress's National Film Registry as "culturally, historically or aesthetically significant."

9. In his autobiography, *A Life to Remember*, producer William MacQuitty wrote, "The film did excellent business besides receiving good reviews. In fact, *Street Corner* came to be Muriel's favorite among all her pictures" (310).

10. The play is described in *The Plays of Benn Levy* by Susan Rusinko: "The play is a debate-of-ideas farce about art, science, psychology, anthropology, sociology, and sex" (132).

CHAPTER SIX

~

Sinéad Cusack

I have inferiority about lots of things, but not my Irishness.

The window in Sinéad Cusack's dressing room at the Bernard B. Jacobs Theatre in New York has been painted shut. But the sounds of the city—horns honking, sirens wailing, brakes screeching—seep into the dimly lit room. So much for the quiet, glamorous backstage habitat of an actor. Because there is no closet, her costumes, like the stockings in Dickens's "'Twas the Night before Christmas," are hung with care on a wheeled rack, which is placed next to a wall with peeling paint.

Born in Dalkey, a seaside community outside Dublin, in 1948, the actress bears a striking resemblance to her father, Irish actor Cyril Cusack. Her two sisters, Sorcha and Niamh (pronounced "Neeve"), from her father's first marriage, are also actors, as is her stepsister, Catherine.

She met Jeremy Irons, her actor-husband of more than thirty years, in the early seventies. She was appearing in London Assurance *at the New Theatre, and he was playing in* Godspell *at Wyndham's Theatre, just across the alleyway. They married in 1978 and have two sons, Max and Sam.*

She settles comfortably into an uncomfortable-looking straight-backed wooden chair just prior to the evening performance of Rock 'n' Roll *by Tom Stoppard. She has been associated with the production, which began at the Royal Court Theatre in London, for about two years.*

Cusack doesn't seem to notice the gloom of her surroundings, but her pleasure and satisfaction at being part of a theatrical tradition and experience is obvious when she speaks about it.

∼

In the beginning?

My parents, Cyril Cusack and Maureen Kiely Cusack, were keen that I should follow an academic route. I was academically inclined at school, and I was good at exams, so they thought an academic career was what I was after.

I was interested in the notion of writing, so I signed up for University College, Dublin, to read English literature. But the summer before I was due to start, and without my parents' knowledge, I auditioned for the Abbey Theatre. I got in. Then I had to face my parents with a fait accompli that I was a member of that company.

What followed was three years of absolute mayhem. I lived academic and theatrical lives simultaneously. In those days, at the Abbey, there were rehearsals, which began at ten in the morning and finished at two in the afternoon. I'd miss the morning lectures at the college. In the afternoon, I'd

Photo by Nick James

scoot up to the university and do my tutorials, and then in the evening, I'd do the show. It was madness. I barely remember it all.

What do you remember about the theatre itself?

I joined the company when it was at a theatre called Queen's, which was, I think, a variety theatre at one point. It was a temporary residence because the old Abbey, which was built at the turn of the century, burnt down in 1951, and the new Abbey was in the process of being built. [It reopened in 1966.] The Queen's was a very old, rat-infested building, but incredibly full of character.

What about your first name and the credentials of being a Cusack?

My name is Jane Mary, and as you can imagine, it wasn't a satisfactory name for a young, aspiring actor. Family members called me "plain Jane," and I never liked that. Also there was a republican spirit at work in me, and Irishness mattered a great deal, so it was at the Abbey that I used the name Sinéad Cusack.

My first schooling—from the age of three to the age of twelve—was in Gaelic, which was practically my mother tongue. At school, I was Sinéad [pronounced Shin-ed], which is Gaelic for Jane. When I left that first school and went to an English convent boarding school, which was run by nuns, I thought it very important to bring my republican Irish credentials with me, and I became Sinéad Moira.

The name Cusack was a name extremely well known in this tiny country of Ireland. Everybody knew I was Cyril and Maureen's daughter. Everybody! There wasn't a single person who didn't know . . . outside the theatre or inside! It was a great responsibility and made everything more challenging, and I didn't meet the challenge until much, much later.

The family still refers to some of your antics as "doing a Janey."

That's extraordinary that you would know that! It's a family reference. They use it in all sorts of contexts, referring to any wrong path that I might take, my faults and frailties as a human being. I make a big drama about things that aren't drama, and I get very stressed by things that there's no requirement at all to be stressed about. It's all about any wrong path I might take.

After your time at the Abbey, you journeyed to London in the early sixties and became a member of the RSC. Why the move to London?

I was aware of my Irish peasant standing, and my father had told me I would never make it as a classic artist, that I didn't have the "equipment." I had seen him as Hamlet at the Gaiety Theatre in 1957 when I was a child and at the Royal Shakespeare Theatre when he played Cassius in *Julius Caesar* in 1963. He didn't do a lot of Shakespeare. I think he should have done more.[1]

I was determined to go against his judgment of my ability, so I decided to go to the RSC to learn my craft. I felt I was too old to go to drama school. I had already been to university, and I'd been part of a national company. I was getting a bit long in the tooth, too. I was, what, twenty-three or twenty-four? The irony of it is [she clears her throat and laughs] that I was too embarrassed to audition for one of the schools. My thinking was, "What would be better than to work with the very best of English actors and directors and *the* playwright, Shakespeare, on whose shoulders we all stand?" And that would be my drama school.

What was your learning curve at the RSC?

My credibility was on the ground when I entered those hallowed portals. I had a Rottweiler mentality. I was determined to prove myself, and I did eventually play a great many of the leading roles there, but not at the beginning. Nobody had any faith in me at all. I was sort of the bimbo type with long blonde hair and blue eyes. I once walked out with footballer George Best.

What was one of the most important elements of acting that you learned during your time at the RSC?

Everything depends on the text. That's the actor's great responsibility. If we're working with a great text, we should honor it. We should not over-decorate it. We should be able to deliver it so that it can be heard, heard in the metaphorical as well as the physical sense, so the ideas, the images can be heard. With Shakespeare, there is room to maneuver because he allows you to do anything. He gives us the potential for at least fifty different characterizations in each moment.

Who finally saw your potential?

Director Barry Kyle was the first one to show real faith in me. Then Terry Hands offered me some great parts, like Beatrice in *Much Ado*. The first Shakespearean role he offered me was Celia in *As You Like It*. That role led to an epiphany for me: I learned I could smile while playing Shakespeare. In those days, I had thought I couldn't smile when I played in Shakespeare. I played Shakespearean roles with this ridiculous reverence and wooden quality. I announced everything. I demonstrated everything. [She flings out her arms.] I spoke with a silly accent. It was hard for anyone to see through that and see what potential I might have.

What recollections do you have about those productions?

I remember *London Assurance* with Donald Sinden. He played Sir Harcourt Courtly to Judi Dench's Lucy Harkaway in 1970, so my taking over from her in 1972 was a contradiction in terms. It simply couldn't be done. I did it, but [she harrumphs] with not much success.

I also recall a production of *Richard III*. I played Lady Anne to David Suchet's Edward IV. I've worked with David many times; he's a wonderful actor, and our friendship was forged during this production. We went to the director, Terry Hands, and asked if we could share a dressing room. He agreed, and for the first time in the history of the RSC, a man and a woman shared dressing room 1A for the entire season. We had a great time.

What about the theatre itself, which was renovated a few years ago?

The old theatre didn't serve the audience, the actors, or the play. I used to feel deeply sorry for the people in the dress circle because they were badly served. Because of its original size and shape—and because there were dead spots—the RSC style was almost dictated by the building. Since clarity of utterance is the only thing that mattered in that theatre, we had to shout to reach the audience in the back; the overhang was terrible.

Although a lot of actors don't like the theatre, I'm different. I love it. I learned my trade on that stage, and I learnt that if I could project there, I could project anywhere in the world, so it stood me in good stead. I'll never forget that. But it did inculcate in me some bad habits because, erroneously, I think, along with others, I felt we were forced to face front and bellow. With the renovation [which was begun in 2007 and completed in 2010], that's all changed now. I'm delighted about it.

Jumping ahead a few years: With regard to theatre venues, you played at the Theatre Royal Haymarket in a production of *Antony and Cleopatra*, which had transferred from the RSC. What are the challenges in transferring from one theatre to another?

The Haymarket is a beautiful theatre, a real gem. It's a love to play there. It's beautiful acoustically and psychologically because it envelops the actors. But we weren't sure how it would transfer. We thought, "How can it work?" when thinking about the breadth and depth of the Shakespeare theatre compared to the Haymarket. But our production transferred remarkably well. If anything, the Haymarket was a great help to the production.

During your time at the RSC, you shared the stage with Derek Jacobi in a production of *Cyrano de Bergerac*. Your role as Roxane almost didn't happen. What finally led to the role?

I was playing Beatrice opposite Derek as Benedick—and with no false modesty, whatsoever—we were a big success in *Much Ado about Nothing* in Stratford and London. When I heard that *Cyrano* was going to be mounted, I went to Terry Hands, who had directed *Much Ado*, and was going to direct *Cyrano*.

I asked, "Can I play Roxane?"

He said, "Don't be silly, Sinéad. You're far too old, and you're *not* a lady!" I was in my midthirties. I left his office, my pride in tatters. He cast Alice Krige for the London end of things.

The production was then going to America, twinned with *Much Ado*; it was decided to recast Roxane. I later learnt that Derek approached Terry, telling him, "I think Sinéad should play Roxane. She's the only one who should."

Terry called me into his office and said, "Sinéad, we'd very much like you to play Roxane in the American production."

"But, Terry," I said, "a year ago you said I was too old."

"You were too old a year ago!"

I have Derek to thank for that opportunity.

What was your interpretation of Roxane in that production?

I decided that she was the other side of the Cyrano coin. They are complete soul mates in every way. She has his bravery, his courage, his recklessness. They both have a poetic sensibility. But she feels she needs a man to validate herself. How ridiculous! She is such a strong and sure person on her own. She ain't a wimp. She's completely wonderful. I love her.

Tragedy or comedy: Which is more difficult?

I try not to differentiate between comedy and tragedy, though. It's the role that's important. In *Rock 'n' Roll*, I have both.

At the end of the day, tragedy is easier than comedy. I think tragedy is underdeveloped comedy. Every tragic moment, if pushed that little bit further, becomes comedic. If you demonstrate your character's dilemma and angst and fear, it's so much more interesting when tears are held back than when tears are shed. Somebody holding back tears is heartbreaking. Somebody shedding tears is sometimes embarrassing.

In comedy, it's more delicate. If you stretch a comedic moment or you do a bit of comedy business three times instead of once, you might lose the audience. Economy in everything! I love economy. I love the audience being allowed into somebody's head and brain without anyone even knowing they're there.

I recently heard that a director in New York apparently posted a notice on the board at the stage door—I won't say what the production was, but it blew me away—that read, "The play is funny. You're not." It was just the most brilliant note.

It's very easy to think if that moment is overdecorated, the audience is shown what's funny, but then you are actually precluding a hundred different reactions to that moment from them. If you deliver the moment with clarity and with intent, you don't have to demonstrate why it's a funny moment. If it plays funny, then the moment will be funny.

Although Chekhov calls his plays "comedies," the great playwrights don't say, "I've written a comedy" or "I've written a tragedy." It's the academics who try to pigeonhole the work.

One venue with which you have been associated for some time is the Royal Court in London. What makes it so different from other theatres?

The Royal Court is a spectacularly [she emphasizes the word and enunciates its five syllables] wonderful theatre. I love it with a passion.

It's primarily a writer's theatre. Look at the history of that theatre and the playwrights who have had their plays performed there. Think of John Osborne and Athol Fugard, Caryl Churchill, Jez Butterworth, David Hare, and those who have been artistic directors.[2] There have been extraordinary moments at the theatre.

That theatre immediately calls to mind three plays for me. The first, the "family affair," was Chekhov's *Three Sisters*; then *Faith Healer* by Brian Friel two years later with Donal McCann, one of the great Irish actors of all time from the Abbey; lastly, *Rock 'n' Roll*. All three milestones in my life.

The refurbishment of the theatre some years ago is a triumph. It's as if everyone got together and said, "Let's retain what's best about the theatre, and let's change what's gotten old and dilapidated." In the modernization, that's exactly what they did. A bee-yoo-tiful balance of the old and new. At one point, Max Stafford-Clark, the artistic director at the theatre then, found me sweeping the steps of the theatre on a press night. There I was with my mop and bucket cleaning away butt ends and other debris. I was just very proud of being there.

What are your recollections of the "family" production of *The Three Sisters* and the challenges of working with your real-life sisters and your legendary father?

It was a traumatizing experience, just astonishing to do it with them. I wouldn't have missed a moment of it. It was difficult—difficult because with three sisters working together, there is a hierarchy, which has been developed over all those years in the real family. We had to throw a stick into that hierarchy. We had the vocabulary of sisters. For us to have that as a given was the single greatest advantage that three actresses could have in those roles. It hadn't happened before on the stage. Our father treated us all as children, so it was very, very difficult.

I played Masha, the middle sister. I should never have been cast as the middle because, in fact, I'm actually the oldest of the three of us. Sorcha played Olga, and Niamh, the youngest, played Irina, who we called "our little sister" in our patronizing fashion. It was the director Adrian Noble's casting choices.

What about the production itself?

The opening had Masha, as always, reading a book, smoking a cigarette, with Olga standing behind looking into the middle distance, and Irina sitting at my knee. All of us were smokers at the time. Niamh had given up cigarettes or was attempting to. But Sorcha and I were still puffing away. In the opening tableau, Niamh used to just put her finger out [Cusack demonstrates], or she would actually take the cigarette from my mouth, or I'd have the cigarette in my hand and pass it to her. This was all done without looking at each other. She'd take the cigarette, puff it, and put it back in my hand. It said sisterhood; it said intimacy; it said knowledge of each other. It was even more of a family affair because my stepsister, Catherine, who is twenty years younger than I am, played my daughter.

Adrian used to watch this ridiculous vignette with these three girls and the cigarette. We weren't full of confidence as a trio. We looked to Adrian for guidance, and, I think, he got the best out of us.

Certainly one of the most challenging of your roles was that of Mai in *Our Lady of Sligo* by Sebastian Barry. Besides a run in New York, the play became your debut at the National. What were the circumstances surrounding that production?

When Max and Sebastian asked me to play Mai, I said, "It can't be done. It's impossible for an actor in terms of learning what has to be done as well as playing it." The character has to hold the stage for more than two hours.

Max said, "I'll help with this process."

What he was referring to was a process, a method, I've used ever since, which he discusses in *Letters to George: An Account of a Rehearsal.* It's a book in the form of letters to the playwright George Farquhar about Max's rehearsal process of *The Recruiting Officer.* It's a great how-to book. Any actor or director should read it. In it, he writes about a method called "actioning," which is not to everybody's taste. At the time, though, I told him I'd heard about the process and that I had no interest in it. "It's not the way I work," I told him. I work on instinct.

He asked me to give the process a chance. I said, "No, I'm just not going to do it."

"Will you do it for just one day?" he asked.

"Yeah," I told him, gracelessly. "I'll give it *one* day."

I knew that at the end of that first day that he was pursuing the same thing I was in pursuit of but with a different, slightly more mechanical route.

The process just gave me wings. We were both searching for all the colors in the tapestry of a character. We took each of the colors and sewed them together [she uses her hands in a sewing motion], but, in the end, none of the stitches matter because all you're seeing is this huge [she flings her arms out to demonstrate the size] riot of color that is a human being, so it is a kind of a method. Some people don't like it and don't respond to the discipline. I was predisposed to hate it. But for me it was the only way I could have done the play. My God, it was so wonderful. It helped that Max is a writer's director, and he knows how important each word is, each phrase is.

One tiny caveat about those matters: There is no *single* method or view about how something should be played or directed, which is wonderful. My methods or views would not suit the DNA of most of the rest of my colleagues, though. Aren't we all so lucky to be in this profession!

What are your thoughts about Tom Stoppard and his work, especially the production of Rock 'n' Roll, with which you have been associated since its opening in London?

The first Stoppard play I saw was original Broadway production of *The Real Thing* in 1984[3] because Jeremy was playing Henry. I must have seen it about a dozen times during the course of the run. I also saw Tom's *Rosencrantz and Guildenstern Are Dead*.

What amazes me about his work is that you never, never—what's the word? I want to get this right because it's so important—he reveals gradually the heart of his plays, so all those references that have sometimes slightly bemused or bewildered the audience throughout the course of the play are suddenly revealed in all their clarity. He does that back to front.

So many playwrights explain at the beginning what their play is about. Tom doesn't do that, particularly in *Rock 'n' Roll*, which I know intimately. Some people would argue that the subjects that he incorporates into his plays are subjects which no brain—except superior intellects who have taken degrees at Oxford or Cambridge—would understand. I would refute that.

In his plays, and I've seen it happen many, many times, young people who have no notion about quantum physics, which he addresses in *Arcadia*, or what Czech politics are about in *Rock 'n' Roll*—or whatever he chooses to address so brilliantly in his plays—at the end of the play, people come out of the theatre with knowledge, which is a gift he's given them. But he also tells wonderful stories.

It seems, then, that your dual role as Eleanor/Esme in Rock 'n' Roll fits into that category?

It's the role I'm most proud of, along with Mai in *Sligo* . . . [and after a pause, she adds] and Cleopatra. It has given me enormous satisfaction and pleasure to play because I think it has to do with a great deal being asked of me as that character, especially as the cancer-ridden Eleanor in the first act. And in the second act as Esme, her grown daughter, I'm given the gift of these women. I don't have to leave the theatre feeling miserable. I leave on a cloud of euphoria because, at the end, my character goes to Prague and finds her man.

You moved into films very early in your career.

My first film was *Alfred the Great*, directed by Clive Donner. The script was pretty dire. Vivien Merchant, who was then married to Harold Pinter, said she would play the part of Freda as a mute. "I won't utter any of that execrable dialogue," she said. I think she was the best thing in it as a result.

As Edith, servant to Prunella Ransome's Aelhswith, I had eleven lines, and ten of them were cut. I was left with one, which was [she doesn't have to think long to recall it] to David Hemmings, who played Alfred: "This is not the Bible as we were taught it."

He replies with the immortal words, "Such a clever answer from a pair of tits."

That was the level of the dialogue.

Did you go to the rushes then . . . or now?

I went one day to see them, and I've never been back. And I never see my finished films. There are more actors than you think who won't see rushes or their films.

In a film, the actors will not know how they are affecting the audience. But there are actors who have the sort of robustness to be able to watch their work on-screen and learn from it. What would happen to me if I watched myself is that I would concentrate on those areas that let me down. That might be as silly as, "Oh, God, I can see my double chin" or "I must hold my head up."

You and your husband seem to have made a conscious decision not to appear on stage together, but you have worked in films as a couple.[4]

The first film we worked on together was *Waterland* in 1992. Our director, Stephen Gyllenhaal, told us that we should live apart during the production. He thought that the couple we were playing was on the edge of an emotional abyss, and he didn't think it would be healthy for us to be actually living together and having to work together and facing those terrible issues they had to deal with. He physically separated us. He told me to "check out of the marriage and into a hotel," which I did. Jeremy stayed with the kids.

I remember *Stealing Beauty* four years later. We worked with Bernardo Bertolucci. He's a genius. It was wonderful to work with him. We stayed at this lovely old Tuscan farmhouse. It was heaven on a stick! As part of the production, Bernardo brought along a huge green tent, which was pitched in the middle of some beautiful countryside; he got the best chef in the area, who produced the most stunning food. The crew and cast all traipsed down to this tent where white linen was laid out with beautiful cutlery. Of course, there was wine.

Costar Liv Tyler really did put on a half a stone [seven pounds] while she was on the picture. When she started, she was slim hipped, and by the end, she was rather Rubenesque . . . as were we all. Liv is so stunning as an actor, and her youth and beauty was so magical.

How do I know this when I said I don't see my films? I have to admit I've seen snippets of the film.

Both of you have worked with director David Cronenberg, but on different projects. This director has a reputation for his canon of horror and science fiction films. What were your thoughts about the script for *Dead Ringers* when your husband was offered the role?

I remember when I read the script, I thought that it was completely horrible: the dual role of twin gynecologists who do unspeakable things to the insides of women and then die in sordid and suspect circumstances. But it became a brilliant film. The Academy of Motion Picture Arts and Sciences gave Jeremy the Oscar for *Reversal of Fortune* the following year because I think they would have found it difficult to give it to him for the two despicable characters in *Dead Ringers*.

And then you appeared in *Eastern Promises,* a different genre than what Cronenberg is known for. What was he like to work with?

You might think, though, looking at his work, that he would be a little grim and maybe a little frightening, intimidating, all those things he could have been. Instead, he is the most wonderful director. He's a complete delight.

I loved the script from the start, and I thought the part of Helen was lovely, but I never imagined I'd be playing it. I thought an American or Canadian might be cast but certainly not me. David came to see *Rock 'n' Roll* and offered me the role.

He has worked with the same crew forever, including the director of photography, Peter Suschitsky,[5] as well as production designer Carol Spier; sound editor Bryan Day; and film editor Ronald Sanders. This reflects well on the director because it means there is a trust and a camaraderie. David generates such a creative climate on the set. It's magical. Everyone is treated as a grown-up, and issues are addressed honestly.

Are there any roles that you'd like to revisit?

Yes, I think I'd like another go at Cleopatra. I was so intimidated in that performance by her iconography, but now, not so much.

Looking at your career, what are your next challenges?

The first challenge is that I'm afraid I'll never get another role, especially as those for older actresses become fewer. What is remarkable is that I thought once when I had reached a certain age, things would start to be less challenging. It's been the reverse. Everything is more challenging.

That's what I find completely remarkable about my luck, and I do consider it luck. Yes, it's talent to a degree, but I've been very lucky.

∽

Selected Credits

Theatre

The Trial, Olympia, Dublin (1959; n/a); *The Importance of Mr. O*, Olympia, Dublin (1959; n/a); Abbey Theatre (at the Queen's; as Sinéad Ni Chiosoig): *Galileo* (1965; Tomas MacAnna); *Kathleen Ni Houlihan* (1965; Tomas MacAnna); *Emer Agus an Laoch* (1965; Tomas MacAnna); *One for the Grave* (1966; Frank Dermody, as Proinnsias MacDiarmada); *Irish Woman of the Year* (1966; Tomas MacAnna); *Conspiracy* (1966; Frank Dermody, as Proinnsias MacDiarmada). **Other:** *Othello*, Ludlow Festival, Ludlow (1974; Philip Grout); *London Assurance*, New (1975; Ronald Eyre); *Arms and the Man*, Oxford Festival, tour (1976; Michael Meacham); *Wild Oats*, RSC at the Aldwych, Theatre Royal, Newcastle (1979; Clifford Williams); *Measure for Measure*, RSC at the Aldwych (1979; Barry Kyle); *Children of the Sun*, RSC at the Aldwych (1979; Terry Hands); *Richard III*, RST (1980; Terry Hands); *The Merchant of Venice*, RST (1981; John Barton); *The Swan Down Gloves*, RST, RSC at the Aldwych, RSC at the Barbican (1981–1982; Terry Hands); *As You Like It*, RSC at the Aldwych (1982; Terry Hands); *Peer Gynt*, RSC at the Pit, Barbican (1983; Ron Daniels); *Much Ado about Nothing*, RSC at the Barbican; George Gershwin, New York (1983; 1984–1985; Terry Hands); *Cyrano de Bergerac*, RSC at the Barbican; George Gershwin, New York (1984–1985; Terry Hands); *Macbeth*, RSC at the Barbican; Tyne Theatre, Newcastle (1987; Adrian Noble); *The Rover*, Swan, Stratford; RSC at People's Theatre, Newcastle (1987; John Barton); *Aristocrats*, Hampstead (1988; Robin Lefevre); *The Three Sisters*, Gate, Dublin; Royal Court (1990;

Adrian Noble); *Map of the Heart*, Globe (1991; Peter Wood); *Faith Healer*, Royal Court (1992, Joe Dowling); *The Tower*, Almeida (1995; Howard Davies); *Our Lady of Sligo*, Theatre Royal Bath; NT, Cottesloe [now Dorfman], Irish Repertory, New York (1998; Max Stafford-Clark); *Antony and Cleopatra*, RST; tour, including Theatre Royal Haymarket; Theatre Royal Newcastle (2002; Michael Attenborough); *The Mercy Seat*, Almeida (2003; Michael Attenborough); *Rock 'n' Roll*, Royal Court, Duke of York's; Bernard B. Jacobs, New York (2006; 2007–2008; Trevor Nunn); *Dancing at Lughnasa*, Old Vic (2009; Anna Mackmin); *The Cherry Orchard*, Bridge Project at the Old Vic; BAM, New York (2009; Sam Mendes); *The Winter's Tale*, Bridge Project at the Old Vic; BAM, New York (2009; Sam Mendes); *Juno and the Paycock*, Abbey, Dublin; NT, Lyttelton (2011; Howard Davies); *Other Desert Cities*, Old Vic (2014; Lindsay Posner); *Our Few and Evil Days*, Abbey, Dublin (2014; Mark O'Rowe); *Splendour*, Donmar (2015; Robert Hastie)

Film
Alfred The Great (1969); *Hoffman* (1971); *Horowitz in Dublin* [a.k.a. *A Likely Story*] (1973); *The Last Remake of Beau Geste* (1977); *Rocket Gibraltar* (1988); *Bad Behavior* (1993); *Sparrow* (1993); *Stealing Beauty* [a.k.a. *Dancing by Myself*] (1996); *Passion of the Mind* (2000); *My Mother Frank* (2000); *V for Vendetta* (2005); *A Tiger's Tale* (2006); *Eastern Promises* (2007); *Crack* (2009); *The Sea* (2013); *Queen and Country* (2014); *Stonehearst Asylum* [a.k.a. *Eliza Graves*] (2014)

Television
ITV Playhouse, "The Square on the Hypotenuse" (1959); *David Copperfield* (1969); *Armchair Theatre*, "The Dolly Scene" (1970); *Thriller*, "The Eyes Have It" (1974); *The Persuaders*, "Take Seven" (1979); *BBC Television Theatre*, "Twelfth Night" (1980); *Performance*, "Tales from Hollywood" (1992); *Oliver's Travels*, five episodes (1996); *Winter Solstice* (2003); *The Strange Case of Sherlock Holmes and Arthur Conan Doyle* (2005); *Masterpiece Theatre*, "A Room with a View" (2008); *Playhouse: Live*, "Crocodile" (2010); *Camelot*, seven episodes (2011); *The Hollow Crown*, "Henry IV, Part II" (2012); *Midsomer Murders*, "Death of the Diva" (2013); *Agatha Christie's Poirot*, "Dead Man's Folly" (2013); *37 Days*, three episodes (2014; Justin Hardy)

Awards and Nominations

The Maid's Tragedy, 1981, Society of West Theatre Awards, Actress of the Year in a Revival, nominee; *As You Like It*, 1981, Society of West End Theatre Awards, Actress of the Year in a Supporting Role, nominee; *As You Like It*, 1981, Clarence Derwent Award, Best Newcomer; *Cyrano de Bergerac*, 1985, Tony, Best Actress in a Play, nominee; *Much Ado about Nothing*, 1985, Tony, Best Actress in Play, nominee; *Our Lady of Sligo*, 1998, *Evening Standard*, Best Actress, winner; also, 1999, Olivier, Best Actress, nominee; 1998, London Critics' Circle Theatre Award, Best Actress in a Play, winner; 2000, Drama Desk, Outstanding Actress in a Play, nominee; *Rock 'n' Roll*, 2008, Tony, Best Featured Actress in a Play, nominee; also, Drama Desk, Outstanding Actress in a Play, nominee

Notes

1. He also played in *The Tempest* (1974) in a National production at the Old Vic, directed by Peter Hall.

2. George Devine, Lindsay Anderson, Max Stafford-Clark, Ian Rickson, Dominic Cooke, and, currently, Vicky Featherstone.

3. At the Plymouth Theatre in New York, directed by Mike Nichols.

4. Cusack and Irons appeared together in an episode of *Performance*, "Tales of Hollywood." Irons and Cusack also appeared in *Mirad: A Boy from Bosnia* (1997), which Irons also directed.

5. Son of cinematographer Wolfgang Suschitsky.

CHAPTER SEVEN

~

Samantha Eggar

The male director is absolutely an inamorato, a lover. If you miss your chance with him or the director of photography, that's your lookout.

It is a warm, verging on hot, July morning in the Los Angeles suburb of the San Fernando Valley. Outside Samantha Eggar's home, two flags flutter in the breeze: the UK Union Jack, with the cross of St. George, and the US stars and stripes.

Although she has occupied this home for a short time, it is already comfortably arranged with career memorabilia and masses of books and family photographs, including a photo of playwright friend Norman Corwin on his 100th birthday and a faded photo of her father in Burma with his Royal Army Service Corps regiment are also near at hand. Two needlepoint cushions featuring English bulldogs are nestled on the sofa. Eggar's own beloved bulldogs, Socrates and Tallulah, recently departed for doggie heaven, are nearby in photographs. A sculpture by Doug Edge in the shape of a tombstone, which reads Humphrey BogART and is composed of thousands of Pall Mall cigarettes encased in plastic with tips that spell out the actor's name, sits on the floor of the den.

In her study, she has copies of all her scripts going back to her earliest theatrical productions. They are bound and interleaved with photographs from the productions. She attributes the collection as being "a matter of discipline."

Eggar is dressed in a diaphanous skirt over black leggings, a black T-shirt, magenta sweater, and black Crocs, which she tosses aside as she sinks into an armchair and curls up. Just over her left shoulder hangs an orange Spanish-style shawl, heavy with fringe, which complements the actress's shoulder-length auburn hair.

"It's a little difficult to remember everything," she admits, "so I've made some notes." Humming "Try to Remember" from The Fantasticks, *she reaches for the papers.*

～

You have a lengthy list of given names. How did you decide on Samantha?

When I was born on March 5, 1939, in Hampstead, I was given six names: Victoria Louise Samantha Marie Elizabeth Therese. I started off as Victoria, the name of a friend of my mother's. I was the only Vicky in school until I was sixteen or seventeen. Suddenly, I met another Victoria, and I was deeply upset. I thought, "I'll use Samantha. Nobody has even ever heard of that name." Now my friends call me "Sam."

Were you relocated out of London during the war?

Yes, when war was declared in September 1939, for safety, we moved to Bledlow in Buckinghamshire, a beautiful village. My future costar, Oliver Reed, lived just down the road. He once told me that I was his first girlfriend. Later, when we did a TV movie together, *A Ghost in Monte Carlo*, I remember the time he spent with my children when we were in Paris before going on location for that film. Anyone who gives time to a child has a huge heart, and he did, despite his hell-raising reputation. I was never sure whether what he became was an act or not.

Your father was in the army. Your thoughts?

He was a brilliant brigadier general but also an extremely shy man. An interesting combination. In his obituary, the papers praised him as leader of his men. I think that what he had learned at Sandhurst was compassion, that and the discipline to lead. Funnily enough, I think that the army and the other services parallel the film business. My father had hundreds of men to move about, as does a film company, which often has as many as 150 people. Those people are controlled by the producer. Those men in the service are controlled by the officers. The entire film, the discipline, the whole organization, and the skill to command is vital to the finances of those productions. Whether war or film, I think there *is* a connection.

You hadn't planned on an acting career. What happened along the way that changed your career path?

It's true. I hadn't planned on acting. Although I received an offer of a scholarship to RADA, my parents—especially my mother—said no. Since I was interested in drawing and painting, I enrolled at the Thanet School of Art in Margate for two years, where I received an intermediate diploma.

I had the idea of a career in fashion. I wasn't ever any good at maths, but I was good at sketching. I thought I might get a job with Norman Hartnell.

You finally did attend drama school, though, and a very prestigious one at that.

I enrolled in the Webber Douglas Academy of Dramatic Art.[1] I learned every aspect of drama, fencing, movement, dance. I never did Stanislavski. I've read him, obviously, and thought, "Can I use that? Can I apply that?" I found my own references, my life's "goody bag" as I call it, that I use to develop character from my own experience.

In one of your first stage roles, you played opposite the formidable Donald Wolfit as Thomas Gainsborough, the painter, in *Landscape with Figures*. It was written by an unlikely playwright, Cecil Beaton, the noted photographer and costume designer. What are your memories of that production and playing opposite one of the last of the great actor-managers of the British theatre?

I was at drama school, and I had a gentleman friend, John Sutro, a member of a Portuguese banking family. He, Graham Greene, and Jamie Thompson formed Pegwell Productions for theatre projects. John also formed Ortus Productions for film; the company name is a reverse spelling of his last name.

The first film they were going to do was Graham's *The Living Room*, with Rex Harrison. The script was ready, but Rex dropped out; then it was going to star Eric Portman, who had appeared in the premiere of the play in 1953 [at Wyndham's, directed by Peter Glenville]. In the end, the picture wasn't made.

John, who was at Trinity College, Oxford, was in that Evelyn Waugh–Somerset Maugham group, who I met through him. He also knew Cecil. Cecil had written the play, originally titled *The Gainsborough Girls*, about the painter, Thomas Gainsborough. It had been produced once before, in 1951 at the Theatre Royal Brighton, and was not a success. Beaton changed the title to *Landscape with Figures*, and in 1959 he brought it back with Wolfit as Gainsborough and Mona Washbourne as his wife. Both wonderful theatre actors. I played Emma Hart, Lady Hamilton.

Cecil took photographs of the production. He did all the costumes and sets. He put me in a Grecian-style costume. I'm not sure if Gainsborough ever actually painted Lady Hamilton [he didn't], and with Admiral Nelson's money and a beautiful house, she had one of the first houses of ill repute. Cecil put her in the play to have a little spice.

It was quite an experience working with Sir Donald. The young actors in the cast—and that included me at the age of nineteen—behaved appallingly;

we were just children. We were relentlessly awful to him. To us, he was old time. I don't remember what age he was then. [Wolfit was fifty-seven.] To us, he was like "grandpa." We laughed at him and teased him, and he terrified us. We were out of his era and out of his league.

The production, again, didn't work. But as a first for me, just being in a production with Wolfit was pretty impressive.

Even though Beaton had worked on the script for years, did Wolfit think there should be changes?

Wolfit had problems with the script, and there was a knock-down-drag-out fight in Newcastle with Wolfit throwing the script onto the stage in frustration. He didn't know that Cecil was sitting at the back of the theatre. He hugely offended Cecil, obviously. I'm not sure how they resolved the issues.

We toured, then closed at the Grand Theatre, Wolverhampton. As with the earlier production, this one didn't work either.

During this tour an incident occurred in which Sir Donald did not make his entrance on cue. What happened?

As the scene unfolds with my "tarts" and me at the opening of the second act, I am holding a goblet to toast him upon his arrival. Sir Donald was to enter from stage right. I actually have my back to him as the scene begins, and I turn toward him as he enters. But on this occasion, he didn't make his entrance.

I said the line, "To Tom." I paused. No Sir Donald.

Then out of the side of my mouth, I asked, "Can anyone see him?" Everyone on stage is singing, and someone is playing the guitar. No reply. So I ad-libbed, "Let's have another drink," And someone refilled the goblets. There was lots of whispering. Finally, I think I walked to the side of the stage and said, "Tom! Tom, where are you?" Then Sir Donald made his entrance, and we carried on.

After the curtain call, I asked, "Sir Donald, could you tell me if you're going to be there tomorrow?" He didn't reply and almost knocked me over on his way to his dressing room.

Shortly afterward, there was a knock on my dressing room door, and I was handed a note, which read: "If you wish to speak to Sir Donald, it will be through the stage manager only."

There was another incident, too. Cecil Beaton had designed that gorgeous Grecian outfit; it was topped with a beautiful purple hooded cape, which flowed out behind me. During one performance, when I walked past Wolfit, he put his foot on my cape, and down I went, flat on my back. Was it on purpose? I think so.

Now not only was I not allowed to speak to him off stage, I also had to avoid him on stage. From then on I made huge circles around him.

I had a certain brazenness then, and I reacted like a pompous, precious child. I thought, "How dare he do that to me?" I even told the press about the incident. Now, I think it's hilarious.

Later in life, I realized what Sir Donald had done for the British theatre, touring with productions of Shakespeare, educating thousands of people in the classical actor-manager role for virtually no money. He really was a wonderful actor.

And then?

I joined the Oxford Playhouse in about 1960 in a production of *Taming of the Shrew*. The Playhouse was under Frank Hauser's brilliant direction at the time. I have a photo album of that production, too. There was Ted Hardwicke, adorable and such a sweetheart; Siân Phillips, who would soon marry Peter O'Toole; and Charles Kay. Brewster Mason was Petruchio.

What were some other early stage appearances?

I worked with David Warner in *Midsummer Night's Dream* and *Twelfth Night*, both at the Royal Court in 1962. We were all so young: Lynn Redgrave was eighteen; Corin Redgrave, twenty-two; Nicol Williamson, twenty-six; David Warner, twenty; Alfred Lynch was the old man of the troupe at thirty-one.

David Warner is a darling. Can you imagine—he had stage fright for thirty years! In fact, the first play he did when he went back on the stage was *Major Barbara* in July 2001. On Broadway, no less! My son-in-law, Brennan Brown, was playing Bilton in that production and understudying two roles.

I gave a first-night party at Café Un Deux Trois in New York and sat next to David. We spoke nonstop, reminiscing about how young we were when we worked at the Royal Court.

David had done the incredible *Hamlet* in 1965 at the RSC. I was in the States by then, and I didn't see the production. Peggy Webber McClory, who is the founder and director of CART [California Artists Radio Theatre], which I'm a member of, had seen it, and, like everyone, fell in love with him. During his stage fright years, he did television, films, and came out to Los Angeles and was part of CART where we worked together. When I listen to those recordings, he was brilliant, even though he was this sort of nonperson; he was so shy. He has conquered his stage fright and continues his stage work.

You first stepped before the camera in *Young and Willing* in 1962.

Producer Betty Box had seen me at the Royal Court in both Shakespearean productions and signed me for the film. It's a college story. I play Ian McShane's girlfriend.

During the production on location at Bishop Grosseteste University in Lincoln, it was very cold. And Betty, who I called "Big Mummy," looked after all of us and brought us warm clothes and taught us all the rules and regulations of filming, including how to behave on a film set. She and the director, Ralph Thomas, who also directed me in *Doctor in Distress*, were both very much of the British institution of film, would say to me, "Stop acting. Bring it down." I was still "of the theatre" at that point.

I was seeing Albert Finney at the time, and he came up and brought me *fraises du bois*. Betty put him in the movie; he's in a scene wearing a college scarf, but he didn't receive a credit.

Albert Finney was just making a name for himself. What role did you play in his life at the time?

We were a couple, a very strong couple, while he was working in London. He was appearing in *Luther* [1961–1962] in the evening at the Phoenix Theatre on Denman Street, and shooting *Tom Jones* [1963] during the day. I saw the play almost every night. He was amazing. We'd go home where I'd have a meal ready in our flat, which was behind the Dorchester.

When Albie and I went to Greece the first time, we stayed at actor Peter Bull's house on Paxos, an island south of Corfu. "Bully," as he was called, appeared in *Luther* with Albie.

Your subsequent film was *Dr. Crippen*, directed by Robert Lynn. You played Ethel Le Neve, the mistress of the notorious wife murderer, played by Donald Pleasence.

I have wonderful memories of *Dr. Crippen*, especially meeting Donald, who was the most unusual, warm, hysterically funny, brilliant demon of a man. Talent galore. Here he was playing a wife murderer.

Look at the people who were in the film: Donald Wolfit—again—and Coral Browne. Fabulous actors. The collaboration was more a theatrical one than a filmic one. It definitely wasn't an MGM-money-out-of-America-coming-into-Shepperton production! It was definitely a British film made on a shoestring. I think it was shot in about three and a half or four weeks at Shepperton.

Nicolas Roeg, who became a brilliant director, was the cinematographer. He made the Old Bailey—essentially constructed of cardboard—look like the real thing.

In one sequence, I am disguised as Crippen's nephew as we're trying to escape to America. Can you imagine! He was the first criminal to be caught by new technology: the telegraph.

Crippen has an image at Madame Tussauds in London . . . but I don't.

In one scene, you and Pleasence play a scene in bed in a seedy hotel. It's a long, long take, no cuts. Just dialogue. We don't see long takes like that in today's films.

That long take was shot because of the time constraints that the director, Robert Lynn, was under. I think the scene carries itself. It works because the dialogue is everything in that scene. We didn't need any fancy camerawork to explain anything. Nic made it look credible.

If you watch some of the older movies on TCM, you can see that the camera doesn't move, and you, as the audience, are drawn in. Today, it's cut, cut, cut, and, I'm sorry to say, I go the other way and am not drawn in. Today, filmmakers think the audience can't possibly listen to a few pages of dialogue without the camera moving about.

You did an about-turn from your bad and ditzy girl roles and became an international star when you appeared as Miranda Grey in *The Collector* in 1965. How emotionally and physically demanding was this role?

Dennis Selinger, who had formed what was CMA [Creative Management Agency] and is now ICM [International Creative Management], was my agent and my Jewish godfather. He had discovered and managed Peter Sellers for years, along with David Niven, Sean Connery, and Michael Caine. He negotiated my contract for *The Collector*. Albie and I had just broken up. He had asked me to marry him, but I said, "I've just got this movie that I have to do."

Of course, I read the book by John Fowles. We rehearsed for a month. I knew it like a play.

The role was hugely physically difficult. First of all, they would wet the leather straps before they bound me every day. There I was in this black leather—S&M, here I come—and with the lights on the set, they shrank. It was sheer hell throughout the four months of filming, but I was tough, as tough physically as anyone in their midtwenties would be. I was physically strong, so it didn't matter what they threw at me. I had the determination and my own professionalism as an actor. It's just the British attitude of pulling up your socks and getting on with it. Look at how much screen time there is for my character; look at the arc that the character has to go through.

Then there was the debacle of no confidence. I was absolutely sucked of confidence. No one spoke to me—cast or crew. Terence Stamp as Clegg didn't speak to me, which was very, very difficult. I had no connection with anyone on the set. Impossible to sustain any relationship because I just wasn't that strong. William Wyler, the director, denied telling everyone not to speak to me during production. It was my first time in America, and I had nobody here, no family, nobody. I faded.

Samantha Eggar in *The Collector* (1965). *Columbia Pictures/ Photofest © Columbia Pictures*

I asked Terence many, many years later why he didn't talk to me. I think I'm quoting him correctly. He said, "You're lucky. There are lots of people I don't talk to."

It seems difficult for you to talk about the film even today.

I was fired from the film.[2] They were right to fire me. I don't think anybody realized what I was going through. I'm not a street kid, and I wasn't strong enough to take all those mental blows. I just dwindled into nothing. I went back to England. They just thought they could get another actress. But they couldn't find anybody else, so they had to rehire me.

It might have been Mike Frankovich, who was Columbia's vice president in charge of production then, who came up with idea of bringing in Kathleen Freeman, who played the elocution teacher in *Singin' in the Rain*. She got me through the movie. Kathy, this premier comedienne, took me and my soul and my body and supported me day after day after day, seven days a week, twenty hours a day. She was a volcaness; she was Wagnerian brilliant. Her attitude, her love of people, her love of the theatre—her parents were in vaudeville—her positive outlook on love, her never-failing positivity was so viable and solid. That's Kathleen Freeman. [Eggar points to a photograph of Freeman on the bookshelf.] Kathy gave me strength to get through it, and, with her help, I was able to take the reins, physically and emotionally.

What about working with William Wyler?

The weight of classic filmmaking just oozed out of him. But this was not a film that was his genre at all. He made just three more films after this,[3] so he was finishing up his career. Today I see him as physically the bravest man I'd ever met, as well as being among the most honored and the most brilliant.

When I was rehired for *The Collector*, I was in Palm Springs at a country club, when Mr. Wyler and editor Bob Swink got up from a meeting and left. I followed along after them like a silly little lamb. There was a swimming pool outside, and I watched the director walk along the very, *very* edge of the deep end of the pool. I thought, "What an extraordinary thing to do. This isn't a circus."

There are stories about his numerous takes on his films, but he didn't do that with me.

"One Take Sam," he called me. But he wouldn't allow me to see rushes.

Did he offer you any advice during the production?

Yes, his pearl of wisdom was, "Never look down. Always show them your eyes."

When Mr. Wyler said that to me, I thought, "Do I need Stanislavski with that remark?"

Despite, or perhaps because of, the trauma of both the role and in production, you received a number of accolades.

I remember when I got the Golden Globe. I was standing next to Omar Sharif. I thanked Mr. Wyler and Kathleen Freeman.

I was also nominated for an Oscar, and I believe that if any actor had played that part under the direction of William Wyler—and I take myself out of the equation—that actor should have gotten the Oscar.[4] If I had won, there was nothing I wanted more than to give that statue to Kathy. I always regretted not being able to give it to her. She knew that.

You returned to a bad girl role in *Return from the Ashes*, directed by J. Lee Thompson.

I never saw the finished film, and when I saw it on TCM, I had no memory of it. That was frightening. Until that moment, I didn't believe people when they said they didn't remember things. I have watched some of my other movies, and I actually remembered the dialogue. I even knew the clothes. I knew what I'd had for lunch on a particular production day. But I didn't recognize a frame of *Return from the Ashes*. I have no idea why. It was a pretty amazing role, and I was very *bad*.

Once I saw it, I remembered Julie Harris, the costume designer, giving me a very funny-looking bikini with a bushel of roses across the front. That costume and the others were absolutely perfect for my character as that little vixen, Fabi Wolf.

In *Walk, Don't Run,* directed by Charles Walters, you played opposite one of Hollywood's greatest leading men, Cary Grant.

I had just had my son, Nicolas, nineteen days before I was supposed to fly to Tokyo. I had been told it would be too dangerous to take the baby, what with germs and all. I asked for a few more days before leaving for the location; Columbia sued me. I immediately got on a plane. By the time I arrived, I had postpartum everything.

We had a blast even though we worked six days a week with a bare-bones script. So much was ad-libbed. I saw the film recently, and I was actually laughing.

I never got the feeling that Cary knew this was going to be his last film. At the time, I didn't put him into his position as film royalty that I should have done. I have a favorite photo of Cary and me where I'm doubled over with laughter listening to something actor John Standing, who is just out of the frame, has said. John's first wife, Jill Melford, was my best girlfriend.

Then there's *The Brood,* directed by David Cronenberg. He tends toward the bizarre, doesn't he?

Despite the fact that his films are referred to as "body horror," Cronenberg, who's a Canadian, is a very warm, very embracing, and embraceable person. That quality allowed me, as an actor, to give my best. I knew it would be a quick flick. The whole film took maybe four weeks, and I was on it for two and a half weeks. We had a wonderful, intellectual, well-read group of technicians.

You continued to test yourself by moving to yet another genre, a musical, *Doctor Dolittle*.

I wanted all these new experiences, scary as they were. I always wanted a challenge. I didn't want to do another "Let me out! Let me out!" film. I wanted to do a comedy and then a musical. That's how I got from *The Collector* to *Walk Don't Run* to *Doctor Dolittle*.

What were the challenges in this new genre?

Two months before we started shooting, we prerecorded the songs with Lionel Newman and 120 musicians so Tony Newley could get his songs down. There I was, sitting in the same studio at Capitol Records where Frank Sinatra recorded, possibly the same stool that Sinatra sat on. I could hardly open my mouth. I was in such awe. This was one of those occurrences that I've stored in my goody bag of life. It will always be there for reference.

I did about 75 percent of my own singing. I'd trained in singing at Webber Douglas. Diana Lee was brought in to hit the high notes, and we shared the songs.

Director Richard Fleischer had a terrible time getting Rex to commit to the film. Rex had said, "Yes. Yes. Yes," to the title role, and at the last minute, he'd say, "No." He did that probably three or four times. But it was finally a "yes." Rex didn't look anything like the short, chubby character in Hugh Lofting's books. Sexy Rexy was tall and slim, but he was brilliant in the role.

During production, we all sang to playback, except Rex. He sang live. It was in his contract. His singing wasn't singing per se. He was talking-singing. Like Tony Newley, Rex didn't have the greatest voice, but they could both sell a song.

The stories about Rex being unhappy about the songs and wanting to redo them are not true. They were a challenge for everyone. I read Richard Fleischer's autobiography, *Just Tell Me When to Cry*, in which he wrote how Rex was really upset with the collaboration between Tony Newley and Leslie Bricusse. It was probably because of Rex's insecurity; he thought the team would write the good ones just for Tony. That would have been absurd because everyone wanted the picture to be the best it could be. The lyrics of the songs were so far ahead of their time, and the genius of both Newley and Bricusse really shines through, the humor and gorgeous melodies.

Rex also had advice for me. "Sam," he once said to me, "never be sung *at*. It's embarrassing." He was referring to the Jeanette MacDonald–Nelson Eddie films where the camera is on her, and he is singing. It looks quite silly.

W. C. Fields advised actors never to work with children or animals. In this film, there were a variety of animals with which you and Harrison had to interact.

Rex handled all those animals very well. Don't forget the trainers, who did a wonderful job. We had to change the chimps every now and again because they grew bigger and bigger; it was the same with the piglets. I wasn't in the scene with the anteater, but it actually escaped one day.

To me, the film shows the awareness of the treatment of animals. Nobody was taking that seriously when the film came out. There were atrocities being done to animals all over the world. I think what will really resonate now with people who watch the film, and especially with children, is how to treat animals properly.

One of the exotic locations for the film was in the Caribbean. What are your thoughts about location filming?

The picture took almost a year to shoot. We shot on the 20th Century Fox lot in Los Angeles; two locations in the UK: Bath and Castle Combe, a beautiful village, which won all sorts of prizes as the prettiest village in England; and on an island in the Caribbean. Oh, what was the name of it? [She reaches for an atlas.] Ah, yes, St. Lucia.

On many films—but especially on location productions—people form relationships, little groups. My group was Herb Ross, who was the choreographer, and his wife, Nora Kaye, the former ballerina; Howard Jeffries, their assistant; Tony; Patricia Newcomb, our publicity rep; and me. Our personalities just jelled, so there was a lot of laughing at dinner and dancing to those wonderful Caribbean drums every night. We were a unit.

Rex's group was just him and his then wife, Rachel Roberts. He didn't want to stay in the little hotel-motel the rest of us stayed in. In fact, he didn't want to stay on the island at all. They stayed on a gorgeous, swank schooner moored miles away from us in Marigot Bay. I'm sure he was jealous of these little groups and relationships that were formed.

This is true on many films, especially on location: people form little cliques, like clubs at school. Rex certainly didn't approve of our behavior. Fleischer wrote that Rex thought Tony and I were "twits when [we] clowned around on the set and disturbed his concentration."

On top of everything, I was about five months pregnant during the production. I remember when we did the song, "There Are So Many Fabulous Faraway Places to See," the costumes had to be continually let out, especially the tops because of the boobs.[5]

You again moved to another genre in *The Molly Maguires,* a film with a political edge to it. What are your recollections of that work?

Martin Ritt, the director, had a gruff voice, but he was the softest, sweetest, warmest, most caring person. Speaking from a personal point of view as an actor, I found him to be just what I wanted a director to be. I would do anything for him. He took care of the cast, like Betty Box had done years before. He made sure we all had dinner because he knew that everybody was away from their families on location in various places in Pennsylvania. When a company is on location, it becomes your family. Even if you have a five-room suite at a hotel, you are still alone, and that loneliness is very loud. Marty never let that happen to us. He was the complete package, the standard of how to be a director.

I'd watch cinematographer Jimmy Wong Howe and Marty work on a setup. I always loved being on the set. I'm technical in that way. I want to know, "What's that?" or "Why are you doing that?" I could see their artistry. It was role reversal as I watched them rather than them watching me.

Sometimes I'd be waiting to go on set in the town of Eckley, in the soft coal area outside of Wilkes-Barre. I would be sitting in one of the real miner's homes waiting to be called. The miner would come in the back door, covered in coal dust, coughing, bowed. The location—and the people—seeped into our being. We were all affected by it. The crew, the actors, the whole unit were in unison with the heart of the project, and Marty[6] said that it was one of his favorite movies. It's a true story, and we were using it in juxtaposition to modern times.

On that film, Sean Connery taught me how to drink scotch, his drink of choice. I remember going to his trailer, and he offered me a drink, Glenlivet. I was about to put Coca-Cola in with it. It was a James Bond moment: "You do it this way," he told me and took the glass and poured in the whisky. I learned how to drink it neat.

Richard Harris, a notorious drinker and hell-raiser, promised Marty he wouldn't drink, and he didn't . . . until one day. Until that day, he was very, very good, and a brilliant actor.

And the story itself was a true one.

We all loved the story of the Molly Maguires about the coal mine labor wars in the mid-1880s.[7] I'd done as much research as I could about the period and the current activism that was going on. My friends in America gave me a quick catch-up on the blacklist, which was fascinating and horrendous and angry making, and I was astounded that this could have been allowed. This may sound naive, that this huge, great country of the United States could have allowed it. I asked, "Where were your balls, people?" Marty's friend and the film's screenwriter, Walter Bernstein, was on the set with him every day.[8]

What are your recollections of David Hemmings, who you played opposite, in Eric Till's *The Walking Stick*?

David was a brilliant human being who spread himself too thin with all the attributes he was given. He was a director, painter, a poet, a writer, even a boy opera singer. Benjamin Britten wrote the part of Miles in his opera *The Turn of the Screw* for David. All these things he could do brilliantly. He just sucked up everything. He was streets ahead of others, a complete Renaissance man. He was magnetic and had such a beautiful face. He died far too young; he was just sixty-two.

It's an interesting story in that my character, Deborah, commits a felony. The story had to have my character put the letter into the letter box, even though she was in love with Hemmings's character. She didn't want to do it. But as far as the censor was concerned, we had to see the police being called.

One of your early television appearances was in the series *Anna and the King*, based on the film versions of *Anna and the King of Siam*.

It was such a sweet series. It was a shame it was cancelled after thirteen episodes.

With my interest in fashion, I always loved seeing what costumes were going to be for a production. I went with the costume designer for the show, and I ransacked the 20th Century Fox costume department. I found Deborah Kerr's costume from *The King and I* [costumes by Irene Sharaff] and Irene Dunn's from *Anna and the King of Siam* [costumes by Bonnie Cashin]. I took pieces of their costumes. I was particularly interested in the shoes; shoes are part of the character. I usually provided my own jewelry. We weren't allowed to use the music for the famous waltz, "Shall We Dance?," so we used another one.

You followed in the footsteps of Barbara Stanwyck in a television version of the iconic film *Double Indemnity*, directed by Jack Smight.

The original 1944 film, directed by Billy Wilder, was so good. I wasn't up to even comparing my role as Phyllis Dietrichson to hers. I remember sitting behind her at some event and told her how much I admired her work. I didn't mention that I'd played the role!

I made this version after my divorce from Tom Stern, and I was not happy. It was a very difficult period in my life, self-inflicted angst. And it showed in my performance.

You returned to the stage in 1985 with *The Lonely Road*.

It is a play by Arthur Schnitzler. Anthony Hopkins and I hadn't been on the stage for years. After a tour around the UK, we hit London's Old Vic, and the critics hated it.

Colin Firth, who won an Oscar for his role as King George VI in *The King's Speech* in 2011, also appeared in the production. He and Tony had been students of the director, Christopher Fettes, at the Drama Centre, which Fettes founded with Yat Malmgren when they broke away from the Central School of Speech and Drama in the early sixties, emphasizing Stanislavski.

Ann Lynn, Tony Newley's first wife, was also in the production.

It wasn't a success.

Looking back at your career and the directors with whom you worked, what have your expectations of a director been?

I think I've always looked for the human affinity. In the case of Mr. Wyler, who was the most brilliant, and Mr. Ritt, who I would have married if he'd asked, I found that affinity. Of course, there was huge respect on my part. I hope there was respect on their side for me even though I was just a nothing.

One of the good things about making movies in the fifties was that I had rehearsal time so at least I got to know that person who was going to be my boss, my general, on the set. I knew the limits I could go to. I knew the restraints, the politesse, the etiquette. I also saw how much he was going to be in control of me and how that was going to affect me personally. Was it going to be intellectual control? Was it going to be sexual control? Was it going to be a give-and-take control? But I don't recall ever being taken advantage of by a director.

All my directors have given me little pearls of wisdom that I remember. I think I'm a very receptive person. And, innocently, I would say, "Oh, all right." I tended to take it all in. I'm not an aggressor, but I do challenge; that's part of being competitive, which an actor has to be.

There's an interesting relationship between directors and actresses. If a woman is in that same relationship with any other man, she'd be considered "fast." With a director, because you know you're not going to sleep with him—or hopefully not—you intellectually make the connection quickly. You don't want to waste time. So I've always looked for the human affinity . . . in anybody. I don't think I would have found that if I'd been asked to work with Mr. Hitchcock, but I wasn't.

What's the difference between working in theatre and film?

When Bob Mitchum was asked that question, he had a wonderful answer: "A quarter of a million dollars." And it's so true. Money aside, an actor doesn't have the same relationship with a theatre director as with a film director. Theatre is a communal experience. The experience is a shared one in the theatre. In film, you are the director's number one wife for a short period of your life. In film you're number one, as long as your beauty and the need for you is paid for. Come the day you're not needed, you're not even in the harem any more.

In theatre, you're part of the harem. Today, you're the number one wife, and then when it comes to notes at the end of the day, you're the number *ten* wife and completely depressed.

The most incredible thing about the alchemy of the theatre is that everybody brings to the theatre that night the day's psyche. If you have a six-month run, you may get one night when everybody's psyche is on a parallel.

And that night, you are so high from the contact. Whether the cast is four or fourteen, it's never repeated because of what's inside of each individual that particular night. It's magic. You try to repeat it, and you never can.

The director on a film is a lover. I'm not sure what the male actors would say about that. [She laughs at the thought.] The male director is absolutely an *inamorato* and so is the director of photography. If you miss your chance with both those men, that's your lookout.

The DP [director of photography] is looking straight at you, watching you eighteen hours a day. Today, sadly, the director isn't even there. Today, they may be watching on a monitor.

When I was making movies, the director was sitting right there in front of my crotch. After a take, it was similar to asking, "Daddy, was it all right?"

And yet another medium: audio recordings. How do you approach this medium in which voice is everything?

I sit for hours with colored pencils and mark out each character. Yellow is the five-year-old, the blue is the nine-year-old, the green is the man. I prep myself for what's coming. It's like radio. We get one rehearsal. Even in the days of radio, they never rehearsed. They had a table read—we're talking about people like Orson Welles, for goodness' sake—and then they'd do it on the day.

I did *Alice I Have Been* by Melanie Benjamin, the story of Alice Liddell. I play her from childhood to old age, as well as her parents, her sisters, Lewis Carroll, and other characters. It's a 430-page novel, and I did at least two weeks of prep and then five days in the studio. I and another actor recorded *Lady in Waiting* by Susan Meissner. It's a divided story about Lady Jane Grey, the nine-day queen, and a modern Jane living in Manhattan, a story about women and their choices. Both were challenging projects.

What is most surprising about being an actor?

I've met these incredible people; I've traveled all over the world. I've found there's a silent connection between actors, no matter what the language. It's a language of understanding life. We don't need things explained. It's a given that you click with whatever somebody is saying or describing; we've been given this intuitiveness. It's a gift.

I never used to give interviews, not because I didn't want to. [She abruptly stops speaking.] What am I saying? Of course, I didn't want to. The publicity people had a terrible time with me, but I think that has to go back to my upbringing. It wasn't part of who I was—to talk about what I did. Whether it was a disadvantage or not, I don't know. When I first started and Dennis was my agent, *I* told *him* what I wanted to do.

I've played different roles to cloak my own personality. Whether it was a mistake or not, I never wanted to be in a box. When I finished a project, I wanted to move on to something different, so after a drama, I wanted to do a comedy; then I wanted to do a musical; then I wanted to do something serious, with passion. That could be a huge detriment in film because the fans—the fanatics—really want to see me play the same role over and over. Looking at the history of women in film, you find those actresses are basically themselves, the "selves" that the fans love.

Then I was told that that's not the way it works. If I wanted to become a film *star*, which I've never become, I was told I'd have to play the same part; in theatre you can do different parts. The idea of always going into something different, jumping about from horror to comedy, I was able to keep a low profile. What that does is build trust in people, especially in a business, which luckily I don't live in now. People would feel comfortable being with me or being part of my life because they knew I would never gossip or go to the posh restaurant. I think privacy is important. You can do your work, absolutely do your work and be private. If you want to be on *Entertainment Tonight* every night, fine, but it's not in my character.

But all in all, an actor's life is just such a damn lucky one.

∽

Selected Credits

Theatre
Landscape with Figures, Olympia, Dublin; Theatre Royal Brighton; Grand, Wolverhampton (1959; Douglas Seale); *Midsummer Night's Dream*, Royal Court (1962; Tony Richardson); *Twelfth Night*, Royal Court (1962; George Devine); *The Lonely Road*, Yvonne Arnaud, Guildford; Old Vic (1985; Christopher Fettes); *The Seagull*, Oxford Playhouse; Theatre Royal Bath (1985; Charles Sturridge); *Auntie Mame*, Candlewood Playhouse, New Fairfield, Connecticut (1992; staged by Karin Baker)

Film
Dr. Crippen (1962); *Young and Willing* (1962); *Doctor in Distress* (1963); *Psyche 59* (1964); *Return from the Ashes* (1965); *The Collector* (1965); *Walk Don't Run* (1966); *Doctor Dolittle* (1967); *The Molly Maguires* (1970); *The Walking Stick* (1970); *The Lady in the Car with Glasses and a Gun* (1970); *The Seven-Per-Cent Solution* (1976); *The Brood* (1979); *Inevitable Grace* (1994); *The Astronaut's Wife* (1999)

Television
BBC Sunday-Night Play, "The Canterville Ghost" (1962); Double Indemnity (1973); Magnum, P.I., "Fragments" (1984); Finder of Lost Loves, "Wayward Dreams" (1984); Murder, She Wrote, "Hooray for Homicide" (1984); Tales of the Unexpected, "People Don't Do Such Things" (1985); Alfred Hitchcock Presents, "Deathmate" (1987); A Ghost in Monte Carlo (1990); LA Law, "Where There's a Will" (1993); Commander in Chief, nine episodes (2005–2006)

Radio
CART: The Strange Affliction (1994); Sherlock Holmes (1995); Alice in Wonderland (1997); Leviathan 99 (1999); Felix and Fanny (1999); Comedy Corwin, "Mary and the Fairy" and "Murder in Studio One" (2010); Shaw's Caesar and Cleopatra; Shakespeare's Antony and Cleopatra (2010); Norman Corwin's 100th Birthday Salute (May 1, 2010)

Awards and Nominations

The Collector, 1965, Academy Award, Actress, nominee; also, 1966, Cannes Film Festival, Best Actress, winner; 1966, Golden Globe, Best Motion Picture Actress—Drama, winner; The Brood, 1979, Genie, Best Performance by a Foreign Actress, nominee

Notes

1. Originally called Webber Douglas School of Singing and Dramatic Art; in 2006, the school became part of the Central School of Speech and Drama.
2. "In somewhat mysterious circumstances, Miss Eggar was suddenly relieved of the part and then suddenly reinstated." "'Collector' Coup for [Producers] Kinberg, Kohn," Los Angeles Times, May 1, 1964.
3. How to Steal a Million (1966), Funny Girl (1968), and The Liberation of L.B. Jones (1970).
4. Julie Christie won for her performance in Darling. Other nominees: Julie Andrews, The Sound of Music; Elizabeth Hartman, A Patch of Blue; Simone Signoret, Ship of Fools.
5. The film was nominated for nine Oscars, including Best Picture and won two: Song, "Talk to the Animals," and Special Effects.
6. Ritt died in 1990 at age seventy-seven.
7. The Molly Maguires was a secret organization in the Pennsylvania coal mining districts pitting the miners, the Mollies, against the mine owners.
8. Both Ritt and Bernstein had been blacklisted by the HUAC in the 1950s.

CHAPTER EIGHT

∼

Stephen Fry

I'm dippy about words and all things digital.

He blogs. He tweets. He acts. He writes. He directs. He hosts a popular television quiz show. To call fifty-seven-year-old Stephen Fry "multitalented" is to minimize his broad range of accomplishments. Perhaps no Englishman of his time has dipped his pen into more intellectual and entertainment projects. His credits range from a book on poetry to hosting a television program on endangered species; from appearing with close friend Hugh Laurie (of House fame) in the comedic television hit A Bit of Fry and Laurie to writing novels and multiple autobiographies, one with the improbable title of Moab Is My Washpot, to numerous film roles. Not to mention he's been named "a national treasure" by the Guardian newspaper.

His life has taken him from a three-month stint in Pucklechurch Prison in 1974 as a teenager for stealing a family friend's credit card to graduating from Queens' College, Cambridge, where he was a member of the famous Cambridge Footlights Dramatic Club.

Fry has scheduled lunch at his club, The Ivy, on West Street, just a door or two away from the venerable Ivy Restaurant. The entrance to the members-only club is discreetly hidden behind a florist's shop, but the uniformed doorman stationed outside betrays its location.

No need to touch a button on the Plexiglas elevator; the doors automatically close, and the elevator rises smoothly to the club's entrance. Since Fry hadn't arrived, a member of staff offers a seat in a deeply cushioned sofa, a drink, and a newspaper.

Seven minutes after the appointed time, Fry rushes in, linen jacket and trousers awash in wrinkles. The Garrick Club salmon-pink-and-cucumber tie is slightly askew over a multicolored striped shirt. He is profusely apologetic. He had been detained by a phone call at home and then walked the five miles to the club in his ongoing challenge, he explains, to keeping his weight down.

He's taller than expected: six feet four inches. A hank of hair falls over his right eye, à la Veronica Lake. He repeatedly flicks back it with his right hand. His world-weary, spaniel eyes sweep the dining room as he enters.

The waiter approaches. In low tones, he and Fry have a discussion about the availability of gulls' eggs, which are in season and a rare treat. Fry is so knowledgeable about this seemingly arcane food that he could easily write a treatise on the topic.

Luncheon items are ordered—including the gulls' eggs. And so begins the interview.

Fry speaks rapidly and sucks in deep breaths of air between sentences. He punctuates his conversation with words like adverts and nonpareil and keen—all very British. He's unexpectedly personable despite his celebrity and streets ahead of everyone intellectually. Regardless of topic, he never, ever talks down to his listeners, whether an interviewer, a waiter, or an admirer.

⌒

What is it about gulls' eggs that make them so rare and delectable?

There are only a few places in London that do gulls' eggs because they are limited in their supply. Gentlemen's clubs—as they're still rather embarrassingly called—have them. They are protected—the eggs, not the clubs—and it is very dangerous to collect them from cliffs. There are a few licensed collectors who go to these traditional London clubs, five-star hotels, and smart restaurants with the eggs. They are creamy and delicious—the eggs, not the collectors. [He demonstrates by plopping an egg into his mouth and savoring it.]

From eggs to your youth: Despite some troubling times, how were you able to turn your life around?

My father, who's a physicist, has a very high doctrine of work because work is what manages the physical universe. It is expressed by physicists as the "erg." It's a force of energy. To him, work is a problem solver. You only change things, unravel things, by working at them. He could see that I was someone who was very gifted in terms of brains, with words and memory, things that are superficially useful for advancement in passing exams. If you can express yourself and remember things, that's really all you need.

I was no good at maths and physics. I couldn't express myself numerically. He used to say to me, "You can't think." He used to drive me mad. It was

Photo courtesy of Stephen Fry

annoying because I read prodigiously, more than anyone else I knew. I knew so much and was passionate about so many things. I felt I was all feeling, and feeling is a deeply important thing. Reason is a kind of emotion, too, sometimes. But I didn't work. I never needed to *work* at learning things. Other people I knew were diligent because things came hard for them; it wasn't easy for them to remember things or learn concepts; therefore, they worked. I thought that was charming, but I wasn't interested in doing it. I thought I didn't have to.

There's a story about Yehudi Menuhin, who was truly one of the great men of his age, and one of the great violin prodigies as a boy; he was world famous as a twelve-year-old. When he was about seventeen, he took two years off from concert performances in order to learn the violin. He realized that he had just done everything on the basis of instinct and gift. He wanted to know how it worked, how to do it properly, the technique. When he emerged, he was a mature player.

That sort of courage and amazing insight, I wouldn't claim for myself because it happened as a result of imprisonment. I was a very disturbed, tormented, deranged, disruptive, unsettled adolescent. I unsettled and deranged those around me, mostly myself. I'm in no better a position to-day to judge why. The point was that after I had been in prison and after subsequent court appearances and I had returned home, I realized that all this literature that I thought I'd loved, I never read properly, so I started to read everything again and to make notes, and I decided I wanted to go to Cambridge. I had to persuade a local college to take me on for a course to prepare for the Cambridge exam, which they wouldn't do, so I had to read and think on my own.

Would you consider yourself an autodidact?

To consider myself an autodidact, no, I don't think so. I'd already had a classic education at that point. If you know more than your teachers have told you, you are an autodidact. It does a disservice to the word.

And those exam questions?

The national essay exams had questions like "Discuss the imagery of the night in *Macbeth*." Cambridge essay exams were famous for something like "Is there such a thing as literature?"

You mentioned the discipline of work. Is that something most people are capable of doing?

Probably they don't realize how hard *work* is. When they try to do it and it doesn't come easily, they think, "Oh, I can't do it," and they stop, not real-izing that the people to whom it apparently seems to come easily just simply work harder than they do. When people say they can't write or can't do this or that, what they're really saying is that they can't focus, can't concentrate. People never want to know that.

I finally discovered an ability to concentrate that I never knew I had.

J. S. Bach, the composer, said that if somebody just copied out what he wrote—not composed it but simply copied it out by hand—it would take sixty-five years or something. He said that to have accomplished what he had done, "All they had to do was to work as hard as me."

People do not understand the extraordinary satisfaction that comes from having done hard work. Yes, there's frustration, too, because it doesn't always produce something good. I remember Douglas Adams, author of *The Hitchhiker's Guide to the Galaxy*, saying this to me years ago when I was starting to write my first novel [*The Liar* (1993)]. I had said, "Oh, God, I don't know if I can do this."

He said, "Well, you can write."

"Yes, I think I can. I've done sketches and articles."

He said, "The one thing that will allow you to write a novel is if you don't get put off by how hard it is. It will come as an enormous shock how much *work* is involved. You'll think, 'I'm having a really good time.' And then after five or six weeks, you'll realize you're not even close, and it will make you almost despair. That's normal."

That's a really good thing to know.

I'm aware that my fifteen-year-old self would be unbelievably thrilled to be doing things I've been able to do. I have to remind myself of that when I'm moaning, which I don't often do.

Speaking of work, how do you do what you do in the time you have? Any one of your projects would be full-time to anyone else.

You're right. I don't know how I do it all. I suppose in the end it has to do with enthusiasm. My mind races sometimes around unhealthy tracks of what it is I'm supposed to be doing, which is why I was seven minutes late today. But mostly it is sheer pleasure. I am delighted that I have the opportunity to do all the things I do. As Oscar Wilde said, "One lives for pleasure." What else should one live for? If pleasure involves an enormous amount of hard work, it doesn't make it any less pleasurable for me—although it might for other people. It's where my appetite is. Of course there are days when I spring out of bed and look at my diary, and my heart sinks at what there is to be done.

But, generally speaking, my life is a picnic. But, as with all picnics, there are wasps. For me the wasps are publicity and the press people, and they've gotten worse. I used not to mind. I did talk shows and interviews with journalists routinely because I was asked to, not because I wanted to. I certainly wouldn't volunteer. Every project I do has a press officer, every one. It's preposterous. Their job is to get interviews. They come to me with piles of interview requests for magazines, books, websites, and blog sites, TV and radio. I *do* a lot; therefore, I have an enormous number of requests. That, to me, that is like a swarm of wasps.

I'd love to do all the filming and all the writing and never have it seen or read if the reward would be that I didn't have to do any of this publicity. The trouble is that if I do 1 percent of what I'm asked to do, I'm still doing too many interviews.

The worst thing, of course, is when it's something I believe in, like some charity thing—because I have, oh, you know, this bloody Twitter thing that everybody goes on about. I have millions of followers on Twitter. It means people constantly want me to mention their charity, which I'm happy to do. I was doing something about water in Africa, and the charity was thrilled because lots of journalists had come to the launch of this charity, but all the journalists wanted to talk about were things that have nothing to do with the project. The problem is that my tolerance gets lower and lower and lower for that side of our business. I wish I could have the strength of some actors I know who simply say no to anybody who wants to interview them for any purpose. Some get away with that.

I feel if I started doing that now, it would be too late. They'd say, "Why is he doing this now?" I know this sounds like a moan. There's no way that it doesn't, but I want to emphasize that 90 percent of my life is a picnic, and just 10 percent is wasps.

Yes, I am pulled in many directions. But life should be full of ambiguity and difference.

I'm not *a* writer. I'm not *an* actor. I'm not *a* broadcaster. I'm not *a* blogger. I'm not *a* noun. I'm undergoing the strange process of being *me* for however many years I'm given on this planet. In the business of being me, I'm no better in interpreting it—and probably much worse—and certainly have no fixed desire to be thought of as one thing or another, particularly. I'm sorry, but I just had to get this off my chest. It's been getting at me. You've just caught me at a bad moment.

What about a better moment at the beginning of your career in 1984 with *Forty Years On*. What are your remembrances of your association with that play?

It was an exciting time. All kinds of new things were happening. It's the first things you do that you always remember. I couldn't tell you what I did two weeks ago. It's the way one remembers.

It was a great joy to do *Forty Years On* by Alan Bennett because I worshipped him. Still do. All of Britain does. I'd heard bits of it on radio and record before video was around. I was pretty fresh out of university, and my agent asked me if I would audition for Alan and Patrick Garland, the director, and John Gale, who ran the Chichester Festival Theatre, where it was going to be put on.

I arrived at the Garrick Theatre and was horrified to see Alan in the stalls with Patrick and John. I had no idea he'd be there. I was nervous as a kitten; I was terrified. The part I'd been asked to read was the part of Tempest, a

Junior Master, which was the part Alan had played in the original production in 1968 at the Apollo with John Gielgud. I was absolutely dreadful at
the audition.

When I got home, my agent called and asked how it had gone. I said, "It
was appalling."

"Well, never mind. Something else will come along," he said.

The next day, he rang and said they wanted to see me again. I didn't know
anything about the world of theatre when I got that "recall."

I went back, and this time it was just Patrick and John . . . or so I thought.
They asked me to read some speeches again, which I did. Then they looked
at each other and said, "I think we can offer you the part of Franklin, a
Housemaster."

"Thank you so much," I said. "I'm so grateful."

Then Alan rose up from behind a seat, and said, "I'm so pleased." He'd
been told that I'd been nervous with him there, so he'd hidden in the stalls.
That was so sweet of him. He was present for the rehearsals a lot and was
absolutely marvelous.

We were in Chichester from about April to July. Then there was a
pause; then we went on to the West End for about six months. In November, I was very anxious because what I had been doing in the summer was
writing and rewriting the book of the musical Me and My Girl, collabo-
rating with director Michael Ockrent. The first night was going to be in
November in the Theatre Royal Leicester. But I was playing in the West
End, so my agent arranged that I could have three days off, a Saturday and,
I think, a Monday and Tuesday. I would have enough time to see a dress
rehearsal and to see the opening. Alan Bennett would take over my part
in Forty Years On while I was gone. I was terribly upset because I would
miss seeing him do it.

Alan asked me, "Would it be all right if I did it on the Wednesday matinee
before, so that I can see if I can do it?"

"Of course," I told him; that meant I could then watch him do it.

When we finished the run of Forty Years On, we were ready to bring Me
and My Girl into the West End.

**Another pleasant association has been with Hugh Laurie. You and he are
now one of the great comedic duos.**

Emma Thompson introduced us when we were at Cambridge. He and I
just instantly realized we had the same sort of sense of humor, the same likes
and dislikes, and different strengths. We have a kind of comic chemistry.

Our association is something I remember about my mother and father:
they did the Times crossword together every day. There were literate clues,

semantic clues, crazy anagrams. I inherited each of their strengths, so I could do it on my own.

Hugh and I are like that with comedy. We have a slightly different way of thinking and expressing things, particularly when we started. We complemented each other rather than being identical.

What was your process in working out routines together? Was it a matter of ad-libbing or writing it out in script form?

In the beginning, all writing is ad-libbing, but then we'd go back and correct bits. In one case, a sketch about Richard Burton, I think we were talking about it over the dinner table, sort of laughing at the preposterous adoration of these ghastly, self-regarding generations of sixties hell-raisers. [Fry lapses into an imitation of Burton with, "Oh, we raised hell!"] Hugh kind of went into the character, and I provoked him into revealing more and more. Then we said, "This is really good. We'd better write it down."

A lot of what we did came from this ad-libbing. We'd improvise to begin with, but we didn't improvise on stage.

In the course of those sketches, with topics ranging from linguistics to making a salad, you have devised some great names. Do you have a favorite?

The one I like best is Mr. Casalingua. It's something that I did actually improvise on stage with Hugh in our first show, *The Footlights Late Night Revue*. I'd only known him for a month or so. We were doing a sketch in which I was a psychiatrist, and he was the patient.

I have a line, "You feel this?"

He says, "How do you know?"

And one night I just added—I was feeling sparky for some reason—"It's my business to know these things, Mr. Casalingua."

It made him giggle on stage, which is always pleasant. Since then, it's been a little joke thing we have between ourselves.

In a hardware store sketch, you make up a number of onomatopoetic words.

Jargon is a rite of passage and one of the things I most enjoy. It's kind of a verbal equivalent of an initiation, being blooded or tattooed into whatever tribe you belong. In our tribe, there are linguistic initiation rites. And it *is* terrific fun. The point is to make the words sound logical, isn't it? We've all felt the mysteries of the tradesmen with their particular jargon. I love it, mocking its oddities and celebrating it.

The special vocabulary that members of a particular group use is not to exclude others; it's to include themselves. I think it's an important difference. A lot of people who object to jargon second-guess the motives of others quite wrongly in the way teenagers always seek pretension where there isn't any.

For example, sailing. Every single part of a sailboat has a name that's quite different from anything on land. That's not to exclude landlubbers; it's to *include* you into the world of sailing. It's a different experience; you use different things, different senses. You see the wind differently; you see air differently; you see weather differently. Everything in a boat is different from what you see and do on land, so it is right to have different names. These things matter. It's not just a "knot." It's a "hitch" because it does a different thing.

Only someone who's afraid of committing themselves would say, "Oh, this is being done to exclude me." Of course, there will always be imbeciles who want to show off their jargon, not to exclude others, but to show how inclusive they are. When we think of biodiversity as a sign of a healthy ecosystem, so is verbal diversity. Surely, richness and diversity are important in language.

Which is your favorite sketch?

The one about language. Absolutely. Oh, what I'm actually doing is expressing pretty common theories of linguistics, structural linguistics. Not that it's relevant to know that, but it's part of my argument. It's a good example, I hope, of how we complement each other because of Hugh's deadpan face when he turns to the camera and says, "We're talking about language." It's so obvious.

I am incredibly wordy with that sketch, which is shameless. It's about words, but it's also a very physical sketch, the way I sit and my hair—it's all part of it. It's just *fun*.

In that sketch and others, you exhibit tremendous breath control. How do you achieve that?

I didn't train at any drama school. It's a technique I discovered doing plays and things. Derek Jacobi and other actors train properly.[1] The technical term is *intercostal diaphragmatic breathing*, sometimes known as "rib reserve." Most people when they breathe move their chest, but actors' chests don't. They fill up lower and more slowly. That breath comes from a very different source. It means they can shout at a candle without moving the flame and talk much longer. Anyway that's the theory, and it seems to work. Having been asthmatic as a child, this technique may have helped increase the size of my lungs.

From your comments and observations, can we conclude you are passionate about words?

Indeed, I am. I'm dippy about words and all things digital.

Having spent so much of your career playing comedy in a variety of media, have you established a philosophy of comedy and its importance?

I once said of someone, "He has no sense of humor." By that I meant to impugn his seriousness. People who don't have a sense of humor are not serious. They do not have a serious view of the world if they don't have a sense of humor because they are incapable of seeing things concretely; they're only capable of seeing things abstractly. Comedy, like poetry, is something that addresses only the essence of things.

There's a very good phrase by G. K. Chesterton, I think it was, about how people are stupid enough to distrust something because it's funny. In fact, they should distrust things that aren't funny, he was saying, because if they're not funny, they're not likely to be true. Examples and analogies of human behavior are likely to make us laugh because they are real. Simply talking in the abstract about virtue and mercy and justice and truth is meaningless. There is no such thing as truth. There's a true thing that happens, and that might be someone falling on their ass, but simply to talk outside human experience, as Woody Allen has said, "Not only is there no God, but you can't get a dentist on Saturdays."

That's incredibly serious. Of course, it's funny, but if we analyze why humor is important, it is because of its truth. It wouldn't be funny if it weren't true.

Whereas talking in the abstract with capital letters—words like *Mercy* and *Virtue* and *Justice*—is simply an exchange of counters, most of which I don't recognize. It's like someone giving me a nine-dollar bill.

When you say "Justice," I don't know what you mean. You think you mean one thing, but it's not my idea of justice.

As Wilde said in *The Importance of Being Earnest*, "[Comedy] teaches one to treat the trivial things in life seriously and the serious things in life in a sincere, studied triviality." The point about Wilde is that almost everything he said is true, and the more we look at it, people will always think that being serious, being earnest, is a sign of truth telling. It's nearly always the sign of the opposite.

What makes you laugh?

So many things. Life.

In terms of people in film, Laurel and Hardy, Woody Allen, although there's not much in common between them. Laurel and Hardy are so influential that there are some Stan Laurel moments in Woody Allen, but not so many Hardyesque moments.

In terms of pure comedy, there are few better performances than Rosalind Russell in *His Girl Friday* or, indeed, even *Auntie Mame*. She's shamefully forgotten as one of the great comediennes. And Lucille Ball. I can watch her Vitameatavegamin sketch time and time and time again, and I will always laugh. Now I like Larry David and Tina Fey. I love Barry Humphries. His Dame Edna is an exhausting persona. Did you know he's a great bibliophile? He has a staggering collection, a scholarly collection of nineteenth-century authors. He's an incredible man, and I worship him.

Other comic heroes? Eric Morecombe, Alan Bennett, and John Cleese. In terms of literary humor: P. G. Wodehouse and, obviously, Oscar Wilde.

Not many actors have the opportunity to play one of their heroes. You had that chance in the film *Wilde*, directed by Brian Gilbert. What challenges were there playing someone who you not only greatly admire but was also a real person?

That's a really interesting point. I had the great good fortune to have Anthony Hopkins remind me of this when I was doing the film. He said, "You didn't have to sit in front of bloody archives all the time like I did with when I played Nixon [1995; Oliver Stone]." Everybody knew how he sounded and how he talked and walked.

I had no such challenge. Obviously, people wrote about Wilde's voice, and there are photographs of him, but nobody knows quite how he sounded. There is a record of someone speaking at the Paris Exhibition in 1900 and is supposedly Wilde, but it isn't. This voice was committed to what was known as Bell's visible speech, a sort of phonetic language [developed by Alexander Melville Bell in 1867 and further developed by his son, Alexander Graham Bell], which aided in Bell's campaign to help the deaf. Professor Higgins refers to visible speech in *Pygmalion*. A student went to one of Bell's lectures in Boston, I think it was, and wrote down as fast as they could what he said and how he said it.[2]

You can't really judge what Wilde's voice sounded like, can you?

That was an advantage in playing Wilde. I didn't have to do an imitation like Jennifer Jason Leigh did in *Mrs. Parker and the Vicious Circle*, who did a really good impression of Dorothy Parker, which is such a good impression that you could have been there.

Parker's voice is on record. She sounds like some ghastly mixture of Katharine Hepburn and a kookaburra. [He proceeds to do a screeching imitation of the two sounds.] Krikey, we don't want to hear someone talking like that now; we really don't. It's very off-putting. That's not how we expect people to speak anymore. It's not very pleasing to the ear.

How would you describe your version of what Oscar Wilde's voice sounded like?

Whenever an actor talks about his "craft" [Fry rolls his r] or "art," it is always open to sounding pretentious. There's the famous remark of Michelangelo about marble that "contained David," and he just had to take away the bits that weren't the *David*. As an actor, I just took away the bits weren't Oscar.

A lot of me is *not* Oscar. There are obviously bits I can't add. I can't add the brilliance and the writing skill, which is fortunate, because it's not something that comes across as an affect that is noticeable. It's not like I'm playing Isadora Duncan, where I have to dance.

So it was about selection, if you like. Which parts of *me* I thought I could get rid of. Funnily enough, I got rid of the most surprising things from most people's view of Wilde. I got rid of the frivolity, the laziness of thought, the brittleness that I have. I'm left with a man who everyone who knew him agrees was as a wonderful man who met your eyes directly when he spoke to you; who made you feel not less intelligent, but more intelligent than you were; who shared his intellect in such a way that it was a feast of soul and reason when you spoke to him. He was kind. Yes, he was foolish and sentimental. He was "big-eyed," if you like, in the way that I'm not.

Then there are all the imponderables that no one ever talks about, which films often leave the audience with an enormous problem: how people behave when they're alone in a room and people who are stiff and upright—wearing waistcoats and a particular way of moving that Victorians had—and even racy Victorians like Oscar Wilde were conventional in most things. But when people left the room, did they sprawl and "break wind" and burp and scratch their testicles like a Hoboken trucker? They are real people; there's nothing realer than scratching balls or not scratching balls. It's a different reality.

We just don't know. By definition we don't know because they were alone. We can't spy on a Victorian woman on her own. Did she still sit "properly"? Did she loosen her corset? There were people, including Constance Wilde, who was a leading light in the Rational Dress Society, who wrote about the immense hardships on women because of their dress.

All those things are meat and drink to actors because they are physical and real; it is quite difficult, though, when you have to make a decision as to how they behave when they're alone.

Wilde might well have been Mr. Blank-of-Nowhere-in-Particular had he lived in the 1920s. [Fry quotes from Thomas Gray's "Elegy Written in a Country Churchyard."]

> Full many a flower is born to blush unseen,
> And waste its sweetness on the desert air.

Sometimes, though, a violet will grow in a dung heap. I'm not saying that Victorian England was a dung heap. But Wilde certainly stood out amongst the sober, black frock coats; whereas, had he been around in the twenties, he would have had less originality perhaps. I don't know. If he'd been earlier, who's to say?

In terms of a personal tragedy, it was certainly a terrible shame. One would love him to see how truly revered he is around the world today.

Wilde was as witty a man there ever was. What's the difference between humor and wit?

Wisdom is the king of wit. It used to mean the ability to come up with a sharp remark. I suppose if someone has wit, they have understanding. If you're witty about something, it's more than a shallow indication; it suggests some sort of penetration of the subject about which you're being witty. It might be unfair and cruel, but it shows an understanding.

You can have people who are witty but not funny. Their wit will make you laugh, but if you saw it written down, it might not be funny. They might not be able to deliver it in such a way that it amuses you.

On the other hand, there are people who make you laugh who may be almost witless. And that's fine, too.

Clowning, you might say, is the opposite. I value them both. Clowning is delicious; good clowning is wonderful. You can have the wit of Groucho Marx next to the clowning of a Harpo Marx. Indeed, Groucho was a pretty good clown when he wanted to be.

Humor, I might argue, is the superset of which those two are subsets. There's humor, and within humor, there is clowning, and there's wit.

There's also humor in its original sense believed to be a fluid, the essence of a person: someone has a good humor. Ben Jonson wrote *Every Man in His Humour* and *Every Man out of His Humour*. He was very interested in his characters having the humors of choler and bile and the others.

Besides Jonson's meaning, humor is what makes us laugh. That is the universe, and there are two planets in it: Planet Wit and Planet Clowning, both in the universe of Humor. Then there's also Planet Satire and Planet Sardonic and Planet Sarcastic. Some of them overlap, and some of them don't. What I certainly don't believe is that one is more important than the other. Or that one is better than the other or that one is more worthwhile than the other.

In terms of our business, it's maybe skewed too much to wit at the moment. Sometimes you need a Jerry Lewis, someone pulling a silly face and being daft, rather than too much wisecracking.

Like Wilde,[3] you visited America. You have also lived and worked in the States. You traveled the highways and byways of America in a black London taxi—not very Wildean—in the series *Stephen Fry in America*.

I love America. I absolutely love it, but I've never understood why, in America, which is a republic founded on a revolution, that the words *radical* and *liberal* seem to be dirty words. Bizarre! I believe you have a socialized army, which declares war on enemies. Isn't poverty an enemy? Isn't ignorance an enemy? Isn't disease an enemy? Why can't you have socialized armies to deal with them? A private army is more logical, frankly, than private education and private health care.

Ben Franklin himself said, "Tax is the price you pay for civilization." If you want a civilized country, you will come together and say, "Let's not have poor people. Let's not have ignorant people. Let's not have the sick. Let's pay for them."

Can't you have a war on ignorance?

Can't you have a war on crime?

Can't you have a war on ill health and disease?

Is that so weird?

I sometimes have to leave dinner parties because I can't trust myself when I hear people I thought I could respect talking about being happy to see people die in their name. It's so alien to me and our culture here in the UK.

But back to the thought: I upped and downed America. I went to every state. I found differences in, say, the South. The Carolinas are different from Alabama; Florida, which isn't really the South at all, is different from Virginia, which calls itself the South.

I came away with a forty-five-inch waistline. But what I really came away with was an even deeper love of America, a love of its physical beauty, its variety, and most importantly, the people.

How does working in the US differ from working in the industry in the UK?

There are huge advantages and pleasure in working in America. For one, the budget. If there's a problem in something in a film or television program you're working on in America, it's simply solved by throwing money at it. And it works . . . usually. Sometimes—and I'm not in any way puritanical—but it can make me gulp. There is always a standard of riches that is always amazing.

Everything is bigger on an American film set. There are that many more cars, that many more trailers, and, of course, they can pay overtime. If something isn't getting done, suddenly we're there till three in the morning. [He flops back into the dining chair, as if it's been a long day's shoot.]

Then there's your writing, one of which is a book not of poetry but about poetry. Why that topic?

I love poetry. I wrote *The Ode Less Travelled: Unlocking the Poet Within* for technical reasons. But it isn't really about poetry, although I describe it as a "self-help book." It answers such questions, for example, as: What's a spondee? What is a dactyl? How does a rhyme scheme work? It's about the forms of poetry. You can't write about free verse because by definition free verse doesn't not follow forms that need to be known about.

Another medium that you're drawn to is the radio. Why is radio still relevant?

I love language and the human voice, and I love using my voice for whatever effects it might have. It's why I do podcasts. The thing I love about it as a performer is that you can take it anywhere you are. You can be in the bath. You can be running. You can be in the car. With the radio, the listener can be doing anything, in bed or beach or boat. It can be in different places with you. It's much closer to reading a book. You can use your eyes for other things and let the voice solace you and amuse you or provoke you . . . or anger you.

When someone is watching a film you've done, they're watching the film. That's all they can be doing. They're listening, and maybe they'll knit or do something else, but then they're not paying attention properly.

One of the glories of BBC Radio 4 is the radio drama, which doesn't really exist in America. The BBC is the biggest commissioner of radio drama in the world and has been for seventy years. It commissions new plays. Tom Stoppard's early work was on radio [*Dissolution of Dominic Boot* (1964)]; Samuel Beckett [*All That Fall* (1956); *Embers* (1959)] and Harold Pinter [*A Slight Ache* (1959); *The Dwarfs* (1960)] wrote for radio early in their careers. Every day there is a new play on Radio 4 with brilliant actors.

⁓

Selected Credits

Theatre
Edinburgh Festival Fringe: *Oedipus Rex*, Adam House Theatre (1979; Peter Rumney); *Artaud at Rodez*, Riddle's Court (1979; Pip Broughton); *Latin! or Tobacco and Boys* (also: dramatist), Riddle's Court (1980; Simon Cherry);

Happy, Happy, Riddle's Court (1980; Oscar Moore); *Dr Heckle and Mr Jibes*, Riddle's Court (1980; Penny Dwyer); *The Roaring Girl*, Riddle's Court (1980; Brigid Larmour). **Other:** *Me and My Girl* (book revised by Fry), Adelphi (1984; Mike Ockrent); *Forty Years On*, Queen's (1984; Patrick Garland); *Look, Look*, Aldwych (1990; Mike Ockrent); *Twelfth Night* (2013), Shakespeare's Globe; Apollo; Belasco, New York (2014; Tim Carroll)

Film

The Good Father (1985); *Peter's Friends* (1992); *I.Q.* (1994); *Cold Comfort Farm* (1995); *A Civil Action* (1998); *Gosford Park* (2001); *Bright Young Things* (2003); *A Cock and Bull Story*, (2005); *Alice in Wonderland* (2010); *Sherlock Holmes: A Game of Shadows* (2011); *Summer Night, Winter Moon* (2012); *Wagner and Me* (2012); *The Hobbit: The Desolation of Smaug* (2013); *The Look of Love* (2013); *The Hobbit: The Battle of Five Armies* (2014); *The Man Who Knew Infinity* (2015); *Love and Friendship* (2015); *Tomorrow* (2015)

Television

The Crystal Cube (1983); *Alfresco*, thirteen episodes (1983–1984); *Blackadder II*, six episodes (1986); *A Bit of Fry and Laurie*, twenty-six episodes (1987–1995); *Jeeves and Wooster*, twenty-three episodes (1990–1993); *Great Performances*, "The Common Pursuit" (1992); *QI*, 139 episodes, host (2003–2013); *Stephen Fry in America*, six-part series, BBC One (2008); *The Borrowers* (2011); *Super Clyde* (2013); *This Is Jinsy*, "Intelligent Hair" (2014); *Marked* (2014); *24: Live Another Day* (2014)

Awards and Nominations

Latin! Or Tobacco and Boys, 1980, *Scotsman* Fringe First Award; *Me and My Girl*, 1984, Tony, Outstanding Book, by L. Arthur Rose and Douglas Furber, revised by Fry, contributions by Mike Okrent, nominee; *Wilde*, 1999, Golden Globe, Best Performance by an Actor in a Motion Picture—Drama, nominee; *The Secret Life of a Manic Depressive*, 2007, 35th International Emmy, winner; *Twelfth Night*, 2014, Tony, Best Performance by an Actor in a Featured Role in a Play, nominee; also, Whatsonstage Award, Best Supporting Actor in a Play, winner

Publications

The Liar (1991); *Hippopotamus* (1994); *Moab Is My Washpot* (1997); *The Ode Less Traveled: Unlocking the Poet Within* (2005); *The Fry Chronicles: An Autobiography* (2010); *More Fool Me: A Memoir* (2014)

Notes

1. Although Jacobi did not attend drama school, he refined his craft at the Birmingham Repertory Company after leaving Cambridge University.

2. In an e-mail to the author on November 15, 2010, Michael Seeney, deputy chairman of the Oscar Wilde Society, wrote, "The 'recording' was supposedly originally a wax cylinder made at the Paris Exhibition. . . . The British Sound Archive did a comprehensive study, proving it wasn't what was claimed."

3. Fry hosted the BAFTA's Britannia Awards in Los Angeles in May 2009. Before he returned to the United Kingdom, he spent the morning at UCLA's William Andrews Clark Library where then head librarian Bruce Whiteman had assembled some two dozen of the library's best examples of Wildeana, including a signed first edition of Wilde's first book, *Ravenna*; the original autographed manuscript of one chapter of *The Portrait of Dorian Gray*; and a copy of *A Woman of No Importance*, inscribed from Wilde to Bosie, Lord Alfred Douglas. Fry was overwhelmed by the opportunity to hold signed copies of the Wilde material. The opportunity was, wrote Fry in a thank-you note, "one of the most important days of my life."

CHAPTER NINE

~

Julian Glover, CBE

I've had just enough recognition to satisfy my ego.

At a trim seventy-nine years of age, Julian Glover moves quickly across his surprisingly large dressing room at the venerable Theatre Royal Drury Lane. He offers a cordial smile and a strong, warm handshake then strides toward a wood-framed, straight-back chair in front of his dressing table. Perched precariously on the makeup table are the requisite pots and tubes of makeup, and, oddly, a packet of dental tape, alongside photographs of his wife, actress Isla Blair, and grandchildren. A poster of a production of King Lear, *in which he played the eponymous role, hangs nearby, a reminder that his early years were spent in Shakespearean productions. In fact, Glover has performed in thirty-one of the Bard's plays.*

Glover is appearing as the benevolent Mr. Brownlow in a revival of Oliver! *His Dickensian-appropriate costume—reddish-orange tailcoat, fawn-colored waistcoat, cream trousers, and a hat with an enormous brim—has been hung on a movable rack, ready for the next performance. The Brownlow role is a 180-degree about-face from many of his polished, graceful cinematic villains in such films as* Indiana Jones and the Last Crusade, For Your Eyes Only, Star Wars: Episode V, The Empire Strikes Back, *and as the monocled Kilkiss in the television series* Q.E.D.

The actor had driven to the theatre from his home in the London suburb of Barnes for a rehearsal with a group of children new to the musical.

Prior to a second interview, this by telephone, he and his wife of almost half a century have just come in from their garden where they enjoyed a late spring alfresco luncheon under their blossoming pear tree. But, he says, pragmatically, "The blossoms will soon be gone, which happens every spring as it does in life."

Glover is now reprising his role as the Interlocutor in the Olivier-nominated London production of The Scottsboro Boys *at the Young Vic, which transferred to the Garrick at the end of 2014.*

⌇

In the beginning?

I was born in St. John's Wood. My father, C. Gordon Glover, was a writer-producer with BBC Radio, and my mother, Honor Wyatt, was a scriptwriter for the BBC Schools Department, which was headquartered in Bristol beginning in 1939 and was very important during the war. We moved there when my parents were estranged. My sister and little brother and I lived with my mother in a house with another family who were also associated with the BBC. During the war years, we were able to get on with our lives.

Photo courtesy of Julian Glover

At what point in your schooling did your interest in the theatre begin?

I attended Bristol Grammar Lower School for about two years beginning in 1942, then St. Paul's School in London from 1948 to 1950, and then we could no longer afford that. I moved to the Alleyn School in Dulwich, where we lived. A terrific school, which is where my interest in acting really began.

The school has an interesting story. It was founded by Edward Alleyn, the most famous Marlovian actor when Christopher Marlowe was writing his plays. He was the first to do *The Jew of Malta* and *Tamburlaine the Great*. Once Alleyn got to a certain age, he decided he wanted to make things right with the man upstairs, and he founded a charity for poor boys in the South of London, which is now what is called Alleyn's College of God's Gift. One of the beneficiaries was the Alleyn's School. It wasn't the public school that it is now.

It is quite relevant why I mention this because when I went there, it had been re-formed after the war when the children had been evacuated. When I attended, a young English master, Michael Croft, had just come down from Oxford, and he decided to revive the tradition of doing Shakespeare at the school. He did an open-air, modern-dress version of *Julius Caesar*. It was entirely because of this wonderful, lovely person that I became an actor. He put me on the road to my career. I'd never done any acting before. It had never occurred to me as I was rather a shy little boy. Would you believe it?

Because I was rather good at reading out loud—I did a lot of that with my baby brother—I got the part of Marc Antony. And the next term, I did the Gilbert and Sullivan operetta, *Iolanthe*, in which I played the comedy leading part, the Lord Chancellor, and did a patter song. I knew then what it was to hold an audience in the palm of my hand.

Until then, I had had no theatrical ambitions. In those days, it wasn't usual for a fifteen-year-old to know what he wanted to do. Never mind that it was something which was—and still is—a dodgy thing. I came home and said to my parents, "This is what I want to do." My parents leapt on the idea as they were artistic people themselves.

There seems to be some discrepancy regarding your association with the National Youth Theatre. Will you clarify the misconception?

It's an understandable misapprehension that I was associated with the National Youth Theatre.

Croft went on to found the National Youth Theatre in 1956. Because I was sort of the first person from the school who, under his auspices, became an actor—later, many did—everyone simply assumed I was with the NYT.

What about an earlier stage appearance in 1953?

Good God. I'd forgotten about that. I was still in school in 1953. It was a holiday job. I played in the panto *Ali Baba* in the scene with the wine casks. I was one of those chaps in the background wearing a turban. That was my very first professional stage appearance.

You went on to RADA and then into repertory. Your recollections?

I auditioned with a speech by Cominius from *Coriolanus* and a silly poem. I didn't finish the two-year course there because I went into the army. It was customary to do a year there, then National Service, and then come back and do the final year. But I couldn't afford the second year and couldn't get a grant.

I wrote letters to various repertory companies and eventually received a reply from Butlin's Holiday Camps, a group of all-inclusive family resorts that had been established throughout the UK by Billy Butlin in 1936. The one I went to was at Skegness, the first camp, in Lincolnshire. Before we went to Skegness for the season, we opened at the Brighton's Palace Pier Theatre, which, sadly, was demolished in 1975.

At the camp, every activity was on a tight time schedule for visitors. Our plays had to be cut to an hour or an hour and a half, which meant there were no intervals, despite the fact that days might have passed in the middle of the story. We rehearsed our productions for only two and a half days. We did a children's play Saturday mornings.

It was an absolutely extraordinary audience. If we overran the play by just one minute, they'd leave, because they had the next entertainment schedule, and we played the last minute to an empty house. They'd just leave as they had a strict program to follow.

Our theatre was placed, as it were, in the middle of a block. On one side was the canteen, which was always noisy; on the other side was the conference room, which seemed to be permanently occupied by the massed bands of the North of England. Then there was also the boiler room with all of that noise. We had to play over all that racket. It certainly got us to *project*. We didn't live in the camp or experience the camp life at all. We had digs outside and came in for the shows. I did that for the one season, 1956. It was a very interesting introduction to the business.

The Royal Shakespeare Company was, then, certainly a step up from the holiday camps.

It certainly bloody was. I'd seen several productions at the Shakespeare Memorial Theatre, before it became the RSC in 1961. I thought, "That's where I want to be."

I auditioned, and I got in. I was a walk-on and worked my way up every season. I played Fisherman in *Pericles*, Albany in *King Lear*, Joiner in *Midsummer Night's Dream*, Roman Citizen 2 in *Coriolanus*, and Montano in *Othello*.

The governor at the RSC at the time was Glen Byam Shaw, and my directors were Tony Richardson and a very young Peter Hall. In our arrogance, we youngsters didn't know what Peter was about. We did recognize that he was brilliant in casting and what a remarkable eye he had for the productions. He cast Olivier, who had never done comedy, as Malvolio in *Twelfth Night*, and Geraldine McEwan as Olivia.

At the same time, John Barton was mucking around as an adviser, but he didn't actually have a position there at the time. When Peter took over in 1960, he gave Barton the position of associate director.

When I was there, we did five productions a year. We finished before Christmas and didn't start up again until March. In between, I had to earn a living, but I always got something, maybe some awful television production where I played a German sergeant. Or I went on holiday.

You joined the highly regarded Prospect Theatre Company, but then left. How did that happen?

It was through Toby Robertson that I joined the company. He had been an actor at Stratford in April 1957 when I understudied him as Giles, Vicomte de Melun, in *King John*. We got to know each other. He left to form the company with Richard Cottrell as associate director and Iain Mackintosh, a very fine theatre designer, as administrator. The three of them had got together at Oxford to form the company. Toby thought back to the people he'd worked with. By then I'd done other things, among them *The Age of Kings* in 1960, which created a great stir. Toby came to me about joining the company. He was certainly the "guv'nor." No question.

Tim West and I would be nowhere without Prospect. He got his first big chance as Dr. Johnson in *Boswell's Life of Johnson*. At the last minute, Toby asked me to play Boswell.

Prospect was going to do productions of *Richard II* and *Edward II*, and I was asked to play Bolingbroke and Mortimer. Unfortunately, I was already contracted to do a film, *The Magus*, directed by Guy Green, which turned out to be a dreadful film. Timmy played those roles. That's a major soreness with me and the biggest mistake of my career.

Toby[1] and I are still very much a family. I'm godfather to his second son, and Isla and I keep up with Iain, and when Richard comes over from Australia, we see him. We also see Sylvia Syms, who was Beatrice to my Benedick in *Much Ado*.

Hadn't you had renewed your friendship with Timothy West before Boswell?

When I was in a production of John Osborne's *Luther* with Albert Finney in 1961 at the Royal Court, he came to see a performance. I played The Knight. In that role, I had bleached blond hair.

He later told me that he said to himself, "I know that head," and snapping his fingers said, "That's the head that used to sit in front of me at Bristol Grammar School."

I've known him for half a century. He's the one who'll do my eulogy when the time comes. He will! We've talked about it. I want it done properly.

One of the roles that interested you was that of the Berlin Philharmonic conductor Wilhelm Furtwängler in Ronald Harwood's *Taking Sides*, directed by Peter Hall. When did you finally have the opportunity to play the role?

That would have been at Chichester in 2004. What was interesting about the play is that the audience is presented with information about Furtwängler, who is being questioned by an American major as part of the de-Nazification Tribunal after World War II to determine the extent of the musician's motives regarding his remaining in Germany during the war. Harwood presents the evidence, but it's the audience members who have to make up their minds about this controversy.

When I got the role, I had to make up *my* mind about whether he was guilty or not. I don't mind saying: I think he was guilty as hell. He also did some wonderful things, but he was guilty in that he hobnobbed with the Nazis. He knew them well enough to get on the phone and say, "There's this chap I want to get out." He did that for many, many people, something near two thousand.

People would line up at his dressing room door to ask for help. He wasn't an Oskar Schindler, but he used his position. He was so terrific at the job he did as conductor of the Berlin Philharmonic that the Nazis evidently looked the other way.

When we toured the play, it didn't do well. We had question-and-answer sessions after performances. We always got the same questions, "What do *you* think?"

I only know what I know from the play. Yes, I did some research, but I think research can often be damaging because you then look at the play and think, "Oh, the playwright hasn't got this right." I certainly wouldn't want to start arguing with the writer, so I can't go into the life of the character too deeply, but I did read about him and his music, especially his music. I looked at a film of Furtwängler, including the famous clip where there is a debate as to whether he was actually shaking hands with Hitler or not. In the end, I had to recognize that Ronnie had written something to be acted.

I had a fantastic actor, Neil Pearson, to work with as Major Steve Arnold, the American who was the interrogator. When I originally saw the play, Michael Pennington was playing Arnold, and Daniel Massey was the conductor. Now Michael is playing Furtwängler, having "changed sides," and he is wonderful.

Ronald Harwood also wrote the play *The Dresser*. You were also attracted to the role of the major character, Sir, who is based on actor-manager Donald Wolfit.

I went to the first night of that play in London at the Queen's Theatre in 1980 and said to myself, "When I'm old enough, I would kill for that part."

When I was old enough at age sixty-nine in 2004, I played Sir for Peter Hall at the Theatre Royal Bath, then toured briefly before moving to the West End. We opened at the Duke of York's in February 2005. Nicholas Lyndhurst was Norman, the dresser. He was wonderful.

It was a great joy to play Sir. Much of the satisfaction came from the play itself. It's a wonderful piece of work. Harwood really knew what he was writing about, as he'd been the dresser to Wolfit. Sometimes the play might seem extreme, but that's the way it was. I couldn't wait to play the role each night. It was such fun.

When I was playing in the West End, it was customary to tip dressers. At one point, I asked Ronnie, "During your time with Wolfit, how much did he tip you at the end?"

He showed me how much by putting his thumb and forefinger together to form a large 0. "The only thing he ever gave me," Ronnie told me, "once, was a cigarette!"

Playing Sir and Furtwängler were infinite joys, both of them. I had fantastic actors with me. Certainly those roles were the pinnacles of my career. Both were extraordinary opportunities.

***Tom Jones* was your first credited film appearance as a villain. Any misgivings about your villainous roles?**

That film sent me on the path to wickedness. I came out of my first three seasons at Stratford having played jolly fishermen and such, and then went to the Royal Court, and then to *Tom Jones*, which started me on the road to villainy. Since then, my career has been mostly based on playing baddies: everything from a Nazi in *Indiana Jones and the Last Crusade* to an alien in *Space: 1999*, and a monster in *Dr. Who* to Aristotle Kristatos in *For Your Eyes Only*. There was also Colonel Breen in *Quatermass and the Pit*.

Only one misgiving: the villain is generally killed off, so there's no chance of repeating the role. Other than that, the villains are often the most interesting characters.

Mr. Brownlow in *Oliver!* is, then, far removed from your villain roles.

Oliver! was my first musical . . . ever. I never thought I'd be in one. I'm not that sort of actor, except that it turned out that I was, particularly with the help of codirectors Rupert Goold and Matthew Bourne.

When someone asked me what I was playing in *Oliver!* I said, "Mr. Brownlow, the kind, old gentleman."

The reply was, "What extraordinary casting."

So it was.

It was a nonsinging, nondancing role, basically straight acting. I enjoyed it so much. I enjoyed the whole life of doing a musical. I saw all these lovely young people working so hard, dancing and singing.

The older I get the fewer parts there are around. I'm getting to play more nice people as I mature.

What observations have you made about that musical as a theatrical genre?

I watched Matthew Bourne all through rehearsals. He's a genius. The show is simply magnificent. It's so well done, from the choreography to the sets to the wonderful performers. The dancers and singers are sublime. Even the lighting by Paule Constable, which, in the old days, was never recognized except by those in the business. Everybody, from the oldest to the youngest in the audience loves the show. Other than that it's—ha!—ordinary!

Then along came *The Scottsboro Boys*. The role as the Interlocutor is quite different from Mr. Brownlow.

In that, I sing. No, that's not the right word, but I do a bit of hoofing. The whole part—just being the person in charge of the whole show. The story is bookended by a minstrel show. It's one of the most original pieces of work I've ever been involved in. It's simply brilliant. His interchange with the characters is really an interesting journey, finding my attitudes to them changing throughout the show, sometimes one way, sometimes another, finally being the person everyone dislikes at the end, instead of just being the jolly Interlocutor, the ringmaster. I loved doing the show.

You had the opportunity to work with the multi-Tony- and multi-Olivier-nominated Susan Stroman on that production. Your recollections?

She had choreographed and directed the production on Broadway, but when it was decided that it would be done here, she was already involved in directing and choreographing the musical adaptation of the Woody Allen film *Bullets over Broadway*.[2] She could only get over here for one week, the last week of our rehearsal, and that was inspirational. She was so sympathetic, so precise about what she wanted. She helped me and the others in that one week right up to our dress rehearsal and saw that the lighting, the sound were right. The person who really got the whole show together was the brilliant associate director, Nigel West.

And then a new production.

Yes, it opened in October 2014, and I'm in it. I wouldn't not do it. I wouldn't miss it. Although I have to say that when you transfer to the West End from the Young Vic, we expect the money to be very good. The money for this, though, is absolutely lamentable.

But I've got to an age now that I do the work I *want* to do and not the work I *have* to do. I really want to do this.

The directors with whom you've worked have ranged from the idiosyncratic to the almost reclusive. For example, Joan Littlewood: a titan in the theatre world in the fifties and sixties and one of the few women directors of Shakespeare then. How true is the legend that she was difficult to work with?

Oh, she was fantastic. She was a completely unique animal, totally powerful, and an off-the-wall director and entrepreneur. She was a short, fat woman. Her company was called Theatre Workshop, and it was run by her companion, Gerry Raffles, who was completely unlike her. He wore a lot of bling. Of course, we didn't call it that then. He wore a wide-open shirt with medallions down his chest, muscles rippling. It was an extraordinary relationship. He did everything from the managing the books to driving the lorry. They had a wonderful relationship, defying all things we think we cleverly know about couples. They adored each other. He was a wonderful, steadying influence on her. When he died in 1975, she went to France and became companion to Baron Philippe de Rothschild and wrote his biography.

Joan ran this totally innovative organization. She got terribly famous and had great success for doing things like *A Taste of Honey* in the late fifties and *Oh, What a Lovely War* in the early sixties. She also had great flops, like the Lionel Bart piece *Twang!* But that wasn't her fault. It was badly written.

Almost deliberately, she chose actors who weren't famous and made them turn corners in their careers. After touring for some years, she eventually moved the company into the Theatre Royal Stratford East.

What I did with her at the Edinburgh Festival in 1964 were two parts of *Henry IV*, which she cobbled together to make one play, lots of cuts and lots of alterations into two and a half hours, much to the critics' annoyance. I played Hotspur. She used to recast people during rehearsals. "You can't play that anymore," she'd say. "You'll play this." She couldn't do that with me because it was written in my contract that I would play Hotspur.

The actor playing Falstaff, George A. Cooper, was a solid, compactly built man. She managed to persuade us that it was a fact that Falstaff, who is described as a huge fat man, a ton of flesh, was actually someone very thin and not the least bit fat; in fact, he was a wiry, strong man. That's an extreme example of what she would get us to do. We accepted it. She would get people to do things they never had any idea they could do. She was ruthless. She would brook no opposition.

There was a young actor, Jeremy Spenser, who was quite a film star at the time. He wanted to move ahead in his career and become a reputable stage actor, and he could well have done. He was cast as Hal in *Henry IV*, and she destroyed him. He couldn't handle Joan saying, "No, no, darling." A minor member of the company took over the part, and Jeremy played Francis.

Joan was rather posh, actually, although she constantly denied it. She always associated with working-class people; that's where her heart was.

Tony Richardson: He spanned both theatre and film productions in which you appeared.

I was in two productions at Stratford directed by Tony: *Pericles* in 1958 with Richard Johnson in the lead, and then *Othello* with Paul Robeson in 1959. I was Robeson's understudy. I rehearsed for two weeks because Paul was ill in Moscow. Tony became *the* Royal Court, along with George Devine and John Osborne. He moved into film, but as a film director, he was thought of as a "loose cannon."

For the casting of *Tom Jones*, he had all Royal Court people: Peter Bull, David Warner, John Moffat, Jack MacGowran, and Rachel Kempson. It's the only film I've been connected with that I could truly call "legendary." We young actors had to stay up with Hugh Griffith and Jack MacGowran at night, keeping them company to make sure they didn't disappear and make sure they got to the set in the morning. We young actors were all gray in the morning because we'd only had an hour's sleep, but they didn't seem the worse for the evening's wear.

One of the famous shots is Hugh Griffith falling off his horse, which wasn't planned. He couldn't stay on the horse because of his previous night out. Thank God, Tony didn't do a lot of takes. But he was having trouble making it all come together. Fortunately he had a brilliant editor, Antony Gibbs, who made it work.

Tony had the idea of having a narrator, which was brilliant. It was a tremendous breakthrough in filmmaking.[3]

What a fantastic summer that was! It was a happy time.

Guy Green: *The Magus,* **1968**

He was a fine cinematographer and a nice man, but he didn't pull this one off. Michael Caine is awful in it, and I can say that because I adore Michael. The film had been made by just putting up a backcloth behind the actor; the actor would say the line; then there was a change of the cloth, and the actor would say the next line. I had a terrible experience with one of the actresses.

Stephen Daldry: *An Inspector Calls,* **1993**

I was in the first takeover when the cast from the National transferred to the Aldwych. I look over the role of Arthur Birling from Richard Pasco. We were all staggered by the production. Absolutely extraordinary; the whole of that first scene is played in an actual house, and the audience cannot see the family, just shadows. What an absolutely fantastic piece of imagination. Stephen absolutely caught what J. B. Priestley meant and made it better.

Woody Allen: *Scoop,* **2006**

I had a quarter of a morning on the film, and he almost ignored me!

Any roles that got away?

At one point, I was a serious contender for James Bond. Sean Connery had just downed his last stirred-but-not-shaken martini in *Diamonds Are Forever* in 1971. But it wasn't to be. I did play the villain, Kristatos, in Roger Moore's James Bond, *For Your Eyes Only.*

In keeping with my villainous status, I would like to have played Coriolanus, such a marvelous, malevolent character. I'm too old now.

I think I would have been well suited to play Louis Mountbatten in the 1986 television series *Lord Mountbatten: The Last Viceroy,* but Nicol Williamson played the role.

You appeared in a production of the Simon Gray play *Otherwise Engaged.*

I wasn't in *a* production of the play. I was in *the* production, the first ever in 1975, with Alan Bates playing the leading role, and with Nigel Hawthorne and Ian Charleson. The production was directed by Harold Pinter. I got the part of Jeff Golding absolutely the first time I went and read for it. They didn't even see anyone else. I was told, "The part is yours." That was fantastically exciting for me, of course, as I was about thirty-four or thirty-five.

I played the drunken journalist. My father was a drunken journalist, and I knew all about the miseries and disappointments in that world. Not only is the character an alcoholic, but like my father, he is also hopeless with women, just like my father. The character is a very louche, very clever sort, the sort you read about in the Sunday papers, those who write those clever, pertinent articles. I knew that part because I knew the man I was talking about.

You were fortunate to know Simon Gray, then?

That production was a milestone in my life and the beginning of a peripheral but very fond friendship with him. Although we weren't best of friends, we delighted in seeing each other. There was a great mutual respect.

One of the most high-profile projects has been your appearance in twenty-two episodes of the television series *Game of Thrones*. How did that role come about?

The story is a good one. I auditioned for three parts and didn't get any of them. Then an actor who was going to play the role of Grand Maester Pycelle got terribly ill, so I got the part. That actor, Roy Dotrice, survived, thank goodness, and he is in the series in the part as Hallyne. I have known Roy since he was at Stratford with me in 1957. His wife was working there as an usherette at the theatre, as was my first wife, Eileen Atkins. But it was due to his not being well that I got the part. It's helping me through my last years in the business.

You took on an interesting assignment on the other side of the footlights.

Yes, that was with a new theatre which opened in Norwich, and the AD, Henry Burke, rang up and asked if I'd like to do a family production of *Hamlet*, with me directing and Jamie, my son, as Hamlet, and my wife as Gertrude.

"And me playing the Ghost?" I asked.

He said he hadn't thought of me as the Ghost, but "Yes."

It was a tremendous adventure, and it was interesting to find things in our lives that we could relate to in the play. Isla and Jamie created such fantastic sparks, particularly the closet scene because of their personal relationship and what they'd been through as mother and son. I won't say it was a triumphant success. It was out of London, and the main critics didn't come, but it was pretty bloody good, a very happy but terrifying—absolutely terrifying—experience directing my wife and son. I had to be on tippy toes.

A couple of your recent projects have unusual titles: *Brash Young Turks* and *Gangster Kittens*. Where do those fit in your CV?

Oh, yeah! I think one of the reasons I received the CBE is not because I'm a brilliant actor but because I like to help people having a go. I'm an ambassador for the Prince's Trust, an organization which Prince Charles founded to help people form their own businesses. I've done about fifteen or twenty films which never see the light of day, but those working on the projects need people like me, not to tell them what to do, but to support the work they're doing. I'm sort of that solid rock.

Ash Mahmood, Naeem Mahmood, the two lads I worked with on these, have a thing about film. They've finished *Brash*, but I don't think it'll get any further. It's quite good. I know I was very helpful to them, and that's why I did it. The other was only half made, about forty minutes, but there was no money to finish it. There are lots of names of funny little films in my CV, which have nothing to do with anything except for the fact that I helped out a student or something like that.

Besides performing, you are now teaching. What challenges does that present?

There's an organization called the British-American Drama Academy, which has a four-week summer session at Balliol College, Oxford, and is accredited to both the Yale Drama School and the University of California, Los Angeles.

We do a Shakespeare or classic play and a modern play. I've done Simon Gray's *Otherwise Engaged* along with *Twelfth Night*. Teaching Simon's play to Americans is wonderful because there are seven parts, which I can split up. With that play, I can really teach about structure and true English wit, which sometimes has to be pointed out to Americans. When they get it, they love it.

The students are gob struck when I say I'd been at Stratford for eight seasons. Understandably, if I went to America, and someone who had worked with Joseph Papp for eight years or had attended Yale Drama School, my face would fall.

I teach at RADA too, but the students there are sort of English worldly wise and more cynical than the Americans. I have to be careful not to play on that. I find teaching very rewarding. The students want everything I can offer, and that's lovely.

After a half century as an actor, what words of advice would you give to young actors?

Don't do it unless you *have* to do it. It can be ghastly, but so can working in the city. I met Isla during our time at the Prospect Theatre Company, and she also knew she *had* to do it. I've been lucky because I haven't been confined to a single medium. I've made big movies but have never become a big star. Just enough recognition to satisfy my ego!

∼

Selected Credits

Theatre
Shakespeare Memorial Theatre, Stratford: *Twelfth Night* (1955; John Gielgud); *Cymbeline* (1957; Peter Hall); *The Tempest*, also at Theatre Royal Drury Lane (1957; Peter Brook); *Pericles* (1958; Tony Richardson); *Hamlet*, tour

(1958; Glen Byam Shaw); *Othello* (1959; Tony Richardson); *Luther*, Royal Court; Phoenix (1961; Tony Richardson). **Other:** *Altona*, Royal Court (1961; John Berry; design: Sean Kenny); *The Lower Depths*, New Arts Theatre Club (1962; Toby Robertson); *Twelfth Night*, Royal Court (1962; George Devine); *Macbeth*, Bristol Old Vic (1969; John David); *Boswell's Life of Jonson*, Assembly Hall, Edinburgh; (1970; Toby Robertson); *Man of Mode*, Aldwych (1971; Terry Hands); *The Oz Trial*, 1971, RSC at the Place (1971; Buzz Goodbody); *The Grand Tour*, Old Vic (1972; Toby Robertson); *Sherlock's Last Case* [a.k.a. *Watson's Revenge*], Open Space (1974; Thelma Holt); *Jumpers*, NT, Lyttelton (1976; Peter Wood); *The Changeling*, RSC at the Aldwych (1978; Terry Hands); *Cousin Vladimir*, RSC at the Aldwych (1978; Jane Howell); *Hamlet*, Old Vic (1979; Toby Robertson); *Henry VI, Parts 1 and 2*, RST Stratford; Theatre Royal Newcastle; Barbican (1991–1992; Adrian Noble); *Cyrano de Bergerac*, Theatre Royal Haymarket (1993; Elijah Moshinsky); *An Inspector Calls*, Aldwych (1993; Stephen Daldry); *Romeo and Juliet*, RSC at the Barbican (1996; Adrian Noble); *Chips with Everything*, NT, Lyttelton (1997; Howard Davies); *In Praise of Love*, Theatre Royal Bath (2001; Deborah Bruce); *King Lear*, Globe (2001; Barry Kyle); *Macbeth*, Albery (2002; Edward Hall); *Man and Superman*, Theatre Royal Bath (2004; Peter Hall); *Man and Superman*, Theatre Royal Bath (2004; Peter Hall); *The Dresser*, Richmond, Theatre Royal Bath, Duke of York's (2004–2005; Peter Hall); *The Voysey Inheritance*, NT, Lyttelton (2006; Peter Gill); *The President's Holiday*, Hampstead Playhouse (2008; Patrick Sandford); *Maurice's Jubilee*, Pleasance Courtyard, Edinburgh; tour (2012–2013; Hannah Eidinow); *The Scottsboro Boys*, Young Vic; Garrick (2013–2015; Susan Stroman)

Film
Tom Jones (1963); *The Girl with the Green Eyes* (1964); *Quatermass and the Pit* [a.k.a. *Five Million Years to Earth*] (1965); *Theatre of Death* [a.k.a. *Blood Fiend*] (1966); *Alfred the Great* (1969); *Nicholas and Alexandra* (1971); *Juggernaut* (1974); *The Empire Strikes Back* (1980); *For Your Eyes Only* (1981); *Heat and Dust* (1982); *Cry, Freedom* (1987); *Indiana Jones and the Last Crusade* (1989); *Troy* (2004); *Young Victoria* (2009); *Backtrack* (2014)

Television
A Midsummer Night's Dream (1959); *An Age of Kings*, fourteen episodes (1960); *Dr. Who*, four episodes (1965; Douglas Camfield), four episodes (1979); *The Wednesday Play*, "For the West" (1965), "Charlie" (1968); *The Rivals of Sherlock Holmes*, "The Moabite Cypher" (1973); *Q.B. VII* (1974); *BBC Play of the Month*, "Electra" (1974); *Thriller*, "Good Salary,

Prospects, Free Coffin" (1975); *Couples*, twelve episodes (1976); *Blake's 7*, "Breakdown" (1978); *Henry V* (1979); *Henry VII* (1979); *BBC Playhouse*, "Journal of Bridget Hitler" (1981); *Q.E.D.* [a.k.a. *Mastermind*], six episodes (1982); *Dombey and Son*, ten episodes (1983); *Kim* (1984); *Remington Steele*, "Steele Searching" (1985); *Mandela* (1987); *Wish Me Luck*, fifteen episodes (1988–1989); *Alleyn Mysteries*, "A Man Lay Dead" (1993); *Game of Thrones*, twenty-two episodes (2011–2014); *Spies of Warsaw* (2013); *Atlantis*, "Pandora's Box" (2014)

Awards and Nominations

Henry IV, Parts 1 and 2, 1993, Olivier, Best Actor in a Supporting Role, winner; *Game of Thrones*, 2011, SAG, Outstanding Performance by an Ensemble in a Dramatic Series, nominee; *Maurice's Jubilee*, 2012, *Stage* Award, Best Actor for Acting Excellence at the Edinburgh Festival Fringe, nominee

Honors

CBE, 2013

Notes

1. Toby Robertson died July 4, 2012, at age eighty-four.
2. *Bullets over Broadway* closed in August 2014.
3. Gibbs recalls that it was Vanessa Redgrave, Richardson's wife at the time, who suggested the idea.

CHAPTER TEN

~

Stephen Greif

Seeing Laurence Olivier in Othello *was everything I ever believed acting should be.*

September 23, 2007, was a cool, dry autumn evening. Hundreds of people were gathered in front of the Royal National Theatre for a gala event: the unveiling of a statue of Laurence Olivier as Hamlet. *The great actor had founded the prestigious company in 1963. Speeches by family members and colleagues preceded the unveiling. Among the actor's colleagues who attended the event were Anna Carteret, Gawn Grainger, James Hays, Charles Kay, Maureen Lipman, Dinah Sheridan, Benjamin Whitrow, and Olivier's widow, actress Dame Joan Plowright. Afterward, the crowd adjourned to the theatre named after the actor for a memorial program.*

Prior to taking my seat in the Olivier Theatre, I strolled by photographs of past productions, including one of the celebrated 1979 version of Death of a Salesman. *Standing next to me in the gloomy corridor and peering closely at the same photograph was a gentleman who looked very like one of the actors in the picture.*

"That's me!" he said, as he pointed to a figure in the group. "I played Biff in that production." We introduced ourselves and chatted about the play and his role in the production.

Stephen Greif had not only appeared in that iconic production but he had also been a member of the National during Olivier's reign and had known the actor and performed with him. Not one to pass up hearing tales about the early days of the company, I asked if we could continue the conversation. We agreed to meet at BAFTA's London headquarters on Piccadilly, which Greif calls his "office."

154

In the graying late afternoon sun, dozens of theatrical and film folk were meeting over coffee. Greif, seated at a table in the far reaches of the large room, waved a greeting. Dressed in a beige shirt with suede elbow patches, a burgundy wool scarf draped smartly around his neck, and a green fedora on the table, it wasn't difficult to imagine him as an actor. His greeting was warm and friendly, and, oh, that voice.

Born in Hertfordshire in 1944, Greif was schooled at various educational institutions. After graduating from RADA with first class honors and several acting awards, he became associated with the three major British theatrical companies: the National at the Old Vic and its subsequent transfer to the South Bank, the Prospect Theatre Company, and the RSC. He played opposite the best of the British acting community: Laurence Olivier, Joan Plowright, Albert Finney, Anthony Hopkins, and Felicity Kendal, among others. He has appeared in scores of television series and films. His voice can be heard on dozens of radio programs and audiobooks. He is, as he calls himself, "a multimedia actor," with more than two hundred credits on his CV.

He is articulate in his assessment of his career choices and eagerly shares anecdotes and adventures about his decades in "the business."

〜

What was your first theatrical performance?
I played Captain Hook in a primary school production of *Peter Pan*. I used a coat hanger for the hook. It was great fun. The Hook hooked me! With that role, I found that villains are the most fun to play.

And from there?
Eventually, I attended Regent Street Polytechnic [now University of Westminster] doing business studies. It was unbelievably boring. I hated it. But I joined the school's amateur dramatics group, and we did a play called *Midnight with No Pain*, written by a student, Ken Chapman. The title comes from Keats's poem *Ode to a Nightingale*. The performances were hits with audiences at Portland Hall, who, I blush to say, laughed a great deal at my performance as the leader of a gang of Teddy Boys. My accent was inspired by my mum, who was born in London's East End.

If I thought that the curriculum at the Polytechnic was boring, I was in for more boring jobs when I worked for Alba, an electronics manufacturing company. Once I nearly killed myself with the equipment. I then was with Brecker Grossmith, an estate agency, for about two years and was quite good at it. I made a lot of money for them and for me. I was only eighteen and was well turned out in a good suit and tie. I was quite charming on the phone. I lost interest after the first year.

Photo from the Stephen Greif Collection

You finally applied to drama school. What was your experience during the audition process?

Despite parental restraint—my father thought his three sons, I was the middle one, would be the next Rothschilds—I applied to RADA in 1964 and did the audition: a bit from *Richard III*, a disaster as I tried to replicate Olivier in the film; and Paul, the pastry cook, from Arnold Wesker's *The Kitchen*. I tried about five times. I was given a note that read, "Thanks."

I left thinking, "Well, that's it. They spotted my talent right away, and I'm in!" About twenty paces down Gower Street, it dawned on me that I was *not* in. I took the rest of the day off and went to see George Peppard in *The Carpetbaggers*.

I was determined to try again. Since I'd never had any coaching, I wrote to John Fernald, who was then the RADA principal, for the name of someone to help me. He recommended Valerie Taylor, a well-known actress who was teaching there at the time. She asked me to come and watch her rehearsal. I enjoyed it because the manner in which she conducted the rehearsal was very businesslike, and I liked that discipline.

When I met with her, she had said she saw "a lot of promise" and agreed to coach me. We worked on a speech by Mark Antony from *Julius Caesar*, a far better choice, and a better contrast to *The Kitchen*. They both suited me.

I took ten tranquilizers before the audition, and when I told Valerie what I had done, she chastised me, "You never ever, ever, ever take anything to dampen your nerves down. Your nerves are the best thing you can have." I've since always heeded that advice.

After the second audition in February 1965, I received a letter saying I was in *if* somebody pulled out. Nobody pulled out. I had also auditioned at LAMDA for the great Hugh Cruttwell, and I could tell at the audition that they liked me. I was accepted. But I wanted RADA. Finally, on the third try, June 1965, I was accepted.

During my time there, Fernald left and Cruttwell became principal [for eighteen years beginning in 1966]. He was the greatest principal RADA's ever had. Not only is he my great hero, but he is also a hero to hundreds and hundreds of students, including Ken Branagh, who used him as a consultant on several of his films. Ken says he remembers going into another stratosphere when he was accepted. He said he walked his dog in the snow and ended up carrying the dog back home because he had walked so far!

Your first visit to America came during a three-month summer hiatus from RADA in 1966. What did you do during that break?

For no reason I can think of, I went to see *A View from the Bridge* at the Sheridan Square Playhouse in Greenwich Village, directed by Ulu Grosbard and starring Richard Castellano, who had taken over the part of Eddie from Robert Duvall. I was so knocked out by his performance that I went to the stage door and asked to see him. He came down, and we chatted for quite a while. I think my British accent fascinated him as much as his Italian–New York accent fascinated me. Castellano's performance was the most powerfully natural performance I had ever seen on stage. Even now, decades later, I can see Castellano with his innate shrugs of uncomprehending bewilderment. It was acting that I instinctively understood and drew me to the works of Arthur Miller. Olivier in *Othello* was the most powerfully *theatrical* performance.

I also walked around New York, played lots of pool, and met lots of girls on Greyhound buses traveling thousands of miles around America.

After graduating, what plans did you have for your career?

Throughout drama school, I saw myself as a serious actor, which meant that the only path was the theatre. I turned down a role in a television series to go into repertory at the Forum Theatre, Billingham, to play Hotspur in *Henry IV, Part 1*. I wanted to play that role because he was my hero as a kid. He is every young man's idea of a hero.

I knew that rep was the right choice. That's the way it was with all of us actors at the time. Film and television could wait.

My agent then was Ben Lyon, casting director in the London office of 20th Century Fox. He wanted me to sign for three years; I wanted only a year. We compromised at two. When I was in Los Angeles in 1969 with the RSC, I saw casting directors at Fox and Columbia; both advised me to hang around as "there'd be work for you." I didn't want to "hang around" and went back to London. I was contrary even then. Those other media waited until a dozen years into my career. I now consider myself a "media actor" who occasionally works in the theatre.

And the next career opportunity?

The Prospect Theatre Company began in the sixties and was one of the three major theatre companies in the UK, along with the RSC and the National. I did, arguably, two of the company's most famous productions, *Richard II* and *Edward II*, with a young Ian McKellen. He was a wonderful company leader, along with Toby Robertson, Richard Cottrell, and Iain Mackintosh.

I read twice for Richard and then again for Ian. I was probably a little young and inexperienced, but they gave me nice parts in both productions: Earl of Pembroke in Marlowe's *Edward II* and Thomas Mowbray and Owen Glendower in Shakespeare's *Richard II*. It was a humdinger of a good job—my second professional gig—and lasted nine months, including appearances at the Edinburgh Festival, British and European tours, two runs in the West End, an audio recording of *Edward II*, and the television production of *Richard II*.

I went straight from there into the Old Vic with Olivier for two years. I auditioned for Laurence Olivier in his office in the Nissen hut on Aquinas Street. It was just him. I was offered to understudy Robert Stephens in *The Beaux' Stratagem* and *Hedda Gabler*. In response to the offer, I wrote a letter saying that more than anything I wanted to join the company, *but* I didn't want to understudy.

Anne Robinson, the casting director, a lovely woman, wrote back saying, "It never ends with that. It will lead on."

But I didn't accept.

A year later, I was working with Faith Kent, wife of Anthony Nicholls, one of the major actors at the National. I was playing Hotspur in *Henry IV*, and she brought me to Olivier's attention again. I found out that Tom Baker, who had played Rasputin in *Nicholas and Alexandra*—my first film—was leaving the National to play the lead in Alfred Hitchcock's *Frenzy* [1972] and *Isabella of Spain* with Glenda Jackson. Barry Foster was cast over Baker in *Frenzy*, and *Isabella* was cancelled. Tom's parts were available. Twenty or so young actors auditioned for his roles. My audition panel was the most wondrous group: Kenneth Tynan, Michael Blakemore, John Dexter, Jonathan Miller, and in the middle, Laurence Olivier. Intimidating? Yes, but it was wonderful.

Two hours later, the casting director phoned and said, "You start on Monday."

The parts were Sir Francis Acton in *A Woman Killed with Kindness*, to be directed by Dexter, and the Prince of Morocco in *The Merchant of Venice*, to be directed by Miller.

Those were the roles, and I got 'em!

The company's productions were presented at the Old Vic. Your recollections?

That theatre was a cathedral. It had an atmosphere that I have never, ever encountered in any other theatre that I've ever played in. It was a shrine. I could have had these feelings because I was young, Olivier was running it, and I had seen him on stage in almost all his performances there.

Of all the Olivier performances that you saw at the Old Vic, which one still stays with you?

The greatest of all the roles I saw him in was *Othello*, directed by John Dexter when I was still at RADA. I've never seen a performance like that. Never. I saw it three times. I wrote to Olivier when I couldn't get a seat for any performance. He wrote back, "Contact the box office. They'll get you a seat."

They did: row F, seat 6.

When he came on, I was pulverized. Afterwards, I walked around the area around the Old Vic, the Cut, and Waterloo like a zombie. It was like I'd been clubbed over the head. It was everything I ever believed acting should be.

I subsequently saw him at the Old Vic in, among other productions, Frank Dunlop's *Home and Beauty* and Jacques Charon's *A Flea in Her Ear*, both in the sixties. How I wish I'd seen him in Glen Byam Shaw's production of *Dance of Death*.

Dangers lurk in every production. In *Woman Killed with Kindness*, you were almost killed. What happened?

It's a vivid memory. I was playing Sir Francis Acton and covering for Anthony Hopkins as John Frankford. At one point during a fight on the raked stage, I fell backward and spectacularly hit the deck. Before I could register any pain or embarrassment, John Dexter yelled out, "Great! Great! Keep it in! Now carry on. Quick!" The cast of the play included Joan Plowright and Derek Jacobi.

You played opposite a Broadway icon, Elaine Stritch.

I did the UK premiere of Neil Simon's *The Gingerbread Lady* at the Theatre Royal Windsor, playing her ex-lover. It was directed by Jerry Harte, also an American. I remember that during rehearsals, which were at the Regent's Park flat of the wealthy producer that Jerry Harte had found, Elaine petitioned him that Jerry be sacked. I pleaded on his behalf that none of us would be there if it weren't for Jerry having obtained the rights to the play and found the producer. I asked that she give him a chance. She did, but truth be told, lovely fellow that he is, he couldn't direct piss into a bucket. But that was that, and we opened in Windsor.

It was the height of summer, and I guess she was thirsty. Even though she was sauced every night, she was brilliant. The last of the red hot mamas. What a gal! What a performer! What legs!

When the plan was to transfer to London's Phoenix, Vivien Merchant bowed out. By then both she and I had enough of Elaine and her drinking. Vivien's marriage to Harold Pinter was on the rocks, and she was frantic to try to save it. She couldn't, and it was the beginning of the end for that lovely actress and friend. At Elaine's request, Vivian Matalon took over the transfer as director. It was a flop, but they kept it on to keep the theatre warm.[1]

How did your association with one of the great American tragedies, *Death of a Salesman* by Arthur Miller, come about?

When I read for director Michael Rudman, who I've now known for over forty years, he said, "I have the duty to offer this role to another actor who played Biff before, so are you interested in playing Happy?"

I told him I wasn't interested in any character except Biff. In the middle of one of the scenes that I read with Warren Mitchell, Michael shouted to me, "Stop! Stop! You've got the part."

It was a wonderful moment. I kissed him, and he said, "I wish you wouldn't do that."

I actually got the role as an indirect result of a recommendation by director Christopher Morahan, who referred me to the great television director Philip Saville when he was casting "Moss," an episode of *Play for a Day*. In that production, Warren Mitchell and I played a Jewish father and son, and since we had already worked together in that, we had a shorthand in place before day one of rehearsal for *Salesman*.

Arthur Miller came over to work with us for a week. I remember this so well. He looked at Warren, who he hadn't seen in performance, and said, "Yeah! Yeah! You *are* Willy." He had written it, not as a big man, as Lee J. Cobb or Brian Dennehy were, but as a smallish man. Warren was a brilliant Willy.

As far as playing Biff, it was a dream come true. I'd been familiar with the play and felt, as many actors do, that I could bring something especially personal to the role. I always bring something personal to everything, but not like that. It was *my* story. Every actor who plays Biff says that it is *his* story. Even Warren had wanted to play Biff when he was younger because it was *his* story then. I'd love to play Willy one day.[2]

The audition process must be both frustrating and fraught with anxiety. Is there an unforgettable one?

The role of Joan Plowright's suspected lover, Luigi, in *Saturday, Sunday, Monday* was definitely memorable. I was called in to read with Olivier and Plowright. I read two or three scenes with Joan, and Olivier read all the other parts, male and female. He did them brilliantly.

Joan was wonderful to me, a real heroine.

That night, I got a call. I had the part.

The part had been offered to Jeremy Brett, Anton Rogers, and Barrie Ingham. They all declined because they wanted billing above the title. They were at that stage in their careers. In the end, Joan's and Frank Finlay's were the only names above the title.

When the play was produced for television, Edward Woodward was hired for the role. Joan wrote a wonderful three-page letter explaining how they petitioned for me to reprise the role, but the director, Alan Bridges, needed to do it his way.

I still have that letter, handwritten and from the heart. Can you imagine someone of her stature doing that today!

Other unforgettable roles at the National?

His Girl Friday was a repetition of the role as Diamond Louie I played years before in *The Front Page*, both for Jack O'Brien. I said I also wanted to do something else, and especially I wanted to be in David Mamet's *Edmond* with Kenneth Branagh, which Edward Hall was directing. I met with Edward, and he asked me what I parts I wanted to play. I told him I was especially interested in the hotel receptionist and, secondarily, the Interrogator. When I read the part, I knew exactly who that receptionist was: one of those terrible box office people who, when you ask, "Can I have a seat for such-and-such a performance?" and the reply comes back, "We're sold out." And you ask, "What about next week?" And the response: "Did you hear what I said. We're sold out." He's a bit fey and hateful with his authority.

That's how I described the character to Ed, and he must have liked the idea because he gave me the part. I played both roles, a nice show-off double. We all played two or three parts, apart from Ken who had his hands full as Edmond. He was on every single page, an hour and a quarter on stage, no interval. He was brilliant. We all fell in love with him, and there was absolutely nothing that we would not do for him. He is the greatest. His courage is astonishing. A thoroughly good egg, as well. Most of what he does works. He has had some things that haven't been huge successes. So what! He tried!

Directors and their styles? How different are they?

Ah, yes, the difference.

Franco Zeffirelli:

I didn't meet him until the first day of rehearsal when he was directing *Saturday, Sunday, Monday*. He was a dictator but a brilliant dictator. He's Italian so he doesn't hold back. He said to Richard Vernon and me after the read through [Greif assumes an Italian accent], "Everybody else is very good. Stephen and Richard—well, you're a problem. I don't know what I'm going to do." We broke for lunch and thought we'd be getting our walking papers when we returned. We didn't.

In the middle of rehearsals, Franco had to leave because of some domestic problem in Italy. Larry came in and announced [Greif lapses into an worthy imitation of the great actor], "Franco has gone home, and I, if you don't mind, will be taking over rehearsals. I have some experience with directing, so let's have a good time."

And we did.

We were under the cosh[3] with Franco. With Olivier, we got our confidence back in about twenty minutes. He was a teddy bear and just fantastic.

Peter Gill:

I found him to be a brilliant director, but had ideas of inflections not just on lines and words, but even on syllables. That made me a little uncomfortable. Had I been the only one at the receiving end of this, I would have walked out, but we all got the same treatment, so I toughed it out. Interesting, Peter kept me waiting a month before he realized there was no one who would play the part better.

Michael Rudman:

On the other hand, there are people like Michael, who are very intimate and friendly. He's with you all the way. I've worked with him many times. We're friends, and we play golf together.

Jack O'Brien:

Not a dictator but a martinet, a benevolent martinet. He, too, is brilliant. We all followed him as a leader, unquestioningly. He has the ability to enlist the faith and trust of his cast, effortlessly. He knows where we're going, and we get to know, too.

I had a line as the Chicago gangster Diamond Louie, in *His Girl Friday*, and during the previews, I would get a woofer of a laugh. On the night before press night, Jack casually suggested that if I shifted the emphasis of a syllable on a particular word, it would get an even bigger laugh. I was wary of changing something that already worked. But he was right. I did get that bigger laugh.

John Dexter:

He was a notorious bully, but his creative and alert mind, together with his uncompromising passion for his productions, overruled other negatives.

Two roles, one in *Fallen Angels* and the other in *George Dillon*, required you to wait and wait for your entrance. How difficult was the waiting?

Director Michael Rudman told me, "Maurice Duclos is the Frenchman in *Angels* who comes on for about ten minutes at the very end of the play, but he's talked about on every single page. And you're going to play him, Stephen."

It was an ordeal waiting well into two hours for the entrance. But it was a very rewarding moment for the audience—and me—when the character finally appears.

The other role was Barney Evans in *George Dillon* with Joseph Fiennes, and again, the waiting was terrible. In this case, it was worse than *Angels* because it amounted to a ten-minute monologue with no run-up. Straight on. Cold. The energy level, everything, goes.[4]

Thanks to Joseph, who was a great source of strength and understanding, I struggled through that scene. He was the best listener in town. Being the brilliant and sensitive actor he is, he was a pillar of concentration and support.

But never again will I wait all evening to make an appearance, no matter how good the part is. My nerves just couldn't stand it. In both, I knew if I let the audience down, I've let the production down as well. They can't be disappointed. If I do let them down, I've gone like this to the cake [he smashes his hand on the table] instead of throwing the cherry on the top.

Your voice is recognizable from your radio and audio work. How different is preparation for roles in those media from film or television?

Preparing a role on radio is no different than preparing for a role in any other medium with regard to character, accent, the objective in a scene.

That's a given. Microphone technique is important, and how little you need to do, which, in a certain sense, is the same as with a close-up in a film or television scene.

On the other hand, John Sessions and I did a scene for BBC Radio 4 of Arnold Bennett's *The Grand Babylon Hotel*. There's a scene when I was showing John's character around the basement of the hotel where all the machines for working lifts, electricity, gas, and water were situated. We both had to shout our lungs out to be heard over the roaring machinery. We had to imagine the sounds, which were added in postproduction. In my view, I made the mistake of giving a television performance on radio. By that I mean I visualized him as any father, who had all the quiet, dignified, "mittle" European charm and Austrian manner, instead of amplifying him just a half a gear more.

I still make fundamental errors in the execution of a performance that I can only detect when I hear or see in playback.

Recurring roles in television series are both a positive and negative in an actor's career. How do you feel about those roles in which you have appeared in multiple episodes?

I'm probably best known as the villain, Space Commander Travis, in the first series of *Blake's 7* on the BBC in the late seventies. I had a patch over one eye and dressed in black leather. I did four and a half episodes. The series, which has taken on cult status, worked because not only was there no British sci-fi on television, except for *Dr. Who*, those characters were so likable.

I did just those few episodes because I'd snapped my Achilles tendon and wasn't able to tape the studio scenes, but I was in the previously filmed location scenes. Another actor was shot from the waist down, and I voiced my lines in the dubbing session.

When I was offered the second season, I didn't want to do it. I didn't want to be remembered as a space villain. But the role gave me a greater profile, for which I am grateful.

At about the same time, I had another series, *Citizen Smith* with Robert Lindsay. I also played a villain, in this case the landlord who terrorizes him in twelve episodes. I remember giving up a holiday in Cornwall and dashing back to London for an interview with the producer, Dennis Main-Wilson; landed the role; and days later was filming. I really had little chance to "get" the character of Harry Fenning, who was both the villain and the comic relief, but I remembered an actor from my childhood who was sinister looking but charming. That's how I played him.

I was scared to death of being typecast. I've turned down more work than I've ever done, which is why if today I were to say yes to everything I'd said no to, I'd do it in a flash. But we can't know then what we know now.

Do you find that acting styles for various roles change for plays, new or classic?

Unless it's Restoration comedy, Greek tragedy, or farce, which require their own style, I don't see the ground rules changing much for most other areas of acting. I don't believe "new plays" are sacred. How can they be? They've never been tried, so that's part of the rehearsal process, to bend, to stretch, and generally to make a fit to this new, unworn material.

When performing in a stage production for a lengthy period of time, how do you keep your role fresh?

It's an energy thing. Some performances are like clockwork because of tiredness or the chemistry between the actors and the audience. Other performances lift off into orbit, often for no apparent reason.

There's a famous story of Maggie Smith and the cast of *Othello* going 'round to Olivier's dressing room one night after a particularly mesmerizing performance he had given. He was in a foul temper, and when Miss Smith asked why he should be feeling that way after such a great performance, he replied in that famous Olivier bark, "I know it was great . . . I just don't know why!"

In the theatre, each performance has a beginning and moves through to the end. In film, the performance is fragmented. How do you develop the character and then maintain it over several days or even months?

In film and television, I do try to ask myself before every scene or setup what my intention is in the upcoming scene—apart from earning my salary! I ask myself, "Where has my character just been, and what is he doing now?"

The first scene I shot in the film *Casanova* as the merchant father of the girl Casanova is seeking my permission to marry, I had never met him before—or for that matter, the wonderful Heath Ledger. In the space of a minute or so I was required to give away the hand of my beloved daughter to the worst and most notorious lecher in Europe.

I had made some kind of decision to make this character a ditherer-buffoon. I had set my character, but I was not altogether happy with it. There was never time to discuss and analyze these ideas with the director, who had his hands full with the cast and crew and the pressure of shooting in a private garden that he has for only one day.

On the rare occasion that I've felt happy with my work in film or television, I mostly feel it was helped by the editing and music.

For a stage character, there is hopefully an uninterrupted journey most nights, and that can bring immediate rewards.

What do you recall about your first film, *Nicholas and Alexandra*?

I have vivid memories. It was produced by Hollywood mogul Sam Spiegel, an Austrian Jew like my dad and was the image of him. We got on well. I met with him several times about playing Rasputin. I was called in a second time to see director Franklin Schaffner. Then a third time to see Spiegel again. In my youthful innocence and ignorance, I had a thought: I had the makeup man make me look as villainous as possible.

It didn't work, and they decided I was too young to play Rasputin. Tom Baker played the monk. I played Martov, a very small role.

The film was cast by the great Maude Spector. I remember she took me into her small office at Horizon Pictures and told me I was going to be a big star. Boy, did she get that one wrong!

The movie was a turkey, but I had a month in Madrid, and the picture led, again in an indirect way, to me being seen by Laurence Olivier and joining him at the National at the Old Vic, one of the greatest and happiest times of my life.

What was your favorite role and, perhaps, the most challenging one?

Going on for a number of performances as Edmund for an indisposed Ronnie Pickup in the National's *Long Day's Journey into Night* with Olivier—in arguably his finest performance as James Tyrone—and Constance Cummings was very special. Olivier had been my hero and inspiration for becoming an actor, so having him fling his arms around my neck and cuddle me in a moment of tenderness in the fourth act in front of eight hundred people was something akin to pride, but nothing at that precise moment had anything to do with the play or performance.

An aside: Although I was physically miscast as Ronnie Pickup's understudy, director Michael Blakemore cast me because the feel and sound were right. And having been part of two of Blakemore's and the National's hits, *Long Day's Journey* and *The Front Page*, there is no explaining what it felt like being a part of these productions. It was literally like walking on water.

Probably the most arduous role—really a double role—was in the National's two-part, six-hour Christmas show, *His Dark Materials*, from the novels by Philip Pullman. It was mercilessly hard work as John Faa *and* President of Consistorial Court, both in rehearsal and performance, to wrench the characters from the books to the stage. There was little in the way of nourishment for us except for audience gratification in seeing their favorite books dramatized and the characters come to life. My admiration for the creative team knows no bounds.

What role still holds some interest for you?

One of the brothers in Arthur Miller's *The Price*. Although I've wanted to play Victor, the policeman, because it's the most sympathetic, it's not really my role. My role is the other brother, Walter, the physician.

You've worked with a disparate group of actors over the years. What is it that makes them memorable as actors and human beings?
Stephen Fry:

I worked with him in a film, *Eichmann*. We had a couple of brief scenes together and dined together on one or two occasions. I think I said to him, perhaps injudiciously, but it came out, that he is "a younger Jonathan Miller." He was quite flattered. He is brilliant at everything; his knowledge is eclectic and amazing.

Omar Sharif:

I worked with him on a forgettable television film, *Lie Down with Lions*, in the South of France over a three-month period in the autumn of 1993. We became friends and dined together on many occasions over the course of filming. He spent all the time between takes in his caravan, poring over restaurant menus deciding where we would dine that evening. He chose the food and the wine. And trying to pay the bill when dining with him was harder than grasping quantum physics. He *always* settled it. No one could beat him to it. He is an old-fashioned movie star with lashings of style.

Albert Finney:

He had a five-year plan. His worked out. I'm still working on mine. I wrote to him twice to be a referee for my green card, which I needed to work in the United States. He gave me a lovely reference.

Anthony Hopkins:

For slaying demons and emerging with another dimension as an actor, he is the best.

Joan Plowright:

For her passion, courage, and devotion to her art.

You are very adept with accents—Italian, Russian, American, among others. Where did your "ear" for them come from?

I've always had an ear for dialect, thanks to my mum, who was born in East London. She used to make up short bedtime stories to tell me. She would ask what country I would like the tale to come from, and then she would tell it in that accent. I don't know why, but my ear told me they weren't quite right. Of course, I never said a word. Later I made it not only my business but also my pleasure to practice them. So, God bless my mum.

I especially adore the American accent in all its variations, of which I had personal experience, first when some American friends of my father's visited, and second, when I toured the States in the late sixties with the RSC.

So, at the point when it came to replicating the Chicago accent in *The Front Page*, I was encouraged by the only real American in the production, David Bauer, the unofficial dialect coach. He said to me, "You don't have to worry. It's the others. . . ." I knew what he meant. Some of them did real comic book stuff, but by the time we opened, he'd got them licked into shape.

According to Blakemore, "Very few of our company had any direct experience of the United States. One of those who did was Stephen Greif, who dressed in chalk-striped suite and grey fedora, played the hoodlum Diamond Louie with authentic, sleazy aplomb. Most of the others, however, derived their knowledge of America mainly from its films and television."[5]

Later, Nigel Havers asked me to participate in a reading of Christopher Hampton's *Nostromo*, directed by Hugh Hudson, at the National Film Theatre, with a who's who of theatre: Simon Russell Beale, Christopher Eccleston, Clare Higgins. Nigel told me an actor was having difficulty with a variety of foreign roles, and he knew I loved doing accents. I did several.

Hudson told me, "If I make this film, you're all in it."

Never got made.

What is VoiceQuality, something you developed for describing voices for the industry?

It came about because I attended the Spoken Word Publishers Association Awards dinner and was speaking to Jonathan James-Moore, then head of BBC Radio Light Entertainment, and we realized that no actor is ever asked to describe their voice. Appearance, yes. Voice, no.

Everyone knows about *Spotlight*, an actors' directory which has a photo, eye color, height, everything except voice. As an actor, if you haven't got a voice, you're a mime.

We both had the idea of a project that would describe voice. We whittled down adjectives to describe the quality of an actor's voice. For example, mine would be "deep, dark, dark-brown; character: avuncular, authoritative, trustworthy."

The website people wanted only one word for each. We hired a panel of six voice experts—a producer, casting director, a voice teacher, and such—who listened to thousands of voices. We came up with twenty, and there is now a link on the *Spotlight* website, which purchased the worldwide rights from us, and actors can hear what they sound like. It's now become the industry standard.

You have a very distinctive voice.

My voice was a birthday present from my father. He spoke with a Viennese accent, in a very deep voice, almost basso profundo. I have his deep voice, which has been trained and stretched over the years.

Now that you're on the audition panel at RADA, how do you see the process has changed since you were accepted?

Where audition pieces used to be one Shakespeare and one "modern," today, "modern" means something written after 1960, and often means texts that no one has ever heard of with every other word an expletive. It's not encouraged, but neither is it verboten. Each selection runs two minutes but not more than three. In the second round now, the candidates have to sing a song.

The most significant change since I auditioned is that there are four rounds instead of one. Just two years ago, there were three thousand applicants for twenty-eight places. When I auditioned there were some nine hundred for eighteen places. The competition is fierce.

Where are you now in your career after almost fifty years?

I'm at an age now where I'm only going to be subsidiary roles in movies, but I'm happy to do that. I've always described myself as a "character actor." I've never played a hero. I may have looked it, but I was much happier in disguise.

With all the negatives to the acting profession, the rejection, among them, why act?

Because there wasn't *anything* else. It had to be that. I felt I was an actor. That's the way I saw myself. I wanted to be other people. I didn't want to be me. I wanted to play act.

When I was ten, I put on my father's coat and hat and put some stuff on my lip as a mustache, because he had one. I rang the bell at the flat where we were living.

My mother opened the door, and I said, "Hello. Is Mr. Greif in?"

My mother, bless her heart, said, "No, I'm afraid not." She was so supportive. Mums are like that. Can you imagine what was going on inside my head? I don't even know to this day.

I have given years of my life to the profession. The repertory system, which was the training ground for every actor who left drama school in my time, has been decimated due to lack of funding. Television soaps or the like seem to be the first destination of graduates or for anyone else who wants to act, for that matter.

Thank goodness, the National and RSC are still here. But today the profession is vastly overcrowded and a much riskier business than it used to be. One thing hasn't changed: you need the heart of a saint and the hide of a rhinoceros because it's a business of rejection. Get used to it—although you never do.

You spent a great deal of time at the Royal National Theatre, but when speaking about it, you refer to "the National," omitting the "Royal" designation.

I feel at home at the National, just the notion of it, what it embodies, what it can do. It's not *Royal*; it's *National*. It still has the aura of Olivier all over it, especially since Nicholas Hytner, to his credit, has made it the best engine room for both new and revival productions and who got rid of the "royal" character of the complex.

I think it's wonderful that the appointment of the next artistic director is Rufus Norris [who became AD in 2015]. He is the first non-university selection. There's no question that graduates from those institutions have enjoyed high-level posts over almost everyone else, so there will now be a much wider range of selection.

You attended the National's fiftieth anniversary gala in November 2013. What were your thoughts about the occasion?

What struck me forcibly was the swift passage of time and custom from those heady days at the Old Vic with Olivier to the National now. There were only twenty-five out of the eight hundred productions from the past used due to time restraints. Obviously, I was disappointed that the three colossal hits that I was in [*A Long Day's Journey into Night*, *The Front Page*, and *Death of a Salesman*] were not mentioned. But that must have applied to many other people who had participated in productions and who had cherished favorites which were not mentioned. It was Nicholas Hytner's party; they were his choices.

∼

Selected Credits

Theatre
King Lear, RST (1968; Trevor Nunn); *As You Like It*, RST (1968; David Hugh Jones); *Dr. Faustus*, RST (1968; Clifford Williams); *Dr. Faustus* and *Much Ado about Nothing*, RSC US tour (1969; Clifford Williams, Trevor Nunn); *Edward II*, UK tour; Mermaid; Piccadilly (1969–1970; Toby Robertson); *The Merchant of Venice*, NT at the Old Vic (1971; Jonathan Miller); *Danton's Death*, NT at

the New Theatre (1971; Jonathan Miller); *Long Day's Journey into Night*, New Theatre; Old Vic (1971; Michael Blakemore); *The Front Page*, NT at the Old Vic (1971; Michael Blakemore); *Richard II*, NT at the Old Vic (1972; David William); *The School for Scandal*, NT at the Old Vic (1972; Jonathan Miller); *Macbeth*, NT at the Old Vic (1972; Michael Blakemore); *Saturday, Sunday, Monday*, NT at the Old Vic; Queen's (1974; Franco Zeffirelli, Laurence Olivier); *The Gingerbread Lady*, Theatre Royal Windsor (1974; Jerry Harte); *Death of a Salesman*, Bristol Hippodrome; Theatre Royal Leeds; NT, Lyttelton (1979–1980; Michael Rudman); *The Paranormalist*, Greenwich Theatre (1982; Alan Strachan); *The View from the Bridge*, Theatre Royal Bath; Old Vic (1984–1985; Peter Coe); *Reflected Glory*, Bristol Hippodrome, Vaudeville (1991–1992; Elijah Moshinsky); *Fallen Angels*, Theatre Royal Bath; Apollo (2000–2001; Michael Rudman); *His Girl Friday*, NT, Olivier (2003; Jack O'Brien); *His Dark Materials*, NT, Olivier (2003; Nicholas Hytner); *Edmond*, NT, Olivier (2003; Edward Hall); *Epitaph for George Dillon*, Comedy (2006; Peter Gill); *Six Degrees of Separation*, Old Vic (2010; David Grindley); *Maydays*, RSC, Stratford (2011; Polly Findlay); *The Hamlet of Stepney Green*, Jewish Museum (2011; Sam Leifer); *Prince of West End Lane*, Globe (2012; Matthew Lloyd); *Lost Hebrew Creek*, Hampstead (2012; Tamara Harvey)

Film
Nicholas and Alexandra (1971); *No Sex, Please: We're British* (1973); *Spartan* (2004); *Casanova* (2005); *Upside of Anger* (2006); *Eichmann* (2007); *Shoot on Sight* (2007); *Boogie Woogie* (2009); *D Is for Detroit* (2015); *The Woman in Gold* (2015); *Bill* (2015); *Clavius* (2015); *Risen* (2016)

Television
Edward II (1970); *The Tragedy of King Richard II* (1971); *Merchant of Venice* (1973); *Return of the Saint*, "One Black September" (1977); *Citizen Smith*, twelve episodes (1977–1979); *Blake's 7*, four and one-half episodes (1978); *The Professionals*, "Lawson's Last Stand" (1982); *Tales of the Unexpected*, "The Luncheon" (1983); *House of Eliott*, two episodes (1992, 1994); *Lie Down with Lions* (1994); *Eichmann* (2007); *Dr. Who: The Infinite Quest* (voice) (2007); *He Kills Coppers* (2008); *MI-5* [UK title: *Spooks*] (2008); *Waking the Dead*, "Waterloo, Part I" (2011); *Silent Witness*, two episodes (2012); *Coronation Street* (2012); *New Tricks*, "Things Can Only Get Better" (2013)

Radio
Saturday Drama, "The Iceman," BBC Radio 4 (2007; Marc Beeby); *Classic Serial*, "Down and Out in London and Paris," BBC Radio 4 (2007; Steven

Canny); *Classic Serial*, "Captain Corelli's Mandolin" (2007; David Hunter); *Drama on 3*, "Hooligan Nights," BBC Radio 3 (2007; Toby Swift); *Classic Serial*, "Witness," BBC Radio 4 (2007; Jonquil Panting); *Afternoon Drama*, "The Babbington Plot," BBC Radio 4 (2008; Sasha Yevtushenko); *Classic Serial*, "The Grand Hotel Babylon," BBC Radio 4 (2009; Steven Canny); *Afternoon Drama*, "Peter Lorre vs. Peter Lorre," BBC Radio 4, (2010; Toby Swift); *Drama on 3*, "Austerlitz," narrator, BBC Radio 3 (2012; John Taylor); *Book of the Week*, "Kennedy's Letters," BBC Radio 4 (2013; Duncan Minshull); *Classic Play of the Week*, "The Castle," BBC Radio 4 (2015; John Taylor)

Awards and Nominations

RADA, 1967, Honours Diploma (First Class); 1967, Kendall Award, Best Actor, winner (Hal in *Picnic*; Inspector in *Gaslight*; Rudolph Kammerling in *Once in a Lifetime*); 1967, Hannam Clarke Award, Diction, winner, and Bossom Award, winner, both judged and presented by Sir John Gielgud; *Saturday, Sunday, Monday*, 1973, London Critics' Circle Theatre Award, Best Performance in a Supporting Role, nominee; *Death of a Salesman*, 1980, Olivier, Best Performance in a Supporting Role, nominee

Notes

1. Stritch died on July 18, 2014. In his tweet, Greif wrote, "Her star quality drenched the stage, oft-times in brandy. Knock 'em dead up there, Elaine."

2. In a 2015 production of *Death of a Salesman* at the RSC to celebrate the centenary of Arthur Miller's birth, Antony Sher played Willy; Alex Hassell played Biff.

3. A bludgeon.

4. Michael Billington, "Epitaph for George Dillon," *Guardian*, September 28, 2005: "In the third act, George is advised by a spivvy producer, brilliantly played by Stephen Greif."

5. Michael Blakemore, *Stage Blood: Five Tempestuous Years in the Early Life of the National Theatre*, 132.

~

CHAPTER ELEVEN

Jeremy Irons

Boredom is something that I'm always fighting against.

The small so-called green room on the second floor of the National Theatre is stacked high with press books, programs, news releases, and other media paraphernalia. Two straight-backed plastic chairs, a small desk, and a shabby, upholstered lounge chair comprise the furnishings. Although it's not meant as an interview space, this is where Jeremy Irons enters, followed by his two bichon frise–mix dogs.

It is now six o'clock. The cigarette-slim actor has been rehearsing his National Theatre debut role as former British prime minister Harold Macmillan in Howard Brenton's Never So Good since midmorning.

He is wearing an olive-green three-quarter-length coat with a pinkish-red scarf crisscrossed theatrically around his neck; his jeans are casually stuffed into his midcalf-high motorcycle boots. A brownish-gray fedora tops his stick-straight hair, but a flap of hair has slipped out from under the hat, which he keeps on throughout the interview.

Irons, one of the few actors who has scored a superfecta of four of the most prestigious acting awards—a Tony, an Oscar, an Emmy, and two Golden Globes—is an ardent cigarette smoker; some sources say as many as forty per day. Out of legal necessity, since there is no smoking in the theatre company complex, he slides open a glass door that leads to a terrace, dragging one of the small chairs outside. He lowers himself into the chair, deftly rolls his own cigarette, lights it, and inhales deeply.

After he admonishes one of his dogs, Dot, short for Dorothea, she of the curly fur, to lie down, which she immediately ignores and continues to frolic, he turns to

the other one, Dora, short for Isadora, she of the straight fur, and points at his feet.
She obediently lies down, head on her paws.

As the knife-sharp cold night air and smoke from his cigarette swirl into the
room, he begins a discussion of topics ranging from colleagues to castles, from
marriage (he's been married to actress Sinéad Cusack for more than thirty years)
to money. Despite the fatigue of a long day, he still moves with actorly grace, is
welcoming, and interested in exploring a variety of topics.

~

In the beginning?

I would describe my childhood on the Isle of Wight, where I was born, as
idyllic. We had three boats, dogs, and ponies. Woods and fields were within
a bicycle ride nearby. What more could a child want?

My father was a chartered account, my mother, a housewife. I have an
older brother and sister. As was the custom, I was sent to boarding school,
where I was dreadfully lonely. Then I went on to the prominent Sherborne
School in Dorset from 1962 to 1966. At the time I thought of becoming
a veterinarian. It never occurred to me that acting was a career choice. I
played the violin in the school orchestra and the harmonica in a band. But
somewhere along the line in my last year there, I made my stage debut as Mr.
Puff in Richard Brinsley Sheridan's *The Critic* and also *Carry On, Hamlet.*[1] So
when I didn't do well enough on my A levels and knew I wouldn't be going
to university, I transferred to the arts.

To support myself, I did some social work at St. Giles' Church, Camber-
well, and I learned a lot about how to deal with people for just over two
pounds a week. I also did some busking in Leicester Square.

I told my father I thought I'd quite like to be an actor. He was very calm
when he heard about my ambition, and I realize now that he didn't really
recommend it, but he wanted me to do what *I* wanted. I appreciated his
uncompromising support.

I answered an advert in *The Stage*[2] and became an ASM at the Marlow
Theatre, Canterbury, a rep company. Even though I wasn't acting—I did
props, scenery, everything else—I liked it, the feeling of theatre, the people,
and the idea of being a gypsy.

Why did you choose to attend Bristol Old Vic Theatre School rather than
one of the London-based drama schools? What are your recollections of
the training that you received during your two years there?

I had applied to RADA and Central School of Speech and Drama but
was turned down by them. I was asked, "Why do you want to be an actor?"

Photo by André Rau

Since I really didn't know why, I said, "I think it would be quite fun." They obviously didn't see me as a committed drama student.

Drama schools are the same but different, but, saying that, depending on who's running them, the ethos is slightly different. And at Bristol, I think the principal, Nat Brenner, must have recognized something in me. He thought I was a bit of a clotheshorse and that I'd probably look all right in a costume because I had the right proportions. That is, if he could get me to stand up straight. He said he thought he could get me the odd role.

There was a weekend audition, two days working with all the tutors. During that time, they'd see how applicants might fit in. One thing about taking people into theatre schools is that they have to think about casting plays, so they have to have a cross section of people. They probably thought I was adaptable, and I was accepted.

"Bristol was where you trained to be an all-round repertory actor, a bloke who could play anything, and subsume himself in the part rather than shine as a star."[3]

After my two years at the school, I was one of several [including Jane Lapotaire, Tim Pigott-Smith, Adrian Scarborough, Patrick Stewart, and Simon Cadell] to join the Bristol Old Vic Company.

What were some of the productions in which you appeared where you honed your craft?

Everything from Shakespeare's *The Winter's Tale* to Joe Orton's *What the Butler Saw* to Noël Coward's *Hay Fever*.

But in the end, I didn't want to continue in rep. Moving from town to town on short contracts. Not for me. I knew I had to get to London and do something, anything, in the West End.

After a number of auditions, you had an opportunity to meet your West End goals with a role in Godspell.

I didn't like auditioning, but I auditioned for everything. I had given myself to the age of thirty to see how I was doing. At just about twenty-five, I auditioned for Godspell, an American show, and got the role of John the Baptist, opposite David Essex as Jesus. We opened at the Roundhouse Theatre, off the West End in 1971, then transferred to Wyndham's in the New Year. I played in that show for two years. It was what I call a good "shop window" for me.

That theatrical production—as well as your current projects—call for performing eight times a week. How do you keep the performances fresh emotionally, physically, and psychologically?

You train! Actors deal with long runs in different ways. I'm actually fascinated by the problem of long runs. I've seen some of the greatest actors coarsen imperceptibly in their performances in a long run because they try to think the same thoughts and be surprised by the same things. In reality, the actor's responsibility is not to know the things we're meant to know until we're meant to know them in the production. How to keep it fresh and alive is really hard.

I remember I was doing The Real Thing with Glenn Close. We had worked together before in Reversal of Fortune, so we knew each other and trusted each other. One day, we were about to do a matinee. At the interval, I said to her, "I'm so bored with this. It's a boring audience, and I'm giving a very bored performance. I think I'm being very boring to the audience."

She said, "I feel exactly the same about what I'm doing."

It's just terrible when something like that happens. It's like wading through mud. I made this suggestion: "When you come on in the second act, I'm going to do everything in my power to make you laugh and to make you forget your lines. I'm going to do everything different. I may even do different lines. I want you to do the same for me."

She came on the stage like a racehorse. We were watching each other to see what was going to happen. The play came alive. We had to break the pattern. In fact, we did nothing differently in that second act, but we were watching, watching to see what the other might do.

I remember seeing Dustin Hoffman in The Merchant of Venice at the Phoenix Theatre, directed by Peter Hall, in 1989. He was working with a very experienced English cast. Hoffman was mesmerizing. I went 'round to see the cast afterwards, and they were all complaining and bitching, saying, "He never does the same thing twice."

I thought, "Well, he was mesmerizing, and you, who were all doing the same thing, were boring."

There are some actors who hit a curve ball, and they'll get that ball and knock it right back to you.

Acting in general is a profession of frequent rejection and ultimate acceptance. What sort of a pact have you made with yourself to deal with those risks?

Acting requires an acceptance of rejection. As a young man, I had a horror of routine. The idea of going into a steady job filled me with dread. I think that there's something about the lack of routine in our business and the constant possibility of failure, which is very, very invigorating. I thrive on risk taking in every area of my life. I ski too fast. I ride horses. I ride a motorbike. The fear of risk is an extra part of life. That extra is when you risk losing all, and, in the end, you gain all. It's not the extra length of life; it's the extra experience of life.

Acting is like lying over the edge of a precipice and looking down and thinking, "I could fall down there." I do that every time I walk on stage. I try to accept work where I *could* fall on my bottom and fail.

So acting is taking risks and what else?

Mike Nichols used to say that acting is like making love. When it stops working, you have to look into each other's eyes, and then it will start again. Actors definitely have to communicate with each other and react to each other. Acting is listening. That's all it is—and reacting to what you hear. But doing it night in and night out makes it very hard to keep that freshness, so we use tricks, as I mentioned with what Glenn and I did. But acting is also storytelling, and that storytelling has many different functions. One of those functions is to teach us that we have a common humanity, to teach us how like each other we are.

What about your expectations of director?

I believe a good director is like a good chef. He chooses the ingredients— the play, the actors—and he knows what he wants to cook. But he's not quite sure how the meal will turn out. He puts everything together and lets it mush around. Then he adds a little salt and pepper and tastes it every now and again. He should also put a little heat under it. At the end, he has the meal that is maybe a little different than he thought he was creating at the beginning. But he has to have the best ingredients and be an enabler.

I have been known to be a problem for directors. In the end, it is a coming together. A director hopefully casts an actor not because the studio or company asks them to, but because they want to. They think you can embody what they want in the character. Then we talk and try to find out if we're all play-ing the same game. I tend to like being very much part of the creative process, sometimes slightly outside my bounds as an actor. That has a bearing on my character. I tend to range quite widely in my interests in the production. That throws some directors.

Herb Ross, the director of *Nijinsky*, which was my first movie, was quite autocratic. I think, though, that he probably recognized what I wanted to do and liked my ideas so he backed off.

I'm now working with a wonderful director, Howard Davies, in *Never So Good* who I worked with at Bristol. He was stage manager then and "on the book," which means he used to prompt us. Then I worked with him on a television piece, *Tales from Hollywood*, and I've been trying to work with him since. He's wonderfully experienced. He lets us work, and gives us notes only when we're ready for them. He's very good at judging when it's the right time.

What do you do to prepare for the role based on a real person such as the former prime minister in *Never So Good*?

This hat that I'm wearing, the fedora [he takes off the hat and holds it at arm's length to check the make], is because I'm trying to encourage my hair to look like Macmillan's, which went straight back. I wear a hat a lot in the play, so I'm just getting used to having a hat. He might have had one like this. He used to like hats.

This play by Howard Brenton is wonderful, and that in itself becomes a support for my preparation. There's a great cast, too: Anthony Calf, Anna Carteret, Anna Chancellor, and Ian McNeice. But again, the risk factor is there, putting myself out there. If it doesn't work, it probably won't work because of *me*!

How long does it take to develop a character? Does it coalesce in rehearsal and continue to develop during the run of the production?

Like many men, I'm blinkered and have tunnel vision. I'm a bit like a dog with a bone in defining a character. At this stage when we're halfway through rehearsal, I get quite edgy and quite tired, but I'm always thinking about it. Even when I leave the theatre after rehearsal and go home, the part is always with me. I don't leave it behind at the theatre. The rehearsal process is all absorbing. But once I begin performances and the character is settled, then I can put it away.

I remember when Juliet Stevenson and I did *A Little Night Music* at the New York City Opera, the Broadway actors came in and were wonderfully professional and very prepared with their performances. Juliet and I didn't know what *we* were going to do.

I asked to the director, "Can Juliet and I just work on this? Could you leave and make some phone calls and come back in half an hour? We'll have something then." He agreed, and when he left, we went about doing our own work and blocking within the set.

The American actors couldn't believe what we were doing. I explained to them that what we were doing was very slowly to knit our emotional chart together. Some actors think it's just a matter of learning the lines and saying them.

For me, it's learning the thoughts, and the thoughts come out of what is spoken to me and how they are reflected, not always, by what I say. We have to weave this very carefully together so it's absolutely real. That for me is what rehearsal is all about. It's the great luxury of theatre. You don't have time to do it in film.

What are the challenges of moving between the medium of theatre and the medium of film?

The audience just gets the raw material with a film. With cutting, the director can quicken the pace, change the emphasis on character. A performance can actually be created in the editing process. That's not possible in the theatre.

Once the stage production is ready, how do you view your relationship with the audience?

Years ago, when I was playing in *Godspell*, I put my understudy on for a matinee because he hadn't ever had the chance. He'd done all this rehearsal but no performance, and I thought he should. I went out and watched the production as a member of the audience. As I sat there, I thought, "Gosh, I've forgotten the excitement of the audience. They're all coming to see our show. They've spent their money, and they've traveled up from wherever. I must always remember that."

When I went back into the show for the evening performance, as I was getting ready and going through my routine, I knew the audience was coming in, having a drink, talking to their friends, finding their seats. The music starts; the curtain goes up. They're really excited. It's really important to remind myself of that association.

You mentioned going through a routine. What does that consist of?

When we're rehearsing, I take a walk before I go in. Once we're in performance, I get ready quite quickly, depending, of course, on makeup and costume. I tend to get to airports and theatres for performances at the last possible moment. Sinéad, on the other hand, likes to get to the theatre early. I use the hurry of being slightly late as an adrenaline windup. While I'm getting my makeup on, while I'm getting my costume on, I'm getting into character so that by the time the curtain goes up, I'm in the place where I should be. For the audience, it's the first time they've seen the production. I have to keep reminding myself of that.

You and your wife have both appeared in plays—although several years apart—by Tom Stoppard: *The Real Thing* and *Rock 'n' Roll*, respectively. What insight can you offer about the playwright and those plays in particular?

Both plays we've been involved with have been rather untypical Stoppard in that they both have a lot of emotional heart in them. A lot of his plays are quite cerebral; they are plays of ideas. Indeed, *Rock 'n' Roll* is that, but it has a central passion throughout, especially with Sinéad's dual character of Eleanor/Esme. In *The Real Thing*, I thought it closest to Tom's heart, and I loved it for that. He's such a clever writer and gives the actor such wonderful fuel.

I think *Rock 'n' Roll* is a play that has to be seen twice. The first time for the information. In fact, some of it is not that important, but he's creating this world of people, some they've heard of, some they haven't. On a second time 'round, we pick up quite different things. I think it's a paean to anarchy. The central truth comes from the play, which seems to be about ordinary people reacting against the loss of small liberties, which will actually set change going. We must never forget that. I saw the production three times in London and three times in New York.

The Real Thing is a more domestic piece. It's about infidelity and affairs and what love is.

And, yes, Sinéad and I discuss the plays we do a lot!

What about actually working with your spouse?

We worked on the film *Waterland* together with director Stephen Gyllenhaall. We were playing husband and wife, and he didn't believe Sinéad and I should live together during the filming, so we went off and lived apart. She joined the film very late, and by then we'd shot about two-thirds of it. The relationship the characters have in the story is very different from our personal relationship. Living apart enabled her to come onto the set, not as my wife, not as Jeremy's wife, but as the character's wife. She was perfect casting for the role of Mary, but the fact that she and I were married was of no help in exploring the characters' realities.

When we did the Bernardo Bertolucci movie *Stealing Beauty* in 1996, we didn't play man and wife. We had a breakfast scene together, and the next day, Bernardo said, "We have to write a backstory for you two because there is an extraordinary chemistry between you, and the audience is going to want to know why."

We wrote a backstory that the characters had been lovers; they'd had an affair, but my character never committed to her, and she had gone off and married someone else. That didn't exist in the script originally. It was added to explain why there was such chemistry between us.

When you hear the title of a film or television project in which you appeared, details must come flooding back. What do you recall about these titles?
Brideshead Revisited, 1981, directed by Charles Sturridge, Michael Lindsay-Hogg:

I have good feelings about playing Charles Ryder. It was a tremendous chance for me because it was eighteen months' filming, thirteen hours of film [eleven episodes], the equivalent of doing six features films back-to-back. I was a central character, so I was always there.

To play the lead role in six films would be quite rare, but to have that opportunity on the television project *and* to make *French Lieutenant's Woman* in the middle of it gave me great experience. Then when they both came out together, that allowed me to sort of be booted skywards out of the magnetic field of actors. There are so many good actors in England that it's very hard to actually launch yourself. But these projects launched me. It wasn't that I was an ingénue of twenty and building a career through films. I was thirty then. I have a huge amount to be grateful for in both of those projects.

The Mission, 1986, directed by Roland Joffé:

To prepare for that role, I read a wonderful book, *Red Gold: The Conquest of the Brazilian Indians, 1500–1760* by John Hemming about the Jesuits in South America. Because my role as Father Gabriel takes place in a different century than my own and has a different experience, a different knowledge, and a different perception of life because of that different time, I tried reading around that so I could know what he would know, take for granted what he would take for granted. I wanted to know the moral and social viewpoints he would have, so I did a bit of research there.

I actually went through the Jesuit induction. I learned about the order from Daniel Berrigan, the Jesuit priest and activist, who was my mentor and got me to a situation, finally, where I could speak daily to God, as part of my daily routine.

That soon went, but at the time, I remember saying to God, "I want You to help me with this scene because if You don't, it will reflect badly on You." I thought, again *at the time*, "You have to help me because You will shine through me if I do it right!"

I learned a lot from Bob De Niro, some of which I rejected. He was finding the role as Rodrigo Mendoza difficult, possibly because it was a period piece. I watched his methods; there are good things in it, but I didn't want to take them directly. It was too slow for me.

De Niro never particularly wanted me in the role of Father Gabriel. The role was actually written for my father-in-law, Cyril Cusack, but it wasn't produced for ten years and by then, Cyril, at seventy-six, was really too old. The producer, David Puttnam, wanted a young man.

David told me, "This is going to be a tough role, and we can't nurse this character through. He's got to drive the part."

Bob wanted a nonactor in order to create the same sort of relationship that Dith Pran [Haing S. Ngor] and the Sam Waterston character [Sydney Schanberg] have in *The Killing Fields* [1984], which was also directed by Roland Joffé. Bob used that aversion to me in the role in the film, which is part of his "method." As a result, the relationship was pretty uncomfortable because we were stuck together in the jungle in several South American countries, Colombia, Argentina, and Brazil. It's quite nice if when your acting colleagues are mates because we can enjoy ourselves in the evening. It didn't work that way, but about halfway through the picture, he came 'round. That was part of Bob's process. Despite what it looked like on the locations, just off camera in most places, there were luxury hotels where we stayed.

Dead Ringers, 1988, directed by David Cronenberg:

I remember that Sinéad read the script and didn't want me to do it. She was uncomfortable about the two real-life characters—twins, Beverly and Elliot—who I would be playing. She said, "They do unspeakable things to the insides of women and then [they] die in very sordid circumstances." The two doctors go mad when they become involved with the same woman. I think she was wrong. That role gave me a great acting exercise. It allowed me to amaze the audience, which I, as an actor, want to do. Actors want to thrill, we want to entertain, and we want to test ourselves. It's hard to find things to tempt myself, and this was one.

The question was how to play these characters. To start with, I asked myself, "How do I make them different even though they look the same?" I gave them slightly different lives, with two different backstories. I went shopping on two different days for costumes and bought clothes for them individually. But when I looked at the rushes after the first two days' shooting, I thought,

"They're too different. No one would have trouble telling them apart," so I discarded the wardrobe idea.

Then I thought, "I'll make them exactly the same physically, but I'll find an *internal* way of making them different." I gave them each a different energy that wouldn't be obvious to the audience. In a rather incomprehensible way, they behave differently. It was very hard to tell why and how they behave differently to the audience.

I had one playing the exterior of the other's behavior. I tried playing one who had his energy in his forehead and one who had his energy in his throat. To increase the difference, I had two different dressing rooms, one for each of the brothers.

Reversal of Fortune, 1990, directed by Barbet Schroeder: You played a real-life character, Claus von Bülow, who was the suspect in the attempted murder of his wife, Sunny.[4] There is still a controversy as to his guilt. Your interpretation was difficult to read in the film. Was he guilty or not guilty?

Initially, I didn't want to play the role. Sunny was still alive and her kids were around. But Glenn Close, who plays Sunny, convinced me. She told me that if I didn't play the role, someone else would.

In order to play a character, I had to *know him*. I have my own opinions about von Bulow's guilt or innocence. I *think* I know the answer, and that's how I played it. I wanted the audience to see the enigma about the man. To say what *I* think would ruin the movie. Without that question mark, there wouldn't *be* a movie. In the end, it's the audience that has to decide.

Kafka, 1991, directed by Steven Soderbergh:

It was great working with Steve, but the film wasn't very successful. I remember when he first showed me the big office set with all the typewriters and my little office. I went to my typewriter and sat at the desk, thinking what a great set it was. There was a paper in the typewriter with a message, "Working with a young director on his second film,[5] that's a risk."

I thought, "Oh, God, whose idea was that?" and sort of ignored it. At dinner that night, Steve asked me, "Did you get my note? The one I left in the typewriter."

"That note was from you?" I would never have thought it was from Steven.

Die Hard: With a Vengeance, 1995, directed by John McTiernan:

My character, Simon Gruber, is a wonderful character, almost too interesting a character. If I'm walking in Calcutta [Kolkata] or Bombay [Mumbai], people shout out, "Ah, *Die Hard*" and point at me. That was a very useful film for getting my movie profile. A lot of my films have a relatively small audience. *Die Hard* is huge.

Lolita, 1998, directed by Adrian Lyne: *Risk* is a word you use in reference to acting. Why did you take the risk of the Humbert Humbert role?

Humbert is also a very interesting character, and it's always interesting to play a character who behaves very badly, but, who in a strange way, is quite likable. I think that's what people found very upsetting because there is this man, who was so out of line, but he was not an obviously evil man. I think that's an exciting dichotomy. I do everything in that film that I'd learned up to that point: there's comedy; there's pathos; there's tragedy. I always say that that role is the work I'm most proud of because of the difficult subject matter.

You mentioned learning—then discarding—ideas from Robert De Niro. What about working with Meryl Streep whose thoughts you did embrace?

I learned a huge amount from Meryl on *French Lieutenant's Woman*. The main thing I remember she said was, "The only thing that matters is the work. That's all."

I realized that the size of the trailer, the size of the car, of the working hours—none of that matters. That's all extraneous. There's a wonderful simplicity about her thinking that and preparing for a role.

Voice work is an important part of your career. How important is "acting" in voice work?

First, I think to the American ear, the British voice is quite pleasing because I think our acting is more literary based, more word based, than American actors. That doesn't mean we're better actors. There is no one better at film than the Americans. I know some wonderful American voices: James Earl Jones, Jack Nicholson, and Meryl's voice is fantastic.

Before *The Lion King*, I'd done voice work before, voiceovers mostly. But this was my first time on an animated film. I was amazed at how different the process was from what I thought it would be. I always thought that you had the picture, and you had to get the words so they sort of worked by lip-synching.

But, no. We recorded it all first, and the artists were there watching us and drawing us and filming us. They had a great storyboard, so I knew what was happening in the story as well as with my character. The artists didn't start drawing until everything was recorded. It gave me huge freedom. Because it was just voice, I could just go wild as Scar. It was like a breath of fresh air.

You've had a number of opening and press nights as well as an Oscar night. Which has been most worrying?

No question that it's the first night in a theatrical production.

It was very nice to be nominated for an Oscar for *Reversal of Fortune*, and I sort of thought I'd win it. Yeah, all the odds were on me. I was nominated with wonderful actors.[6] I know it has nothing to do with measuring one performance against another. It's just somebody's time, and it was my time.[7]

Away from filming and the theatre, you have an interesting hobby: you're a "restorationist." You restore furniture, and you have even restored a castle in Ireland. Like your roles, which you bring to life, you bring those treasures back to life.

When I was at Bristol, none of my colleagues thought I'd do anything or even remain an actor because I was always buying and selling furniture. They thought I'd become an antiques dealer. I used to go to auctions between classes and on weekends. I'd refurbish what I'd bought, sometimes keeping it, sometimes selling it. I still have furniture I bought while I was at Bristol. I love putting life back into a piece.

I've started doing that with houses now that I'm a bit richer. I have a house in Oxfordshire and a house in London, but I think my heart lies with my house in southwest Ireland, an historical place, a castle, really, on a property on an island near Skebreen in County Cork. Kilcoe Castle is connected to the mainland by a causeway. It was built in 1458, and the English brought it to ruin in 1602. I spent six years bringing it back to life. I stopped working for two years to restore it, and then I went back and did about a film a year just to pay for it.

It's furnished with an eclectic grouping of Moroccan rugs, Indian fabrics, and memorabilia from travels and films. [He takes out a small photograph of the property with a boat in front of the mainland.] I love it there because it's right on the sea. I have my horses there. It's a great place to get away. Great people. No crowds. Cities are all right, but I don't like lots of people for long.

I have a house in Dublin which, when I finish it, I hope that will be *it* in terms of restoration. I have a lot of property, too much, probably more than I need. But it's very nice, and we can move around and still be home wherever we are.

With more close to fifty years in film, television, and stage, what have you learned about acting and about yourself?

I think there was a period in my career when I was trying to seek perfection. As I get older, I realize that perfection doesn't exist, and the most important thing when I am in a group telling a story is that we all enjoy each other and ourselves. If that is the case, it's an easy atmosphere; everybody does better work. It's better not to care—no, that's not the right word; it's better not to *worry* so much because what is "perfection"? It doesn't exist, so chasing it is a highway to *nothing*. [At the word *nothing*, he tugs at the scarf for emphasis.]

What I'm interested in is not showing my proficiency as an actor but moving the audience and making them feel, not watching *me* feel. That's the area I'm interested in, bringing a truth to the audience and letting them recognize that truth in themselves. What I've tried with my career is to flit about so I can't be categorized because I am categorized to a certain extent: tall, English. As I become older, I've changed, so I can offer something different.

As actors, we, as artists, should hold up a "mirror to nature" and show people our situation. As an artist, I think actors have a real responsibility, and the stories we tell should be anarchic and stir up sediments. I've never really worked for work's sake. I don't work as much as I could because I love doing other things a lot. I have a very full and colorful and interesting life.

～

Selected Credits

Theatre
Little Theatre, Bristol (1968–1970): *School for Scandal* and *What the Butler Saw* (Mark Woolgar); *Hay Fever*, *A Servant of Two Masters*, *Oh! What a Lovely War*, and *The Merry Gentleman* (John David); Bristol Old Vic (1969–1970): *Major Barbara*, *The Devil's Disciple*, and *As You Like It* (Val May); *The Taming of the Shrew*, Theatre Royal Bath (1970; Val May); *Godspell*, Roundhouse, Chalk Farm, Wyndham's (1971–1972); *Wild Oats*, RST, Aldwych, Piccadilly (1976–1977); *The Rear Column*, Globe [now Gielgud] (1978); *An Audience Called Edouard*, Greenwich (1978); *The Real Thing*, Plymouth, New York (1984–1985); *Richard II*, RST, Stratford; Barbican (1986–1987); *The Winter's Tale*, RST (1986–1987); *The Rover*, RSC at People's, Newcastle; Mermaid (1987); *A Little Night Music*, New York City Opera (2003); *Camelot*, Hollywood Bowl, Los Angeles (2005); *Embers*, Duke of York's (2006); *Impressionism*, Gerald Schoenfeld, New York (2009); *The Gods Weep*, Hampstead (2010; Maria Aberg)

Film
Nijinsky (1980); *The French Lieutenant's Woman* (1981); *Moonlighting* (1982); *Betrayal* (1983); *Swann in Love* (1984); *A Chorus of Disapproval* (1989); *Damage* (1992); *The House of the Spirits* (1993); *M. Butterfly* (1993); *The Man in the Iron Mask* (1998); *Callas Forever* (2002); *Being Julia*

(2004); *The Merchant of Venice* (2006); *Appaloosa* (2008); *Pink Panther 2* (2009); *Margin Call* (2011); *The Words* (2012); *Night Train to Lisbon* (2013); *A Magnificent Death from a Shattered Hand* (2014); *The Man Who Knew Infinity* (2015); *High-Rise* (2015); *Batman v Superman: Dawn of Justice* (2016); *Race* (2016)

Television
The Rivals of Sherlock Holmes, "The Case of the Mirror of Portugal" (1971); *The Pallisers,* six episodes (1974); *Notorious Woman,* two episodes (1975); BBC2 *Play of the Week,* "Langrishe, Go Down" (1978); BBC *Play of the Month,* "The Voysey Inheritance" (1979); *Danny, Champion on the World* (1989); *Tales from Hollywood* (1992); *Mirad: A Boy from Bosnia* (1994); *Longitude* (2000); *Elizabeth I* (2005); *Georgia O'Keefe* (2009); *Law & Order: Special Victims Unit,* two episodes, "Totem" (2011), "Mask" (2011); *The Borgias,* twenty-nine episodes (2011–2013); *The Hollow Crown,* "Henry IV, Parts 1 and 2" (2012)

Documentary
Trashed, as narrator, executive producer with Titus Ogilvy, Tom Wesel, et al. (2012)

Awards and Nominations

The Rear Column, 1978, Clarence Derwent Award, Best Male in a Supporting Role, winner; *Brideshead Revisited,* 1982, BAFTA, Best Actor, nominee; also, 1983, Golden Globe, Best Performance by an Actor in a Mini-Series or Motion Picture Made for Television, nominee; *The Real Thing,* 1984, Tony, Best Actor in a Play, winner; Drama Desk, Outstanding Actor in a Play, nominee; *The Mission,* 1987, Golden Globe, Best Performance by an Actor in a Motion Picture—Drama, nominee; *Dead Ringers,* 1988, New York Film Critics Circle, winner; Best Actor; also, 1989, Genie Award, Canada, Best Actor, winner; *Reversal of Fortune,* 1990, Academy Award, Actor in a Leading Role, winner; also, Golden Globe, Best Actor—Motion Picture—Drama, winner; New York Film Critics Award, Best Actor, nominee; *Elizabeth I,* 2007, SAG Award, Outstanding Performance by a Male Actor in a Television Movie or Mini-Series, winner; also, Golden Globe, Best Performance by an Actor in a Supporting Role in a Series, Mini-Series or Motion Picture, winner; *The Borgias,* 2012, Golden Globe, Best Performance by an Actor in a Television Series—Drama, nominee

Notes

1. According to the school's alumni officer, Irons was part of the winning team in the Shout, the school singing competition, in 1965, and took part in a reading of *Playboy of the Western World* with the James Rhoades Society.

2. The longest-running entertainment and performing arts publication in the United Kingdom.

3. Shirley Brown, *Bristol Old Vic Theatre School: The First 50 Years, 1946–1996* (Bristol, UK: BOVTS Productions, 1996), 52.

4. Claus (also spelled Klaus) and Sunny are, oddly, two characters in *A Series of Unfortunate Events* by Daniel Handler (a.k.a. Lemony Snicket).

5. Soderbergh's first film was *Sex, Lies and Videotape* in 1989.

6. Kevin Costner, *Dances with Wolves*; Robert De Niro, *Awakenings*; Gérard Depardieu, *Cyrano de Bergerac*; and Richard Harris, *The Field*.

7. In his acceptance speech, Irons thanked director David Cronenberg, who had directed his previous film, *Dead Ringers*.

∼

CHAPTER TWELVE

Sir Derek Jacobi, CBE

It ain't what you say; it's the way wot you say it.

Sir Derek Jacobi has just completed a Sunday matinee performance as Malvolio in the Donmar Warehouse production of Shakespeare's Twelfth Night *at the Aldwych Theatre. Because there is no evening performance on Sunday (in fact, unlike many Broadway shows, which have Sunday performances, occasional Sunday matinees are new to the West End after decades of darkness), the theatre staff is eager to lock up, so the interview, scheduled for the cluttered green room, is moved to the restaurant across the alley from the theatre.*

Blinking into the darkness of the busy bar area, the gray-bearded and mustachioed actor appears much taller on stage than he actually is. His gray beard is neatly trimmed, and his silvered hair is in what might be called a crew cut. At age seventy-three, his skin is surprisingly wrinkle-free—and pink. He wedges himself into a seat behind a corner table. No one takes notice of the soft-spoken actor as the waiter takes his order for a glass of chardonnay.

Considering that Sir Derek, just a half hour before, had taken a company curtain call for the eighth performance of the week that, as the saying goes, brought down the house, he is full of energy and enthusiasm and eager to talk about his craft, and his blue eyes sparkle each time the word theatre *is mentioned.*

∼

In the beginning . . . Is there a touch of the Cockney in your voice?

Could have done. My parents were both Cockney. They talked like that. When I get excited—or a bit tired—I have been known to lapse into it. You can take the boy out of Leytonstone, where I was born in 1938, but . . . [he hesitates but does not complete the adage].

I was a happy youngster. I started acting in school. I don't know where that interest came from; my parents certainly weren't theatre oriented. The earliest performance I remember I was in was at the local library in *The Prince and the Swineherd*, in which I had the dual title role. Later I won a scholarship to read history at St. John's College at Cambridge, all the while combining acting with academia. At the end of my time at Cambridge, I wrote letter after letter after letter to repertory companies. I finally was accepted into the Birmingham Rep, beginning in 1960. I was there for three years. That rep was my drama school; they were very traditional and based in the classics.

At one point, I was asked to audition for the RSC at Stratford. John Barton, Peter Brook, Peter Hall; all of them were there. I was handed the script of *The Tempest* and minutes later was asked to read Ariel. Quite badly, I must admit. I wasn't accepted into the company. My first *big* disappointment.

Back I went to Birmingham, which had kindly released me for the audition, and there I was offered the roles of Henry in *Henry VIII*, Troilus in *Troilus and Cressida*, and Aaron in *Titus Andronicus*.

Laurence Olivier came up to see one of the matinees of *Henry VIII* in which I was appearing. After the performance, there was a knock on the dressing room door. It was Olivier. He didn't recognize me because I was already out of my costume. When he finally did recognize me, he asked me to join him at Chichester in a production of George Bernard Shaw's *Saint Joan*. That company was the first incarnation of the National Theatre. I then became a founding member of the National when the company moved to the Old Vic in 1963. Eventually I was asked back to Stratford.

So, the first eleven years of my career I was never out of work. I did three years in repertory at Birmingham and then nearly eight years with Olivier. I never had to wait on tables or any of those things actors do while waiting for work.

Your role as Malvolio in the 2008 production of *Twelfth Night* is not your first in the play.

That's true. In 1973, I played Andrew Aguecheek with the Prospect Theatre Company, which was a touring company formed by Toby Robertson and Richard Cottrell in 1964. Ian McKellen was part of that company in their first production of *Edward II*, which put him in the forefront of actors.

Photo courtesy of the author

Donald Sinden's performance as Malvolio is one of the most memorable performances of that character. How did his "presence" affect your interpretation?

Donald's was the Malvolio I remember in 1970, directed by John Barton, with the famous business with the sundial and the watch he wears. He got a humungous laugh with the gag in which he compares the sundial to his anachronistic watch.

When I was asked to play Malvolio by Michael Grandage for the Donmar production, I found that throughout rehearsals I could feel Donald's presence at my left shoulder. [Jacobi turns to look over his shoulder as if Sinden is still there.] I was very aware of Donald *all* the time. I knew I couldn't do the business with the watch. I knew I couldn't do anything like that. That was his creation. I had to think of some other things to do.

We got to the very first preview on December 5, 2008, the first time in front of a paying audience, and I was terrified. My second line was gobbledygook. I didn't know what I was saying. I got through it, just.

After the performance, I was in my dressing room. There was a knock on the door. In walked Donald Sinden. I told him, "If I'd known you were there, Donald, I wouldn't have gone on. I was frightened enough, but to know you were sitting out there would have been too much." He was very sweet and said he enjoyed it.

But the gist of the story is that I was very aware of him throughout rehearsals and thank goodness I didn't know he was there in the audience. It would have affected me . . . badly.

I had a scene [Act II, scene v] with the words: "I frown the while; and perchance wind up my watch, or play with my—some rich jewel . . ."

Some members of the audience got the gag, and I got some quite nice laughs during that moment. The great gag of the evening in our production was right at the end when Malvolio gets the wrong Olivia. It's a wonderful gag. I'd never seen it before. It was the biggest laugh of the evening. Another audience approval with laughs has to do with Malvolio's costume—the yellow costume with garters at the seaside. It looks like I'm ready to go to Bermuda in that outfit.

They want to take the production to Australia, but [he says this under his breath] I couldn't face it. I don't want to do it until June, having been with it since the end of October. We have another seven weeks here. I adore Australia, but not another ten weeks. I'm too old and too ugly. I need a holiday.

What makes a comedy like _Twelfth Night_ such a challenge, perhaps even more so than tragedy?

We need an audience's reaction. We can kid ourselves in a drama that the audience's silence is not because they're asleep but because they're holding their breath. We can't do that with comedy. We've got to _hear_ them. We have to be aware of that in order to time the next line.

It's that strange dichotomy that an actor has to have: to be entirely inside what you're doing on the stage and at the same time have a third eye that's sitting halfway down in the stalls watching. We have to know and feel that we're part of the audience as well as performing. We have to _feel_ that. Our antennae have to be very, very sharp.

The actress who taught me that was Maggie Smith, who, on stage, thinks at the speed of lightning. You have to think that way. You _have_ to. Maggie, by the way, is one of two actors who call me by the nickname "Del." The other was Edward Hardwicke, also a member of the National; we appeared together in _Royal Hunt of the Sun_ and _Love for Love_.

You just mentioned that you are "too old and too ugly." How can that be?

I've never liked the way I look. I never have. I've been blessed with many things. But one of the things I've been unblessed with is a round face. I'm an actor, and round faces are not good for [he searches for the right word, and then it comes to him] suffering. Round faces don't suffer well. A lot of the best parts have to do suffering. Every year, I ask Father Christmas for cheekbones, not my two front teeth, but cheekbones, and he has never granted my request.

Among your colleagues is Kenneth Branagh; you have worked on several of his film projects. You were filming his _Henry V_ and appearing on stage concurrently. How did you manage both?

It was an interesting time because I was filming at Shepperton, and I was also in the theatre playing *Richard II* and *Richard III* in tandem at the Phoenix Theatre. Film work and theatre work back-to-back, all on the same day, all Shakespeare. It was fascinating.

My abiding memory is begging Ken every day at about five o'clock, "Pleeeeease let me go as I have to get to the theatre."

He would say, "Oh, just one more take. Give me one more." I was frightened most of the time—very frightened—that I would never make it into town.

I would say, "But, Ken, what about traffic?" I had to get from Shepperton to Charing Cross Road, about fifteen miles. I like to be at the theatre early. I don't like just going into the theatre and walking straight onto the stage. But I always got there on time.

What is the most obvious difference between working in the theatre and in film?

It's a vocal difference. On film sets, I have a microphone practically down my throat. Whereas at the Phoenix, for example, I had to serve it up. As a theatre actor, I'm used to bigness, and it's much easier for me to find smallness, to pare away. It's much easier for a stage actor to pull back on vocal technique and not do so much. For a film actor, it's much more difficult to find that voice to fill up the big space in a theatre. They're used to filling no space at all because there is always that microphone. They can whis-s-s-s-per the entire role, and it will still be picked up.

Using a microphone on stage gives an actor's voice a falseness. I was appalled when they decided to mic the actors at the National several years ago. I don't know whether they still do.[1]

When I was a member of the RSC, we came to the States in 1984. I played Benedick in *Much Ado about Nothing* and Cyrano in *Cyrano de Bergerac* for a twenty-two-week schedule in Washington, DC, and New York. We were at the Gershwin Theatre, which is as big as an airport hangar,[2] and as Brits, we were used to not having microphones. After a week, we were all losing voices. I begged them to find me a voice teacher, which they did: Clyde Vinson, a Texan. He was the most miraculous voice teacher I ever met. Within minutes of working with him, I had a virtual microphone in my mouth. He taught me how to make my voice stronger, louder, deeper, higher. He did it all. He was wonderful! Wonderful![3]

One thing that distinguishes one actor from another on stage is rhythm, tempo, timing. That is falsely created in the editing room. The editor of a film creates the rhythm of your performance. Performances can be created and improved by the editor, but they can also muck up a performance. On stage, you do it yourself in front of an audience and adapting the performance to the audience.

I have said that I have more control of the roles on stage than in film. Film is all about photography. It's about a picture, what's in that picture, and which bit of you is going to be seen. In film, unless you are a mega-star, you are just fodder.

Is *Cyrano* one of your favorite plays?

Hmmmm. I think *Cyrano* [which he pronounces CyRANo, dictated, he explains, because of the scansion] *is* my favorite play. It's a genius of a play. We were using the Anthony Burgess translation. I found when I was reading it—before I'd even rehearsed it—I had to keep putting it down because I was in floods of tears. I found it *so* moving. There is every, every nuance of language and of phrase and of emotion in the translation. It's miraculous. It's quite amazing that I can feel that way about a translation, and it's not the original, which must be staggering. I did try to read it in the original, but my French isn't quite good enough.

Hugh Whitemore wrote *Breaking the Code* with you in mind as Alan Turing. Why did you initially not want to take on the role as the famed code breaker?

That's true. Hugh, who had taken a year off to do the research about this enigmatic genius, sent the script to me saying he had written it with me in mind. I read it, and my heart sank. Of course, I was honored and flattered, and I could see that it was an interesting concept, the breaking of the German Enigma code during World War II.

But there were endless speeches about mathematical theory, about how computers work—page after page. I wasn't worried about learning it. I thought, "People in the audience will have been at work all day; they will have dragged themselves to the theatre, and this is going to send them screaming out of the theatre with boredom."

Hugh asked me, "What's the last play you've done?"

At the time, it was *Cyrano*.

God bless Hugh when he said, "Then you must believe that when Alan Turing is talking about mathematic theory, computers, numbers—it's Cyrano talking to Roxane, writing to Roxane. The speeches are sexy and exciting."

He also said, "It doesn't matter if the audience doesn't understand *exactly* what you're talking about."

That's so true of every part an actor plays: what the audience responds to is the excitement in telling them about the subject you love. Turing loved numbers. When he talked about them, he was excited, and the audience

Derek Jacobi as Alan Turing with Jenny Agutter and Michael Gough in the 1987 Broadway production of Hugh Whitemore's *Breaking the Code*, directed by Clifford Williams. *Photofest*

responds to that emotion, to his excitement. [Sir Derek becomes excited just talking about the character and the role.] I castigated myself for not having seen that and having to have that pointed out to me by the playwright: It ain't what you say; it's the way wot you say it. It's fundamental to acting, absolutely fundamental.

Then is that true with Shakespeare as well?

Particularly with Shakespeare, which is archaic, to say the least. In Shakespeare, the audience may not be familiar with a particular word, but it's how you say it, the intonation and attitude. If the audience is aware of your attitude as an actor to what you're saying through body language, by facial expression, by intonation, they'll know what you're speaking about.

What about the rehearsal process? What happens when you walk into the rehearsal room?

For the production of *Twelfth Night*, we rehearsed for five weeks. But I knew I was playing Malvolio months before. It's not the biggest part in the world, but it's a good one. I started studying it and learning it in May or June, and we began rehearsing at the end of October, beginning of November.

By the time we started, I knew what to say, but I didn't know *how* to say it. I knew the lines. I'd learnt them as I always do; they're there by rote. I don't have to waste time looking at the book, so the rehearsal process is revelatory and wonderful. The rehearsals teach me why I'm saying the words, where the words are coming from, what the words mean, how they're attached to emotion, what I'm feeling when I say them, what the other person has said that makes me ask: "Do I mean what I say? Am I lying? Am I telling the truth?"

All the answers to those questions are things that I learn in rehearsal, but they're all predicated on the fact that I know the words. But in the beginning, they are just that: words. They don't have any context. With Shakespeare particularly, the meanings are many layered. I realize there are many ways of saying a line, many, many alternatives. I can make the words mean all sorts of things, whatever I want, which is why I think Shakespeare has survived for four hundred years.

If the lines are going to be purely on rhythm—da-de-da-de-da-de-da and so on—forget it. That truly is boring. But with a healthy disrespect for punctuation, I can make the line mean what I want it to, according to the stand I take with the character—not just with my character but with the other characters around me.

Once you have the lines learned and have established their meaning, how do you move into the character and his motivation?

One of the problems with actors is that they say things like, "Oh, my character wouldn't do that." I believe that if the character is in any way part of the human race, he would do *anything*. What motivates the character is situation. Given the right situation—or the wrong situation—the character could kill someone. That is what controls character: situation.

People have said, "Oh, Derek's acting out of character."

No, I'm *not*. I'm *reacting* to a situation that you, my friend, have never seen me in before.

That's all. Absolutely, the situation makes the character.

How do you expect a director to assist you in preparing the character?

There are many different types of directors. The worst kind for me are the ones who believe than an actor's creative juices only flow when the actor is in a state of abject terror. Terror of the director. They terrorize a performance out of actors. I think they are fulfilling in some weird way their own neuroses. That kind of director can be much more neurotic than the actors they're working with.

I need a director like Michael Grandage. He is the perfect director. In rehearsal situations, he is the benign dictator. There are a lot of laughs, a lot of fun, a lot of messing about, but behind it all is a great strategy and a discipline and a security which he gives, making me feel that if I haven't got it today, I'll find my way tomorrow. He surrounds us with safety nets.

When we were rehearsing *Twelfth Night*, each scene was rehearsed on its own. If an actor wasn't in the scene, he or she wasn't allowed in the room. When we came to the first run-through, we all sat there watching each other. Michael would then—in the rehearsal room situation—give us all our costumes. We could then know how long changes were going to take. Then when we eventually got on the stage in a technical situation, we'd had the costumes for a week and knew how long it took to get out of one and into another. It was so much smoother, much less stressful.

I've never known another director to do that. I think Michael is unique in doing that partly because he was an actor himself. He knows how an actor feels in those circumstances: frightened, nervous.[4]

Curtain calls are an interesting theatrical convention. What's your thought about this custom? The *Twelfth Night* curtain call had an ensemble feel to it.

Yes, yes, it did. I generally hate curtain calls because they get down to who's best. Hate it. Hate it. Won't do it. They are often so manufactured.

When I did *The Tempest*, Michael and I had a bit of a row about it. He ultimately said, "If you don't take a solo curtain call, you are insulting the audience." I took a solo call. But I'm not good at it.

The evening belongs to the company. The audience have been watching everybody all evening; even if what an actor has been doing is minimal, we couldn't work without them. We need *everybody* on stage. A company saying "thank you" is much more exciting than an individual's "thank you."

For the *Twelfth Night* curtain call, we all stood silhouetted, which was very effective, and then the lights came up and as one, we walked down stage, and the audience immediately reacted. By doing this, we weren't saying, "He's the best" or "She's the best," or "He was better than she, so we'll give her a bigger hand."

One of the best curtain calls I ever saw was at Her Majesty's with Lauren Bacall in *Applause*. She was fine, but it wasn't a particularly wonderful evening. There was first the company curtain call. Then one for Bacall on her own. The applause was . . . substantial. The curtain came down. The curtain went up again, and she was there again in a different dress. The applause went up. The curtain came down. And up again. She had yet another dress on. The curtain calls were the show. Brilliant!

Several actors have said that Prospero, who you have played, is a run-up to King Lear. What is your thought about those two roles?

I've heard that. I don't agree with it. I think Prospero is much younger than he's normally played. I think he's about forty-five. There's a line of text where he says that he has given Miranda, his daughter, "a third of mine own life" (Act IV, scene i).[5]

I also think it's more interesting if Prospero is still a sexually aware man. This is why he's so hard on Caliban and Ferdinand. There's that undertone that Miranda is the only woman on the island, and she's becoming pubescent. If he's a younger man, it adds textures and other depths to what he's saying and who he is. That's how I played him.

Your association with the Donmar resulted in one of the more interesting productions, *Voyage round My Father*, where the playwright, John Mortimer, was a participant in the rehearsals. Your recollections of the man?

He was quite a character. Very funny, very amusing, and very supportive. Very often, he'd come to rehearsals and sit in his wheelchair. On occasion he would change a couple of things, a word, a phrase. I played his father, and in the last act, I was wheeled in *my* wheelchair, passing him in his wheelchair. It was very odd.

Let's go back to that initial National Theatre production at the Old Vic.

Oh, yes, please. Let's do. I've been a company man all my life. Being part of an ensemble is what I like.

That first night of the National Theatre was the 22nd of October 1963. It was my twenty-fifth birthday. I was playing Laertes to Peter O'Toole's Hamlet at the Old Vic. In 2013, the National will be fifty years old. I shall be seventy-five. I think there should be some sort of celebration organized!

I've never worked at the building on the South Bank. Never been on any of those stages, the Olivier, the Lyttelton, or the Cottesloe [now the Dorfman]. I've got to. I want to.[6]

What do you recall the most about Olivier, the person?

What I remember is how very supportive he was of the kids in the company. I remember the first time at the very first rehearsal of the very first play I did, *Saint Joan*, he and his wife, Joan Plowright, arrived at the rehearsal. We were all lined up, and he came down the line, shaking hands with all of us. He eyeballed each one of us. My shirt was sticking to my back, I was that nervous. He became my friend, certainly my mentor, director, fellow actor, god figure, my employer. I adored him. I owe so much to him, so-o-o-o much. I couldn't have had the start I had without him, and what a fantastic start it was.

At one point, Olivier asked you not to look him in the eye when you were on stage together. Is that true? Was it stage fright?

Yes, but it was apropos of a certain time in his life when he had stage fright. We didn't know he had it. But I remember him saying it to me when

I was playing Gratiano to his Shylock in Jonathan Miller's production of *The Merchant of Venice* in 1970 at the Old Vic not to look at him.

He called me into his dressing room and said, "I don't want you to look in my eyes. Look at my ear, nose, anything else." If I looked him in the eye, he told me, it would distract him.

I didn't understand what it was like then, but now, having had stage fright myself, I do. It's a fear, a terror that is catatonic and can't be controlled. I've called it an "industrial disease." You think you're going to fall over; you can't remember your lines; you can't stand up. It's awful. I had it for more than two and a half years. I didn't do theatre during that time. I did film and television. Thank goodness I could earn my living in that way. But I didn't stand on the stage.

How did you finally cure the "disease"?

It was the RSC that got me out of it. I had always wanted to be part of that company. I was in Bavaria playing Adolf Hitler in a television film. A phone call came through from Terry Hands, who was then artistic director of the company, inviting me to come to Stratford to play Benedick in *Much Ado*, Prospero in *The Tempest*, Peer Gynt in *Peer Gynt*, and Cyrano in *Cyrano*. I knew if I didn't accept that amazing offer, I would never get on the stage again.

I said yes, but it was a terrified yes.

The first one was *Much Ado*. I went on that first night. I was catatonic with terror. It was awful. But I got through it. And gradually it got better.

In 1960, *The Hollow Crown* was conceived by your Cambridge colleague, John Barton. Your participation in that piece came much later.[7]

I first met him when I was an undergraduate, and he was a don at King's College and directed productions. He was famous for chewing razor blades during rehearsals. He was a very frightening man. One of his great attributes was that he was an expert fencer, and he would teach fencing to all the undergraduates in the plays that he produced. I was scared of him as well as many others were . . . in those days. Later he was a bunny rabbit, but then he was pretty scary. He was known to make actresses cry.

In 1975, I did his *The Hollow Crown* with Michael Redgrave, and we literally went 'round the world to about two dozen venues. We flew from London to Ft. Lauderdale and worked our way across America, across the Pacific, across the Far East, Israel, for four months. It was the most fantastic job. I last did it in 2002 in Australia with Donald Sinden, Ian Richardson, and Diana Rigg. And twenty-seven years later, it still worked. The concept is timeless. The way John seamlessly put it together is amazing.

You mentioned that you are a "company man." As a member of the National in its earliest incarnation and with the RSC, what do you see as the major differences about what they do, where they are today, and what they might be doing in the future?

The RSC has a stricter remit on what it can do because it is the Royal Shakespeare Company. It has the cachet that it has to maintain: presently mainly Shakespeare. On the whole, I was against it leaving the Barbican as its London home in 2002. I enjoyed the Barbican and was sad when we left. I truly can't say why the company left, as I wasn't part of the decision.[8]

The RSC has some marvelous actors, some marvelous directors. It's doing great work. The National, also with Royal in its title, on the other hand, has a much broader remit. It can do all sorts of things. They can do a greater variety of plays. Both companies are incredibly successful. Both are vibrant at the moment and doing wonderful stuff.

With your long association with Shakespeare, have you come to a conclusion about the authorship of the plays? Are you a Stratfordian or an Oxfordian? That is, do you believe that William Shakespeare was the author of the plays or that it was actually Edward de Vere, the 17th Earl of Oxford?

There is a hugely controversial issue about the authorship, but I believe that de Vere, who was a poet and a courtier, did more than just dabble in poetry. I believe he wrote all the plays attributed to Shakespeare. De Vere wrote them anonymously and allowed Shakespeare to stage the plays and take credit for them.

Stepping off stage into the television studio: Since diction and enunciation are crucial to an actor, your role as the stammering Claudius in the series *I, Claudius* must have presented interesting challenges. How difficult was it to play a role in which the character has a speech impediment?

I didn't know when we started that there is a difference between a stutter and a stammer. Claudius had a stammer. A stutter is like a machine gun: ta-ta-ta-ta. A stammer is when you can't get the word out. If I had stammered for real, each episode would have been two hours long. I had to modify the stammer. I had to know when to cut it off, so it is a theatrical stammer by necessity.

When the scripts were first sent to me, the writer, Jack Pullman, had written the stammer in. If I had to say the word *please*, it would have three *p*'s before it. After about the third episode, they decided to save on typewriter ribbon and just left it to me to stammer when I wanted.

Claudius was a definite challenge, a huge challenge. It was very concentrated, very dedicated work. Each episode took a fortnight. We rehearsed for ten days; we recorded for two, and then we had a day off in order to learn the next script. That was over six weeks. Very intense.

How did you maintain the integrity of the character in the fragmented shooting schedule of such a series?

With difficulty. In that series, we did it in sequence. Episode one is the first time we see Claudius; he's sixty-four years old, so for all departments—makeup, costume, wigs—we have to present an old man who the audience isn't going to grow into for thirteen episodes. We hoped that the old man presented at the beginning of the first episode would be the same old man we were going to see in the last episode. It was very difficult.

By the time he was older, he didn't twitch so much. He didn't stammer so much. The link was the same, but those two characteristics had to be modified as Claudius aged. It was really a close collaboration between the director, Herbert Wise, and myself to say, "No, don't do too much."

Almost two decades later, you appeared in the *Cadfael* series. Any differences?

Cadfael was much easier. It was a doddle compared to *Claudius*. We also did thirteen episodes in all. They were all made in Budapest. We'd go there for ten weeks, and we'd do three or four episodes. Then we'd come back a year later and do some more.

Do you have plans for your next project?

I'm going to be waiting on tables! [He laughs, knowing that's not going to happen.] I don't know. I truly don't know what I'll do when *Twelfth Night* finishes. What I absolutely need is a holiday. I'm going to go to Los Angeles to see my new American agent there and then to Hawaii or Bora Bora.

I'm doing a radio play, *Mayflies* for *The Afternoon Play* on BBC Radio 4. It's about a man who's a retired astronomer, and there's been a message from outer space, which needs a reply. It's a very philosophical story.

I always feel that the part I'm about to embark on, whatever it is, is the one that's going to find me out, that I'm going to fail. I don't think I've ever actually said, "I want to play so-and-so." It's always been somebody coming to me and asking, "How do you feel about playing so-and-so?"

I constantly think, "I'll never work again."

That sounds as if you're a bit superstitious.

Yes, I am superstitious in that I have a routine before I get onto the stage that I've *got* to repeat. Certain things I have to do, certain places I have to be, but no details. It's more of a routine because it's different with each play.

It usually has to do with my journey from my dressing room to the stage. It has to be the same each time.

What would you like to do?

I would like to do a prestigious telly or a film for a lot of money. *Twelfth Night* was lovely, and it's a Donmar production, which is a stunning place to work, but you pay *them*!

On a personal note, you and your partner, Richard Clifford, have been together for decades.

I've been with Richard for more than thirty-five years. Pretty good, isn't it? I'm older by seventeen years, which now that we're older, the difference has kind of closed. When we met, I was coming up to forty. I was set in my ways. I had my life. It was difficult for both of us, but it seems to have worked out. We did the civil partnership ceremony in 2006. We live in Primrose Hill, a lovely area of London, which has now become very chic.

～

Selected Credits

Theatre

Hamlet, English Youth Theatre, Edinburgh Festival (1957; n/a). **Birmingham Rep:** *Hobson's Choice* (1960; David Buxton); *The Caretaker* (1961; Bernhard Hepton); *Getting Married* (1962; John Harrison); *Look Back in Anger* (1962; David Buxton); *Henry VIII* (1963; David Buxton). **Other:** *Saint Joan*, NT at the Old Vic (1963; John Dexter); *The Workhouse Donkey*, NT at CFT (1963; Stuart Burge); *Hamlet*, inaugural NT production at the Old Vic (October 22, 1963; Laurence Olivier); *The Recruiting Officer*, NT at the Old Vic (1963; William Gaskill); *Saint Joan*, NT at CFT (1963; John Dexter); *Andorra*, NT at the Old Vic (1964; Lindsay Anderson); *Hay Fever*, NT at the Old Vic (1964; Noël Coward); *Othello*, NT at CFT (1964; John Dexter); *Trelawny of the "Wells,"* 1965; NT at CFT (1965; Desmond O'Donovan); *As You Like It*, NT at the Old Vic (1967; Clifford Williams); *Tartuffe*, NT at the Old Vic (1967; Tyrone Guthrie); *Three Sisters*, NT at the Old Vic (1967; Laurence Olivier); *Much Ado about Nothing*, NT at the Old Vic (1967; Franco Zeffirelli); *The Advertisement*, NT at the Old Vic (1968; Laurence Olivier, Donald MacKechnie); *Love's Labour's Lost*, NT at the Old Vic (1968; Laurence Olivier); *Back to Methuselah*, NT at Old Vic (1969; Clifford Williams); *The Idiot*, NT at the Old Vic (1970; Anthony Quayle); *The White Devil*, NT at the Old Vic (1970; Frank Dunlop); *The Merchant of Venice*, NT at the Old

Vic; Cambridge Theatre; (1970–1971; Jonathan Miller); *A Woman Killed with Kindness*, NT at the Old Vic (1971; John Dexter); *Twelfth Night*, Prospect Theatre Company at the Round House (1973; Toby Robertson); *No Man's Land*, NT at the Old Vic (1975; Peter Hall); *Antony and Cleopatra*, Prospect Theatre Company at the Old Vic (1977; Toby Robertson); *Hamlet*, Old Vic (1977; Toby Robertson); *The Suicide*, ANTA Playhouse, New York (1980; Jonas Jurasas); *Cyrano de Bergerac*, RSC at the Barbican; George Gershwin, New York (1983–1984; Terry Hands); *Much Ado about Nothing*, George Gershwin, New York (1984–1985; Terry Hands); *Breaking the Code*, Yvonne Arnaud, Guildford; Theatre Royal Bath; Theatre Royal Haymarket; Neil Simon, New York (1986–1988; Clifford Williams); *Mad, Bad and Dangerous to Know*, Ahmanson at the Doolittle, Los Angeles; Ambassadors (1989, 1992; Jane McCulloch); *Kean*, Old Vic (1990; Sam Mendes); *Becket*, Theatre Royal Haymarket (1991; Elijah Moshinsky); *Macbeth*, RSC at the Barbican, tour (1993–1994; Adrian Noble); *God Only Knows*, Vaudeville (2001; Anthony Page); *The Tempest*, Old Vic production transfer from Sheffield Crucible (2003; Michael Grandage); *Don Carlos*, Gielgud (2005; Michael Grandage); *A Voyage round My Father*, Donmar at Wyndham's (2006; Thea Sharrock); *Twelfth Night*, Donmar at Wyndham's (2008; Michael Grandage); *Shakespeare's Women*, one-off fundraising performance for Almeida (2010; Michael Attenborough); *King Lear*, Llandudno, Wales; Donmar; UK tour, BAM, New York (2010–2011; Michael Grandage); *Heartbreak House*, CFT (2012; Richard Clifford); *Romeo and Juliet*, Garrick (2015; Kenneth Branagh)

Director
Hamlet (1988), Renaissance Theatre Company on the Road tour with Kenneth Branagh as Hamlet; also at Elsinore, Denmark; Phoenix

Film
Othello (1965); *Interlude* (1968); *Three Sisters* (1970); *Day of the Jackal* (1973); *Enigma* (1983); *Little Dorrit* (1988); *Henry V* (1989); *Dead Again* (1991); *Gladiator* (2000); *Gosford Park* (2001); *Margot* (2009); *The King's Speech* (2010); *Anonymous* (2011); *My Week with Marilyn* (2011); *Effie Gray* (2014); *Grace of Monaco* (2014); *Cinderella* (2015)

Television
BBC Sunday Night Play, "She Stoops to Conquer" (1961); *Much Ado about Nothing* (1967); *ITV Playhouse*, "The Photographer" (1967); *Budgie*, "Do Me a Favour" (1972); *The Pallisers*, eight episodes (1974; Ronald

Wilson, Hugh David); *The Rivals of Sherlock Holmes*, "The Secret of the Fox Hunter" (1974); *I, Claudius*, thirteen episodes (1976); *Philby, Burgess and Maclean* (1977); BBC Television Shakespeare, *Hamlet* (1980); *Tales of the Unexpected*, "Shin" (1980); *Inside the Third Reich* (1982); *The Secret Garden* (1987); *The Tenth Man* (1988); *Cadfael*, thirteen episodes (1994–1998); *The Old Curiosity Shop* (2007); *Frasier*, "The Show Must Go Off" (2001); *Dr. Who: Scream of the Shalka* (voice), five episodes (2003); *The Borgias*, two episodes (2011); *Last Tango in Halifax*, six episodes (2013); *Vicious*, six episodes (2013–2014)

Radio

Afternoon Drama, "Mayflies in the Afternoon" (2009; Neil Gardner); *Afternoon Drama*, BBC Radio 4, "The Last Tsar" (August 28, 2009; Jeremy Mortimer); *Afternoon Drama*, BBC Radio 4, "Gerontius" (2010; Martin Jenkins); *Classic Serial*, "I, Claudius" (2010–2011; Jonquil Panting)

Awards and Nominations

The Suicide, 1981, Drama Desk, Outstanding Actor in a Play, nominee; *Much Ado about Nothing*, 1983, *Evening Standard*, Best Actor, winner; 1985, Tony, Best Actor in a Play, winner; Drama Desk, Outstanding Actor in a Play, nominee; *Cyrano De Bergerac*, 1984, Olivier, Best Actor in a Revival, winner; also, Drama Desk, 1985, Outstanding Actor in a Play, nominee; *Breaking the Code*, 1988, Tony, Best Actor in a Play, nominee; also, Drama Desk, Outstanding Actor in a Play, nominee; *Uncle Vanya*, 2000, Drama Desk, Outstanding Actor in a Play, nominee; *Frasier*, "The Show Must Go Off," 2001, Emmy, Outstanding Guest Actor in a Comedy Series, winner; *Twelfth Night*, 2009, Olivier, Best Actor, winner

Honors

CBE, 1985; Knight First Class, Order of the Danneborg (Denmark), 1989; KBE, 1994

Publications

As Luck Would Have It (2013)

Notes

1. In an e-mail to the author on October 5, 2011, Lucinda Morrison, NT's head of press, wrote, "Sound technology is a complex tool for directors and sound designers and an area rarely understood by laymen, including actors! . . . We occasionally use mics in all our theatres where the needs of the production warrant it—must usually for musicals or shows where there is pronounced use of music and sound effects underneath dialogue. It's very rarely for simple amplification purposes."

2. The theatre seats just over 1,900, more than any other theatre in New York.

3. In an interview with Vinson in the January 1989 *Text and Performance Quarterly* (vol. 9, no. 1), he said of Jacobi, "I had never worked with an actor who was so willing to try new things and work on himself in the middle of the run of a show and I had never worked with one with such mental acumen."

4. Among productions in which Grandage appeared on stage was the 1985 production of *The Scarlet Pimpernel* at Her Majesty's with Sir Donald Sinden as Sir Percy, directed by Nicholas Hytner.

5. Sir Derek played Lear to great acclaim in Michael Grandage's Donmar Warehouse production in 2011.

6. On November 2, 2013, a fiftieth anniversary gala was held on the National's Olivier stage with a who's who of British theatre, which included scenes from some of the eight hundred productions at the complex since its opening in 1963. Among those actors who participated—and had all been on the National's stages at some point in the last fifty years—were Simon Russell Beale, Benedict Cumberbatch, Dame Judi Dench, Ralph Fiennes, Rory Kinnear, Dame Maggie Smith, and Penelope Wilton. Sir Derek finally appeared on a National stage in a scene from Harold Pinter's *No Man's Land* with Sir Michael Gambon, in which he had appeared in 1975 when the National's productions were presented at the Old Vic.

7. *The Hollow Crown* was originally devised and directed by John Barton as a one-off piece for the RSC. It is composed of speeches and music about British kings and queens from William the Conqueror to Queen Victoria.

8. It was a highly controversial departure at the time, and now under its current artistic director, Gregory Doran, the company returned to the Barbican for the 2014–2015 season as part of a two-year partnership.

∼

CHAPTER THIRTEEN

Felicity Kendal, CBE

Shoes make a character. No question about it.

The stage door to the Trafalgar Studios Theatre is just off an alley, a few steps from the square of the same name. As Felicity Kendal enters, the bright sun puts the actress in silhouette. She allows George, her caramel-colored spaniel, to precede her into the semidarkness of the stage door manager's confines. Without hesitation, the dog races up seventy-eight stairs to the actress's dressing room. She follows him up, not quite as friskily. That means that for every performance, the actress climbs seventy-eight stairs for makeup and costume; seventy-eight down for the perfor-mance; seventy-eight stairs up during the interval; down the stairs for the second act; seventy-eight up at the close of the performance; and finally down another seventy-eight and home after the curtain. At sixty-three, it's no wonder she has kept her youthful figure.

Barely five feet tall and with a distinctive husky voice, she could play a sexy pixie or perhaps even a female Puck. Seated in front of her makeup table, in the room that smells distinctly of fresh paint, she runs her hands through her hair—stylishly short and beautifully blonded; even when it falls in rumpled tendrils, it's attractive. Her makeup box sits atop a bright orange sari, which falls gracefully to her feet. Although not superstitious, "Foo," as friends and family refer to her, has two decades-old keepsakes in the box: a slip of paper from a fortune cookie she received early in her career: "You may not be a star, but you need not be a cloud" and a skull that had originally dangled from a key chain that her beloved older sister, Jennifer,[1] gave to her.

Born September 26, 1946, in Olton, Warwickshire, the actress recalls her childhood as "magical." As a baby, she went out to India with the family's troupe of actors, touring during the last days of the Raj. Traveling from Bombay [now Mumbai] to Darjeeling, Lahore to Delhi, Mysore to Calcutta (now Kolkata), she learned Hindi, which she can still speak fluently. The troupe was affectionately called "the Firm" by Kendal's father, who led the company; he had fallen in love with India during an ENSA tour. Their repertoire included Shakespeare and Shaw and Sheridan, all of which were performed for audiences of students, nuns, British colonials, and maharajahs. India's prime minister, Jawaharlal Nehru, attended a number of performances as did Lord and Lady Mountbatten, all of whom became patrons of the company.

Kendal's first stage appearance was A Midsummer Night's Dream when she was just a few months old; at five, she played the changeling in the same play; at the advanced age of nine, she played one of her first gender-reversed roles as Macduff's son in Macbeth; and at twelve, she played her first major speaking role as Puck in Dream.

"How now, spirit! whither wander you?" was her mantra as an itinerant actor for more than a dozen years with the family firm. At seventeen, after attending thirteen convent schools, she left India and returned to London during the swinging sixties to try out her talent in film and theatre. Since then, she has appeared in more than fifty theatre productions and two dozen television series.

Kendal, known for such disparate accolades as the Evening Standard Award's Best Actress to the Rear of the Year award, was just completing a run of The Last Cigarette at the Trafalgar Studios. The production had just exhaled its last puff of smoke, and the closing notice had been posted. The play premiered earlier at the Minerva Theatre, Chichester, and then transferred to London, where critics gave it less-than-positive reviews. The play, by Simon Gray, was adapted by Hugh Whitemore from his friend's The Smoking Diaries and reflects on the writer's early life and then death in 2011.

Three actors play the writer: Nicholas Le Prevost (with whom Kendal had appeared more than a decade previously in Absolute Turkey, directed by Peter Hall), Jasper Britton, and Kendal, in one of her gender-bending roles. The actors all wear the identical costumes: blue work shirts over white T-shirts, chinos, and soft-soled shoes. As Gray the writer, the actors tap away at a trio of typewriters; as Gray, who smoked sixty cigarettes a day, they smoke the herbal variety on stage, lighting up and puffing in unison.

～

How do you take on the obligation of a production such as *The Last Cigarette*, which becomes very personal during the rehearsal and performances, and then closing notices are posted?

I think it's wonderful that we're doing this play, a very difficult one. Actually, it's not a play: it's a "piece." I had known Simon and agreed to do the play while he was still alive. I have a most wonderful postcard from him, which I received not long before his death. He wrote that he was so glad we were going to do it and that I was going to be in it. This has been a tremendous opportunity to make this production an homage to him.

It's the nature of the business that you commit to something, and then . . . it's over; it's ephemeral. That's part of being an actor. If you want security and want to hold on to something, don't be an actor.

Photo by Brian@brianaris.com

Everything is new: a new show, a new dressing room. To be quite honest, in an ideal world, I would never do anything for very long anyway. First of all, to me, the joy now is reading the script and thinking, "I want to do it." Then it's the joy of working with these wonderful actors, like Nicholas and Jasper. The rehearsal process is the highlight to me. Then opening it and honing it and getting it well oiled and getting the energy that's needed to get out there and do it. To me, ten to twelve weeks is exactly perfect.

How do you feel about the closing notice?

It's unfortunate that we didn't get the audience that we should have had. We were thinking of taking it to the Royal Court after Chichester, but there wasn't space for it there. At the Royal Court, it would have had an audience that doesn't expect just entertainment for their money; that's a theatre where they expect more thinking entertainment, thought-provoking entertainment on the stage, which this is. For this show—in this theatre—our audience hasn't picked up on some of the things that we expected them to do normally, so it is a bit disheartening. It's very easy just to say to yourself, "Uh, oh," but we still give 100 percent.

I'm comfortable, though, because I don't have to prove anything to anybody except myself. I used to have a passion for how I was being observed, how I was being judged. I think you have to have that as a young actor. I feel, now, like I come into a production with an awful lot that I've done before, so how I'm judged on a particular evening—or matinee—isn't so vital to my whole body of work, as long as I know I'm doing my best. I'm in a position now where I can say that because I've got more work behind me, there is still more ahead.

In the beginning, you were a member of your family's traveling troupe of actors. Your family's travels were part of a long tradition, even as that tradition was coming to an end.

We were sort of on the cusp of the British Raj world, a period that had already ended, but we extended it in a way because my father had a foot in each camp. He knew the British counsels and also those who were to be the future of India, and the democracy that was on the horizon.

In the old days, the actor-manager, in this case my father, would ordinarily have left his children in the UK. But he brought my sister and me out with him. He and my mother, Laura Liddell, were the stars of the company. It became more or less like a circus troupe, or, like snails, we took our house with us. We had trunks and trunks of costumes and props, scenery: everything we needed to survive as a touring rep company.

I've been back to India several times, and I realize nothing like what we did could be replicated today.

Your mother gave you some acting advice, which you still follow to this day.

That's absolutely true. She told me, "Never give less than 100 percent, even at matinees."

There were three people in the audience on a recent Sunday matinee here, and just the week before, I'd said to the boys in the play [referring to Le Prevost and Britton], "My mum said, 'There's always *somebody* out there.'"

Your mother also had a process for learning lines, which she passed on to you. How does that method work?

She taught me a very old-fashioned way of learning lines. It comes from the repertory companies where they were performing a different show every week, and they had to find a way to learn the lines quickly. They found that if something was actually written down, the brain remembers better. If the lines are written in red, you can remember more, so I tend to write in two colors: red and black.

What I do is copy out cues on one side of the page and lines on the other side. That is my mother's technique. I still do that, but, funnily enough, I didn't do that on this current production.

Your father gave you several theatrical aphorisms. What are some of those that you have incorporated into your roles?

One of most helpful was "The curtain always goes up and always goes down. What happens in the middle is your affair."

It's too true. It's easy in a long run to think, "Oh, it was a bad house tonight because they weren't laughing as much." It's really up to us, the actors, not to allow anything to alter the journey through the evening.

By nature, we, as actors, might say, "I wasn't good because of this or that," but that's the job. In a funny way, maybe that's why I like short runs. I really do have to do *every single night* as if it's the first time I'm going to do it, which becomes progressively more difficult as the weeks go on.

I've already taken into account that every night is fresh, but as we come to the end of a run, there's something that happens: it becomes more precious, so we automatically do it as if it's fresh. That's our training. We will take extra care because these will be the last few performances. Does that make sense? It becomes much more difficult to actually think, "This is the first time." I have to think, "I'm here in the present," and then it *is* the first time.

Another bit of advice my father gave me was "Rehearse in the shoes that you'll wear for a role." But it's more than the shoes. If I'm lucky enough to be with some top designer, their concern is at the fittings of what I'll be wearing. Only after that do they ask what size shoe I wear. But because of my father's advice, I go for the shoes first. The shoes *have* to be right. I can't play someone who's wealthy and aristocratic in ordinary shoes. They have to be beautiful shoes because then I'll walk in a special way, walk in a different way. The shoes make a character. No question about it.

In *The Last Cigarette*, our shoes are very important. We're wearing the same kind of shoes that Simon wore, the only shoes he wore, sort of espadrilles. If we were wearing different shoes, the way we move would be different.

Shoes were also important when I was playing in *On the Razzle* at the National. I was playing a boy, Christopher, and I realized I needed to have some big boy's boots. I got them, and everything came together. As soon as I was literally "in the shoes" of the character, it made a difference.

What other pithy bits of advice did your father offer?

There were quite a few:

"Always give yourself the luxury of time before and after a show."

"Don't forget to breathe. Breathe deeply before you go on stage."

"Remember that your stock in trade is your voice and your body."

And an especially amusing one: "In love scenes, remember that the audience must be thrilled, not you."

How important is your father's counsel for an actor to "listen to the whole play, not just your role"?

Absolutely important. It may sound old-fashioned, but it's a classic observation. One of the reasons is that as part of the whole, I can't think for a minute that it's *my* scene. If I don't listen to the whole, I—or any of us—won't know how it went before we come on or the rhythm of it when we are on. How do we know what note to come in on if we're not listening? How do we know what energy we should be providing for the entire piece if we isolate ourselves?

When you finally left "the Firm" and came to London from India on your own, you had to learn to audition. What was the audition process like for you then and now that you have had a career?

At that point, I was young and vulnerable. I needed a job. I needed the money. Auditions are cruel, but it's important to do them because it makes you brave. It's like bungee jumping: you have to be able to jump. Basically, an audition is going into a situation where there are forty people trying to win the role, and thirty-nine of them are going to lose.

I personally never got any good jobs from an audition, except for *Minor Murder*. I auditioned for Olivier just before the Old Vic moved to the National. I was terrified—terrified—at the audition, which was in a temporary hut. And I did *not* get the part.

[In her memoir,[2] Kendal recalls that audition:]

I knocked on the door of one of the Nissen huts that were office and rehearsal rooms for the Vic. . . . [Olivier] was charming . . . and much taller than I had imagined. His two hands shaking mine were warm and reassuring. He introduced me to Kenneth Tynan. . . . I had no idea who he was. [I found out later that] Tynan had reviewed *Shakespeare Wallah* [Kendal's debut film] for *The Observer*. He loved the film and described me as Buckingham's daughter: "their Ophelia is charmingly played by the dumpling-faced Felicity Kendal."

I might have worked on stages all over India from the age of five, but I was totally unprepared for the trauma of auditioning for the great actor. . . . I launched into Ophelia's madness [scene] with a sinking heart, then swept straight into *Saint Joan*. . . . My legs began to shake uncontrollably . . . and by the time I got to Viola [*Twelfth Night*], my voice, once quite strong but weakened by lack of practice, had deteriorated into a high-pitched squeak. I got to the end. I knew that I had failed miserably.

Even within the last ten or fifteen years, if I go in to discuss a role or do one of those video things, I never get the part. I think there's something, a psychological block. When I walk in, I think I must project, "I hate this." So I don't get the role!

Your body of work has included plays by some of the most famous of contemporary playwrights. How would you compare the dialogue of such disparate writers as David Hare, Tom Stoppard, and Alan Ayckbourn, among others?

They all have such different styles.

David Hare's dialogue is probably the most difficult to learn. On the page, it looks very naturalistic—it sounds naturalistic—but it's actually very structured. Alan Ayckbourn's is lovely, and Michael Frayn's is witty, so it's fun.

Tom's isn't hard to learn. What *is* difficult is that he endlessly inserts something—maybe physics—which you don't know anything about until you do your homework. He always gives you something that you don't know . . . yet. The physical research absolutely has to be done, either by yourself or possibly by the director. That's certainly true in *Arcadia*.[3]

The interesting thing about Simon's *The Last Cigarette* is that what he wrote in his *Diaries* was written to be read. He was a clever enough writer to write in two different forms. If he wants a laugh, for instance, his structure is different in a play than in book form. In a book, the reader can go on and on and on and doesn't have to stop.

In a comedy, you need a feed line, and then another line to leave space for the audience to "get it" and then laugh. This varies quite often. In this play, sometimes the audience will laugh in one place one night, and in other nights, they don't. It's not structured to signal the audience to "laugh here." If there's no laugh, we just have to keep going. We can't play it as if there's going to be a laugh because it may not come. So going back to what my father advised: listen.

Is there a clue about playing for laughs?

One of the things I've learned over the years, depending on the cleverness of the playwright, is that if it *is* comedy, the less you do *your* bit and the more you do *his* bit, the better. I remember talking to Tom Stoppard, and we were saying that an actor was working to make the scene funny. Tom said, "If only the actor would stop trying to be funny and let *me* do it." That is great advice. If you've got a great playwright, you don't need to do anything but be true to what you're saying. If it's not a great script, you may have to embellish it, but with a good one, you shouldn't have to.

Besides those playwrights, you have worked with some of the iconic directors of the British theatre, including Peter Hall, for at least three decades. What makes his style of directing something you continue to find inspiring?

I've worked with him a number of times. I've actually lost count. My first work with him was in his production of *Amadeus* with Paul Scofield. That's more than thirty years ago. His process of working is as a great theatre director would be. First, he loves actors but not in a "lovey" way. He creates an atmosphere of absolute comfort. He's not the slightest bit nervous about anything. Projecting this is what makes an actor very brave. He never overburdens an actor, but he knows when to tell an actor to push further.

He has a totally democratic manner. If somebody who has just come in to help move the furniture says, "I think this, that, and the other," he will listen to the suggestion, not only with politeness but also with genuine openness. He has the ability to listen to *every* point of view. There are directors who are bullies and dictatorial. Peter's not like that at all. He has something to offer every actor, and if the actor doesn't want it and will not work *with* him but works *against* him, the role is going to go to someone else. If an actor fights Peter's talent, that actor will lose. He will either be ignored or will have to move on.

Peter has the ear of a musician, so he's passionate about dialogue being correct and being heard. He also has the wonderful ability to push, to nudge us a bit. He loves naturalism, but, on the other hand, he has worked with productions using masks.

I've worked with him on a tiny production, Samuel Beckett's *Happy Days*, and then he'll go and do operas or other huge productions. It's all those things that make him a great director and bring me back to work with him again and again. He's a rainbow of a director.

Speaking of *Happy Days*, it's a claustrophobic challenge for an actress. How did you overcome that?

That was one of my favorite roles, not in the sense that it was fun but certainly favorite in that it was an experience that I would have given anything not to have missed with Peter. He had done the first production with Peggy Ashcroft at the Old Vic in the seventies, and he knew the play. He had asked me to play Winnie three or four years earlier and I said, "I can't." Then he came back again, and I read it once more and realized the poetry of the piece. So, so real. I again said, "I can't *not* do this."

Halfway through as I was learning it, I suddenly thought, "I can do the first bit but that last twenty minutes . . . when she is buried up to her waist in sand, I get claustrophobia." It really made me scared, but then this is the wonderful thing about the theatre: you just do it.

In fact, in the end, it became quite easy [to be buried]. It wasn't that I was buried up to here [she raises a hand to her chest]. It's that I mustn't move. To me, that's the ultimate claustrophobia.

Many actors believe that once they have finished a production, they will never work again. Do you share that attitude?

No. I think there was a time that I felt if something didn't go well, then I didn't know what I'd be doing next. But now I know that's not true. It's not that I'm insecure about the next thing. But that feeling can stay with you forever.

Do you read reviews immediately after press night or wait until further in the run?

I usually read reviews the week *after* the play has opened, when I have everything together, after I've cleaned the debris from the last job, or even preparing for the next one. It is an extraordinarily psychological thing, which is quite amazing.

I find that I don't quite believe the good ones, and I absolutely believe the bad ones. When a critic writes, "She's just not up to it," I think, "Right. You've spotted it."

Or another one might write, "Tonight she was magic," and I think, "Yes, it was, but I'm not sure I can re-create it," or "Maybe it's because the critic liked my work before."

If I read something about what I've done early on and if it's alarmingly upsetting, that's not good. If I read the same words about the same night, which is over anyway, they don't have the same power.

How important are critics in the theatrical scheme of things?

Critics are very important to us, the actors, but I wouldn't have their job for anything in the world. I do think it's important that we know what people think about our work. We do have some very good critics today [but she won't name them]. I think they truly want to believe more than anything that what they're going to review is going to be a great evening; they've seen so many that aren't. They don't go in thinking, "This is going to be a disaster." They have very high expectations because they've been bored too many times. Very rarely are they completely wrong. Artistically, if the whole lot of reviews is taken together, the critics are usually right.

If critics can pinpoint the positives and negatives of a production, should they try their hand at writing a play?

Oh, no! They're not that kind of writer. It's also much easier to act in a play than to write one. Writing a play is a really difficult thing to do.

What's the most surprising thing about being an actor, about the art and craft of acting?

What still surprises me in the theatre after all these years is how it makes me very glad to be in the business. It's how, with all the technology and all the advances that we have, people will still collect together, sit in the dark, are quiet, and meditate on somebody else's thoughts. This concept of coming together is deep in our psyche. It still surprises me about the people who turn up at the theatre and, for whatever reason, they're happy to let us go on and trust us for that period of time. We want to do that as human beings. That's my answer to anyone who asks, "Is the theatre dead?" It's all sort of magic, and it is always a surprise.

Your memoir is entitled *White Cargo*. What is the significance?

My father was performing in Leon Gordon's play with that name when I was born.

In the memoir, you refer to your father as "Geoffrey" rather than "Daddy." Why?

It was purely a decision for the book that I didn't refer to him as "Daddy." It was to give him his character and the respect as a person I felt he deserved. "Geoffrey" is who he was, whereas "Daddy" is not. The book is about Geoffrey Kendal—who had changed his surname from Bragg—not Daddy. It would have been a different book if I'd called him Daddy.

At the age of about nine, you were playing Macduff's son, your first speaking role. You panicked and ran toward a "chink of light." Before you got

too far your father grabbed you and threw you onto the stage. Are you running toward something or from something even today as an actor?

The thing about writing is that you write what you feel at that moment. It's absolutely true for the moment. I probably wouldn't write that now.

I've always wanted to go from one job to another, one house to another, one place to another. That's how I grew up. It was natural for me because that's how I started out, traveling from place to place with my parents' theatre troupe. If you need to know where you're going to be next week, don't be an actor. If you embrace that, each surprise leads you to another. You could get very frightened of change, and that can't work in this business.

Your memoir takes your life and career up to 1998. Is it time to write another volume?

No, not for some time. I wrote everything I was interested in for *White Cargo*. Up to that point, I told all the important bits about the people and places in my life. I have to get to another phase of my life to look back again. It's been ten years. I think it needs another five.

⌣

At this point, with George now snoring contentedly at her feet, the actress turns her attention to the makeup table and begins the process of becoming one of the Simon Grays.

Selected Credits

Theatre

Tour with parents' company, Shakespeareana, in India and elsewhere: *The Merchant of Venice, Hamlet, A Midsummer Night's Dream, Twelfth Night.* *Minor Murders*, Strand (1967; Reginald Denham); *Back to Methuselah*, NT at the Old Vic (1969; Clifford Williams); *Midsummer Night's Dream*, Regent's Park (1970; Richard Digby Day); *Much Ado about Nothing*, Regent's Park (1970; David Conville); *Kean*, Globe [now Gielgud] (1970; Frank Hauser); *'Tis a Pity She's a Whore*, Actor's Company at Arts Theatre, Cambridge (1972; David Giles); *The Norman Conquests*, Greenwich, Globe [now Gielgud]; Apollo (1974; Eric Thompson); *Evening Light*, Bristol Old Vic (1975; Richard Cottrell); *Arms and the Man*, Greenwich (1978; Robert Chetwyn); *Clouds*, Duke of York's (1978; Michael Rudman); *Amadeus*, NT, Olivier (1979; Peter Hall); *Othello*, NT, Olivier (1980; Peter Hall); *On the Razzle*, NT, Lyttelton (1981; Peter Wood); *The Second Mrs. Tanqueray*, NT, Lyttelton (1982; Michael Rudman); *The Real Thing*, Strand [now Novello] (1982; Peter Wood); *Jumpers*, Aldwych (1985; Peter Wood); *Made in Bangkok*, Aldwych (1986; Michael Blakemore); *Hapgood*, Aldwych (1988; Michael Codron); *Much Ado about Nothing*, Strand (1989; Elijah Moshinsky); *Ivanov*, Strand (1989; Elijah Moshinsky); *Hidden Laughter*, Theatre Royal Brighton; Vaudeville (1990; Simon Gray); *Heartbreak House*, Theatre Royal Haymarket (1992; Trevor Nunn); *Arcadia*, Theatre Royal Bath; NT, Lyttelton (1993; Trevor Nunn); *An Absolute Turkey*, Globe [now Gielgud] (1994; Peter Hall); *Indian Ink*, Aldwych (1995; Peter Wood); *Mind Millie for Me*, Theatre Royal Haymarket (1996; Peter Hall); *Waste*, Old Vic (1997; Peter Hall); *Alarms and Excursions*, Theatre Royal Bath; Gielgud (1998; Michael Blakemore); *Fallen Angels*, Theatre Royal Bath, Apollo (2000; Michael Rudman); *Humble Boy*, Gielgud (2002; John Caird); *Happy Days*, Theatre Royal Bath; transfer to Arts Theatre (2003; Peter Hall); *Amy's View*, Theatre Royal Bath (2006; Peter Hall); *Amy's View*, Garrick (2007; Peter Hall); *The Vortex*, Apollo (2008; Peter Hall); *The Last Cigarette*, Minerva, Chichester; transfer to Trafalgar Studios (2009; Richard Eyre); *Mrs. Warren's Profession*, Theatre Royal Bath; transfer to Comedy [now Pinter] (2009–2010; Michael Rudman); *Relatively Speaking*, Theatre Royal Bath; transfer to Wyndham's (2012–2013; Lindsay Posner); *Chin-Chin*, Theatre Royal Bath; UK tour (2013; Michael Rudman); *Hay Fever*, Cambridge Arts; Theatre Royal Bath; Queensland Performing Arts Centre, Adelaide Festival Centre, Australia; Duke of York's (2014–2015; Lindsay Posner)

Film
Shakespeare Wallah (1965); *On the Razzle* (1983); *Valentino* (1997); *Parting Shots* (1999)

Television
The Wednesday Play, "The Mayfly and the Frog" (1966); *ITV Play of the Week*, "Person Unknown" (1967); *The Man in the Suitcase*, "Blind Spot" (1968); *The Good Life* [a.k.a. *Good Neighbors*], thirty episodes (1975–1978; John Howard Davies); *Edward the King*, seven episodes (1975); *ITV Sunday Night Drama*, "Now Is Too Late" (1976); *Clouds of Glory: William and Dorothy* (1978); *BBC Television Shakespeare*, *Twelfth Night* (1980); *Solo*, thirteen episodes (1982); *The Mistress*, twelve episodes (1985–1987); *The Camomile Lawn*, four episodes (1992); *Honey for Tea*, seven episodes (1994); *Rosemary and Thyme*, twenty-two episodes (2003–2006); *Dr. Who*, "The Unicorn and the Wasp" (2008)

Awards and Nominations

Norman Conquests, 1976, Variety Club Award, Most Promising Newcomer, winner; *Amadeus*, 1980, Clarence Derwent Award, Best Female in a Supporting Role, winner; *Much Ado about Nothing* and *Ivanov*, 1989, *Evening Standard*, Best Actress, winner; *Fallen Angels*, 2001, Variety Club Award, Best Actress, winner

Honors

CBE, 1995

Notes

1. Jennifer Kendal, thirteen years older than Felicity, married Bollywood star Shashi Kapoor. They had three children. Jane, as the family called her, died from cancer in 1984 at the age of fifty-one.

2. Felicity Kendal, *White Cargo*, 244–245.

3. Kendal had a long-term relationship with Stoppard and starred in productions of several of his plays, including *Jumpers*, *Hapgood*, *Indian Ink*, and *The Real Thing*. She has since reunited with her former husband, director Michael Rudman.

~

CHAPTER FOURTEEN

Sir Ben Kingsley, CBE

As a stage actor, I was a landscape artist; as a cinema actor, I am a portrait artist.

The interview with Sir Ben had initially been arranged to take place prior to the premiere screening of his film Fifty Dead Men Walking *in London. But the traffic from his home in the Cotswolds into London was bumper to bumper, and the interview had to be cancelled, as he went directly to the theatre.*

However, several months later, the actor was in Los Angeles to attend the Academy Awards, and the interview was rescheduled at the famed Hollywood landmark hotel, the Chateau Marmont, where writers are hunched over their PCs, tapping out their next scripts on the crowded sun-dappled patio. Groups of people are huddled together, talking in low tones about their next "deal." A few tourists are discreetly snapping photos. Inside, the logs in the fireplace burn brightly, and guests and journalists lounge on overstuffed sofas, reading the trade papers and drinking midmorning coffees.

Upon arrival, Sir Ben is escorted to a table by a receptionist. The actor is wearing a black V-necked T-shirt topped by a brown corduroy jacket. He is sporting his trademark interpretation of a Vandyke beard and mustache, which he wears both on-screen and off; his head is shaved as it has been for decades. When his order for a pot of tea arrives, he pours a full cup, but puts aside the packet of French acacia honey that accompanies it.

His Elegy *costar Patricia Clarkson unexpectedly stops by to greet him. In a courtly manner, he introduces the interviewer. "He's a great kisser," she laughs over her shoulder as she turns away.*

After the conversation has begun, an admirer interrupts, and the actor courteously excuses himself to her, indicating he is in the midst of an interview and is unable to chat.

Sir Ben answers questions about his life and career seriously and responds thoughtfully to each question. His distinctive voice and his dark eyes reveal an actor who is committed and dedicated to his craft.

～

In the beginning?

I was born December 31, 1943, in Snainton, near Scarborough, North Yorkshire, to Rahimdulla Bhanji and Anne Goodman. My mother was a British actress, and my father, a physician, was Indian. I have a brother and two sisters. Some years after my birth, we moved from Yorkshire, across the Pennines to Salford, near Manchester, where my father established a practice.

I had what I consider a privileged childhood. We traveled, and I attended Manchester Grammar, a rather high-end, very competitive school. It was where I met Robert Powell, who became a great friend and is a fine actor. I studied the sciences, physics, and chemistry. At the time, I had the grand idea of going to university and studying medicine like my father.

Where I was brought up, we had brass bands, silver bands, operatic societies, orchestras, dramatic societies, and such. This was before television, so the community had a marvelous way of providing its own entertainment.

When I left grammar school, I was recruited into an amateur dramatic society, the Salford Players,[1] a really wonderful group. I did three plays with them, and, by the end of the third one, I was the star! I also found at that time that I was interested in music. I wrote rock songs and sang them on the radio, accompanying myself on the guitar. Musicality still plays a part of my life now as it helps me with my dialects and gives me a sense of balance, which I need as an actor.

What about higher education?

I didn't attend university. All my degrees are honorary. When I was awarded an honorary doctorate from the Scarborough campus of the University of Hull, Virginia Baroness Bottomley, the school's chancellor, introduced me as "doctor—sir," with a huge grin on her face.

What prompted you to make acting your career?

We were living in Salford when my parents took me—I was about eight—to a film entitled *Never Take No for an Answer*, directed by Ralph Smart and

Sir Ben Kingsley in honorary degree robes, 2008. *Photo courtesy of University of Hull, Scarborough campus*

Maurice Cloche, about a young Italian boy and his donkey. I looked like the boy Peppino,[2] and everyone at the cinema that day thought I was the child actor. I enjoyed the attention.

Years later, when I was about nineteen, the idea of becoming an actor cemented itself in my mind when I bought a standing room ticket to see Ian Holm in a Royal Shakespeare Company production of *Richard III* at Stratford, directed by John Barton and Peter Hall. That was a turning point. Within about two years, I was asked to join the RSC!

The anecdote about your audition at RADA is worth retelling.

My birth name is Krishna Bhanji, which I dutifully wrote on the school application. On the day of auditions, I, along with a large group, waited to be called and for the process to begin. I heard an assistant call out, "Christina Blange." I thought it was the young woman sitting next to me—who I fancied—who was being called. No one replied. The name was called again. Then I realized that because of my terrible handwriting, I was the one being called. In the end, handwriting aside, I wasn't accepted.

There are distinct Yorkshire and Mancunion accents to which you were exposed as a youngster, but you don't have either. But with your musical ear, you have been able to use some of those regional accents in your characters.

We didn't have an "accent" as such at home. At school, the accent wasn't strong, but I find that the accents are like playing a musical composition in different keys, and I've been able to use them in several of my roles. The Manchester accent is one I enjoy doing. In *Fifty Dead Men Walking*, I use that accent as my character is from the Lancashire police force. The accent I used in *Sexy Beast* is a South London accent.

In Brad Anderson's *Transsiberian*, I spoke Russian. I learned it phonetically and had mixed reports from people. One woman I met at a party took it upon herself to tell me how terrible my Russian was and how it ruined the film for her. Why do people take the trouble to tell you how bad something is? It's extraordinarily rude.

What was the trajectory of your career in the early 1960s?

Sometime after the fiasco at RADA, and after a short time with an educational theatre group, I went up to Stoke-on-Trent, where I reunited with my school chum, Robert Powell. We were actors and acting ASMs at the Victoria Theatre. When we were introduced, he didn't recognize me. He thought he was going to see his friend "Krish."

At my father's suggestion, I had changed my name from the ethnic-sounding one to the one that has stood me in good stead since. I took his school nickname, Ben, and for my last name, I took the one that my grandfather was known by, so it wasn't surprising that Robert didn't recognize me when I was introduced as Ben Kingsley.

And the interest in music continued?

Yes, and it almost changed the direction of my career. Robert and I appeared in a play by Alan Plater about 1966 that we reshaped into a play with music called *A Smashing Day*, but it was not a *proper* musical. We wrote the music. I played the guitar, and Robert played the harmonica. We opened in a little theatre in the North of England. Our director, Peter Cheeseman, somehow got onto the Beatles' manager, Brian Epstein, who came up to see the show, and he liked it so much, he eventually brought us into the West End at the Arts Theatre.

One evening, Brian brought John Lennon and Ringo Starr to see the performance. They didn't actually come backstage; I met them at the back of the auditorium where they said [Sir Ben lapses into an incomprehensible Liverpudlian accent], which I think the gist of what they said was, "'ave a go!"

I think Brian thought they could convince me that he could shape my future as a rock star and wanted me to see the famous Beatles' Northern Songs publisher, Dick James. I met with him, and whilst cigar smoke drifted around me, I thought, "No," and went on to the RSC. Although I didn't choose that path, music has continued to be part of my life.[3]

You appeared at the Chichester Festival Theatre for a season, and then you auditioned for the Royal Shakespeare Company. Who did you audition for at the RSC, and what were your audition pieces?

This was just after the Chichester productions of *The Cherry Orchard* and *Macbeth*. At the age of twenty-three, I auditioned for Trevor Nunn, then artistic director of the RSC.[4] I think I did something from *Luther* by John Osborne, a speech from *Richard III*, and I think something from *Little Malcolm and His Struggle against the Eunuchs* by David Halliwell.

One of your earliest appearances with the RSC was in a production of Sean O'Casey's *The Silver Tassie*. What do you recall about that production?

That production included Patrick Stewart and Helen Mirren. They have done very well, indeed! It was an extraordinary role for me. As the Croucher, I was a shattered piece of meat from the World War I trenches. Bits and pieces of my character were held together with bandages. During rehearsal, I asked the director, David Jones, if I could rehearse with a paper bag over my head. He agreed. Once I put the bag on, my voice changed, and it came out as sort of a metallic roar. I don't know where it came from, but that bag gave me the character.

As a note, I spent more than a decade with the RSC, but not a continuous decade.

Once you were part of that prestigious company, you participated in several iconic Shakespearean productions, one of which was A *Midsummer Night's Dream* in 1971, in which you played Demetrius.

It is *still* famous. We usually had somewhere around six or seven weeks, but I think for this production, we had ten weeks in Stratford, a very generous rehearsal period. The director, Peter Brook, and the company really felt we were custodians of this remarkable piece of information locked in a play that was crucial to the seasons, life, our relation to the earth, all in a spiritual and intellectual way. It was all held together by the genius of Shakespeare and his extraordinary grasp of mythology far older than his time. We became the caretakers of this living, breathing piece of urgent information about life. We were able to convey it urgently to our audience.

Peter's concept is that if an event, in this case the play, lacks any urgency, then it isn't worth participating in the event, and it certainly isn't worth presenting it to an audience. I had probably seen other interpretations of the play, but I can't remember them. And now I'm unable to watch any production because ours is the only one I know.

Your interpretation of Hamlet in the 1975 RSC production was, to say the least, unexpected. You actually left the theatre in midperformance. Where did that concept originate?

Yes, I came up with that idea. We were in the original Other Place in Stratford, so, after the speech that begins, "O, what a rogue and peasant slave am I . . ." [Act II, scene ii] and as I said, "Fie upon't . . . ," I walked through the audience down the central aisle and left through the doors at the back of the building. The audience heard these doors close with a crash. Then I, as Hamlet, decide to rejoin the play at one of the many fulcrum moments.

Many actors and directors consider the central moment in the play as "To be or not to be . . . ," but there are other instances where Hamlet wonders whether it really is worthwhile to remain. I decided that *my* Hamlet would leave the play, but return seconds later, completely refreshed and invigorated by a new set of ideas that he shares with the audience with that terrific urgency that I mentioned. Physically, the idea worked very well.

The beautiful thing about that role—one of the many beautiful layers in the creation of the character—is that the actor is able to inhabit it so fully, thanks to the genius of the writing. The journey of the actor on stage exactly parallels the journey of the character across his landscape, so that the play does logically begin with Hamlet announcing to the audience that he is completely incapable of getting to the end of the play with any kind of resolution. Then, in the middle of the play, he debates leaving the play forever. At the end of the play, he declares that he has completely expressed himself, and there is nothing more to say.

With my leaving the theatre, then, I think the audience did understand that this was something quite visceral, for both them and the actor. The role provides the actor with an extraordinary architectural journey, and if the actor is able to weld himself to that part, then the part will take him, and he won't know if he's saying Shakespeare's lines or his own lines. He won't know whether he *is* Hamlet or if he is an actor *as* Hamlet. It was a sublime experience to play the role.

Besides the RSC, you appeared at the Royal Court, a London theatre with a reputation of presenting cutting-edge, avant-garde plays. What was your association with that theatre?

I was part of the Athol Fugard season under his direction at the theatre in *Statements after an Arrest under the Immorality Act* as Errol Philander in 1974, with Yvonne Bryceland, his favorite actress. She was to Athol what Billie Whitelaw was to Samuel Beckett. There was that symbiotic relationship. Athol not only directed this wonderful play but he also became a great friend.

This was at the height of apartheid, and I had to be guided by Athol because I had no experience whatever with South Africa. I'd been there once, briefly, after apartheid ended. I was in two of his other plays, *Hello and Goodbye* with Janet Suzman, which he didn't direct, and later I did his *Dimetos* with Paul Scofield and Bryceland.

What about a playwright, such as Athol Fugard, as a director? And as a person?

Although you wouldn't think so, he's amusing, witty, and fiercely intelligent. He's tremendously articulate and has a grasp of the absurdities of apartheid, its ludicrous, hideous nature.

As a director, he's very participatory. He finds ways of joining in without showing the actors anything. He becomes an emotional ingredient in the rehearsal room rather than just the objective eye and is able to measure the emotional urgency and emotional temperature of what we, as actors, are attempting to convey.

As an actor, either in a one-man show such as *Kean* or sharing the stage with others, everyone in the theatre—actors and audience—has to enter into a conspiracy to participate in the action of the play and understand the characters. How does that happen?

It's terribly hard to talk about acting without talking utter crap. It really is. It's a struggle to try and articulate it because there are so many young actors blundering into this relationship between audiences and themselves, and they are utterly clueless about the urgency of knowing the history of mythology and storytelling in our society.

That "conspiracy" never takes place in the rehearsal room. It will only take place with that unique chemistry with the "tribe"—the audience—surrounding the storytellers—the actors. I've been told by people in the audience after a performance that the boundary between them and the actor was transcended and became something else altogether.

There is the shrinking of our social skills and our ability to empathize with one another because of these little plasma screens now being the primary relationship in a young person's life. That in itself is very, very threatening. It's spawning a generation of what I can only describe as "wannabe" actors who have no sense of urgency about being prepared to tell stories. If you want to be an actor, there has to be that compulsion to tell stories. If that isn't there, all the rest is bunk.

Acting has to be spontaneous and come from the subconscious. Otherwise it looks conscious and studied. I can tell when actors are doing that. I want to say, "Go back to your dressing room. Stop showing off! Come back when you can show us something that we can recognize as a human being."

Not only have you played real-life characters but also characters who were in tragic circumstances. How do you work within those parameters, which could be personally and professionally intimidating?

I don't know. I just don't know. But I do have a relationship with a terrible, indigestible part of European history in terms of my work. It has been terrifying in some instances. In some cases, the impossible was put on film.

My first experience with playing that type of character was when I played Simon Wiesenthal more than twenty years ago in *Murderers among Us*, directed by Brian Gibson. I had the privilege of meeting the Nazi hunter in Vienna and spent quite a lot of time with him. I grew tremendously fond of him, and, I believe, he grew fond of me. He used to introduce me with, "He's like a son to me." He'd say this with his arm around me. [Sir Ben makes the encircling gesture as he says this with a Viennese accent.] Wiesenthal was one of our great prophets; he was an Old Testament prophet walking around in a suit. We ignore him at our peril.

I was at the receiving end of him as a remarkable storyteller, a shatteringly moving storyteller. Recollections, memories, and, again, those causes and effects. He was watching me as I was filming the liberation of Mauthausen concentration camp, and I was crawling across the ground. Brian called, "Cut."

There was Simon in tears. I went to him, and sat with him and held his hand. It was like a transfusion from that man to me.

Wiesenthal's story was not the only Holocaust-themed story in which you were involved. How difficult was it for you to accept the role of Itzhak Stern in the highly acclaimed film *Schindler's List*, just a few years later?

It was harrowing. I had to be persuaded to take the role. I didn't want to visit the Holocaust again so soon. When director Steven Spielberg asked me to play Stern, I asked him, "What do you want me to do? What is my narrative function in the film?" I need to know that in any piece I do.

I had a word in the back of my head, and Steven said he had a word too. My word was "witness."

His was "conscience."

I knew then, we were off and running. Those words would be the relationship to that work and the Holocaust and the character.

Many of the characters you've played—from Don Logan, the sociopath-psychopath, in *Sexy Beast*, to Fagin in *Oliver Twist*, to the doctor in

Death and the Maiden, among others—are villains. But there is a touch of sadness in these characters. Was that a conscious character-driven interpretation, a decision to aid you as you developed the character?[5]

I'm not sure. I think it's locked inside the creation and interpretation of the character. I believe that happiness and balance and calm is so undramatic as to be utterly boring. You have to have that drama that has that salty taste, that little thorn in the flesh. That's where the drama is. The sadness is in the character I see on the page, and it's that which makes it dramatically compelling. Without that ingredient, audiences would not be interested.

In good drama, there's humor, there's sadness, there's something slightly dislocated in the character that the actor presents to the audience. The audience needs to leave the cinema or the theatre with their own sense of order, which has been dismantled and reassembled. That's what storytelling is. That's why I'm here.

My mission statement as an actor is to tell a story. It's simple and enormous at the same time.

In *Sexy Beast,* your character covers his sadness with a bravado that complements the violence.

I loved the Logan character and the dialogue on the page immediately on reading the script. There's the scene in which I, as Don Logan, want the Ray Winstone character, Gary Dove, to do one last heist, and he doesn't want to do it. Ray and I decided on the speed of the dialogue we have between us. It's very, very fast. It was almost impossible to play it slowly. Learning those lines that were written by Louis Mellis and David Scinto was really a lesson for actors.

I've been asked if we improvised that scene. I despair at the thought because if we had improvised it, it would have been a miss. It's written word-for-word with a block of the word *no* eight times and the word *yes* thirteen times. That much I remember. It's so well written that the audience responds to the flawless rhythm. It has the rhythm of a Jacobean tragedy.

In *Elegy,* you were directed by Isabel Coixet. What does a woman director bring to the story that perhaps a male director might not?

Isabel was able to bring that feminine eye to the story about the central male character, who I played; he is in a male predicament in terms of his relationships with his son, Peter Sarsgaard; his best friend, Dennis Hopper; his longtime mistress, Patricia Clarkson; and the love of his life, Penelope Cruz.

As a director, Isabel brought a symmetrical eye to the story, and that eye includes operating the camera. She literally *was* the eye. Therefore, there is a balanced film in terms of empathy. The camera's eye is the gods looking down and seeing a man who's committed to escaping from intimacy as long as possible. Then the gods send him a situation that will be difficult for him to wriggle out of.

When my character climbs into Penelope's hospital bed—which was my idea—Isabel came out from behind the camera, saying, "Cu-u-u-t" in a rather high-pitched voice. She had tears in her eyes, which was a great measure of appreciation of what we were doing. Isabel understands the symmetry of storytelling that I love and brought it to the story.

Fifty Dead Men Walking was also directed by a woman, Kari Skogland. What were the differences with this subject matter?

Kari always films the man in context of being *seen* by women and children to prove something or to set an example. The canvas of this film has to do with violence in Northern Ireland, and it's pretty much male-driven violence. But the canvas includes great tenderness from the women. There are many scenes with children in the corner, in one's peripheral vision. The context of the film is, again like *Elegy*, beautifully balanced, which again suits my appreciation of symmetry.

I think that a male director might *not* have had those ingredients: women and children in almost every scene, so when there are scenes of men torturing each other in a garage, it's more shocking because there's that absence of tenderness.

Life is all right if you can see women and children going about their lives. Suddenly, in a scene, they're gone, and there are men with pliers! It's a brilliant juxtaposition and, again, the balance.

And yet another female director, Phyllis Nagy, and her approach in _Mrs. Harris_?

Yes, that's a television film in 2005 when I played the Scarsdale Diet doctor, Herman Tarnower, with the wonderful Annette Bening as Mrs. Harris, his lover. Phyllis, who also wrote the screenplay,[6] was able to bring a balance to him, revealing his terror of intimacy and inner loneliness, which she was able to divine about him. I didn't judge him, but I call him a misogynist.

Can you look at some of the other characters whom you have played and evaluate them?

I see in many roles the beautiful landscape, the rich mythology, that takes us back thousands of years and is dramatically hardwired into my system.

In the big Jerry Bruckheimer film *The Prince of Persia*, directed by Mike Newell, I play another baddie. My wonderful character, Nizam, brother to the king, is a man completely inhabited by envy and regret. I believe if a person's life is motivated by those two forces, it will consequently end in a very bad place. There is nothing guiding you to any kind of future. I used that cause and effect, that equation, in the role: if you start life with a clenched fist as a weapon, you will eventually fall upon it.

I see so much Shakespeare in some of the roles. For example, when I did Don Logan in *Sexy Beast*, I saw Iago. When I filmed *The Wackness*, I saw Falstaff and Prince Hal. As Luke, Josh Peck ultimately has to ban my character, Dr. Squires, as Henry banishes Falstaff [*Henry IV, Part 2*]. All those characters are there in Shakespeare's work, and I can see them in my current work.

In *Death and the Maiden*, your role is more a physical one than a verbal one, until the conclusion. It's a terrifying piece of work and leaves the audience in a quandary as to whether your character is or is not culpable and capable of the crime. What is your opinion as to the character's innocence or guilt?

I wouldn't ever say to the audience what my thought is about the situation. I wouldn't answer their question, "Does she have the wrong guy?"

I'd ask, "What do you think?" That's what the film is about.

I played it throughout as if the Sigourney Weaver character definitely has the wrong guy. Definitely. To director Roman Polanski, I said the way I would play it is, "She's got the wrong guy."

He responded, "Good. It's a wonderful way into the character. Let me film that."

As an actor, I had to have a tool in which to open the can of my character, and that can opener was that she's got the wrong guy. The rest is completely handed over to the audience, and they are pretty well split down the middle as to whether I'm guilty of what she says I've done or not. But I will never reveal which way I think.

You have appeared with a variety of outstanding actors. What do you expect from your colleagues, whether Michael Caine in *Without a Clue*, Dennis Hopper in *Elegy*, or Leonardo DiCaprio in *Shutter Island*? Or your female costars?

Every one of those men has a very highly developed capacity to listen and react. I would meet that with my own capacity to listen and react. At best in our scenes together, one doesn't really know what's coming next. Martin Sheen as Vince Walker and I had that in *Gandhi* in that remarkable scene sitting on the wall. I also became very close to that with Téa Leoni in *You Kill Me*, who has that comic genius, sharp as cut glass but with warmth and angular genius.

Then there is your magnum opus, _Gandhi_. By the time you played that role, you had played at the RSC, Chichester, Royal Court, and the National, as well as roles on Broadway, television, and a few films. That's quite a journey for an actor.

I was a fifteen-year overnight sensation in that film. When I walked into Dickie Attenborough's office, I had been in the business that long. I was "discovered" when Dickie's son, Michael, saw my Hamlet when it transferred from Stratford to the Roundhouse in London. Physically, I looked like Gandhi, but I had to lose weight on his vegetarian diet, and I held my body differently. My voice is very like Gandhi's. In fact, I used to listen to his voice on tape. I remember I recorded a speech and gave it to the soundman, a lovely guy. He put on the headsets to listen and said, "You see, Ben, that's what you've got to sound like." As if to say, "You'll never do it!"

I told him, "You've just listened to me." I was so happy.

Gandhi is one of the best examples of my work and how I, as a cinema actor, consider myself a portrait artist.

What would you like your legacy to be?

If a documentary about my life and work was made after my death, the filmmaker could probably edit some parts of my films together, and using those roles, the audience would see _me_. If it were edited in a certain way, you could see my journey.

There is a story, which may be linked to my legacy, and the essence of it is, to me, to be treasured. What happened is an example of things that have occurred in different guises along my journey with different characters, and different people have said it to me in slightly different ways.

When I was performing _Hamlet_, I was walking across the fields where Shakespeare used to walk. A lovely young woman approached me from the other side of the field. In order not to be an oaf, I moved to my left; at the same time, she moved to her right. I moved again; this time to my right; she turned to her left. She was tracking me. Eventually, she was completely face-to-face with me, and there was nothing I could do.

She looked at me and said right into my eyes, "I saw _Hamlet_ last night. How did you know about me?"

That's the best thing anyone could ever say to me about my acting. Others have said the same thing about different roles in different plays I've appeared in.

My answer? "I've done my job. Thank you."

What I'm doing is "holding the mirror up to nature." That's what _the man_ himself said!

In an October 22, 2013, interview in the Yorkshire Post, *Sir Ben announced that it would be "very, very unlikely indeed that you will ever see me on stage again."*

Selected Credits

Theatre
Victoria Theatre, Stoke-on-Trent: *Five to a Flat*, (1965; Peter Gallagher), *As You Like It, The Three Musketeers, Three Lodgers, Pygmalion, Tartuffe, Mata Hari; A Smashing Day*, also New Arts (1965; Peter Cheeseman; produced by Brian Epstein). **Other:** *Macbeth*, CFT (1966; Michael Benthall); *The Cherry Orchard*, CFT (1966; Lindsay Anderson); *As You Like It*, RST (1967; David Hugh Jones); *The Relapse*, RSC at the Aldwych (1967; Trevor Nunn); *King Lear*, RST (1968; Trevor Nunn); *Troilus and Cressida*, RSC at the Aldwych (1969; John Barton); *King Lear*, RST (1969; Trevor Nunn); *Bartholomew Fair*, RSC at the Aldwych (1969; Terry Hands); *The Silver Tassie*, RSC at the Aldwych (1969; David Hugh Jones); *Much Ado about Nothing*, RSC US tour, including Ahmanson, Los Angeles; Curran, San Francisco (1969; Trevor Nunn); *Richard III*, RST (1970; Terry Hands); *The Tempest*, RST (1970; John Barton); *Troilus and Cressida*, RSC at the Aldwych (1970; John Barton); *Measure for Measure*, RSC (1970; John Barton); *A Midsummer Night's Dream*, RST; Billy Rose, New York (1970–1971; Peter Brook); *Enemies*, Aldwych, (1971; David Hugh Jones); *Occupations*, the Place, London (1971; Buzz Goodbody); *Hello and Goodbye*, King's Head (1973; Peter Stevenson); *Statements after an Arrest under the Immorality Act*, Royal Court (1974; Athol Fugard); *Hamlet*, RSC at the Other Place; Roundhouse (1975–1976; Buzz Goodbody); *Dimetos*, Nottingham Playhouse; Wyndham's; Comedy [now Pinter] (1976; Athol Fugard); *Volpone*, NT, Olivier, (1977; Peter Hall); *Merry Wives of Windsor*, RST; Aldwych (1979; Trevor Nunn, John Caird); *Baal*, the Other Place, Stratford; Gulbenkian Studio, Newcastle (1979–1980; David Hugh Jones); *The Life and Adventures of Nicholas Nickelby*, RSC at the Aldwych (1980; Trevor Nunn); *Edmund Kean*, Studio Theatre, Harrogate; Lyric Hammersmith; Theatre Royal Haymarket; Brooks Atkinson, New York (1983; Alison Sutcliffe); *Othello*, RST; Barbican (1985; Terry Hands); *Melons*, RSC at the Other Place, Stratford; the Pit at the Barbican (1984–1985; Alison Sutcliffe; *Waiting for Godot*, Old Vic (1997; Peter Hall)

Film
Fear Is the Key (1972); *Gandhi* (1982); *Betrayal* (1983); *Turtle Diary* (1985); *Without a Clue* (1988); *Pascali's Island* (1988); *Bugsy* (1991); *Schindler's List* (1993); *Death and the Maiden* (1994); *Sexy Beast* (2000); *House of Sand and*

Fog (2003); Oliver Twist (2005); Elegy (2008); Transsiberian (2008); Fifty Dead Men Walking (2008); The Wackness (2008); Shutter Island (2009); Prince of Persia: The Sands of Time (2010); Hugo (2011); A Common Man (2012); Ender's Game (2013); The Physician (2013); Iron Man 3 (2013); Walking with the Enemy (2013); A Birder's Guide to Everything (2013); Eliza Graves (2014); Robot Overlords (2014); Learning to Drive (2014); A Doll's House (2014); Exodus (2014); Night at the Museum: Secret of the Tomb (2014); Selfless (2015); The Walk (2015)

Television
Coronation Street (1966–1967); Orlando (1966); The Love School (1975); BBC2 Playhouse, "Thank You, Comrades" (1978); "Every Good Boy Deserves Favour" (1979; Kean (1983); Murderers among Us: The Simon Wiesenthal Story (1989); The Tale of Sweeney Todd (1997); Anne Frank: The Whole Story (2001); Mrs. Harris (2005)

Awards and Nominations

The Merry Wives of Windsor, 1980, Olivier, Comedy Performance of the Year, nominee; Gandhi, 1982, Academy Award, Actor in a Leading Role, winner; also, BAFTA, Actor in a Leading Role, winner; BAFTA, Most Outstanding Newcomer to Leading Film Roles; 1983, Evening Standard British Film Award, Best Actor; Bugsy, 1992, Academy Award, Actor in a Supporting Role, nominee; Golden Globe, Best Actor in a Motion Picture, winner; Schindler's List, 1993, BAFTA, Best Actor in a Supporting Role, nominee; also, 1994, Evening Standard British Film Award, Best Actor, winner; Sexy Beast, 2001, Academy Award, Actor in a Supporting Role, nominee; also, Golden Globe, Best Performance by an Actor in a Supporting Role in a Motion Picture, nominee; House of Sand and Fog, 2003, Academy Award, Actor in a Leading Role, nominee; also, Golden Globe, Best Performance by an Actor in a Motion Picture—Drama, nominee

Honors

CBE, 2000; KBE, 2001 [some sources say 2002]; Star, Hollywood Walk of Fame, 2010, 6931 Hollywood Blvd., Hollywood; Cinema For Peace Honorary Award, 2008; BAFTA-LA, 2013, Honoree, Albert R. Broccoli Britannia Award for "Worldwide Contribution to Entertainment"

Notes

1. Now the Salford Arts Theatre; Albert Finney and Christopher Eccleston were also associated with the company.

2. Played by Vittorio Manunta.

3. Sir Ben wrote the music for a 1979 production of Brecht's *Baal*.

4. Nunn has described seeing "an element of danger and recklessness" in the young actor.

5. In an interview on May 2, 2013, on *The Colbert Report*, promoting *Iron Man 3*, Sir Ben commented on what it's like to play a villain: "When you're playing a villain, the last thing you must do is play him villainously. He must have a sense of righteousness. As bizarre and crazy as his political message is, he has to believe he is right."

6. From Shana Alexander's book *Very Much a Lady*.

~

CHAPTER FIFTEEN

Dame Angela Lansbury, CBE

It's true: tragedy is easy; it's comedy that is hard.

As a five-time Tony winner, three-time Oscar nominee, fifteen-time Emmy nominee, and six-time Golden Globe winner, Angela Lansbury has had roles that have placed her opposite the greatest names in the business: Laurence Olivier, Spencer Tracy, Orson Welles, Paul Newman, Joanne Woodward, and Judy Garland. Her characters have been regal, zany, threatening, and murderous with such performances as saucy Nancy in Gaslight; *the villain, Mrs. Iselin, in* The Manchurian Candidate; *dotty Madame Arcati in* Blithe Spirit; *the eponymous* Mame; *the pie maker, Mrs. Lovett, in* Sweeney Todd; *and her most beloved role, author-detective Jessica Fletcher in* Murder, She Wrote.

Dressed casually in beige pants and blouse, topped with an olive-colored cardigan, Dame Angela greets visitors personally at the door to her Brentwood, California, home, thousands of miles away both personally and professionally from her cottage in County Cork, Ireland. She has already prepared tea—a mixture of loose Typhoo and loose Lipton, and earlier in the day, she had gone to the local bakery to purchase an assortment of coconut, chocolate, and lemon curd pastries. She opens the traditional pink box and places them on a flowered plate. (No personal assistant attends to these details!)

A 1950s portrait of her mother, actress Moyna Macgill, watches over the proceedings in the living room. Yellow daffodils and tulips spill out from a crystal vase. Although many family mementoes were lost in a 1970s fire at her home in Malibu, she has collected others, and they sit atop a baby grand piano.

Lolly, her cat, who, she says, "walked in off the street," leaps up on the sofa and eyes the treats. Dame Angela places the tea tray on a higher table, shoos the purring feline away, waves to the gardener, and begins her reminiscences.

~

You were born on October 16, 1925, to actress Moyna Macgill and businessman Edgar Lansbury. What are some of your earliest memories of your family life in England?

My mother was one of the most fascinating and beautiful women imaginable. She gave up working in the theatre in 1930[1] when my twin brothers, Edgar and Bruce, were born. We lived well, but at my father's death in 1935, there wasn't much of an income, and we were financially hard-pressed, so she returned to the West End stage where she appeared in *Killicreggs in Twilight* by Lennox Robinson. I helped her learn her lines because it was difficult for her, having been away from the stage for some time. Working with her was my first serious introduction to being involved in reading a play.

I had been interested in doing theatrical bits and pieces with my older half sister Isolde, who later married Peter Ustinov. As children, we were always dancing, singing to records of Bing Crosby and Jessie Matthews, and dressing up in paper costumes. Even in these playlets, I realized I had the ability to characterize, which my mother recognized and encouraged.

When the war came in 1939, I was going to be evacuated from London, but I didn't want to leave my mother. I put my foot down. She agreed to let me stay and arranged for me to have lessons at home in English, French, and mathematics, at which I was hopeless. I could add, and I thought that was enough. My mother tutored me as the nurse in a scene from *Romeo and Juliet*, and I auditioned and received a scholarship to the Webber-Douglas School of Singing and Dramatic Art. That was a pretty good trick because they gave boys preference, as there were never enough young men in drama schools. I went there for one term during the Sitzkrieg, the so-called phony war, of 1939. During that year, my mother was a member of the ARP as an ambulance driver. She told me she remembered taking those who were more than slightly inebriated to hospital because there were fewer casualties than expected. It was no joke because subsequently the casualties were terrible in London.

Your grandfather cut quite a political swath in the early part of twentieth-century Britain.

George Lansbury was my paternal grandfather. For decades, he was a leader of the Labour Party and a member of Parliament. I remember him as

Photo by Stephen Paley

a bigger-than-life figure. I went to political meetings just to hear him speak. Such passion! I wish I had the passion he had. I'm rather apolitical. But perhaps some of my theatrical enthusiasm came from him. He loved children and used to take us to see pantos and buy us boxes of chocolates.

At the beginning of World War II, your mother made a life-changing decision for the family.

Mother decided that she, my brothers, and I had to leave England for America, and she sold everything. Isolde was then married to Peter Ustinov, and they remained in England.

As luck would have it, we left on the last ship out of Liverpool before the city was bombed, so I wasn't in London during the Blitz. I had no dramas of that sort. I missed all of that. Only just. We came across on the SS *Duchess of Atholl* in a convoy. I remember the excitement of being on a ship, traveling second class with loads of children, being seasick, and having lifeboat drills. There was this spirit, this camaraderie that we were going to a new world, which overshadowed the belief that we would go down. We were never actively terrified.[2]

What were those first days in America like?

When we arrived in New York in August 1940, we were met by my mother's first husband, Reginald Denham, who was by then a Broadway playwright [*Ladies in Retirement*, 1940] and later a director.[3] We stayed at the Algonquin Hotel for about three days and went to the World's Fair before we took a flat on Morton Street in Greenwich Village.

My brothers were enrolled in school. Mother and I earned extra money visiting young ladies' schools doing scenes from Shakespeare. Mother would recite Alice Duer Miller's "The White Cliffs of Dover" and Gene Fowler's "The *Jervis Bay* Goes Down" for twenty-five dollars. That was a huge sum then. Lamb chops were just thirty-three cents a pound! Imagine!

At one point, I stayed with Mrs. George Perkins, a wealthy lady on East Ninety-Fourth who took me to the theatre where I saw Helen Hayes [possibly *Twelfth Night* or *Candle in the Wind*], Lynn Fontanne [possibly *There Shall Be No Night*], and even Arturo Toscanini.

What about continuing your training in those first months in New York?

Through the efforts of the American Theatre Wing, I received another scholarship, this one to the Feagin School of Dramatic Art in Rockefeller Center. When I finished there, I got a job in Montreal for about four weeks in a cabaret called the Samovar, a haven for Russian émigrés. I was only sixteen, but I told them I was nineteen. I was earning sixty dollars a week. Big money at the time. One of the songs I sang was Noël Coward's "I Went to a Marvellous Party." I also did impressions of Bea Lillie, Gracie Fields, and others.

Where was your mother at this time?

She had obtained a green card and was able to work. Through her former husband who was directing the play, she appeared in a small role in *Yesterday's Magic* [1941]. Then she accepted a role that would take her on tour through Canada in Coward's *Tonight at 8:30* with Herbert Wilcox and Anna Neagle, in a production to raise money for the Royal Canadian Air Force. So while I was in Montreal, mother toured all the way to Vancouver. When she arrived there in August 1942, she told me to close up the New York flat, enroll my brothers in the Choate School in Connecticut, and take the train, *The Challenger*, to Hollywood, where she would meet me.

That was a second major journey within two years. What was your reaction to arriving in Hollywood?

My introduction to America had been through films of the stars who I had read about in the movie magazines like *Modern Screen*. I had the worst crush on Errol Flynn, and I admired Robert Donat and Bette Davis. They represented something very special and magical. I had only really been exposed to theatre, so when I came to Hollywood, everything was sort of supra-glamorous. The opportunities were overwhelming.

I arrived at Union Station. The excessive dry heat in Southern California in August was something I hadn't experienced. And those palm trees. I'd never seen them before. We moved into a flat in midtown Los Angeles near Wilshire Boulevard, where I slept on a pull-down bed. There was no smog, and we could actually see the Hollywood Hills. We had to have a car, so we purchased a fourth-hand 1936 Ford convertible with a rumble seat. Being island folk, the first thing we looked for was the sea, and we drove to the beach. It was really a journey of discovery.

What connections did your mother have with the British acting contingent who were in Hollywood at the time?

Mother knew a great many of the British group already in Hollywood: Basil Rathbone, who had played Iago to her Desdemona in a London production of *Othello* at the Court [1921]; Ian Hunter; Sara Allgood; Una O'Connor; and Queenie Leonard—they were all there. In those days, people would give letters of introduction to a director, and that was how you got roles . . . maybe. Mother found an agent and worked with a theatrical group run by, among others, Edgar Bergen, where she played the lead in *Maya*, a play with George Coulouris, directed by Peter Godfrey, who later directed me in what I refer to as "the Skid Row of my films," *Please Murder Me* [1956]. I took tickets at the Beachwood Theatre on Beachwood Drive in Hollywood.[4] I didn't yet have the cachet to get a role!

At Christmastime, we needed money. It was decided that I should get work at the famous Art Deco department store, Bullock's Wilshire, and I worked there as cashier, then in sales in the cosmetic department.

Your recollections?

Gaslight at MGM was my first *acting* job. Louis B. Mayer wanted to change my name to Angela Marlowe. That wasn't going to happen.

The mood on the set was very warm, and I felt secure. Coming on a set—the entire film was shot on soundstages, even the exteriors—for the first time can be a very daunting experience, that sense of strangeness. But it was a great atmosphere. Ingrid Bergman and Charles Boyer went out of their way

Angela Lansbury at seventeen in her 1944 film debut in *Gaslight,*
directed by George Cukor. *Photo from the collection of Dame
Angela Lansbury.*

to be welcoming. Boyer played the evil husband to a fare-thee-well, but he
was just the opposite, a kind and genuinely nice person. Because Bergman
was so tall, I wore high heels so I could look her in the eye. Also, I still had a
slight teenage figure, so my costume was padded to give me "heft."

How did director George Cukor encourage you in that first role?

I was just seventeen when production began, and, even though I wasn't
an amateur, that first role could have been very intimidating, but Mr. Cukor
was patient and helpful. He called me by my middle name, Brigid, or Miss
Lansbury. He made sure I wasn't treated as a bit player. He would indicate to
me how my role as the very cheeky Nancy would react in a particular scene,
but he wouldn't do a reading. He wouldn't tell me *how* to do a line. He gave
me encouragement to give the performance I did. He felt the actor's attitude

toward the role was important. He was very rigid about actors being ready. That had a lasting impression on me.

But because of my English background and training, I was able to come on the set prepared. I had a tremendous grounding in the values of my work. I had no sense of fear that I wouldn't be able to do what was expected of me. I certainly was not an amateur at that point. I had already done my professional work as a performer. I've always minded my p's and q's. To celebrate my eighteenth birthday, they had a lovely cake for me on the set.

What is your most memorable learning experience on that first film?

I learned one *big* lesson on that film. I had a scene with Barbara Everest, a fine English actress, who played Elizabeth, the housekeeper. I finished a scene, and since she was finished, and we thought neither of us was needed until after lunch, off we went to the commissary. We left the set before lunch was called. When we returned, it turned out that she had been needed for a scene. Cukor gave me a dressing-down in front of the company. I haven't told anyone to leave the set since then.

In May 1944, the trade paper the *Hollywood Reporter* reviewed your performance in *Gaslight* as "a debut of great promise. Her talents . . . stand out in such company." That role earned you your first of three Oscar nominations for Supporting Actress.

I remember thinking I couldn't possibly win. I was dazzled by my competition.[5] My mother and brothers accompanied me to the Oscars, which were held at what was then the Grauman's Chinese Theatre on Hollywood Boulevard.

Following this auspicious beginning, you went into two other high-profile films.

I was immediately cast as Elizabeth Taylor's sister, Edwina, in *National Velvet*, directed by Clarence Brown. From that, I played Sibyl Vane, a music hall songstress, in *The Picture of Dorian Gray*. And, can you believe it: I was again nominated for an Oscar as Supporting Actress for that film with an impressive group of actresses.[6]

Youngsters working in Hollywood went to school on the studio lot. What type of schooling did you have there?

Although there was always a social worker on the set until I was eighteen, I didn't go to school on the lot as other young actors did. I took a competency test to prove that I had learned what was necessary for a high school diploma. Remember, I had been out of formal school since the age of twelve. I call my education a "Hollywood education," which meant I kept my eyes open. I learned a lot that way.

You established yourself early on in character roles rather than as ingénues. Didn't that give you much more flexibility as an actress?

That's absolutely true. I never would have had the career I've had had I only played ingénue roles.

Kay Thorndyke in the Frank Capra–directed *State of the Union* was one of the first roles in which you played older than your years.

Even to this day, I remember that it was an extraordinary fluke that I got that role. It was quite an undertaking. I was only twenty-three. Katharine Hepburn had championed me for the role. I was blown away by her originality and was terribly, enormously flattered to work with her, and I had to work like hell. I had to lower my voice, as it didn't have the "weight" for the role. I've always tried very much to match the voice to the character, whether it's a shopgirl, the girl next door, or any of the disreputable characters I seemed to have been attracted to. In this I was playing a forty-year-old and had a twenty-three-year-old voice.

Spencer Tracy was all seriousness toward his work. And Frank Capra had an easygoing manner and told jokes while we were working. I've been lucky. I've always worked with the best people.

What about the singing roles?

Even though as Sybil Vane I sang "Yellow Bird" in *Dorian Gray*, it was odd, even ironic, that MGM had my voice dubbed by Virginia Rees in *The Harvey Girls*, because they thought it "thin," and the part of Em needed to be throaty. Thinking back, I believe the studio was right, because I didn't have the voice to do the character at the time. My own voice was used again in *Till the Clouds Roll By* in the musical number, "How'd Ya Like to Spoon with Me." When I went on to all those wonderful stage musicals, I had to learn how to "belt" a song.

But what goes around comes around?

Yes, years later [she laughs] I dubbed dialogue for Ingrid Thulin in *Four Horsemen of the Apocalypse* [1962]. Uncredited!

MGM loaned you out to Paramount for *Samson and Delilah* with director Cecil B. DeMille. What differences did you notice between MGM and Paramount?

I left MGM after eight years and found that working at Paramount was like being let out of school early. While we were held on a short rein at MGM—they wanted their people to keep within the framework of the studio, whether it was hair, makeup, clothes, attending premieres—Paramount was an easygoing country club.

You received a third Best Supporting Actress Oscar nomination for *The Manchurian Candidate*,[7] again playing an older woman, a role you almost didn't get.

Frank Sinatra, the film's star, had the power to dictate casting. He wanted Lucille Ball for the role of Mrs. Iselin, opposite Laurence Harvey. I later found out that director John Frankenheimer asked Sinatra to see me in *All Fall Down* in which I played Warren Beatty's mother.[8]

I never understood how they could remake the picture because people already knew who the villain of the piece was. In the original, no one knew. The cat was already out of the bag in the remake.[9]

This wasn't the only role in which you were your costar's mother and only slightly older than your "son."

Besides playing opposite Laurence Harvey as his mother—I was only three years older than he was—I played older character roles several times, once as Elvis Presley's mother in *Blue Hawaii* in the early sixties; I was just ten years older than he was. I was Carroll Baker's mother in *Harlow* and just six years older than she was, and was Warren Beatty's mother in *All Fall Down*; I was twelve years older than Warren.

As early as 1950, you ventured into live television. What was the attraction of that new medium?

I never thought of television as a comedown from theatre or film, especially *live* television. There was a sense of excitement, like a theatrical opening . . . except we only got to do it once. In those days, the programs that were done in New York had very high standards.

My earliest appearance was in 1950 in an episode entitled "The Citadel" on *Robert Montgomery Presents*, directed by Norman Felton. Montgomery never showed up for rehearsals, even though it was his show. He had a stand-in who played his part, and then he came in during the first run-through and dress rehearsal, and then did the show. That process was very difficult for those of us working with him.

There was an episode of *Lux Video Theatre*, "Operation Weekend," in 1952 where I played a nurse opposite Richard Kiley as a surgeon. There was even an appearance on *Your Show of Shows*, in 1954, which had a sense of the ridiculous about it.

Earnings then were anywhere from $750 to $1,000 each, which included airfare to New York, rehearsal time, and the production. At one point, I was grateful for television roles as they paid for groceries for a summer!

You stepped onto the Broadway stage in 1957 and began accumulating Tonys. What are some of the backstories about the roles and the productions?

If movies were my first career, then theatre was my second. I first went into *Hotel Paradiso*, a farce with Bert Lahr and directed by Peter Glenville. But it wasn't a musical. What I learned from Bert Lahr was a lesson in playing comedy. He taught me how to control the audience, to milk a laugh, to wait for a laugh.

My first musical was *Anyone Can Whistle* in 1964. It was also my first association with Stephen Sondheim. Unfortunately, no one whistled for tickets! It ran for just nine performances!

I played Joan Plowright's mother in *A Taste of Honey*. The play was already a hit in Britain, where it had been done very successfully. At thirty-five, I was much too young to play the role of Helen. But it was a great experience for me. Tony Richardson, who had directed the play, asked me to play the role in the film. I turned it down even though he was adamant I should do it.[10]

I refer to *Mame* in 1966 as the beginning of my "glamorous years." It was that show that turned the tables in my career. A thrilling time for me, even though Josh Logan, the director, had me audition three or four times! *Mame* played two years! Two years! It ran for more than 1,500 performances—on Broadway, in two theatres. Then we opened in Los Angeles mid-1968. Now the run of most productions is just several months or even just a few weeks.

Part of that glamour of that production were the costumes by my very dear friend, Barbara Matera, who would go on to create just about all of my costumes for *every* show I ever did on Broadway. It was also the beginning of my long association with composer-lyricist Jerry Herman.

Were you considered for the role in the film version?

I don't think Warners felt I was a big enough name. It was a terrible disappointment. Lucille Ball played the role.

You moved on to playing a less-sophisticated role in a Disney film.

I was lured into *Bedknobs and Broomsticks* [1971; Robert Stevenson] because I saw the chance to play to a presold audience. The role of Eglantine Price, an apprentice witch, was just acting by the numbers; every shot was completely preplanned. The role was rather different from the previous film, *Something for Everyone*, in which I played the morally corrupt Countess von Ornstein. It was only one of two films that Broadway director Harold Prince directed.[11]

What prompted your return to your London roots for a role in _Hamlet_ for the National's inaugural season?

Before that, I had returned in 1972 to play in Edward Albee's _All Over_, directed by Peter Hall, in an RSC production. But I was anxious to play a Shakespearean part, as I'd never had the opportunity. Queen Gertrude in _Hamlet_ seemed the ideal chance. And I had the opportunity to work with Peter Hall and play opposite Albert Finney as Hamlet.

We began the run at the Old Vic [December 10, 1975, to February 28, 1976], where the theatre company had been housed since its founding in 1963,[12] and then the production transferred to the Lyttelton for the remainder of the run [March 16, 1976, to July 27, 1976].

Then came the role of Mrs. Lovett, the pie maker of grisly ingredients in _Sweeney Todd_, which took a bit of the sting out of the _Mame_ rejection.

Stephen Sondheim tailored the part of Mrs. Lovett in _Sweeney Todd_ for me once I accepted the role. His work is probably the most difficult in terms of lyrics, which are very demanding but very haunting. His music is a mixture of the complex and the simple. It's as close to opera without being opera as a work for the theatre can get.

For the last several years, you have been playing the ditzy Madame Arcati in a revival of Noël Coward's _Blithe Spirit_. How did you become associated with that project?

My agent told me, "They're going to do _Blithe Spirit_ next season [2009] on Broadway, and Michael Blakemore is going to direct. Producer Jeffrey Richards thought you might be interested in playing Madame Arcati."

I just paused for one moment, and then I said, "Gosh, I wouldn't mind having a crack at playing that role. Yes, I'm interested." We took it from there.[13]

I knew that Christine Ebersole had brought the project to Jeff. I thought she would be interesting casting as Elvira, the ghost of Charles Condomine's first wife. I'd seen her in _Grey Gardens_ [2006; Michael Greif]. The character of Ruth, Charles's current wife, was difficult to cast, and we didn't quite know how we were going to do that. I say "we" because I was given the chance to put in my two pennies' worth as to who was going to play her. We discussed a lot of actresses who Michael was interested in using. Many of them were British because it _is_ a British play; there was the thought that we ought to have a Brit playing the role. We lucked out by finding Jayne Atkinson, whose parents were British. She was able to bring off the Englishness required in that role and was extremely good at bringing that sensibility to the role.

How relevant is Coward to contemporary audiences?

I feel that Coward had managed in 1941 to really write probably the first sitcom. If you look at the play and put it all together, it plays like a sitcom. There are the situations and the payoff. The jokes and the payoff, and on it goes. That's what keeps the audience on the edge of their seats because they really don't know what's going to happen next. There are many universal—and contemporary—truths in the play in what he has to say about marriage, what he has to say about relationships between husbands and wives and the fact that wives [ahem, she clears her throat knowingly] do tend to override their husbands, but they don't realize it. The scenes with the two main characters in the play bickering about who did what to whom is all very "today." It's prevalent in current television shows.

And audiences—the elderly, the middle aged, the young marrieds, and kids are most appreciative. The kids enjoy it as much as the elders. I notice when I come out of the theatre in the evening and talk to the youngsters who've come to see the show and then ask for my autograph, they'll tell me they did it in high school. Some fifteen-year-old will tell me, "I played Madame Arcati." It's a sweet thing.

The character of Madame Arcati generates many laughs. How much do you listen to the audience in order to know when to encourage them to laugh? Or do you need to hold off because you have a bigger laugh coming?

That's an interesting thing that you learn to do when you're doing comedy. There are a great many—I won't say "secrets," but as has been said, "Tragedy is easy; comedy is hard," which is true. You have to experiment. Keep delivering the lines, and sometimes a line will have two laughs in it. You have to decide whether you're going to go for the two laughs or whether you're prepared to override the first and go for the second, which might be bigger. These are technical things that actors learn after years of doing it.

The pause is one of the greatest ways of giving the audience a chance to digest what they've just heard. First, they get it, and then they laugh. It often depends on the line and how it connects with them. There are times when you get a laugh three nights running, and on the fourth, nothing. We come off stage and ask each other, "Where are they tonight?" We can hear them breathing and coughing, but we don't hear them laughing." I wonder, "What did I do differently?" or "What's wrong with me tonight?"

Then someone says, "Oh, don't worry. They're all having a good time. They're all smiling."

The costumes you wear in *Blithe Spirit* give an added dimension to the character.

The play's costume designer, Martin Pakledinaz, did an amazing job gowning me. We had a lot of fun putting all this stuff together. He would say that it was a mutual effort on our parts, but he has an ability to find fabrics that I didn't think were any longer available, and he picks them up in the darnedest places. He has this huge supply of bits and pieces, which he brought in, and I'd wonder, "Where did he get that?"

The one used in all the promotional photos is kind of "gypsy-wear." The fabrics are colorful and topped off with the clunky jewelry.[14]

The other one I love is the tweed outfit. You have to realize she's always on her bicycle, so whatever she's wearing has to lend itself to not getting caught in the spokes. You can imagine what it was like in England in the 1930s—in my young days—when women would wrap their skirts around themselves very carefully when they were on their bicycles so they wouldn't show too much leg.

Madame Arcati reflects the physicality of the role when she says, "You have to put your back into it." How do you keep the up the physical part of the character?

The thing about that character is that she *is* very physical. I'm loosening up all the time. When I'm in the dressing room, I do stretches because of the dancing around that I do. That is part of my regimen. I wrote a book.[15] The book is still around and fans send it to me to sign. That kind of attitude towards keeping in shape is simple, straightforward, and still works for me all these years later. Of course, I've got a lot of artificial joints now, two knees and two hips. I'm the bionic woman. If I hadn't had those replacements, I wouldn't be able to do what I do. Since I do the eight shows a week, I take excruciatingly good care of myself. That's the only way I could. I have a lot of stamina, but I have to save it.

In this role, and others, I remember my mother's sense of humor and lovely kind of lightness to her, which I try to sort of get into sometimes and use remembering it. I'm much more of a character person than she was. I'm a bit heavy duty compared to her.[16]

With just about every entrance and exit you make, the warmth of the audience flows right across the footlights. How does that affect you?

It is heady, to say the least, and most heartwarming. I'm enormously grateful for their acceptance and understanding of the fact that I'm there and back on Broadway again. Also, they're so excited because they know me through

Murder, She Wrote, basically, although some of them know me from some of my movies. Their greeting is stunning. It really is. It's a most beautiful feeling to know that that many know me. I hope it's because they enjoy what I do within the context of the play, and this extraordinary character I play. Madame Arcati is no ordinary lady. I play it, shall we say, very large. They kind of appreciate and enjoy that. It's what I love to do. I'm a character actress and also a comedienne; so the combination of the two, which is inherent in that role, allows me to really have some fun. And to give the audience that sense of enjoyment in what I'm doing is tremendous. It's a great part. It was another of those wonderful character roles that have given me a lengthy and flexible career as an actor.

How do you feel about applause?

Applause is thrilling, very thrilling. But I'm ambivalent about the idea of the now-common standing ovation. Audiences feel it's necessary to rise to their feet all the time. There is no longer a measure of understanding the performance. They think it's expected. They should save that wonderful gesture for something truly deserving. After all, it's my job!

On June 7, 2009, you received an unprecedented fifth Tony Award for Best Featured Actress in a Play for your role as Madame Arcati.

I didn't expect it in a million years, but there was always a chance. I was up against some fantastic performers. You just don't know until that last moment when it's announced.[17]

At the same Tony ceremony, Jerry Herman received a Lifetime Achievement Award. Your renditions of his songs have become standards. What is it about his music and lyrics that make him so special?

He knows how to put together lovely lyrics with a lovely melody, and they go together like ham and cheese. He starts with the lyric, and then he puts the music under it. Honestly, I think some of his songs are the best ever. There are songs that people don't even know that are so beautiful, like the ones from *Mack and Mabel*, which is a terribly underrated show even though it won eight Tonys[18] but only lasted sixty-six performances. That song, "I Won't Send Roses," is one of my favorites.

I played in *Mame*, one of his great successes, with songs such as "Mame" and "If He Walked into My Life." My second Tony, again with music and lyrics by Jerry, was *Dear World*, which had some gorgeous songs in it—"Dear World," "And I Was Beautiful," and "One Person." He's a one-off. I'm very upset that he's never been recognized by the Kennedy Center Honors. How could his talent and contributions be overlooked?

Within five months of *Blithe Spirit* closing on Broadway, you appeared in a revival of *A Little Night Music*. That was your third production in three years, a daunting schedule. What brought you back?

As Madame Armfeldt, how could I pass up singing Stephen Sondheim's wonderful song "Liaisons"?[19]

What incidents have happened during a performance that were completely unexpected?

Well, I've never been sitting in my dressing room and I hear, "You're on! You're on!" That's every actor's nightmare. I haven't had that experience.

I had one rather hair-raising experience with Len Cariou in *Sweeney Todd*. It happened during a preview. I could see from the corner of my eye that a huge part of the set—weighing maybe a ton—was slowly dropping. This bridge was upstage, and Len and I were almost under it. We moved downstage. The audience certainly noticed as it moved lower . . . and lower . . . and lower until it finally clunked onto the stage. All the while, I'm singing, "Nothing's gonna harm you/Not while I'm around." Talk about irony. The audience reacted and went wild. We could have been seriously hurt.

You're still performing eight times a week. How do you continue to prepare yourself for that rigorous schedule?

The main ingredient, I must say, is rest. I really don't do anything except the show. I go to lunch occasionally. Or I go out to do a little bit of shopping, but other than that, except for publicity, which I have avoided rather strictly on this show because of the nature of my part. I really couldn't handle too much alongside the actual doing of the show. I just said, "Don't count on me to do a lot of early morning publicity on television. I can't do that and the show." The producers were very accommodating in that respect.

The Tuesday night performances on Broadway now start at seven o'clock. It gets people in and out earlier during the week, and it's quite a good idea, but it takes a little adjustment because I have to be at the theatre earlier than ordinary. The car picks me up at 5:50 p.m. for the show and 6:50 p.m. for the eight o'clock show. I live very close to the theatre. I look at the mail and chat with my assistant. I have a very good dresser [Maevefiona Butler], who is my right hand in the dressing room. She takes care of the mail and flowers that come to the theatre. We discuss what needs to be taken care of. Then I start to put my makeup on, and the hairdresser and I put my wig on. Then the costume, and off I go.

We have Monday completely free, which is supposed to be our rest day. We also have Sunday night off. It allows those of us who work in the theatre to have a break. We can go out on a Sunday evening with friends or have friends in. Just sort of have a more social kind of existence.

I keep chocolates and fruit and nuts in my dressing room for my colleagues and guests and anybody else who needs a lift.

With matinees and evenings on Wednesdays and Saturdays, what do you do between shows and in the evenings?

On Wednesdays, I come home and have a quiet time. It's more restful there although it means that extra little bit of travel, but it's worth it to me. Otherwise, the theatre takes up too much of your mind-set, and I just need to get home and check my e-mail and mail. Fortunately, it's a pretty straight shot from the theatre to where I live, and I have a wonderful driver who gets me home and to the theatre on time.

On Tuesday and Thursday nights, I will often go out to supper with friends who have made a date beforehand and have come to the show. I get home about 11:30 or midnight. But I don't usually get to sleep before 1 a.m. any night. I wake around 9:30.

What do you see as your responsibility to the audience?

I do feel a responsibility to *my* audience. I use the word *my* because I know there is an audience out there that will follow me. It's mainly because of *Murder, She Wrote*. That is the door that opened the way for me to reach an enormous worldwide audience. It was not easy to face the fact that the show was the reason I have this tremendous base. I discounted it for ages. I thought, "That's just something I did, and we do these things as annuities." That was true in my case.

When you returned to television in 1984 with *Murder, She Wrote*, you stayed for a dozen years. Why the return to this medium?

I got tired of working nonstop in the theatre and on national tours. At that point, I was in my late fifties, and my husband, Peter Shaw,[20] and I made a decision: it was the time for me to move to television. That's what I did. I became a businesswoman and an actress. Housekeeping and producing are complementary work.

I'm enormously grateful I did. At the time I was doing *Murder, She Wrote*, I felt that I was selling out in a curious way. Although I liked the character of Jessica Fletcher, and except for the daily grind of it, I realized that Jessica reached an across-the-board audience, which turned out to be a good thing. The audience found that the qualities of the character of Jessica Fletcher reflected on me. Certainly the audience saw *me* as that person. I didn't lose those people who had enjoyed my work in movies and theatre. They finally put it all together and said, "This is what she does. When she comes back to the theatre, we'll go and see her."

And they did. The affection with which I am received is lovely. Sometimes the audience mixes me up with the character of Jessica Fletcher. They think I *am* Jessica Fletcher. It's very odd.

How has Broadway, as an idea, changed in the decades since you first appeared?

It's changed so much. I can't even begin to go into all the ways. First of all, it's the economics. The cost to mount a Broadway show today is astronomical. We're talking about millions of dollars to mount a play, depending on what's involved, such as special effects, etc. Whereas in the days when I started, it was manageable. One was paid more than a living wage in the theatre, nothing huge. You never made a lot of money in the theatre. The cost of living in those days was less. The cost of a ticket was negligible compared to what it costs today. From that point of view, it's a whole different scene.

The thing that I find most changed, because the way the world has changed so much in more than sixty years, is the attitude of young people coming into the theatre. It's quite different than it was in my early days. In those days, we really started at the bottom and crept our way up to getting better and better parts. This wasn't necessarily true in my case. I didn't have to start playing tiny little parts, walk-ons, doing something that youngsters in those days did to get started. I was fortunate enough to start off in high gear in a role with the great Bert Lahr. We were prepared to do that, though.

Today, they come through the drama courses at universities and acting studios, and they expect to play featured roles right off the bat. They're not really quite ready to put up with a cold-water flat on Tenth Avenue like my generation did. Today, everybody wants immediate stardom. It all has to do with these television programs that make "stars" overnight.

Once a film is "in the can," it's permanent and doesn't change, but theatrical performances are ephemeral, a "one-off." Is that a disappointment or a positive element of theatre performances, which can be changed daily?

Maybe that's the thing about theatre. It's what you experience at any given performance that you remember. It's different for everyone for every performance. It's very sad that we can't keep theatre performances on film, but there are records at the Billy Rose Library for the Performing Arts at Lincoln Center. For us performers, we find ourselves turning up on YouTube. It's amazing the amount of film that has filtered into the Internet of shows that I've done that I didn't think anybody had ever photographed. Thank God they did, otherwise nobody would know what I did in *Gypsy* or what I did in *Mame*.[21]

You've kept the curtain up for a long time. Are audiences going to be able to enjoy seeing you in the future?

Undoubtedly. Absolutely.

⌒

Selected Credits

Theatre
A Taste of Honey, Lyceum, then Booth (1961; Tony Richardson, George Devine); *Anyone Can Whistle*, Majestic (1964; Arthur Laurents); *Mame*, Winter Garden; Broadway (1966–1970; Gene Saks); *All Over*, Aldwych (1972; Peter Hall); *Sondheim: A Musical Tribute*, Shubert (1973; Burt Shevelove); *Gypsy*, Piccadilly; Shubert, Los Angeles; Winter Garden, New York (1973–1974; Arthur Laurents); *Hamlet*, NT at the Old Vic; NT, Lyttelton (1975–1976; Peter Hall); *Sweeney Todd: The Demon Barber of Fleet Street*, Uris (1979–1980; Harold Prince); *A Little Family Business*, Ahmanson, Los Angeles; Martin Beck, New York, (1982; Martin Charnin); *Mame*, revival, Gershwin Theatre (1983; John Bowab); *Deuce*, Music Box (2007; Michael Blakemore); *Blithe Spirit*, Shubert; Gielgud; Ahmanson, Los Angeles; Golden Gate, San Francisco; Washington, DC; Toronto (2009–2015; Michael Blakemore); *A Little Night Music*, Walter Kerr (2010; Trevor Nunn); *The Best Man*, Schoenfeld (2012; Michael Wilson); *Driving Miss Daisy*, Australian tour (2013; David Esbjornson)

Film
National Velvet (1944); *The Picture of Dorian Gray* (1945); *The Harvey Girls* (1946); *Till the Clouds Roll By* (1946); *The Private Affairs of Bel Ami* (1947); *The Three Musketeers* (1948); *State of the Union* (1948); *Samson and Delilah* (1949); *Kind Lady* (1951); *The Purple Mask* (1955); *The Court Jester* (1956); *Dark at the Top of the Stairs* (1960); *Blue Hawaii* (1961); *All Fall Down* (1962); *The World of Henry Orient* (1964); *Harlow* (1965); *Something for Everyone* [alternate titles: *The Rook; Black Flowers for the Bride*] (1970); *The Mirror Crack'd* (1980); *The Company of Wolves* (1984); *Beauty and the Beast* [voice] (1991); *Nanny McPhee* (2005); *Mr. Popper's Penguins* (2011)

Television
Robert Montgomery Presents, "The Citadel" (1950); *Lux Video Theatre*, four episodes (1950–1954); *Screen Directors Playhouse*, "Claire" (1956); *The Man from U.N.C.L.E.*, "The Deadly Toys Affair" (1965); *Little Gloria . . . Happy*

at Last (1982); *A Talent for Murder* (1984); *Murder, She Wrote*, 264 episodes (1984–1996); *Magnum, P.I.*, "Novel Connection" (1986); *The Shell Seekers* (1989); *Mrs. 'arris Goes to Paris* (1992); *Law & Order: Trial by Jury*, "Day" (2005); *Law & Order: Special Victims Unit*, "Night" (2005)

Awards and Nominations

Gaslight, 1944, Academy Award, Supporting Actress, nominee; *The Picture of Dorian Gray*, 1945, Academy Award, Supporting Actress, nominee; *The Manchurian Candidate*, 1962, Academy Award, Supporting Actress, nominee; *Mame*, 1966, Tony, Best Actress in a Musical, winner; *Dear World*, 1969, Tony, Best Actress in a Musical, winner; *Something for Everyone*, 1971, Golden Globe, Best Motion Picture Actress—Musical/Comedy, nominee; *Gypsy*, 1974, Tony, Best Actress in a Musical, winner; *Death on the Nile*, 1978, National Board of Review, Best Supporting Actress, winner; *Sweeney Todd*, 1979, Tony, Best Actress in a Musical, winner; *Murder, She Wrote*, Emmy, 1985–1996, Outstanding Lead Actress in a Drama Series, nominee; also, Golden Globe, 1985, 1987, 1990, 1992, Best Performance by an Actress in a TV Series—Drama, winner; also, 1986, 1988, 1980, 1991, 1993, 1995, nominee; *Deuce*, 2007, Tony, Best Actress in a Play, nominee; *Blithe Spirit*, 2009, Tony, Best Featured Actress in a Play, winner; *A Little Night Music*, 2010, Tony, Best Featured Actress in a Musical, nominee; *Blithe Spirit*, Olivier, 2015, Best Actress in a Supporting Role, winner

Honors

Hollywood Walk of Fame stars, 1960: motion pictures, 6623 Hollywood Blvd., Hollywood; television, 6259 Hollywood Blvd., Hollywood; Grand Marshal, 104th Tournament of Roses Parade, 1993; CBE, 1994; Disney Legend, 1995; Lifetime Achievement Award, SAG, 1997; Kennedy Center Honors, recipient, 2000 (with Mikhail Baryshnikov, Placido Domingo, Clint Eastwood, Chuck Berry); BAFTA-LA, 2003, honoree, Britannia Award, for Lifetime Achievement in Television and Film; Academy of Motion Picture Arts and Sciences Governors Award, November 2013; DBE, 2013

Notes

1. Among the earliest productions in which Macgill appeared included *Love in a Cottage*, Globe (1918); *As You Like It*, Lyric Hammersmith (1920, directed by Nigel Playfair); *Will Shakespeare*, Shaftesbury (1921, directed by Basil Dean); *Getting Mar-*

ried, Everyman (1922, directed by Norman MacDermott); *Dear Brutus*, Wyndham's (1922, directed by Gerald du Maurier); *Little Eyolf*, Everyman (1928). She appeared at the Everyman in Muriel Stuart's *The Bond* in 1930.

2. The ship was torpedoed and sunk on October 10, 1940.

3. *Sherlock Holmes* (1953), *The Bad Seed* (1954), and *Hostile Witness* (1966).

4. According to *Balancing Act*, the authorized biography of the actress by Martin Gottfried, Macgill appeared in a production of *Horror Tonight*, at the Gate Theatre in Hollywood.

5. Ethel Barrymore won for *None but the Lonely Heart*. Other nominees: Jennifer Jones, *Since You Went Away*; Aline MacMahon, *Dragon Seed*; and Agnes Moorehead, *Mrs. Parkington*.

6. Anne Revere, who played Lansbury's mother in the film, won. Other nominees: Eve Arden, *Mildred Pierce*; Ann Blyth, *Mildred Pierce*; Joan Loring, *The Corn Is Green*.

7. Patty Duke won for *The Miracle Worker*.

8. "Once Sinatra saw her, conversation over. The role was hers," said Frankenheimer during an interview at an event at the Museum of Television and Radio in Beverly Hills (now the Paley Center for Media) on September 24, 1997.

9. In the 2004 remake, Meryl Streep played the Lansbury role as Eleanor Shaw; Denzel Washington played the Frank Sinatra role; Liev Schreiber played the Laurence Harvey role.

10. In the 1961 film, Dora Bryan, who was also thirty-five, played Helen.

11. The other film was *A Little Night Music* (1977) with Elizabeth Taylor.

12. With Laurence Olivier as its first artistic director.

13. Lansbury is the most recent in a long list of actresses who have played the eccentric medium on stage, including Margaret Rutherford, who originated the role in a production directed by Coward in 1941; Mildred Natwick, in the first American production (1943); Geraldine Page (1987); and Penelope Keith (2004); among others.

14. One reviewer wrote that Lansbury's wig looks like "a pair of braided bagels on either side of her head," rather like Mrs. Lovett or even Princess Leia (from *Star Wars*).

15. *Angela Lansbury's Positive Moves: My Personal Plan for Fitness and Well-Being*, with Mimi Avins (1990).

16. Macgill played in a Broadway production of *The Boy Friend* (1954), directed by Cy Feuer.

17. In her acceptance speech, Lansbury said, "This is amazing. . . . Who knew at this time of my life that I should be presented with this lovely, lovely award! I feel deeply grateful. I can't believe that I'm standing here. And because I am standing here and some of you are standing there, I must take this moment to send my love and my congratulations to the other nominees in this category. . . . I am the essence of gratitude and happiness and joy, and being back on Broadway and being with all you Broadway-ites is the greatest gift in my old age that I can possibly imagine. Thank you for having me back!"

18. The original production in 1974 was directed and choreographed by Gower Champion.

19. On December 13, 2009, *Variety* reviewer David Rooney wrote, "The production's real jewel is Angela Lansbury as [Catherine Zeta-Jones's] worldly mother. . . . The actress has sparkled in plays in recent seasons, but seeing her in a Sondheim musical is something quite special. Regally coiffed and outfitted, and with a strength of character undiminished even in a wheelchair she occupies for much of her stage time, her Mme. Armfeldt can inject tart flavor into a single, 'La la la.'"

20. Lansbury was married to Shaw for fifty-four years before his death in 2003.

21. In a September 16, 2013, e-mail to the author, Patrick Hoffman, director, Theatre on Film and Tape Archive, New York Public Library, wrote that the archive "has video recorded and preserved *all* of her performances since she returned to Broadway in 2007 . . . nearly all of her award-winning performances in musicals received original cast sound recordings so *Anyone Can Whistle*, *Mame*, *Dear World*, and *Gypsy* live on indelibly." The archive holdings are free to the public to view by appointment, but nothing may be copied or borrowed.

CHAPTER SIXTEEN

~

Sir John Mills, CBE

Everybody needs luck, especially actors. But we have to work our pants off, too.

The first of two interviews with Sir John Mills took place on a warm August afternoon at his daughter's, actress Juliet Mills, home in a suburb of Los Angeles. She was folding laundry, and a new puppy was scampering from room to room.

Sir John decided to step out of harm's way and find a comfortable chaise longue in the garden. He is wearing white shorts and polo shirt, slip-on shoes, a terrycloth hat pulled low over his brow, and sunglasses. A bottle of water and a container of Coppertone sunscreen are near at hand.

He had recently presented his one-man show to a sold-out audience at the Academy of Television Arts and Sciences Theatre in North Hollywood, California, where he showed no signs of slowing down. His ensemble for the performance included a purple brocade waistcoat under a white dinner jacket; black tuxedo trousers and black patent pumps covered all but a sliver of his lucky red socks. He carried a silver-headed cane, more for effect than balance.

A second interview with the actor took place in a very different setting: the ninety-year-old actor's three-hundred-year-old home, Hills House in Denham, Buckinghamshire, where he has lived since 1975. The three-story home, which fronts Village Road, looks out on several acres and abuts St. Mary's Church where the actor and his wife, Mary, renewed their marriage vows a short time ago.

His attire there conformed to the cooler weather: black turtleneck, olive-green corduroy trousers, and an ivory shawl-collared sweater. Hamlet, the spaniel, cavorted at his feet. Hobson, the aging corgi, and Gus, the cat, dropped in for a brief *visit, then padded silently out. Sheet music by such disparate composers as Noël Coward, Leslie Bricusse, and Tchaikovsky are open on the grand piano. Memorabilia is displayed on every surface and wall: photographs of the actor with Her Majesty Queen Elizabeth II; a signed photograph from Lord Louis Mountbatten; a Christmas card from Elizabeth the Queen Mother; and a photo of the actor and his wife on their wedding day, January 16, 1941. His Oscar for Supporting Actor in* Ryan's Daughter *sits on the mantel.*

Despite having lost much of his sight, he still gets around both homes with the grace and ease of the dancer he was more than seven decades ago. The actor wears all these garments comfortably, illustrating how easily he has crossed over from film and theatre roles as diverse as Willie Mossop in Hobson's Choice *to Lieutenant Colonel Barrow in* Tunes of Glory *to T. E. Lawrence in* Ross, *and even to Gus, the Theatre Cat, in the made-for-television version of the musical* Cats.

You have just celebrated your ninetieth birthday. With some seventy years in theatre, film, and television to look back on, can you offer a potted version of how it all began?

First though, I have to tell two amusing stories that just recently took place: I was shopping in Los Angeles, and some ladies approached me. They were certainly over eighty. They advanced toward me, and one of them said, "Is it really you? It's so great to see you looking so well."

I thanked them and said how kind it was to be remembered. As they moved on, they made this parting comment to me: "You take care of yourself, Mr. Fairbanks." So much for being in more than a hundred films and dozens of stage productions.

Secondly, I received a birthday gift from my great friend, Stephen Fry. He gave me the black quilted velvet dressing gown with gold trim that Noël Coward wore as Elyot in *Private Lives*. I have it hanging on the back of the door in the guest loo. I think Noël would find it amusing to see it there. It's one of my treasured possessions.

But more to the question: In the beginning, I was born February 22, 1908, in North Elmham in Norfolk, where my father was a schoolmaster. I was given the daunting name of Lewis Ernest Watts Mills. I credit my sister, Annie, for later suggesting that I change it to the more marquee-appropriate John.

There was never a time that I didn't want to be an actor. My first performance was at the age of six, dressed in a sailor suit, and I brought down the house—and the flap on my pants—with my routine. I appeared in performances with the Felixstowe Players and the local vicar's dramatic society. Annie gave me my first acting lessons, and years later, she gave me a letter

Photo courtesy of the author

of introduction to Zelia Raye, who ran a dancing school in London. Between tap dance lessons, I took a job as a salesman, selling, among other things, toilet paper. Fortunately, I was sacked, which gave me time to audition.

At the suggestion of Miss Raye, I teamed with Frances Day, who became the sex symbol of her day, and we auditioned for the chorus in *The Five O'Clock Girl* at the London Hippodrome. When we were both offered places in the 1929 production, I eagerly accepted the four pounds weekly that I was offered. Frances turned down the show. She told me that she had bigger plans.

Another audition, another show, this one with a group of young actors in a so-called concert party, the Quaints. I got a wonderful part, Raleigh in R. C. Sherriff's *Journey's End*, for which I was paid the magnificent sum of seven pounds a week. We toured for eighteen months in the Far East beginning in 1929. We played Calcutta, Rangoon, Penang, Malacca, Kuala Lumpur, Bombay, Singapore, and other exotic locales, sometimes just one-night stands.

What a quaint name for a type of theatrical troupe that doesn't exist anymore. What is the history of that company?
R. A. Salisbury started the troupe in the 1920s. It was a company of about a dozen who originally performed songs, dances, and sketches at piers at all the seaside resorts in the UK during the summer. There were about a dozen in the troupe, including a soubrette, a comic, a singer, dancers. These concert parties were all the rage for some years.

By the time I joined, the company had graduated to performing not just *Journey's End* but *Mr. Cinders* and even *Hamlet*, in which I played Osric and the second grave digger—not a great double in which one could make a reputation—as well as *Funny Face* and *So This Is Love*. The repertoire was a combination of musicals and dramas designed to please the British population living abroad, as well as the locals. Most productions were directed by Jimmy [James Grant] Anderson, a real character, who had worked for years in small parts with some of the old-time greats of the theatre: Sir Herbert Beerbohm Tree, Mrs. Patrick Campbell, and Sir Charles Hawtrey, names that today no one remembers.

Through that company, you met people who played important roles later in your personal and professional lives. Noël Coward was one of them. What do you remember about the first meeting with the noted playwright-actor?
I met Noël by chance when we played Singapore in 1930. He had arrived there with his traveling companion, Jeffery Amherst, who was hotel bound, having come down with dysentery. So Noël was on his own, tootling around the city in a rickshaw. He stopped in front of the Victoria Theatre where he saw the theatre bill announcing "The Quaints in *Hamlet*."

He is reported to have stopped dead in his tracks and exclaimed, "I don't believe it. What does it mean?" He decided he had to see it.

Unbeknownst to Noël, we had to switch to *Mr. Cinders* because our leading man got plastered at lunch. When we were told the great man was going to attend the performance, I said, "So's God!" We were all very nervous. It was a bit of luck for me, though.

I had such a fit of nerves that when I made my entrance on roller skates, I made it at a much faster speed than usual. I tripped over a rough spot on the stage and sailed into a perfect somersault, and splat, landed flat on my back. It stopped the show; then I carried on. Coward came backstage afterwards to congratulate me on the fall and told me to keep it in. I thanked him for the compliment, addressing him as "Sir."

He retorted, "Don't call me 'Sir.'"

"What should I call you?" I asked.

Without so much as blinking, Coward replied, "Master."

That night he hosted the full cast to supper at the famous Raffles Hotel. And he took our entire troupe everywhere, including to a party at Government House given in his honor. In fact, his one stipulation on accepting invitations to any event in his honor was that he bring along his friends, the Quaints!

While waiting for his traveling companion to recover, Noël convinced Salisbury—or at least someone associated with the company—to allow him to play Stanhope in *Journey's End* for several performances. On his departure, he generously told me to contact him when I returned to London. When I eventually did return in late 1930, as requested, I phoned the number he gave me and spoke to Lorne Lorraine, his secretary, who told me that a ticket would be at the box office for me that night at the Phoenix Theatre to see his new play, *Private Lives*. Noël couldn't play character parts, but he was brilliant at the things he wrote for himself, including Elyot in this production with Gertrude Lawrence, Laurence Olivier, and Adrienne Allen.

In 1974, I appeared at Her Majesty's Theatre in *The Good Companions*, a musical version of a J. B. Priestley novel, which was really the story of the Dinky-Duos, a Quaints-like touring concert party, which Ronald Harwood, Andre Previn, and Johnny Mercer put together with an amusing story and songs. I was back to my tap and singing roots. Judi Dench was my costar. It was, as they say, déjà vu all over again in that production.

The Quaints' tour brought you to the attention of a young lady. What was the result of that meeting?

In Tientsin, China, Colonel Hayley Bell, the commissioner of Maritime Customs, who was in charge of two anti-smuggling gunboats, invited the company to luncheon with tennis afterwards. I played alongside a young lady who had flaming red hair, and I was trounced soundly. This lovely person was Bell's fifteen-year-old daughter, Mary, nicknamed Paddy.[1]

Eight years later, in 1939, Mary had achieved success as an actress in the London production of *Tony Draws a Horse*, replacing Diana Churchill when the play transferred to the Comedy later that year. We met again at a party given by my good friend, director Anthony Pelessier's mother, the renowned actress, Fay Compton. I'm ashamed to say, I didn't remember her. She told me she had seen me as George in a matinee of the production of *Of Mice and Men* in which I was appearing.[2]

260 Chapter Sixteen

I asked her if she had a good seat. "Yes," she said, "in the gallery." I told her she must come again, and I arranged a seat in the stalls. We had strawberries and cream in my dressing room afterwards, and that fixed it. We fell madly in love. We had both been going through problems with personal relationships: my marriage was crumbling; her fiancé had run off to marry another.

When Mary was asked to appear in the New York production, we made the heart-wrenching decision that she should go. She said, "If I survive this, we're really meant to be together forever." She made it across the Atlantic in a convoy chased by U-boats.

The play opened at the Playhouse Theatre with a new title, *Billy Draws a Horse*. After the opening, all the players went to Sardi's, the traditional restaurant where actors gathered to await reviews. The papers arrived. Someone read Lucius Beebe's *New York Herald Tribune* critique, which went something like, "The play called *Tony Draws a Horse* should be called *Billy Draws a Blank*." Champagne glasses were lowered, and the party went dead. There were a dozen more performances, and it closed. She sent me a telegram that read, "Darling. Wonderful news. Play a flop. Coming home. Mary."

We were married in Westminster Register Office, Caxton Hall, on January 16, 1941. I had a forty-eight-hour leave from the army where I had enlisted in 1939 in the Royal Engineers as a sapper [engineer]. Just a few months later, I was later invalided out of the service because of ulcers.

Immediately following our marriage, Mary insisted on giving up her career. "Only one actor in the family," she told me. Then we found out she was a gifted writer. She wrote three plays in which I appeared: *Men in Shadow*, *Duet for Two Hands*, and *The Uninvited Guest*. Her most famous work is the novel, *Whistle Down the Wind*, which was published in 1959 and became a film [1961] and then a long-running musical by Andrew Lloyd Webber, which played at the Aldwych [1998–2001].

I have to brag a bit. Every year on our anniversary, Mary and I renew our vows at our neighboring church, St. Mary's. To celebrate the occasion, I wear the sports jacket that I wore when I was courting her. It's had two lots of elbows and two lots of piping down the front, but I can still do up the middle button. We've been married sixty years.

Noël Coward wove his way in and out of your career for the next several years. What were some of the highs—and lows—of your work in his productions?

After C. B. Cochran's production of Noël's *Revue of 1931* surprisingly flopped, Noël rescued me both professionally and financially with a role he had written with me in mind: Joey Marryot in *Cavalcade*. The production at the Theatre Royal Drury Lane featured some four hundred cast members. There's never been a production like it since.

Hollywood came calling and offered me the same role in the film at the enormous salary of £100 a week. Noël advised me not to accept, explaining the pros and cons of going to California. On his advice, I turned it down.[3] I've never regretted it. But I did wonder what my life would have been like if I had accepted. It wasn't until years later that I worked in Hollywood.

Noël was at the top of his game when he wrote *Words and Music*, which opened in '32. Everybody got to rehearsals half an hour early for that show. We didn't want to miss a minute. He brought all the excitement and verve and thrill to the theatre.

He had originally set me to sing "Mad Dogs and Englishmen" in that revue, but, rightly so, he realized that at twenty-three, I was too young to sing it. Romney Brent, about a decade older than I was, sang the song, which has remained one of the top songs in the Coward canon.

Coward was a completely unique person. He was magic in the theatre. The "Master" remained a professional mentor and personal friend over the next decades.

Fortunately for your career, when you were invalided out of the army, Noël Coward again stepped in and offered you another memorable role, Shorty Blake in *In Which We Serve*. Some consider this Coward's cinematic magnum opus. What was the genesis of your association with that film?

Noël was a great patriot and wrote a screenplay to honor his great friend, Lord Louis Mountbatten, and the story about the sinking of his ship, the HMS *Kelly*, which was sunk on May 23, 1941, during the Battle of Crete. Noël planned to play the Montbatten-type role, Captain Kinross. There was great opposition to his playing that role, not from Lord Louis, as we referred to him, but from others, including Lord Beaverbrook,[4] publisher of the *Daily Express* and the *Evening Standard*. The story of the film, in fact, was a brilliant piece of propaganda and would inspire great patriotism. Mountbatten often came down to the set at Denham. Using his connections, he also supplied real navy extras when needed, as well as matériel needed for the sets.

I was very flattered that Noël had written the role for me as one of the survivors clinging to Carley floats. Along with Noël; Dickie Attenborough, who became a lifelong friend; Bernard Miles; and others, I spent hours and hours in the tank at Denham Studios, which was huge, about the size of an Olympic swimming pool, but square, and covered in synthetic fuel oil to resemble oil from the sinking ship called the *Torrin* in the film. It was absolutely ghastly working in the tank full of muck, and it stank. For three weeks, we spent every day in that filth.

One morning, the Master came out of his dressing room and saw us standing around, shivering, before diving into the tank. "What are you hanging about for?" he said. "Come on. Get in the water," and, showing off, he dove in. He came up, smothered in goo and, gasping, said, "Dysentery in every pore."

Ordinarily the actors didn't attend the rushes. There was the thought that to see what we had done the day before might affect our performances later. But at the request of the Master, I was in the screening room and seated just behind him one morning. We watched the scene where Kay Walsh and I are in a railway carriage. Noël enters the carriage and introduces us to his wife, played by Celia Johnson. When we were shooting, I was desperately nervous knowing Noël was in the scene—just as I had been so many years ago in Singapore. Strangely, on this occasion *he* was nervous. Take seven or eight had been printed.

The scene came on, and it was obvious that Noël was *not* good at all. The screening finished. There was a pause. No one spoke. Noël turned 'round to me and said, "All right, dear. Daddy knows."

He was marvelous about it. He was quick to recognize there was a problem with his performance. He knew. He always knew when something worked and when it didn't. We reshot the scene.

At one point, there is a scene in which the survivors are attacked by German aircraft. How to simulate the explosions of the bullets hitting the water? One of the brilliant technicians came up with the idea of filling condoms with an explosive powder and attaching hundreds of them to a sort of trellis contraption just under the water. The mechanism was attached to a control panel.

"Action," called David Lean, the director. The electrical contact was made and voilà! A good effect of machine-gun fire.

Just as David called, "Cut," bits and pieces of the condoms rose to the surface.

Everything worked out frightfully well. Many attribute the rise in enlistments in the Royal Navy to our film.

The first Mills family "production" made her debut in that film. Other productions followed in their parents' footsteps.

Mary's and my first "production," Juliet, was born in 1941; her godfather was Noël, and, yes, she made her debut in *In Which We Serve* as my character's baby. It wasn't until years later, though, that she caught the family acting bug.

It happened in 1949 when I was producing and starring in H. G. Wells's *The History of Mr. Polly*. One afternoon, I was reading the script in the garden, and a little voice said, "Is there anything for me in it, Daddy?"

I explained there was, indeed, a part of a six-year-old little girl—and Juliet was six.

I gave her a three-page scene to learn. She came back in about three minutes and performed the scene perfectly. She did a test and was terrific, and she played Little Polly, directed by my old friend Anthony—I called him "Ant"—Pelissier. At one point during production, I dried, and *she* prompted *me*.

A decade later, she auditioned for Sir John Gielgud for a role in *Five Finger Exercise*. At the time the great actor was directing the play and was unaware who her parents were. Once she won the role of Pamela Harrington, he asked, "Is that Mills girl any relation to John Mills?" Gielgud was then told who her mum and dad were. The play ran in London in 1959 and later went on to New York. She was nominated for a Tony as Best Featured Actress in a Play for the role.

Our second child, Hayley, was born five years later. One day, she was messing about on the lawn when director J. Lee Thompson was visiting to discuss his next film, *Tiger Bay*. Thompson had in mind a major character change in the story: instead of a twelve-year-old boy, why not, he suggested, a twelve-year-old girl? I would be playing a detective who investigates the murder, which she has witnessed.

"Where," I asked him naively, "would we get a girl who would meet the requirements for the part on short notice?"

"Over there," he said, pointing to Hayley. Hayley and I not only appeared in that film, but also together in three other films: *The Chalk Garden*, directed by Ronnie Neame; *The Truth about Spring*, directed by Richard Thorpe; and *The Family Way*, directed by Roy Boulting.

So began the next Mills progeny's career as a thespian. Hayley's career really took off when Walt Disney saw her in the first film and signed her to a multipicture contract. She made seven films for Disney and was named a Disney Legend even before I was.

Our youngest, Jonathan, who was born in 1949, is a writer and producer.

With the success of In Which We Serve, Noël Coward, David Lean, Anthony Havelock-Allan, and Ronald Neame wanted to continue with various projects with their production company, Cineguild. How did you fit into their plans?

First, there was another Coward play-to-film, *This Happy Breed*, directed by David Lean. I was again in a navy uniform.

John Mills with daughter Hayley, with whom he appeared in four films. Los Angeles Herald-Examiner/*Los Angeles Public Library Collection.*

David rang again after that and said he was doing another movie. He was by then a hot property. Everybody wanted to work with him. He said, "I've got a part I would love you to play. It's sort of a 'coat hanger' role, where a lot of marvelous characters hang all over you."

He didn't tell me the role or the title of the film, but I asked, "It wouldn't be Mr. Pip in *Great Expectations*, would it?"

"That's what it is," he replied and didn't seem terribly surprised that I knew.

He was right about the wonderful characters, both in real life and in the script: Martita Hunt as Miss Havisham; Finlay Currie as Magwitch; and young Jean Simmons as Estella. Bernard Miles was Joe Gargery; as Baron Miles, he was later known for his work establishing the Mermaid Theatre.[5]

I remember telling Mary after the first day's shooting that I had just worked with a shy, nervous but brilliant young actor as Mr. Pocket: Alec Guinness.

One of the most memorable scenes—and one of the most difficult to shoot—was the one in the room where I, as the adult Pip, have come to visit Miss Havisham. She is in the dining room at Satis House where her molding wedding cake is laid out on the table with its rotting lace cloth, cobwebs, mice, all the accoutrements of decay. It had taken five hours to set up the room, brilliantly done in perspective by production designer John Bryan. In the scene, Miss Havisham tells Pip it was she who encouraged Estella to leave him. I rush out, and as I'm going down the stairs, I hear her screaming. I dash back upstairs to see that a log has fallen from the fireplace, and her rotting dress is alight. I heroically try to save her by pulling off the tablecloth and throwing it over the flames that are engulfing her, but I can't save her.

Just before we started, producer Ronald Neame came on the set. He said to David and me, "If you can get this done in one take, it would be great."

"Why?" I asked.

"Because it will take another five hours to set the bloody thing up again."

It was sheer luck that everything went as planned.

There's a lesson to be learnt in the script for *Great Expectations*. David and Ronnie, who had shacked up together in some small country room, cut down this enormous novel to a size that didn't lose any of the qualities of the original. They came out with a bloody marvelous script. It can't be faulted.

What were the physical and professional challenges you faced playing Captain Robert Falcon Scott in *Scott of the Antarctic*, directed by Charles Frend? You played a real-life character rather than a "reel" one.

One of the problems with playing historical characters is when members of that person's family are still alive. This was particularly true in the case of Scott. I discovered a lot about him from Peter, his son, but the family didn't want to show anything they would consider even slightly detrimental to his character or show any weakness in their relation with him.

Scott had a very bad temper, but I wasn't allowed to show that. It wasn't a vast problem, but I felt I just couldn't be quite as honest as I'd have liked to be with the character. I believe it makes the person more heroic when he overcomes aspects in his character, which, perhaps, he'd rather not show. He was a human being, wasn't he? So I could show his physical strength and courage, but not his temper. He was a marvelous man, very much a leader. It didn't really prevent me, as an actor, from a full portrayal because I sneaked things in.

How dangerous were the locations on that shoot?

We all—cast and crew—suffered from frostbite on location in Norway. In Switzerland, there were just two of us, James Robertson Justice, playing Edgar

"Taff" Evans, and me. We shot on the Jungfrau where I almost lost my life when I slipped into a crevasse.

The film was a good one, but not a great one.

Ronald Neame went on to direct *Tunes of Glory* with you as Lieutenant Colonel Barrow, arguably one of your finest roles and your first venture with him as director. What are your recollections of the project?

I was surprised to find that Ronnie was a fine director, sure and firm. He had photographed me in *In Which We Serve*, produced me in *Great Expectations*, and those productions worked out all right. But he had never directed me. He told me, "If you do the magic that I've seen you do, I promise to be in the right place at the right time."

When he offered me the role, he said, "Barrow is right up your street, but he has to be hard, like Monty."

I told him I'd done shows for Field Marshall Bernard Montgomery just before D-Day. Mary and I had entertained troops on ships during the war. To his credit, Ronnie gave me some advice: "Keep the dialogue very crisp and clear, and speak up." That suggestion was a tremendous help.

What I didn't know then was that Ronnie had first offered that role to Alec Guinness, who felt it was too similar to the Colonel Nicholson character he'd played in his Oscar-winning performance in David Lean's *The Bridge on the River Kwai* three years earlier. He wanted to play Jock Sinclair, the red-headed boozer. It was Alec who suggested that I take the role of Barrow. I am indebted to him for that. It was casting against type, a role reversal for both of us. We looked forward to working together again after almost a decade.

How did Neame follow up on his promise to be the support you needed for this change-of-pace role?

One example is the party scene with Alec where I explode, blow my top, and go absolutely raving mad. I embarrass everyone, shouting at all the guests. All this from having been in complete control earlier.

I knew that these big, emotional scenes are best on the first take, but I also knew how difficult it would be to get appropriate reaction from extras. There were about eighty in the scene.

Take one. Ronnie looked at me and said, "Action."

The scene went very, very well.

Ronnie called, "Print."

We were about to move to the next setup when I saw the soundman beckon to Ronnie. I saw them talking, talking, talking. Ronnie came to my side, "We have to go again. The soundman told me that the needle was banging on the edge of the meter when you went into a rage."

"Ronnie," I said, taking him aside, "I really don't want to do it again. It *should* sound a bit raucous."

To Ronnie's credit, he told the soundman, "We won't go again." Another director would have tried to convince me to do another. If I had gone again, I couldn't have guaranteed that it would have been as good as the first. That take was a bloody good one. Ronnie knew it was the right one, and he knew I'd be worried if I did another. At that point, he showed that he made the decisions on the set.

Neame also directed you and Hayley in *The Chalk Garden*, a far different story. Were there any difficulties with the film being overseen by a Hollywood producer?

Hayley played Laurel to my Maitland, the butler in this, our second film together.

It was produced by the very successful American Ross Hunter. He was what I would call a "lush" producer, very Hollywood. Everything was artistic, but hardly realistic. Everything had to be gorgeous. Nothing looked like the old English house where the story takes place, so Ronnie couldn't quite get what he wanted for the film. He didn't get the reality he would have liked. I don't mean anything in a derogatory manner. It just wasn't real. That's what upset Ronnie. It was an odd duo: Ronnie the quintessential British filmmaker; Ross Hunter, a model Hollywood producer. Hunter was, as Ronnie said, "where the money was."

An interesting casting note: Although it was understood by Ronnie and Ross that Gladys Cooper would play Mrs. St. Maugham, the story goes that Dame Edith Evans visited with them at Ross's suite at the Dorchester and basically announced that she was playing the role! Gladys understandably blamed Ronnie for her not playing the role.

During the production, Dame Edith bestowed a charming nickname on Ronnie: Ron-Pon. Someone—can't recall who—made a needlepoint pillow with that sobriquet on it. Ronnie kept it in his Beverly Hills home.

On several occasions, you worked with David Lean. What was his working method?

David was very different from Ronnie. Ronnie's work was unobtrusive, smooth and professional. He loved actors and appreciated them, unlike David Lean who would ask everyone on the floor about a take . . . except the actors.

One incident I remember, but can't remember which film: After a take, David turned to the cameraman and asked, "Was that all right for you?" Then he turned to the soundman and asked, "Was that all right for you?" He continued asking other crew members for their approval of the take.

Finally, I couldn't have it. "What about the damn actors, David? Was it all right for us?"

With David, we're talking about someone who was a genius. He never wasted film. Never. His preparation took forever. David would give his cameraman, Freddie Young, who was on several of his films, the setup and leave for a bit. David would come back and ask, "What have you done, Freddie?"

"Just what you wanted, David," he said.

"That's *not* what I wanted," he'd admonish the great cameraman and give him further directions.

He was a fantastic director, so one can forgive some of the personal drawbacks he had. He often treated people terribly, but he was forgiven because what he produced was quite extraordinary.

Lean must have known what you were capable of when he cast you as Michael in *Ryan's Daughter*.

He must have had faith in me. He asked me if I thought I could play a village idiot.

"Typecasting," I laughed.

He also asked, "Have you ever gotten an Oscar?" He well knew I hadn't. He told me, "You will with this role."

He was right. I got the Supporting Actor Oscar for playing the mute, Michael. Before this, I'd spent all my time learning dialogue, and for this, I get an award for not saying anything!

I remember I asked him what the schedule would be, and he said twelve weeks. Well, knowing David, I doubled that and instead of staying in a hotel with the cast, I took a house in the local village and brought the family over. I was right. It was an eight-month shoot.

You returned to your musical theatre roots in the television version of *Cats*. How did Andrew Lloyd Webber bring you into the production?

When Andrew decided to do a television version, he had to cut at least twenty minutes. There was one section that he wasn't too mad about, which was with Gus, the Theatre Cat. Gus does a number, which, supposedly, Andrew was never very keen on. The story about how I got involved goes like this: He was having dinner with his wife, Madeleine, and he said, "I don't know what the hell I'm going to do with the old cat. I want an old actor, and what *old* actor can do musicals?"

There was a long pause. Madeleine waited and then said, "Johnnie . . . Mills."

Andrew said, "Oh, he wasn't a musical star."

"Oh, he certainly was," she told him. "He was a song and dance man."

That's how I came back to the musical stage where it all began. We shot it at the Adelphi Theatre where, in 1932, I'd appeared in *Words and Music*.

With your career bridging theatre and film, how would you compare the two?

I just love the stage. I love being in the theatre. It's not the same as film. I don't get the excitement I get in the theatre in any way.

You don't walk onto a soundstage and wonder whether you'll get tomatoes thrown at you or get applause. You don't get any of that working in film. You know that you'll do the very best you can. What you feel is sort of an excitement at the start of a new film; the adrenaline flows.

In the theatre, you're in the loo most of the evening from sheer fright. Olivier was in a state on first nights, an absolute state. It's that terrific excitement you can't get with film.

I was on the phone to my best friend, Dickie, now Lord Attenborough,[6] and we were talking about how different things are in the film business today. It's not as personal as when we started out. The people who ran the studios then knew films and loved them. Now accountants have gotten into the act, and they really don't know anything about film. Back then, I could be halfway through a film without a contract; we would have just shaken hands. Now we have to sign on the dotted line before we appear in front of the camera for two seconds. It was more like a family then, a golden time with people like Alexander Korda and Micky Balcon.

Sir John died on April 23, 2005, at age ninety-seven. His wife died just eight months later. They had been married for sixty-four years.

Selected Credits

Theatre

Charley's Aunt, New (1930; Amy Brandon Thomas); *Cavalcade*, Theatre Royal Drury Lane (1931; Noël Coward); *Words and Music*, Adelphi; (1932: Noël Coward); *Jill, Darling*, Saville (1934; Francis M. Collinson); *Floodlight*, Saville (1937; Beverley Nichols); *She Stoops to Conquer*, Old Vic (1938; Tyrone Guthrie); *Of Mice and Men*, Apollo (1939; Norman Marshall); *Men in Shadow*, Vaudeville (1942; Mills, Bernard Miles); *Duet for Two Hands*, Lyric (1945; Herbert Darsey); *The October Man* (1947; Roy Ward Baker); *The Damascus Blade*, Bristol Hippodrome, Theatre Royal Newcastle (1950; Laurence Olivier); *Top of the Ladder*, St. James's (1950; Tyrone Guthrie); *Figure of Fun*,

Aldwych (1951–1952; Peter Ashmore); *The Uninvited Guest*, Bristol Hippodrome (1952–1953; Sydney Phasey); *Charley's Aunt*, New Theatre (1954, John Gielgud); *Ross*, Eugene O'Neill, New York (1961–1962; Glen Byam Shaw); *Separate Tables*, Apollo (1971; Michael Blakemore); *Veterans*, Royal Court (1972; Ronald Eyre); *The Good Companions*, Her Majesty's (1974; Braham Murray); *Goodbye, Mr. Chips*, Chichester (1982; Patrick Garland); *Little Lies*, Wyndham's (1983; Tony Tanner); *The Petition*, NT, Lyttelton, (1986; Peter Hall); *Pygmalion*, Plymouth, New York (1987; Val May); *An Evening with John Mills*, Academy of Television Arts and Sciences, North Hollywood, California (March 15, 1999)

Film
Midshipmaid [a.k.a. *Midshipmaid Gob*] (1932); *The Ghost Camera* (1933); *Those Were the Days* (1934); *Car of Dreams* (1935); *Born for Glory* [UK title: *Forever England*] (1935); *The Green Cockatoo* (1937); *Cottage to Let* [a.k.a. *Bombsight Stolen*] (1941); *The Black Sheep of Whitehall* (1942); *Land of Promise*, voice [Paul Rotha's Films of Fact] (1945); *Total War in Britain*, voice [Paul Rotha's Films of Fact] (1945); *Waterloo Road* (1945); *The Way to the Stars* [a.k.a. *Johnny in the Clouds*] (1945); *Scott of the Antarctic* (1948); *The Rocking Horse Winner* (1950); *Morning Departure* (1950); *Mr. Denning Drives North* (1952); *Hobson's Choice* (1954); *Escapade* (1955); *Above Us the Waves* (1955); *The End of the Affair* (1955); *The Vicious Circle* (1957); *Ice Cold in Alex* (1958); *Swiss Family Robinson* (1960); *The Singer Not the Song* (1961); *Tiara Tahiti* (1962); *The Chalk Garden* (1964); *King Rat* (1965); *Operation Crossbow* (1965); *The Wrong Box* (1966); *Sky West and Crooked* [a.k.a. *Gypsy Girl*] (1966); *The Family Way* (1966); *Oh! What a Lovely War* (1969); *Ryan's Daughter* (1970); *Oklahoma Crude* (1973); *Gandhi* (1982); *Bright Young Things* (2003)

Television
Producers' Showcase, "The Letter" (1956); *DuPont Show of the Week*, "The Interrogator" (1961); *Dundee and the Culhane*, thirteen episodes (1967); *Young at Heart*, eighteen episodes (1980–1982); *Sherlock Holmes and the Masks of Death* (1984); *A Woman of Substance* (1985); *A Tale of Two Cities* (1989); *The Lady and the Highwayman* (1989); *Night of the Fox* (1990); *Martin Chuzzlewit* (1994); *Great Performances*, "Cats" (1998); *The Gentleman Thief* (2001)

Director
Angel, 1947, Strand; written by Mary Hayley Bell; *Sky West and Crooked*, 1966

Awards and Nominations

Hobson's Choice, 1955, BAFTA, Best British Actor, nominee; *Tunes of Glory*, 1960, BAFTA, Best British Actor, nominee; also, Venice Film Festival, Volpi Cup, Best Supporting Actor, winner; *Ross*, 1962, Tony, Best Actor in a Play, nominee; *Ryan's Daughter*, 1971, Academy Award, Supporting Actor, winner; also, BAFTA, Best Supporting Actor, nominee; Golden Globe, Best Supporting Actor, winner

Honors

CBE, 1960; KBE, 1976; BFI Fellowship, 1995; Disney Legend, 2002; BAFTA Fellowship, 2002

Notes

1. In her autobiography, *Anna Lee: Memoir of a Career on* General Hospital *and in Film*, actress Anna Lee, who was traveling with her aunt then, remembers meeting Mary in Hong Kong: "We galloped around Kowloon in rickshaws, complete with pointed bamboo hats, all of which we rented from their owners. We generally behaved in a rather unladylike fashion. In fact, we behaved so badly that we received a call from one of the governor's *aides-de-camp* who scolded us saying, 'Young English girls do not behave in such a manner.' But, oh, did we have fun" (59).

2. Also in her autobiography, Lee recounts meeting Bell, at which time she said she would like to meet Mills again. She told Bell, "You know he's married." Bell said she knew, "but that makes no difference because I'm going to marry him one day" (100). The meeting at the studio was arranged.

3. The film, released in 1933, was directed by Frank Lloyd and starred Frank Lawton in the role of Joey Marryot.

4. In his autobiography, *Straight from the Horse's Mouth*, Ronald Neame, who was the cinematographer on the film, recalls, "[Beaverbrook] wholeheartedly disliked Noël Coward [and] demanded to know how the effete matinée idol could possibly play such a role. . . . Noël didn't seem to take any notice of the scathing press other than to comment, 'I don't care what they say about me as long as they go on talking about me'" (62).

5. The theatre closed in 2008 to be "redeveloped."

6. Lord Attenborough died August 24, 2014, at age ninety.

CHAPTER SEVENTEEN

∽

Alfred Molina

I don't think I've ever been anybody's first choice for a role. That's not a bad thing.

Alfred Molina lives in a restored 1920s house on a quiet street above the Sunset Strip. Elegant old trees form a canopy over the sidewalk. The front garden is awash with blooming plants: roses, agapanthus, and geraniums. An enormous copa de oro leans toward a vintage stained glass window. In the backyard, a waterfall burbles down a side wall, and dozens of pots await planting by the actor's wife, actress-author Jill Gascoine.

Molina makes a tardy entrance, stage right. He apologizes, "I was hiking in Griffith Park and got lost. I followed an interesting trail that led to another, and before I knew it . . . I couldn't phone because there was no reception."

The sixty-two-year-old actor disappears to change clothes, and in less than five minutes, he has caught his breath, apologizes again, and settles his six-foot-three-inch frame into an armchair. Just as he is about to begin his discussion about his career and thoughts about the acting profession, he sees a busload of gawking tourists, cameras at the ready, slowly lurching past the house.

∽

What led you down the path to acting?

To be honest, I'm not really sure. Family legend has it that my mother remembers that at the age of nine, I said, "I want to be an actor." Let's assume that's true. At that age, I wouldn't have had any serious idea what that involved. I wouldn't have understood the subtleties or implications. I do

Photo by Kevin Lynch

remember seeing *Spartacus* in 1960 and it having a very strong, visceral effect on me. It wasn't Kirk Douglas, although if I ever meet him, I want to thank him. It was seeing someone in my innocent eyes who seemed like a real person. I've since seen the movie and appreciated other performances, but it was something about that central character. I saw a hero, and I responded to that. But I had no idea what acting meant.

My teacher, Martyn Corbett, at the Cardinal Manning Secondary Public School for Boys, told me that I wasn't a very good actor, but I was a wonderful showoff. He told me if I was serious, I'd have to work at it. I had a kind of naive fearlessness, but I didn't know what I was doing. Corbett eventually coached me for my drama school audition.

You enrolled in Guildhall School of Music and Drama. Why there?

I had applied to RADA, Central School, all of them. Guildhall was the only one that replied and gave me an audition. It was only after I accepted my place at Guildhall that the others wrote that I'd been accepted.

Do you recall your audition pieces?

I remember exactly. My Shakespeare piece was the Chorus from *Henry VI, Part 2*: "Open your ears . . ." [Molina can quote the speech at length.] I also prepared a speech from Brecht's *Caucasian Chalk Circle* and a speech from a play by J. P. Donleavy, *A Fairy Tale of New York*. In that, I played a boxing coach who has a chat with the main character who has just returned from Ireland. I used my American accent, and I remember the line "He's been tellin' me about the wimmin over dere. You don't have to marry 'em. They do it because they like it." I also prepared a poem, a chunk from Robert Browning's *My Last Duchess*.

What was the learning trajectory at drama school?

When I was acting in drama club productions at the end of term at secondary school, I was the big fish in a very small pond. I was the one star actor at the school only because four other kids and I bothered to turn up. We ended up taking all the big parts because the teachers knew we'd be there. I got one of the leads because I was there, and I loved it. We did Brecht's *The Caucasian Chalk Circle*, but I never really understood it when we did it.

It was only when I went to drama school when the education became formal, and I really had to study rather than rely on enthusiasm. Demands were being made on me. It was then I started thinking about acting in terms of things I would have to work on. It was often accents I didn't know, like Russian or German accents. We did a production of a play where a whole chunk of dialogue was in German, and we were learning the German phonetically.

The instructor said, "You've got find a way of knowing exactly what part of Germany your character is from. The way you speak German has to have some kind of authenticity." So we started studying more specifically. I always found myself loving that kind of work. It was never boring. The technique of it absolutely hooked me, and I got really excited about it.

When did your ear for accents begin to take shape?

I've always been good at accents. I don't think there's any particular genius for them on my part. I think it was just a happy confluence of the accidents of my birth. My father was Spanish, my mother Italian. They learned English at the same time I did. I lived with their accents. I was brought up in Notting Hill, which, in those days, was very working class, Irish, Caribbean, Spanish, Italian, Portuguese. The kids at school were sons and daughters of these people, and I heard their parents talking. I remember playing in the street—those were the days when you could—and we would mimic what we saw on television. Probably as much as 50 to 60 percent of television was American. We would copy those accents as we played cowboys and Indians or cops and robbers: "Head 'em off at the pass" or "Ya got me, copper." Maybe because of my proclivities for showing off and wanting to live in that fantasy world, I soaked up the sounds just a bit more. As far as the American accent, I've had the advantage of living here for the best part of twenty years, so I'm surrounded by it.

How challenging are the variations of the American accent?

I have always been fascinated by all things American and particularly the sound of the American accent. I've always felt at home with it and had a real affinity for it. It's always come fairly easily. There's a rhythm to it, a musicality, a vibrant, percussiveness to it. Whenever I've played an American in a British theatre production, I've always had a good time.

The Chicago accent is really tough. A New York accent, which is the one I feel most at home with, is probably the one I've heard the most and the one I've used the most. But even within New York, there are variations. With that level of specificity, I need a coach.

I got pulled up once: a sweet woman came to see *Red* and asked, "May I make one observation?"

"Of course," I said.

"There's one word that you say that has the wrong emphasis: television." She explained that in America the accent is on the first syllable, and in Britain, it's the second half. I'd never spotted it. As soon as she pointed that out, I could hear it. It's tiny things like that that you have to keep an eye—and ear—out for.

The thing that's very interesting about accents: When an American speaks, you get a sense of where he's from and not much else. When an English person speaks, their accent is redolent of all kinds of information: their class, their education, background, and where they come from, all kinds of subtle codes. That's even before you listen to their vocabulary.

It's interesting from an acting point because we "hold the mirror up," and that sort of stuff is wonderfully useful and illuminating. When you get it right, you're telling a whole other story and telling it in a more authentic way, which is why I think accents are crucial. The wrong accent can take you out of the moment, and you may never get back in again. The other side of that is when an actor gets so obsessed with the accent that the performance becomes all about the accent.

Younger American actors have a much better time with foreign accents than perhaps actors from ten to fifteen years ago. British actors are perceived as having a better American accent than Americans having a good British accent, probably because as children growing up, we were exposed to much more American product than our counterparts in America watching British programs. In England, we couldn't escape American programming. The Americanized twist in language is so pervasive in all aspects of culture, music, fashion. The only time you see British television in America is when you watch BBC America or PBS, and a small number watch those programs.

When my daughter, who lives in London, was in her late teens, she went through a phase when she had a London accent, and everything ended with a question mark. [He raises his voice at the end of the sentence to demonstrate the concept.] It was all from watching *Ally McBeal* and *Friends*.

British drama schools taught RP for years.

Received Pronunciation was an attempt to rid anyone of any accent. Today, that's for the most part been discarded; regional accents are more accepted.

What followed once you completed the course work at Guildhall?

I went into rep. My very first job was working in a children's theatre company. We toured doing potted versions of *Midsummer Night's Dream* and *The Jungle Book*. I did two stints with companies like that, doing two shows a day in schools. It was an interesting period, hard work, but it was fun. It was the sort of work we all knew wasn't what we wanted to do permanently. We were all dreaming of other things.

I remember being in a pub in the Midlands reading in *The Stage* magazine about an actor who had just signed a contract to do a play in the West End for the glorious sum of £100 a week! In 1975, that sounded like a lot of money. We were working for £17 a week, the Equity minimum.

Various rep companies followed: Newcastle, Leicester, Liverpool. By the time I hit the rep circuit, it was still a major employer for actors. Most cities still had one rep theatre; Leicester and Manchester had two; Birmingham had three, one rep and two commercial houses. The Royal Exchange and the Manchester Library, which was slightly smaller and a bit more risqué, was where people went to see new plays by playwrights nobody ever heard of. But the notion of hiring a company of actors for a season of three or four or five plays for a period of three or four months was already dying.

With the closing down of these companies, there was a rise in new theatre companies that didn't have a building, so they had far less overhead. These new companies applied to the British Arts Council for what were called "project grants" and received £25,000 to put on a play; where it was put on and how it was paid for came out of that grant.

My generation of actors was lucky in that there was this huge explosion of grassroots theatre, which put on essentially agitprop productions. There were companies such as the Red Ladder; the 7.84, which took its name from the evidence that 7 percent of the population own 84 percent of the wealth in the country; and Common Stock—a whole flurry of left-wing groups doing radical plays, new plays, and reworking classics. I joined the RSC in 1977 and left in 1978. I worked for Belt and Braces at the Albany Empire in Deptford, South London, one of these fringe companies. That was my world for five or six years. Although I now make my living as a film actor, I go back to the theatre every year.

What are some of your recollections of your season with the RSC?
The RSC used the Aldwych as their London home, and I appeared there in *Bandits* and *Days of the Commune*, both directed by Howard Davies; also *Troilus and Cressida* with Michael Pennington.

Young spear or lantern carriers like me had maybe one or two lines, such as, "Hark, they come."

It was a season where the RSC also used the Donmar when it was still really a warehouse and used as their experimental theatre. I was in Edward Bond's *The Bundle* with Patrick Stewart.

Besides Shakespeare and experimental plays, you also appeared in musicals.
We did *Destry: The Musical* in 1982, with director Rob Walker, who effectively stole the screenplay. Not stole, really; he borrowed big chunks from the movie. We weren't allowed to use the song "See What the Boys in the Backroom Will Have" from the movie in our production. It was a good little show. That production is where I met my wife, Jill Gascoine, who played the Marlene Dietrich role.

Two years before, I was Jud Fry in *Oklahoma!* at the Palace, Cameron Macintosh's first big musical. Jud is a good part, and there's more to it in the stage version than there is in the film. The one song everyone knows, "Pore Jud Is Daid," is in the film and the musical, but Jud's solo, "Lonely Room," sort of a dirge, was not included in the film. Our director, William Hammerstein, Oscar's son, absolutely insisted on keeping everything intact in his father's shows, so every night for a year, every other song was met with a burst of applause, apart from mine, which no one knew, because no one ever heard of it.

What do you expect from a director?
My facetious answer? I expect the director not to get in the way. I always hope that the director will know more than I do about the play and the playwright's intention and will have a deeper, more detailed understanding of the play.

As an actor, I read a play over and over and over again. My intelligence is limited, but I have a great imagination. I can think of all kinds of places to take the character, but I need the intelligence of the director to point me in the right direction. Getting lost in the canyon as I did today is a perfect example of what I'm talking about. Imaginatively, I had no problem thinking, "Oh, I'll go down this path. This looks like a good way to go." I just leap into it, but I need someone to tell me which path to take. That's what I hope to get from a director who is smarter than I and says, "No, no. That's a dead end. Let me tell you why."

I know a lot of actors look at directors in a rather adversarial way; they see the struggle between the actor and director as essentially one dominating the other. I've always gotten on very well with directors—in the main—because I rely on them. I find myself getting lost without them.

As Satipo in _Raiders of the Lost Ark_, you received your first real on-screen credit. What are your recollections of the director, the role, and your furry costars?

It was a big event for me because it was my first film. My daughter was about to be born, and I was broke, so the movie money came in very handy. The whole thing was a massive learning curve for me. I was so green about filming. I didn't even know about hitting my marks. It all had to be explained to me. I was getting notes from carpenters!

Steven Spielberg was already a star director in 1981. I was in awe of him. He was very generous and patient with me. On the set, he established a familial feeling. Although he didn't realize it, he both got my film career off the ground but also on a more personal basis, he saved my bacon. I've always publicly thanked Steven for that.

My costars were long-legged, furry tarantulas. They get a very bad reputation. Despite being ugly, horrible looking, and squirm-making, they're effectively harmless; they scratch, and they bite, but they're not poisonous. And, yes, they were all _real_. That made it great fun. Today, they would be CGI [computer-generated imagery], but this was more than thirty years ago.

I was only on the production for about a week in London and about a week in Hawaii. I didn't have a lot to do, but I was thrilled beyond measure getting the chance to do it.

The chunk that I did was right at the start of the movie and basically set up the character of Indiana Jones, so it was constantly being used in clips and trailers. It gave my friends and family the impression that I had this huge role. The trailer was all about Harrison Ford and me! It was a lovely thing to film and very exciting but had nothing to do with the plot.

By the time you played Dr. Octavius, the arch villain, in _Spider-Man 2_, you were a name to be reckoned with. When playing a comic book character, how do you refrain from the role becoming "camp"?

I had just auditioned for Tevye in *Fiddler on the Roof* when I got the role in *Spider-Man*. Because the director of *Fiddler* left, the whole thing was in a state of flux, and we weren't quite sure whether it was going to happen at all. I really couldn't turn down the Dr. Octavius role.

During the early part of filming, everything for *Fiddler* came together, and the producers said they would wait for me to finish the film. Once I finished, I went to London to see my daughter, who was expecting her third child, then straight to New York for eighteen months as Tevye. I had the best of both worlds.

In terms of the character in *Spider-Man*, you have to know what medium the character is based on. That determines how you play it. Because the character happens to be a comic book figure, you don't have to play it like one. You avoid it being camp by playing it for real. All great villains are written seriously to create tension and conflict for the hero.

The audience felt sympathy for Doc Ock, didn't they?

That's typical of many of those Marvel characters, unlike the D. C. comic characters, who live in a much more absolutist moral world; Batman and Superman are good and never have a moment's failing. What made the Marvel characters so interesting—especially when I was reading them as a child—is that they all have a moral ambiguity. Many of the Marvel heroes are reluctant heroes. They're people to whom something has happened, and they're placed in this position, which they don't always enjoy.

Doctor Ock is one of those villains who starts as a good person; he's a serious scientist. Then he has this terrible accident, which affects him in a bad way. At the end of the movie, though, he has a moment of redemption.

I think that's a tribute not so much to my acting as to the complexities written into the character to start with. I got hold of story lines from the original appearance of Doctor Octavius in the early sixties. There were lots of the comics floating around in director Sam Raimi's office. There was no shortage of research material. He was drowning in it. I saw this strain of moral ambivalence and conflict was there all the time. When I'm offered a big part like that, I have a responsibility to have a handle on what I'm doing.

The film version of *The Tempest* was directed by Julie Taymor. What is the difference between working with a female director versus a male?

I enjoy working with women directors because they do have a sensitivity and awareness of the material that is unique. That's not to say male directors don't. But there is a difference in tone and energy. I like that feminine attitude, in the sense of female. I find their particular type of energy very supportive. When there's a room full of chaps with a male director, there is always a tendency of getting testosterone heavy, which is fine sometimes. That can be a lot of fun. But there's a different kind of energy with the woman director. Certain projects just lend themselves to a feminine approach.

In the film, the play has been redefined. Prospero has been refashioned as Prospera. What about refashioning Shakespeare?

I love it. I like to think that Shakespeare wouldn't mind. I think it's perfectly in the spirit of Shakespeare. He certainly wasn't above refashioning existing material. He had no qualms about stealing from the occasional Italian novel or Roman play and adapting to his use. Because the plays are so good and so full of good material and writing, beautiful words and thoughts and deep, dense ideas, they stand up to scrutiny, to rethinking, to retooling. Conceptualizing Shakespeare is dangerous; reworking him, putting it into a different setting that somehow highlights elements in the story or illuminates a hitherto unseen strand, can be acceptable.

The only time it doesn't work is when it's done with a devil-may-care attitude, when someone might say, "Oh, we're going to do a production of *Titus Andronicus*, and we're going to make Titus Irish. . . ." Or when Shakespeare is sacrificed for some kind of concept that the director has. A perfect example of that reworking is Ian McKellen's 1995 Richard III as a Fascist, which he and Richard Loncraine refashioned. The *Macbeth* that he did at the Donmar some years earlier, which director Trevor Nunn boiled down so that it became more intense, more concentrated, also worked.

What Julie did with *Tempest* by changing Prospero to Prospera is to completely redefine and clarify the relationship between her and Miranda. The drive of Prospera to do right by her daughter in terms of having denied her a normal life by retreating to this lonely paradise, wanting her to reenter the world as a thoroughly formed grown-up, intelligent woman and not this wild nature child, that becomes her priority. It wasn't that we were inventing a new story; it was always there. Plus, those undercurrents of racism and colonial oppression in the play just suddenly bubbled to the surface.

Your role as Stephano was also refashioned.

I thought I knew the play. I've seen umpteen productions in which Stephano and Trinculo are often played as a comedy duo, a couple of antics. In this reworking, they're all of that, but they become opportunistic, malevolent, sort of thieving rip-off merchants, and they exploit the possibility of making money out of Caliban. Stephano says something to the effect, "If I can get this creature back to Italy, I'll make some money." Exactly like the story of *King Kong*. I'd never quite appreciated that notion before. I had only seen Stephano and Trinculo as a couple of drunken, comic figures.

Moving back to your theatre work, which you said you try to do yearly: Your opening line in John Logan's *Red* is "What do you see?" What do you see in a role that attracts you to it and you make the decision to accept it?

I'm not sure that I know. I was always a character actor, never a Romeo. There are certain roles by dint of reputation that people say, "When you're a certain age, you'll be ready for . . ." I'm sixty-two now, and there's a whole generation of parts out there that I can play. For instance, Big Daddy in *Cat on a Hot Tin Roof*, some great parts in Miller's *Death of a Salesman*. Those are something to aim for.

When I read a part and I get this feeling that I just know I have to do it—it's never one of those punching in the air moments when I say, "Yes, I just found the part." It's actually a sinking feeling because as I'm reading this part, I can feel all my options disappear. It's a delicious state to be in.

There's an actor's joke: There's only one thing better than work and that's being available. Somehow being available for work is somehow a more delicious state than actually working. The offer is invariably the best part of the job. You say yes, and from then on it's a slow, diminishing return.

When *Red* came along, pretty much out of the blue, it had been almost two years since I'd been in a play. I'd done movies and television, but I was looking for a play. Before I got to page 21, I just knew I had to play Mark Rothko. I've now played the role for more than two years.

How did you become associated with *Red*?

It all happened in a rather casual way. I'd met Michael Grandage, who was then Donmar Warehouse artistic director, when he brought *Frost/Nixon* to New York in 2007. A friend of mine was in the play, and I went to see it, and met Michael then. We got on very well, chatting and gossiping about what was going on in London.

Then in 2009, I was in New York again, and I got a phone call saying that Michael was also in town and wanted to meet me for a drink. My first thought was, "Yeah, we'd got on ever so well before. This is another chance for us to have another gossip about what's happening."

We met, and he asked, "I know you worked at the Donmar in *Destry*. What are your memories of it?"

I told him I have a soft spot for it, that it's a bloody wonderful place. That's where I met my wife, and blah, blah, blah. I'm on my second cocktail by now, thinking, "This is a lovely evening. Perhaps we should go and have dinner."

"I'm glad you have those memories of the Donmar," he said. Then he slipped a FedEx envelope across the table to me.

I suddenly thought, "I think I've just been set up." He went off to an appointment, and I pulled out the script and sat down to read John Logan's play.[1]

Whenever I read a play that I love, I phone Jill. My contention is that when a husband phones his wife, especially if it's long distance, and starts the conversation with, "Darling, there's something I need to tell you," the wife will invariably go to the darkest place. She'll think, "It's another woman," or "You've spent the kids' college money," or "You've been arrested."

I phoned her and said, "Darling, there's something I have to talk to you about."

Jill's response: "Oh, shit, you've read a play."

Red transferred from London to New York, but Equity has a rule about British actors on Broadway as those roles might be available to American actors. How did that affect Red?

It's a movable feast. It depends on who it is, what it is, how long it's there for. It's a kind of reciprocal method. For instance, the season when Eddie Redmayne was doing Red on Broadway and getting a dispensation to do it, American actors Jeff Goldblum and Mercedes Ruhl went to London to do Neil Simon's The Prisoner of Second Avenue.

I think there's a kind of give-and-take. In my case, I'm an American citizen now, so I can work on Broadway whenever the opportunity arises. Even when I worked on Broadway for the first time in Art, I was a green card holder.

I think the reason why Red had a dispensation was because it was a Donmar production, and it was a specific transfer of a preexisting production coming to Broadway for a limited run. Had the producers wanted to license the play for an indefinite run under their own auspices, I think Equity would have put its foot down. I think they would have let me do it, but possibly not Eddie.

In Red, you are already on stage when the audience comes into the theatre. That's not in the published version of the play. How did that come about?

In the published script, the playwright has Rothko staring out through the fourth wall at a painting. Michael and John wanted to create a sense of the audience entering the studio. We felt that having the audience coming in with me already in place, contemplating a painting, which they can see, was more conducive to creating that sense.

At one point I asked, "Would it work if I were already on stage as the audience came in?" Michael said that thought had crossed his mind, but he remembered a production he had done a few years before when he had one of the actors on stage "behaving." It drove that particular actor crazy. The audience thought the play had already started. It was counterproductive. I argued that if I'm already there, sitting and looking at a painting, not even facing the audience, with my back to them, they might not even notice I'm there. A few people did, but they just carried on waiting for the show.

At the Donmar, which seats about 250, I was on stage around fifteen to eighteen minutes. At the Golden on Broadway, it was about half an hour. The first couple of nights I had to time going to the bathroom—as there is not an interval—and make sure I didn't drink anything an hour before the show. But I got into it, and I found it a very useful half an hour because it helped me get into the play each night. It also helped me to read the audience. I got the sense about what kind of mood they were in as I sat listening to them.

As Rothko, you performed a physically demanding eight performances a week. Dr. Octavius in *Spider-Man 2* was, in its way, just as demanding. What are the demands on you as an actor in a play versus a film?

That film made far less demand physically than the eight shows a week. It's basically because on film, we're working in very small increments. It's a bit like making a big mosaic out of tiny tiles. Also, in those sorts of films, the actor is a small cog in a much bigger machine. The actor has to embrace that fact, and once he can do that, it ceases to be hard work. At worst, it becomes tedious. The hours are long, and I do get tired, but it's not the same kind of intense physicality that *Red* was.

The only time film is hard work is when you're working under duress, under conditions that are not conducive to the work itself. Say you're shooting a movie, and it's unbearably hot weather, and things are going wrong, the food doesn't arrive, everything is falling apart—that's when it's really hard work. It becomes not only physically but also morally and spiritually difficult.

Most of the time, when I have that huge infrastructure of a film around me, my every need is taken care of. I don't have to think about anything. I wake up in the morning, have a shower, and my driver, who's also my assistant, is outside with the car; when I get into the car, there's a cup of coffee waiting for me and all the newspapers; when I arrive at the studio, I have time to get my stuff out and hook up my computer. Then someone comes and says, "We'll come and fetch you in five minutes to get made up." And there is always fruit and muffins available!

To be a film actor is a very privileged, comfortable, wonderful life. No three ways about it. Any actor who complains about working too hard in movies really ought to get a reality check.

Red was unique in the sense that it was an hour and a half of nonstop verbal and physical action, which didn't let up until the end. Even at the very, very end, Eddie was pulling records, cleaning me up, picking stuff up, plus the big central motif of preparing the canvas. I was far more tired at the end of the week in *Red* than I ever was during *Spider-Man 2*.

What's the motive for you to continually return to the theatre? The environment is hardly luxurious: dressing rooms are small; paint is peeling from the walls; carpets are threadbare.

Every night, when we go on stage, something is at stake. The theatre actor is in the midst of it. For a film actor, all that happens way after the event. If the film opens next week, I was paid a year ago, and I may already have two films in the can before the first one opens, so my relationship to that initial product is completely removed.

My relationship with theatre material has a much stronger impact on the quality of my life. It's also why most actors can't make a living in the theatre. We keep going back because that's where we live. That's the medium that still belongs to *us*. The great thing about doing the play is that it belongs to us, the actors.

As has been said, "Film is the director's medium; theatre is the actor's medium."

How does the pay for film and theatre differ, not just the amount but the frequency of payment?

The theatre separates the wheat from the chaff. It's all to do with the fact that we get paid by the week. If actors on film got paid by the week or got paid according to how successful the film was in the same way theatre actors get paid according to how successful the play is, well . . . [he doesn't have to complete the thought].

When we sign for a play, we don't get paid until we start playing. We get some money for rehearsal. We might have signed on for twenty thousand dollars a week, but only *start* getting that amount when we're performing, not while we're rehearsing for the four or five or six weeks. If the play isn't successful and the actors are terrible in it and the audience doesn't turn up, it closes. That's it. Movie actors get paid up front. Whether the film is successful or not, the actor gets paid.

Before playing Mark Rothko on stage, you played Kenneth Halliwell in the film *Prick Up Your Ears*. What elements do those characters have in common, especially in the way that one character outgrows the other?

That's an interesting observation. The Halliwell-Orton dynamic was in a way similar to the one between Rothko and Ken. It's about the point where the master is overtaken by the student. It's that moment. It can be a very domestic moment, in which one lover has outgrown the other, or it can be on a much bigger, more epic scale where one culture takes over another. Or in the case of *Red*, where an artistic movement overtakes another.

It's that moment when the world—whatever world we're in—of two men in a room or two cultures or the world of two movements in an artistic sense—it's the moment when all the tectonic plates shift and things change. It's a huge thing in life. We all go through that crucial thing.

The reason *Red* was successful for me was that I've reached a point in my life as an actor where I have passed the baton to another generation of actors. I play the "dad" role now.

An actor friend of mine said, "It's the point when you stop going up for the part of the sexy lawyer and realize you're being considered for the judge." [Molina chortles heartily at the realization of the truth of that statement.]

It's very hard for people who have been creative all their lives and have called the shots; then everything suddenly shifts. It can be very, very tough. It happens to women in a much more cruel way. It's about outward beauty or youthfulness for them. For men, it's more inner, their potency or virility. I don't mean that in a biblical way, but intellectually, in the sense of still being viable.

There was a long gestation period to that film, initially bolstered by your performance as the Maniac in Dario Fo's play *Accidental Death of an Anarchist*, in 1979.

The Maniac is such a showy part. It was a great step in my career. Originally, Ian McKellen was going to play Halliwell in the film; Keith Allen was going to play Orton. This was about four or five years before our version. In 1979 or '80, I had an interview to play one of the men Orton picks up. I didn't get the job, and that version didn't get made. Later, when it got rebooted, Ian was approached again about playing Halliwell, but he felt he was too old; the moment had gone. Keith Allen had moved on.

Then it became Gary Oldman as Orton, and I was approached about playing Ken. I was asked to do a screen test. There was this agonizing week waiting to hear whether I was going to do it or not. In that week, there was a great deal of hemming and hawing about whether I was a big enough name, which I clearly wasn't. Stephen Frears was very loyal, and he wanted me for the part. I wasn't everyone's first choice. I don't think I ever have been. I've never been the first choice for anything. That's not a bad thing.

That "first choice" thing came up again on *The Sorcerer's Apprentice*. I had a wonderful relationship with Jon Turtletaub, the director. After I did a scene, he came up to me and said, "That's fantastic. Who knew my third choice would be so good!"

Yet another artist, Diego Rivera, in *Frida*, again directed by Julie Taymor, is part of your canon. How does he complement your thoughts about Rothko?

Interestingly, both Rothko and Rivera speak to me in very different ways. I've always found Rivera's paintings very moving because they appeal to the sentimentalist in me: people working and going about their business, the honesty and weight of those figures, the sense that there is real, physical work being done. That's always struck me as rather beautiful. The scope, the scale of his murals is incredibly imaginative. They take me to some fantastic places.

With Rothko, it was precisely the opposite. It was the simplicity of the work. Getting to know and love his work was not the most pleasant of experiences. "Big color fields in a rectangle. So what!" I thought. Here was a man struggling with a difficult vision. His was the paradox of art versus commercialism. The whole thing about him was that he wanted to be taken seriously by his "viewers."

Eddie and I went to see some of Rothko's work at the National Gallery in Washington, DC. I'm off to Pittsburgh for a film next week, and it's a five-hour drive from there to Detroit. Since I've got a five-day break, instead of coming home, I'm going to Detroit Institute of Arts to see some more of Rothko's work that I've only ever seen in books.

Before we began production on *Frida*, we got to Mexico a few weeks early, and while we were rehearsing, we did all the trips to all the big sites where the murals are.

It's interesting that not only have you played artists, but in Yasmina Reza's play *Art* you play an art "critic," one of three friends who come together to evaluate a piece of art that one of them has bought. What does *Art* have to say about the artist and the critic?

Art is the kind of play that flatters an audience, and *Red*, in a way, is the same. *Red* is the kind of play that doesn't condescend to the audience.

In *Art*, the painting was being discussed through the filter of three friends responding to each other and judging each other, the way friends do. A lot of critics asked, "Is this play an intellectual piece masquerading as a boulevard romp?" or "Is it a boulevard romp masquerading as a piece of intellectual theatre?"

In *Red*, art is discussed through the prism of a man at the end of something, trying to make sense of what's left, discussing with a young man who is at the beginning of everything. Rothko was on the way down and running headlong into a generation that was coming up.

But, really, I thought, it doesn't matter because *Art* and the success of *Red*, in a way for the same reason, was based on the fact that something important was being discussed.

Both plays have something in common: the notion about how we are perceived. *Art* was not only about the painting but also how the friend who bought the painting was perceived by his friends. In *Red*, Rothko is as obsessed about how he's going to be perceived by his peers as he is obsessed with the work.

What attracted you to the role of Richard Susskind, who collaborated with Clifford Irving on a fake autobiography of Howard Hughes in *The Hoax*?

Hoax is one of my favorite films, along with *Chocolate*, which Lasse Hallström also directed.

I think Susskind is a bit of both a tragic and comic character. I saw him as noble, not in the Shakespearean sense, but noble in the sense of a rather ordinary man trying to be decent in a world where it's often more expedient and profitable to be indecent. He's ultimately comic; his tragedy wasn't the same as Clifford Irving, whose tragedy was his inability to live in a real world. Dick was seduced and got ruined by his loyalty to his friend. In the end, he survived, redeemed himself, and had a pretty decent career writing children's books. He is the other side of the coin as the hero.

What made it slightly more confusing was that the hero in this case was an antihero. In many ways, as far as that relationship was concerned, Susskind was the moral center of the story.

There's something that Lasse played out in the scenes that Clifford makes up, his fantasies and his lies; he becomes so convoluted that he starts to believe them. At one point, Dick says, "You weren't there. It didn't happen."

I think Lasse found a good way to tell that story without having endless scenes with actors reciting exposition. I'm all for less talk. In a movie, there's no need to say, "Oh, the water's cold." If I've just put my hand in water, I can *act* that the water is cold.

What about Hallström's directing style?

His style is very simple and matter-of-fact. He's not one of those directors who talks in big concepts. Some directors say, "This scene is a rock with a crack in it, and you are ice water working your way through that crack." You can't play that.

Lasse loves the actors to come up with things. His priority is story: does that pause or the removal of a line tell the story? If it does, then he's happy to entertain the idea. Lasse is not the father-figure type of director. No, not at all. He's far too polite and far too gentlemanly. He's a very quiet man. He directs by stealth. He doesn't like a lot of noise. He's not a powerful, booming presence. He sometimes gives the impression that he's not prepared, but I saw through that. He just doesn't want to impose himself; he likes a sense of egalitarianism on the set. He is impeccably prepared.

You appeared in a spin-off of the long-running television franchise *Law & Order*. How did your role as Ricardo Morales in *Law & Order: Los Angeles* develop?

We didn't do a pilot for the show. NBC bought it, ordered thirteen episodes, and then cast it. I think I was on a short list of two or three actors, again probably not the first choice!

The development process of the character, deputy DA Ricardo Morales, was an interesting one. The backstory of my character was that his parents were immigrants. I am a first-generation American. My father is a groundsman at a posh country club. I am the first member of the family to go to college. Morales is a smart guy, very savvy, with a little bit of a chip on his shoulder, maybe a bit touchy about his modest background, not that he's ashamed of it; he doesn't want to trade on it. He doesn't want to be the kind of guy who'd say, "I come from working-class stock." He likes to wear nice clothes; he'll go without a few lattes in the morning so he can buy himself a pair of nice cuff links. He may have political ambitions one day. A people pleaser. All these things we discovered about the character were grace notes.

I was fond of the idea of his character being the first one in his family to go to college. I can relate to that. I'm the son of immigrants, and I've become an immigrant myself now that I'm in the United States, which is partly why the character appealed to me. He's achieved the American dream. But it placed a certain responsibility on him.

I remember when I saw Sonia Sotomayor being sworn in as a Supreme Court justice. Her mother was there and was deeply proud. I thought what a great weight is being placed on Justice Sotomayor. People were thinking, "Now you've done it. Now you've got to prove you're worthy of it."

What do you see in Morales's—and your—future?

I said to the series creator, Dick Wolf, "I'm fifty-seven, and if this runs for five or six years, I'll be my early sixties, so by then, I expect you to promote me to the Steven Hill character, the DA in the original series." Steven is one of Jill's and my favorite actors. From my mouth to God's ear.[2]

Sir Donald Sinden thought about his career as an actor: "Actors tend to be larger than life. You come across quite ordinary, nondescript people in daily life. I don't see why we should be subjected to them on stage." Do you agree?

I think from an audience's point of view, there's a taste, an appetite for something a bit more out of the ordinary. Equally, there's a great tradition of what we might put in quotation marks as being "realistic" or "naturalistic" acting. I always try to avoid those terms because at the root, there is nothing real about acting. We're not in the business of being real so much as being, hopefully in some way, authentic. We create an authentic experience for an audience, but everyone is aware of the contract they've entered into, but they're never fully unaware that they're sitting in a darkened space with hundreds of others watching something that has been presented night after night, eight times a week.

I remember seeing Peter Gill's production of *Juno and the Paycock* in 1989 at the National's Lyttelton; my friend Linda Bassett was in it. The set was very realistic: a room in which everything worked. They had a real gas fire, and they even had plumbing. At one point in the play, one of the characters goes to the sink and turns on the tap and out gushes water; he fills up a bucket, then he turns off the tap. I remember being completely knocked out by this. It was all so real. I didn't think that this was something that was completely manufactured. There was nothing "real," but it was authentic.

Donald is right in that—it's a relatively new phenomenon—it was only mid- or late-nineteenth-century theatre where the curtain would go up and audiences were greeted with facsimiles of their own lives. Oscar Wilde, Ibsen, and Shaw were part of that whole new generation of writers who were cutting edge, writing realistic plays. The audience was seeing themselves for the first time. That must have been quite shocking in a way. I can only guess what it was like. It must have been quite a surprise to suddenly see your own world reflected. Even then, though, it was larger than life because the people on stage were presumably wittier or smarter or more entertaining than your average upper-middle-class person.

So, yes, I agree.

～

Selected Credits

Theatre
King Lear, RSC at the Aldwych (1977; Trevor Nunn); *Troilus and Cressida*, RSC at the Aldwych (1977; Barry Kyle); *The Bundle*, RSC at the Warehouse (1977; Howard Davies); *Accidental Death of an Anarchist*, Half Moon (1979; Gavin Richards); *A Short Sharp Shock*, Royal Court; Theatre Royal Stratford East (1980; Robert Walker); *Oklahoma!* Palace (1980; William Hammerstein);

Destry Rides Again, Donmar Warehouse (1982, Robert Walker); *Can't Pay? Won't Pay!* Criterion (1982; Robert Walker); *The Taming of the Shrew*, RSC, Stratford (1985; Di Trevis); *The Cherry Orchard*, Odyssey, Los Angeles (1986; Jack Stehlin); *Serious Money*, Royal Court, (1987; Max Stafford-Clark); *Speed the Plow*, NT, Lyttelton (1989; Gregory Mosher); *Molly Sweeney*, Roundabout, New York (1996; Brian Friel); *Art*, Royale, New York; UCLA's James A. Doolittle, Los Angeles (1998; Matthew Warchus); *Fiddler on the Roof*, Minskoff, New York (2004–2005; David Leveaux); *Howard Katz*, Laura Pels, New York (2007; Doug Hughes); *Red*, Donmar Warehouse; John Golden, New York; Mark Taper Forum, Los Angeles (2009–2012; Michael Grandage)

Film
Ladyhawke (1985); *Letter to Brezhnev* (1985); *Enchanted April* (1992); *Maverick* (1994); *Species* (1995); *Mojave Moon* (1996); *Boogie Nights* (1997); *Magnolia* (1999); *Frida* (2002); *The Da Vinci Code* (2006); *The Moon and the Stars* (2007); *An Education* (2009); *Pink Panther 2* (2009); *Prince of Persia: The Sands of Time* (2010); *Sorcerer's Apprentice* (2010); *Abduction* (2011); *We'll Never Have Paris* (2014); *Love Is Strange* (2014); *Road to Capri* (2015); *Paint It Black* (2015)

Television
Reilly: Ace of Spies, "Gambit" (1983); *Miami Vice*, "The Big Thaw" (1987); *Screen One*, "The Accountant" (1989); *Screen Two*, "Virtuoso" (1989); *El C.I.D.*, thirteen episodes (1990–1991); *Murder on the Orient Express* (2001); *Ladies Man*, thirty episodes (1999–2001); *Law & Order: Trial by Jury*, "Day" (2005); *Law & Order: Special Victims Unit*, "Night" (2005); *Law & Order: Los Angeles*, sixteen episodes (2010–2011); *Harry's Law*, three episodes (2011); *Monday Mornings*, ten episodes (2013); *Matador*, "Quid Go Pro" (2014); *The Normal Heart* (2014); *Angie Tribeca* (2015)

Radio
Copenhagen, LA Theatre Works, UCLA (2011; Martin Jarvis)

Awards and Nominations

Oklahoma! 1980, Olivier, Most Promising Newcomer of the Year in Theatre, nominee; *Speed the Plow*, 1989–1990, Olivier, Comedy Performance of the Year, nominee; *Art*, 1998, Tony, Best Actor in a Play, nominee; also, Drama Desk, Best Featured Actor in a Play, winner; *Fiddler on the Roof*, 2004, Tony, Best Actor in a Musical, nominee; also, Drama Desk, Outstanding Actor in a Musical, nominee; *The Hoax*, 2008, London Critics' Circle Film Award, British Supporting Actor of the Year, nominee; *Red*, 2010, Tony, Best Actor in a Play, nominee; also, Drama Desk, Outstanding Actor in a Play, nominee; Drama League Award, Distinguished Performance; *An Education*, 2010, London Critics' Circle Film Award, Best Supporting Actor of the Year, nominee; *The Normal Heart*, 2014, Primetime Emmy, Outstanding Actor in a Miniseries or a Movie, nominee

Notes

1. *Red* takes place in 1958 in Mark Rothko's studio with a fictional assistant, played by Eddie Redmayne, who won the Tony for Best Featured Actor in a Play. Rothko has been awarded a major commission, for which he has conflicting feelings. Dialogue between the two about art versus commerce, the elder-statesman artist versus the new artist are the some of the issues in the play.

2. *Law & Order: Los Angeles* was cancelled in May 2011.

$\sim$

Lynn Redgrave, OBE

Actors have to take risks.

The hills on both sides of steep Topanga Canyon Road, north of Los Angeles, are covered in masses of yellow mustard seed and purple Mexican sage; cactus plants poke their spiny heads up through the flora, compliments of a recent El Niño. The road curves higher and higher to large homes that sit on huge parcels of land. This environment is geographically and emotionally distant from Lynn Redgrave's childhood home in London where she was born in 1943. But it is here that she has made her home for several decades.

The actress's pet Rottweilers, Portia and Hogarth, are at her heels as she meets her guest at the gate. Rather than entering through the front door, she enters through the service area leading to the kitchen where John Clark, her husband of more than thirty years,[1] stands amid a heap of kitchen utensils, pots, and pans, awaiting workmen to begin demolition of the pantry floor due to dry rot.

Moving into the sitting room, where the furnishings are reminiscent of a West End play set in a country house, Redgrave lifts a floral quilted cozy from the pot, and pours two cups of her favorite libation: Marks and Spencer's Extra Strong tea.

The actress, who looks remarkably like both her father, the great actor Michael Redgrave, and her older sister, Vanessa, sits on the edge of a wicker chair. A needlepoint pillow, on which the words "God couldn't be everywhere so He created grandmothers" are stitched, is nestled at her back. This is in reference to her several grandchildren. On the wall behind her are posters of The Three Sisters, in which she appeared for the only time on stage with Vanessa; another poster, Shakespeare *for My Father, her acclaimed one-woman show, is hanging just slightly askew. A whimsical touch is a chess set made by her younger daughter, Annabel, with fairies, gnomes, and toadstools as the game pieces. There is a comfortable clutter about the room.*

As she sips her tea and speaks about her family and career, her blue eyes sparkle.

⌒

You come from a long, long line of thespians. How many generations have there been?

We're into at least our fourth generation. My grandfather, Roy Redgrave, and grandmother, Daisy Scudamore, were on the stage at the end of the nineteenth century. My father, Michael Scudamore Redgrave—he was knighted in 1959—was an actor; his middle name is homage to his mother. My mother was Rachel Kempson, also an actor. My middle name is Rachel, after her. She was still trouping at age eighty-seven playing, as in real life, Vanessa's mother in *Déjà Vu*, directed by Henry Jaglom.

My brother, Corin, and my sister, Vanessa, are actors. My brother's wife, Kika Markham, is in the business. And there are nieces and nephews: Carlo Nero—his middle name is Redgrave; Joely Richardson; Jemma Redgrave; Natasha Richardson;[2] I'm aunt-in-law to her husband, Liam Neeson. And my daughter Pema [born Kelly] studied at drama school and appeared with me in a television film, *Calling the Shots*.

So there we are: Redgraves have been treading the boards for more than a century. Not many families can boast that. There is something to be said for inheriting the right genes.

Growing up a Redgrave must have meant that many famous contemporaries of your parents passed through your life. Who were among those who visited with your family?

Peggy Ashcroft was my mother's best friend and Dad's too, so we knew her well. We saw a certain amount of Vivien Leigh and Laurence Olivier. Vivien was always very sweet to me when I was growing up. In fact, my husband and I went to visit Vivien at her home on Eton Square the day before she died in 1967. I remember she was wearing a beautiful negligee and smoking a cigarette, very elegant and looking absolutely beautiful despite her illness.

You had the genes to be an actor, but it was not what you wanted to do as a child, is it?

I grew up in a household where "the play was the thing," but I wasn't interested then. It was all about horses. I had a chestnut named Rosalinda. I think my parents were amazed and dismayed that I showed no signs of taking

Photofest

up the family business. My brother and sister showed signs early on. It rather snuck up on me, and once I knew, at the age of fifteen, that I wanted to be an actor, I never again didn't want to be. It actually felt late for me.

What prompted the change?

I think it was after seeing *Twelfth Night*, directed by Peter Hall at the Royal Shakespeare Theatre, about 1960, with Ian Holm and Geraldine Mc-Ewan. The idea of mistaken identity, of being someone else, appealed to me.

Did you apply to drama school?

I followed Vanessa into Central School of Speech and Drama. I had to ignore the pressures that came with being from such an illustrious family.

People kept wanting to compare me to my parents and my siblings. I just cut myself off from that, partly because nobody was expecting anything of me. I had doubts about being good enough. In a way that was sort of a protection. Today, I would probably get bored with being told that I sounded exactly like or looked like someone in the family.

Having the "acting gene" wasn't enough, then? How much training is necessary to hone the art and craft of acting?

I don't think acting is all about the training. Training *is* absolutely vital, but the essentials of what it is to be an actor are in there or not. They can be brought out and nurtured in the school environment, but along with that, there has to be this fantastic addiction. If you don't have that, you won't survive the rest of it, especially the downside: rejection.

What was the next step after Central School?

My stage debut was Helena in *Midsummer Night's Dream* in 1962, directed by my then brother-in-law Tony Richardson at the Royal Court. I had a role, a very small role, in Tony's film, *Tom Jones*. I went on to Dundee Rep in *Rookery Nook* and *The Merchant of Venice*.

Your career-changing opportunity came when Laurence Olivier founded the National Theatre in 1963.

Yes, he invited me to become a founding member. I found him to be wonderful with young actors. But there was a curious thing about him: he wanted the very best around him, the very best. He wanted it . . . and then he didn't. It was almost jealousy. It was a very strange syndrome. Of course, he did assemble the greatest theatre company. Look at who the members of the company were: Maggie Smith, Derek Jacobi, Peter O'Toole, Albert Finney, and so many others.

Olivier was a bit too much like a godlike figure to be a friend to me on a personal level, but he certainly was very good with the company. He loved good work, but he ended up not being so great for me.

There was a particular time in a production when the director was going through a phase of making *me* the problem. I went in despair to Olivier, and he went through the scene with me and helped me enormously. But, finally, it was Olivier who let me go from the company. Up to my dismissal, I had always played wonderful supporting roles. I auditioned for a role in a production at the Old Vic of *The Storm* by Aleksandr Ostrovsky that was being directed by John Dexter. After several auditions, they decided not to give me the role. The excuse was that I was too young and inexperienced, and the role was played by Jill Bennett.

Olivier said to me, "I can't give you this role. You're brilliant, but I cannot perceive of the day when you're going to play leading parts." He called me his "flopsy bunny actress."

I cried for several hours. Of course, he hadn't bargained for *Georgy Girl*, which I had made several months before. Vanessa and I were in competition that year for the Oscar in the Actress category, Vanessa for *Morgan!* and me for *Georgy Girl*.[3] Neither of us took home the statue.

But to give the great man his due, I ran into him shortly after leaving the company, and he recanted. It was awful then because I was the first person with the company to be given a three-year contract. I was the first long-term artist. I'd done two years. I left and never looked back, but at the time it was heartbreaking because I imagined my whole life bound up with the company as a founding member.

But maybe he did me a favor. If he couldn't see me in leading roles, maybe I would have stayed too long playing supporting roles. And that happens sometimes. There was a wonderful actress who came up through the ranks while I was there, but who stayed too long, ten years. And now she's out of the business.

It's wonderful to be part of a company, but it can become too comfortable, too cozy. Actors have to take risks.

You wrote *Shakespeare for My Father*, which was about your relationship— or lack of it—with your father. That was risky. What is the genesis of that work?

It began when the Folger Library in Washington, DC, asked me to read a bit of Shakespeare, tell a few stories about the family, and answer a few questions. I had been trying to come up with a little play of my own, and I thought maybe I could write something but not tell them what I was going to do. I wasn't sure it would be any good.

Obviously, what they wanted was Shakespeare. I began to explore how I could write a play where the Shakespearean pieces became so woven into the story that it wouldn't be "And now I'll do this and then this and this." I didn't think it was going to be a piece that would release the demons that pursued me about my father. But it did become the ultimate expression about my dad and me. At first, I thought it was going to be a play about my dad. I later realized that it was a play about *me*. It was not a consciously cathartic act, where I said to myself, "I must get my feelings out." But it was a way to give up the grief over not being able to communicate with him. I wrote about what interested me and what I thought could make a theatrical story that would appeal to audiences.

What are some examples of Shakespeare's words that became part of the piece?

It was fun searching for the material. It was extraordinary that during the research, I discovered that Shakespeare's characters often were speaking directly to me. For example, *Macbeth* seemed an unlikely play to contain themes that would be part of *my* story. But I found Malcolm's words to Macduff in Act IV, scene iii, when he has just received the news that his wife and children have been killed—"Give sorrow words; the grief that does not speak/Whispers the o'er fraught heart, and bids it break . . ."—spoke volumes to me.

I opened a book of Shakespeare's sonnets and thought, "I've never seen this one before." After all, he wrote 154 of them. When I read number 115, I found it to be perfect, and yet I had missed it before. [Without missing a beat, Redgrave launches into the sonnet from memory.]

> Those lines that I before have writ do lie,
> Even those that said I could not love you dearer;
> Yet then my judgment knew no reason why
> My most full flame should afterwards burn clearer.
> But reckoning time, whose million'd accidents
> Creep in 'twixt vows and change decrees of kings,
> Tan sacred beauty, blunt the sharp'st intents,
> Divert strong minds to the course of altering things;
> Alas, why, fearing of time's tyranny,
> Might I not then say, "Now I love you best,"
> When I was certain o'er incertainty,
> Crowning the present, doubting of the rest?
>   Love is a babe, then might I not say so,
>   To give full growth to that which still doth grow?

In *King Lear*, there's another example of Shakespeare's words speaking for me when Cordelia asks in an aside, "What shall Cordelia speak? Love, and be silent," from Act I, scene i. All these selections were in reference to my being unable to speak to my father and him being unable to speak to me. Mainly, the purpose of the piece was to speak to him through Shakespeare. Inside myself, I could say all these wonderful things, but what actually came out was not my voice, until I assembled those bits and pieces.

Again, there was familial acting competition, this time for a Tony in 1993.

That's right. My niece, Natasha Richardson, and I were nominated for Best Actress in a Play. She was nominated for *Anna Christie*, and I was nominated for *Shakespeare for My Father*. We lost to Madeline Kahn for *The Sisters Rosenzweig*.[4]

What about the other theatrical pieces you've written that were inspired by a family member?

Rachel and Juliet is about a woman who is now old. We meet her first as she falls apart with a nervous breakdown, and we discover the truth about a long-past affair. It's very loosely based on an incident my mother told me, probably about my grandmother. Much of it is speculation, invented. But the spark came from something she once told me. It's really an homage to my mother. Another family-related and woman-oriented piece is *Nightingale*, about my father's mother. I also pay tribute to my mother in *The Mandrake Root*, which is a drama for seven actors, rather than a one-woman piece. So family is very much a part of what I write.

How do audiences react to theses plays?

During the nine-month run of *Shakespeare for My Father* on Broadway, people told me they would return again and again because they found so much in it about themselves. It had an extraordinarily powerful effect on the audience because people saw themselves in the work. They found a release. They laughed and cried.

Speaking of audiences, is there a difference between American and British audiences and their response to what is happening on stage?

American audiences are generally more demonstrative than English audiences. If American audiences aren't hooked right away, they talk or even leave. If they're hooked, they let you know, and if they don't like it, they also let you know. They tend to leap to their feet much more than British audiences. It's become somewhat of a cliché. They think that's what they're supposed to do if they enjoy a performance.

I remember playing *Shakespeare for My Father* in Wilkes-Barre, Pennsylvania, where the audience was kind of an oil painting. No reaction, no movement, nothing. My heart was sinking. Maybe they were quiet since they were not used to going to the theatre. I didn't get a lot of feedback during the performance. It was not an easy night, but afterwards, people came up to me and told me about parts of the play that really affected them. Maybe it had something to do with the theatre itself, which was a bit of a bummer because it was one of those converted movie houses where the front row is miles away and is not conducive to live productions.

Are audiences in general ready for live performance?

Most audience members are not used to live theatre. I'm not sure how much they realize that live theatre is a participatory sport. That's the wonderful thing about the theatre. Perhaps they're intimidated, a little reserved and think that theatre is where they mustn't react, mustn't do anything. What they don't realize is that they need to prepare for it. For instance, I wouldn't go and watch a play having had a drink, because—I'm alone in this because most of the audience usually does have a drink—generally it softens your reflexes and makes it a little fuzzier to respond. I want to be attentive to what's going on on the stage. I'm a good audience. I go partway toward the play and the actors because I enjoy doing that. That's what I mean when I say, "Theatre is a participatory sport."

Obviously, there will be variations in audiences. I can see that the audience's point of view is more sophisticated in the bigger cities, but theatre is universal.

Sometimes that 8 p.m. start is even a bit later than that stated time because audiences are late. It's great when there's a bit in the program that says, "No latecomers will be seated." On very rare occasions when management puts its foot down, people amazingly get there on time. It's only because they know that the time is pushed back that they get lazy about getting there. It's a courtesy to the performers and to your fellow audience members who do get there on time. And I would no more think of having a drink before I step on stage!

You were exposed to Shakespeare at school and had the opportunity to see productions as a youngster. What are some of the important aspects of teaching Shakespeare?

At school, Shakespeare is badly taught and can be boring. We tended to learn things by rote. I can still do "Tomorrow and tomorrow and tomorrow" from *Macbeth*, but now, of course, I know what it means. At the time we didn't explore; we didn't delve into character or language. We read it out loud a bit and learned chunks. I think to a certain extent schools are still like that. I was lucky. I learned to love the Bard early on because I saw my parents in productions. I was seeing Shakespeare beautifully played throughout my earliest years and learned to love the plays. Not everybody has that opportunity. I was lucky. By the time I was thirteen, I had seen all the plays, save one, *Timon of Athens*. Not everybody sees a play "on its feet." When I was about ten, I remember seeing my mother and father in *King Lear* in 1953 directed by George Devine at the Shakespeare Memorial Theatre.

I think it's wrong to think the children should just see pantos and ballets. I did a class at the Tennessee Performing Arts Center in Nashville, which is a huge venue, and I had 1,500 kids at each session. We had ten guinea pig kids who were sort of prepared ahead of time to get up on stage. I had them do the scene from *Romeo and Juliet* when Benvolio tells the Prince about the fight. It's not complicated, and it's something that any high school student could understand: explaining how your best friend by mistake killed this guy in a brawl.

The first Benvolio who got up had the attitude, "This is Shakespeare," and was intimidated. But the minute he had this physical problem of having to be heard and understood over a crowd, it changed how he said his lines. It changed his body, and suddenly he was extremely persuasive. It's amazing what these kids can do if the material is presented the right way. We got the whole place being the Capulets and the Montagues. It was wonderful.

What I would suggest is for teachers to get the students up on their feet. That's what I do when I do classes in high schools and colleges. I find that the only time they are up is when it's the school play.

If you start off teaching them iambic pentameter, you'll bore the wits out of them. They'll go, "Argh!!!" and never know what it's *about*. Story and character and what is being said come first. But the minute I get the students up on their feet with something to act, it's amazing how it works. It's not impenetrable at all. They have to have an action. They can't sit there with a bunch of words. You have to start with what the scene is about and get 'round to the far more complex material—delving technically to the verse and all of that. If students could see the plays performed, that would be wonderful.

You have moved between theatre and film for most of your career. What are the major differences in those areas?

Working in film is very different than being "on the boards."

Films today can be very challenging, considering the speed in which they are made. The most difficult part of filming is being ready for "the moment," which may be our only chance. We haven't got tomorrow's matinee to get it better. We work terribly long hours. We might do a really difficult scene at one thirty in the morning, and we're tired. I get panicky that I just won't be "there." But I have to do it come hell or high water because maybe tomorrow they'll lose the location or the other actor. There are always constraints.

The odd thing is that sometimes when my resistance is lowest, my acting becomes truer. I just abandon myself to it in some peculiar way. It's not always a bad thing to work when you're tired. Sometimes the work is really good; it's just not very pleasant.

In the theatre, we have the sustained performance, which is very helpful, enormously helpful, because we haven't been sitting about dissipating our energy all day, waiting to do a scene we thought we were going to do three hours ago.

Do you have a routine when doing a theatre production?

I love the ritualistic side of working in the theatre. Like an athlete, I have an absolutely regimented day when I'm doing theatre. At a certain point on performance days, I stop talking. I won't take any more phone calls. When I get to the theatre to warm up, it's all organized. Everything becomes the countdown to being ready to leave the starter's block. I always get to the theatre at least an hour ahead. Depending on what the show is, it might be more. It's not so much as how long it takes to do makeup and hair and putting on the costume as it is leaving the day behind. There are some actors who appear to be able to walk off the street and go on stage. I don't know how they do it. I can't, so I don't.

I always nap before a show, not only because I need my energy but also because it does separate what's happened before. I nap, eat, and go to the theatre, and nothing can disturb that. I might watch the news, or not, probably not. It would depend on what's on the news!

What is your responsibility once you have accepted a role? How do you develop a relationship with the director?

It's the actor's job to come up with the character. If the director has something totally different in mind than my take on the character, that's something that we need to find out *before* we work together. If I'm playing a leading role and I'm planning to do it with a certain director, I have to be sure my ideas mesh with his, or it could be nothing but pain. That's what is known as "artistic differences."

Actors should not be puppets. They absolutely should not be having their strings pulled. The director should be aiding and abetting the development of the character. But saying that, having cast the actor, the director should already know what sort of actor he's dealing with.

Very few good actors ask the director, "What do you want in this character?" I believe actors, in the long run, have to be the keepers of their craft. They are the guardians of their characters.

How often do you have to use a microphone in a stage performance?

That's an interesting question. Appearing on film and television and theatre is a physical job and requires a flexible voice. Unfortunately, actors aren't told that until too late. "Oh, I don't need a voice. I'll have a microphone," is their excuse. But you do need that voice.

I've used a microphone for *Shakespeare for My Father*, but it depended on the size of the theatre and the acoustics, particularly the converted theatres, especially the old vaudeville houses and movie houses. It's lovely to see these venues brought back, but generally they are very poor acoustically. They tend not to be actor friendly.

There has been an ebb and flow of your career, moving from one medium to another. How do you account for that?

I've had a little film renaissance because of my role as Gillian in Scott Hicks's *Shine*, so I played that out. Films are fickle and for a bit, things are good, and then it could all change. At the moment I'm getting such interesting film roles, having not been on film much in the years before. I don't want to pass that up because, lifestyle-wise, it is also much easier. With a film, you're away for four weeks, then you're home, but with a play, if it's going well, you're there every night for the run of the piece, which could be for months.

Media pundits have cried that theatre is a dying art form. Do you agree?

They said television would kill film, and film and television would kill theatre. It actually didn't happen. The more remote we become from each other, the more we need live theatre, and the more people flock to it. People are desperate for a shared experience. People are alone so much—in the car, in front of the computer. Even though we have big-screen televisions, it's not the same as sitting in a movie theatre and sharing the experience. Going to the theatre is even a greater shared experience.

You mentioned being alone in front of a computer. Is that how you do your writing?

I don't use a computer when I'm writing. I write in longhand, and my husband puts it on the computer. I do have a laptop.

Your brother and sister have been vocal about controversial political issues. In your own, quiet way, you were involved in a contentious litigation.

I had a famous lawsuit against Universal Television in 1981, during the run of *House Calls*. I was dismissed from the show because I wanted to bring Annabel to the lot and breast-feed her in my dressing room. It developed into a long lawsuit, which we lost, but it eventually did change working conditions for women at studios.

I didn't suspect or want to go through that many years—almost thirteen—of litigation, but I'm glad that one can work positives. I heard that director Bill Condon met an actress who had a newborn, and this woman knew that I was responsible for the change. She said she called it "the Lynn Redgrave law." That was more touching than anything, just one person remembering that it could have been different. It's heartening to know that I made a difference.

I also took Actors' Equity to the National Labor Relations Board regarding the one-on-one exchange of performers between the States and Britain. At the time that exchange didn't exist. It took a couple of years to persuade Equity that this was an issue. It had to do with aliens who already had been allowed to work in the States being charged huge dues.

Actors' Equity claimed it was their way of keeping jobs for Americans. I had already been admitted here as a resident alien, but I didn't physically have my green card, so Equity levied a huge sum on a summer theatre tour I had done. Of course, because of the suit, I was threatened with nonemployment. But out of all this came the one-on-one exchange, which at least allows American actors of nonstar status to go to England, and English artists to come here. It's not as good as a free exchange of artists, though.

You now carry dual citizenship papers, US and UK. What was the motivation to become a US citizen when your roots—and much of your career—are in the UK?

For a long time, there were many aspects of my thinking I would like to become a citizen. I'd been here in the States for more than half my life, and my husband had become a citizen some time before. I wasn't forced into it. I could have had a green card for the rest of my life. But I couldn't vote. Now I can!

Finally, the combination of working out how long I'd been here and thinking that I live here, I'm now part of it. I'd stuck my neck out on several issues. If I became a citizen, people couldn't say, "If you don't like it, go home," because now I *am* home. To say my voice is equal to everyone else's is, by law, a nice position to be in. I now have the full rights of everybody else. I like that. After some twenty-five years of living here, I became a citizen through the naturalization process.

If there was a single person who was responsible, it was actually General Colin Powell who inspired me. I had met him a couple of times and thought he was a wonderful man and admired his career. In 1995, when he announced at a press conference about his reason for not running for president, I was so struck by the fact that not one political-speak word came out of his mouth, none of those carefully couched phrases that too often come out of politicians. He didn't speak with that gloss of a politician. He sounded like a real person, a human being. I admired him for having the guts and knowledge of himself not to run.

And the naturalization ceremony?

It took place on Ellis Island in the big hall. Ray Charles sang "America the Beautiful." It was awe inspiring.

~

After a seven-year battle with breast cancer, Redgrave died on May 2, 2010, at age sixty-seven, at her home in Connecticut.

Selected Credits

Theatre
National Theatre at the Old Vic: *Hamlet* (1963; Laurence Olivier); *The Recruiting Officer* (1963; William Gaskill); *The Master Builder* (1964; Peter Wood); *Andorra* (1964; Lindsay Anderson); *Hay Fever* (1964; Noël Coward); *Much Ado about Nothing* (1965; Franco Zeffirelli); *Love for Love* (1965; Peter Wood); *Mother Courage and Her Children* (1965; William Gaskill); *Love for Love* (1966; Peter Wood). **Other UK:** *A Midsummer Night's Dream*, Royal Court (1962; Tony Richardson); *The Merchant of Venice*, Dundee Repertory (1962; Piers Haggard); *The Tulip Tree*, Theatre Royal Haymarket; UK tour (1962; Glen Byam Shaw); *The Two of Us*, Garrick (1970; Mark Cullingham); *Slag*, Royal Court (1971; Max Stafford-Clark); *The Three Sisters*, Yvonne Arnaud, Guildford; Queen's (1990–1991; Robert Sturua); *Noises Off*, Piccadilly (2001; Jeremy Sams); *Aren't We All?*, Theatre Royal Haymarket (1984; Clifford Williams); *Shakespeare for My Father*, Theatre Royal Haymarket (1996; John Clark). **Other US:** *Black Comedy/White Lies*, Ethel Barrymore, New York (1966–1967; John Dexter); *My Fat Friend*, Brooks Atkinson, New York (1974; Robert Moore); *Mrs. Warren's Profession*, Vivian Beaumont, New York (1976; Gerald Freedman); *Saint Joan*, Goodman, Chicago; Circle in the Square, New York (1977; John Clark); *The Two of Us*, Huntington Hartford, Los Angeles (c. 1970s; John Clark); *Thursday's Girls*, Coronet, Los Angeles (1981; John Clark); *Aren't We All?*, Brooks Atkinson, New York (1985; Clifford Williams); *Sweet Sue*, Royale, New York (1987; John Tillinger); *Les Liaisons Dangereuses*, Ahmanson, Los Angeles (1988; Peter Wood); *The Master Builder*, Belasco, New York (1992; Tony Randall); *Shakespeare for My Father*, Helen Hayes, New York (1993; John Clark); *Moon over Buffalo*, Martin Beck, New York (1995; Tom Moore); *The Notebook of Trigorin*, Playhouse in the Park, Cincinnati, Ohio (1998; Stephen Hollis); *Broadway '98*, Hollywood Bowl, Los Angeles (1998; conductor: John Mauceri); *The Mandrake Root*, 2001, Long Wharf, New Haven, Connecticut;

2002, San Jose Repertory Theatre, California; 2003, Little Shubert, New York (staged by Warner Shook); *The Constant Wife*, American Airlines, New York (2005; Mark Brokaw); *Nightingale*, Manhattan Theatre Club at City Center, Stage 1, New York (2006; Joseph Hardy), Mark Taper Forum, Los Angeles (2009, Joseph Hardy); *The Importance of Being Earnest*, BAM, New York (2006; Peter Hall); *The Fairy Queen*, Folger Library Consort, Washington, DC (2007; Richard Clifford); *Grace*, Lucille Lortel, New York (2008; Joseph Hardy); *Rachel and Juliet*, Kay Playhouse, Hunter College, New York; Folger Shakespeare Library, Washington, DC (2009; n/a)

Film
Tom Jones (1963); *Girl with the Green Eyes* (1964); *Georgy Girl* (1966); *Every Little Crook and Nanny* (1972); *The National Health* (1973); *Getting It Right* (1989); *Shine* (1996); *Gods and Monsters* (1998); *The Next Best Thing* (2000); *My Kingdom* (2001); *Unconditional Love* (2002); *Charlie's War* (2003); *The White Countess* (2005); *The Jane Austin Book Club* (2007)

Television
House Calls, forty-one episodes (1979–1981); *The Seduction of Miss Leona* (1980); *Murder, She Wrote*, "It's a Dog's Life" (1984); *The Bad Seed* (1985); *Chicken Soup*, twelve episodes (1989); *Whatever Happened to Baby Jane?* (1991); *Calling the Shots* (1993); *Varian's War* (2001); *Law & Order: Criminal Intent*, "Folie à Deux" (2009); *Ugly Betty*, "The Butterfly Effect, Part I" (2009)

Awards and Nominations
The Girl with the Green Eyes, 1964, BAFTA, Most Promising Newcomer to Film; *Georgy Girl*, 1967, Academy Award, Actress, nominee; also, 1966, Golden Globe, Best Actress—Motion Picture Musical or Comedy, winner; 1966, New York Film Critics Circle Award, Best Actress, winner; *Misalliance*, 1977, Sarah Siddons and Joseph Jefferson Awards, Chicago; *House Calls*, 1979, Primetime Emmy, Outstanding Lead Actress in a Comedy Series, nominee; *Mrs. Warren's Profession*, 1976, Tony, Best Actress in a Play, nominee; *Saint Joan*, 1985, Tony, Outstanding Actress in a Play, nominee; *Shakespeare for My Father*, 1993, Tony, Best Actress in a Play, nominee; also, Drama Desk, Outstanding One-Person Show, nominee; *Shine*, 1997, BAFTA, Best Performance by an Actress in a Supporting Role, nominee; *Gods and Monsters*, 1998, Academy Award, Actress in a Supporting Role, nominee; also, Golden Globe, Best Performance by an Actress in a Supporting Role, winner; SAG, Outstanding Performance by a Female Actor in a

Supporting Role, nominee; *The Constant Wife*, 2006, Tony, Best Actress in a Play, nominee; also, Drama Desk Award, Outstanding Featured Actress in a Play, nominee; *The Witches*, 2006, Grammy, Best Spoken Word Album for Children; *Nightingale*, 2010, Lucille Lortel Awards, nominee

Honors

OBE, 2001

Publications

Journal: A Mother and Daughter's Recovery from Breast Cancer with Annabel Clark (2004)

Notes

1. Redgrave filed for divorce from her husband, John Clark, after more than thirty years of marriage when she discovered that he had had a child with her personal assistant.

2. Rachel Kempson died in 2003 at age ninety-two. Corin Redgrave died in 2010 at age seventy. Richardson died after a skiing accident in 2009 at age forty-five.

3. For the first time in twenty-five years, two sisters vied for the top Oscar. At the 1941 Academy Awards, Olivia de Havilland was nominated for *Hold Back the Dawn*; her sister, Joan Fontaine, won for *Suspicion*. The year the Redgraves were nominated, Elizabeth Taylor won for *Who's Afraid of Virginia Woolf?*

4. The other nominee was Jane Alexander for *The Sisters Rosensweig*.

CHAPTER NINETEEN

∽

Jean Simmons, OBE

I've not had a bad career for a kid from Cricklewood.

On the walls of the sitting room in Jean Simmons's Santa Monica, California, home is an array of photographs. In one, she's curtsying to Queen Elizabeth the Queen Mother, standing along with Greer Garson, Rosalind Russell, and Ralph Richardson. "My knees were going a bit on this one," she laughs.

In another with Laurence Olivier, both in costume from Spartacus, she is holding a cigarette. "Isn't it awful? I've just quit . . . again," she sheepishly admits. In a photo from The Grass Is Greener, she is surrounded by costars Cary Grant, Robert Mitchum, and Deborah Kerr.

A prized possession is a painting of her at age seventeen by Sir Matthew Smith. "I don't know how to light it properly," she says, contemplating the portrait. "I grew into it, and now I've grown beyond it. I asked him why he painted me with such a sad face. He told me, 'I saw sadness in your face.' I wish I looked like that now!"

A vintage Underwood typewriter that belonged to her second husband, writer-director Richard Brooks, sits on the desk beside her computer. "It works fine, except for one letter, the m," she notes, striking the recalcitrant key, which doesn't respond.

Settling into an overstuffed chair in the sunlit den, the actress speaks about her decades-long career, her marriages to actor Stewart Granger and Brooks, her triumphs, and her regrets.

∽

You grew up in Cricklewood, a suburb of London.

Mummy used to tell me, "If anybody asks, say we live in Golders Green, not Cricklewood." She got very piss-elegant when she said "Golders Green," which she thought sounded posh. Cricklewood ain't so posh! Six of us, my parents, my sisters, Edna and Lorna, and brother, Harold, lived in a little, semidetached house. My daughter, Tracy, and I went back to see it some years ago. The people who owned the house asked us in, but I had to get out rather quickly. Too many memories. The saying "You can't go home again" is too true.

What were your experiences with your family during World War II?

My father had been in the 1912 Olympics in Sweden and took third place in gymnastics, and he became a gymnastics instructor at the Regent Street Polytechnic. He and his students were evacuated to Somerset during the war, and Mummy and I joined him. She became weary of not being in London and said, "If I'm going to die, I want to die in my own bed." Back to Cricklewood we went. It was very brave of us. We slept under the billiard table, which was not very wise. We could have been cut to pieces if a bomb had hit. Curiously, I wasn't afraid. But then nothing can happen to you when you're twelve or thirteen. It was just an annoyance. I went to school every day and came back in the blackout.

There were ack-ack guns in the parkland around us. The noise from the guns was horrific. We were just a block away from the Handley Page aircraft factory, which was producing the HP.52 Hampden. When the Germans tried to hit the factory, more noise. We could hear the doodlebug bombs approaching, but once the noise stopped, they'd fall. It was frightening because we never knew whether it was going to fly further or drop immediately. If we heard it explode, we say, "Oh, thank God, it isn't us," not thinking about the people who had been hit. Looking back, I guess it was a bit nerve-racking.

What about your schooling and your eventual "discovery"?

My grammar school was Orange Hill School for Girls. I left at fourteen and enrolled at the Aida Foster School of Dance, which had quite a good reputation. My siblings were older and were already working.

After about two weeks, Mrs. Foster said, "I want you to come with me tomorrow." She dragged me to see director Val Guest. I read a few lines, and all of a sudden, I was in a movie, *Give Us This Moon*, which he was directing. I play Margaret Lockwood's sister. I didn't know what to expect. I was told what to do, and I did it. It was just fun and games. I didn't take it seriously. I had just been in the right place at the right time.

And following that?

I was in one scene in *The Way to the Stars*, directed by Anthony Asquith, singing "Let Him Go, Let Him Tarry," an old Irish song with my arms akimbo, and I laugh all the way through the number. I am credited as Singer. I have no idea why they shot the scene or, after it was shot, why they kept it in because I didn't have a scene with any of the stars. The £5 a day I got was very nice. It wasn't until later with *Great Expectations* that I decided to take acting seriously.

What were the films that prepared you for some of the important roles later on?

I met Gabriel Pascal when he was directing *Caesar and Cleopatra* in 1945 and got the part as Harpist. I'm in a scene for a split second. I was also Vivien Leigh's double in the film and almost drowned in one scene. I was screaming, "Help," but the crew thought I was acting.

They were saying, "Oh, isn't she good."

When I went down for the third time, they realized I was in trouble and rescued me. I also rode a camel in a scene in which Gaby insisted on being the camel driver. The camel didn't like him and jumped off the eight-foot-high dais—with me on it. When it fell, I bent my coccyx. It was painful.

Pascal wanted to put me under contract, and then, all of a sudden, J. Arthur Rank also wanted me under contract. Gaby had half of me, and Rank had the other half. When I met Rank, as young and naive as I was, I didn't understand his importance in the British film industry then. Of course, now I'd like to go back to those days so I could pay more attention . . . and be a lot younger. And especially know what I know now.

I loved Gaby, but then he and Rank sold my contract to Howard Hughes. I asked, "Why, Gaby? Why? You didn't even ask."

He told me, "I needed the money." At least he was straightforward in his answer. He was quite a character.

In *Black Narcissus*, I played Kimchi. I tested with Sabu, and I had to crawl up his leg. I got the giggles. "Well, I've ruined that one," I thought. Oddly, though, I got the part but didn't have a single word in the picture, and my makeup looks like I'd been in a tanning booth.

That was a great cast, especially Kathleen Byron, who was to die for. A sweet lady, too. What her character Sister Ruth does was such a shock for those days, the sensuous clothes, the makeup, the madness! And she was playing a nun!

What are your recollections about your experience with David Lean in *Great Expectations*, your first major film role?

I was just sixteen when I played the young Estella. Valerie Hobson played the adult Estella. I remember David—who seemed like a god—as attractive and charming, gentle and kind and sweet and wonderful to Anthony Wager as the boy, Pip [John Mills played the adult Pip], and me. We were a couple of kids rushing around on the set and misbehaving, tearing up and down corridors. We generally made nuisances of ourselves.

In one scene, Anthony and I had to go up and down the dark stars in Miss Havisham's Satis House with me holding the candle. I remember it was late at night, and we had done several takes. I was so tired. I must have held the candle too close to my costume, a pinafore, and it caught on fire. The crew stood there aghast, but Anthony came and tore my pinafore off and put out the fire. This boy! He saved me.

Everyone remembers my famous line, which I say to Pip, "You may kiss me if you like," and I turn my cheek to him! What a little snot!

And Martita Hunt as Miss Havisham?

She was great but terrifying, just terrifying to us two young innocents. Although she didn't mean to be, she *was* Miss Havisham, for God's sake.

Can you believe that some forty years later, I had the guts to play Miss Havisham in a television production of *Great Expectations*, directed by Kevin Connor? When I was asked to do it, I said, "I can't do that. Are you mad?" Then I reread the script, and I thought I'd have a go. Martita Hunt was always over my shoulder. I couldn't get anywhere near her performance. It was fun trying, but you can't beat the original.

Still a teenager, you played Ophelia in *Hamlet*, opposite Laurence Olivier, who was starring and directing. Your recollections?

I was working at Pinewood on *The Woman in the Hall* when Laurence Olivier came to audition me in a studio dressing room. I'd prepared a speech from the play.

"Do it for me now," he commanded.

While he stood in a corner, I said the speech, which begins, "I was sewing in my closet . . ." [Act II, scene i].

It is mind-boggling when I think about it—doing the scene in a dressing room. I remember hearing a huge bang while I was playing the scene. I didn't pay any attention to it. I just continued on. Maybe it was my concentration or that I was absolutely paralyzed that impressed him because after I finished, he came over and gave me a hug. God, he was so handsome. I got the role, and Larry got me released from another picture for Rank I was scheduled to do. He had enough clout to do that.

Although he was starring in and directing *Hamlet*, he had another actor on the set, his great friend, Anthony Bushell, who was sort of a "shadow director," who's credited as "assistant producer." He would discuss scenes with Larry and then stand by the camera when Larry was in a scene. This gentleman would point out if I made a boo-boo, which Larry might not have seen.

I had hated Shakespeare at school because they made it so boring, but Larry got me the most wonderful coach, Molly Touraine, who worked with me and got me to understand what I was talking about. He had put his trust in me and that amazed me.

Katina Paxinou, whom I had recently played opposite in *Uncle Silas*, had given me some acting advice, which I took very seriously. "When you want

Jean Simmons as Ophelia in her "mad" wig by Vivienne Walker, with Laurence Olivier in his 1948 production of *Hamlet*. *Universal Pictures/Photofest © Universal Pictures*

to look afraid, hold your breath," she had told me, so at one point in *Hamlet*, I had to look afraid. I held my breath. Larry broke up, laughing, and asked, "What *are* you doing?"

"I'm holding my breath to look frightened. Katina Paxinou told me to do that."

"No! No! No! Don't do that," he said. I have never done it since.

I remember the wig that the wonderful hairdresser, Vivienne Walker, made for me for the mad scene, braids and a wreath of flowers, everything to make me look mad. It was she who convinced Larry not to wear a wig but to dye his hair blond, which made all the difference in his characterization of the Dane.

Did Olivier have you watch rushes during the production?

Larry asked me to see the rushes of the mad scene. He said, "I think you'll be very pleased."

I obediently went into the screening room. When the scene came on, I started to giggle when I saw this looney. I thought everybody else would laugh too. Nobody else was laughing. Suddenly, I heard him say, and pardon my language, "Get the fuck out of here." Larry was so angry with me because of the way I behaved.

Some actors can see themselves in the third person, which is wonderful because they can learn by watching. I can't watch myself objectively. I just want to curl up and die. I just can't watch myself. It's impossible.

I knew that Larry was a giggler, too, but not while watching rushes. In the midst of shooting a serious scene, he would crack up for some reason. Laughter was a tremendous release from the tension of the production.

You received a number of positive reviews for your role.

I especially appreciate James Agee's review now more than I did when I was younger. He wrote [she reads from the review from *Time* magazine, June 28, 1948], "She plays the sane scenes with baffled docility, a faint aura of fey, and a tender suggestion of nascent maturity. . . . Compared with most of the members of the cast, she is obviously just a talented beginner. But she is the only person in the picture who gives every one of her lines the bloom of poetry and the immediacy of ordinary life."

There were numerous awards and nominations for that film, including several for you.

Yes, and it's still amazing to me that I received an Academy Award Supporting Actress nomination. I didn't attend the ceremony. I won the Volpi Cup at the Venice Film Festival in 1948.[1]

You had been in Hollywood two years earlier to collect Oscars for some of the British nominees if they won.

I was asked to accept for the winners, as many of them couldn't attend. I flew in from Fiji with a terrible coral cut on my leg I got while filming *The Blue Lagoon*, and I was limping badly. When I went on stage to accept the award for Jack Cardiff [Cinematography—Color; *Black Narcissus*] and then again when Guy Green won [Cinematography—Black and White; *Great Expectations*], I tried not to limp. I again accepted for John Bryan and Wilfred Shingleton and Alfred Junge. It became a joke with the audience because I went on stage to collect one Oscar and then another and another. Finally, all I could say was, "Thank you."

What I do remember clearly is that, as a typical teenager at the Oscars, I rushed around with my autograph book getting signatures of Elizabeth Taylor and Ingrid Bergman and lots of others. It was all too much for me. I even remember what I wore: a strapless black velvet dress. And I was chaperoned like crazy.

I brought the Oscars back to London where there was a special ceremony at the Odeon Leicester Square, which Lord Mountbatten attended. But it's all a vague memory.

Years later, in 1958, I collected the Oscar from presenter Cary Grant for Alec Guinness when he won the Acting award for *Bridge on the River Kwai*.[2]

In 1949, you stepped onto the London stage for the first time in a less-than-successful production.

The play, directed by the wonderful Peter Glenville, was *The Power of Darkness* [Vlast' t'my] by Tolstoy. My soon-to-be husband, Stewart Granger, and I had pre–West End performances in Glasgow, Liverpool, and, I think, Manchester. It wasn't very good. The whole thing was a disaster and was on and off very quickly at the Lyric Theatre in London. I couldn't get into the mood of the piece because I didn't see me playing Alkoulina, a deaf half-wit. It put me off the stage for a long time.

The reviews were terrible. [She reads a portion from a newspaper review:] "This was an ill-advised production. . . . [Stewart] Granger thought he and Jean Simmons would be applauded for choosing such a challenging project . . . but it was disliked by audiences and regarded as another example of Granger's arrogance and pretensions."

Years later, you were a great success in A Little Night Music. What brought you back to the stage?

Glynis Johns, my great friend, was playing Desiree Armfeldt in New York, where I had seen the production. I was asked to take over the role for the

London production at the Adelphi Theatre in 1975. But I wouldn't take the role without asking her. I called, and she told me that she wasn't well enough and said, "You go ahead." Before I went to London, I did a national tour in the States with Margaret Hamilton as Madame Armfeldt. What a smashing lady!

The male lead in London was Joss Ackland, also a friend. We got along fine up to a point, until, for some reason, we had a bit of a row and ended up not speaking to each other for some time. That apparently showed on the stage. Now we're great buddies again and have worked together in the television film, *Daisies in December*, directed by Mark Haber.

I was never considered a singer, so I took lessons from George Griffin on how to present a song. Sondheim's music and lyrics are difficult and complicated, but how beautiful! For my character, my songs were simple and funny, but some of the lyrics between the husband and wife are counterpoint. There really are no "singable" songs, except maybe the showstopper, "Send in the Clowns," which could almost be spoken.

It was the music, though, that held me up for those eight shows a week. Sometimes I was tired or not in the mood to go on. Suddenly, I'd hear the music, and it would pick me up. Music does that to both the performers and the audience. Also, once I was in costume, which was bloody uncomfortable, it made me stand and walk in a different way. And away I'd go. It was always very motivating to know there was an audience out there who'd paid to see the show.

Funnily enough, it would be my first role as a character named Desiree, the other as the title character in the film *Désirée* with Marlon Brando.

Speaking of Brando . . .
Oh, yes, please, do.

You played opposite him in two films.
Marlon played Napoleon and was wonderful, but the film was all about *my* character, Désirée Clary, who had once been Napoleon's fiancée. It should have really been more about Napoleon.

And we sang and danced together in *Guys and Dolls*. We had wonderful rehearsals with choreographer Michael Kidd. When we finally had to shoot them, we were sad because we wouldn't be able to rehearse any longer. It was the joy of learning and being with Michael. He made it fun. We got comfortable with all the movements we had to do. Yes, I went to dancing school, but I'm talking about Michael Kidd stuff. He was heaven, absolute heaven.

A decision was made to dub my voice and Marlon's. Then someone heard us rehearsing because, of course, we had to practice the songs along with the dancing. Director Joe Mankiewicz suggested that maybe we should do our own singing.

Jean Simmons snuggles up to Marlon Brando in the Joseph L. Mankiewicz–directed film *Guys and Dolls* (1955). *Goldwyn/MGM /Photofest © Goldwyn/MGM*

Sam Goldwyn told Brando and me, "Well, you don't sound so good, but it's you."

Brando's voice was just right for the character of Sky Masterson. It was so charming. Who could have looped him? Imagine a baritone coming out of his mouth? But that's what was done in the German version where they left his speaking voice, but put in a singer with a deep, deep voice.

I can't believe Marlon's gone. When I saw him in *The Score* in 2001 with Robert De Niro and he smiles, I thought, "Oh, God. He's still got it." [As she reminisces about her costar, Simmons's voice catches; she pauses and takes a deep breath before she can continue.]

Some years earlier, 1951, you appeared in *The Clouded Yellow*, directed by Ralph Thomas. The character played by Barry Jones was initially written one way and then rewritten. How did that change affect you?

When we started the film, wonderful Barry Jones was *not* the villain. Then in the middle of shooting, there were script changes. He and I had been cozy and friendly off the set. But once his character was changed, just the look in his eye frightened me. He was terrifying and scared me to death. I knew he was acting, but it was kind of creepy. It was quite marvelous to see.

I remember that Trevor Howard, who played the hero, was, in real life, such a cricket fan that he had it in his contract that wherever he was in the world, he could return to Lord's Cricket Ground for the games. Like Jack Nicholson and the Lakers. I played in Trevor's last film in 1988, *The Dawning*. My costumes were by Julie Harris, one of the best designers in the business.

Director Otto Preminger had a reputation of being difficult. What was your working relationship with him on *Angel Face* in 1952?

It was horrible shooting that film because of Preminger. If there was one word to describe his directing style, it would be *sadistic*.

Robert Mitchum and I had a scene in which he slaps me. For each take, he'd cheat the slap. Preminger argued, "No, it looks fake. You've got to *hit* her."

Bob, bless him, helped me through the scene. He was on my side. But he *did* hit me. We did the slap in long shot, over the shoulder, close up, and then the reverse. He had a hand like a bunch of bananas, but he was, surprisingly, a very gentle man. After each take, Preminger, who was standing behind the camera, said, "It doesn't look real. Do it again."

By the time we finished, I thought my jaw was broken. The crew saw what was happening, and I think they were going to drop something heavy on Preminger. If it hadn't been for Bob, I would have talked to Howard Hughes, who owned RKO then, and insisted that he get me out of there. Off the set, I went to dinner with Preminger; he was absolutely charming, but on the set . . . [she lets the thought vanish].

That film was one of the few in which you played a villain.

Yes, I usually played a goody-goody. But as a villain, I could let out all the ugly bits of my personality. I found things about myself that I wasn't too happy with. It's much more fun to play a nasty role, just as I did as Estella.

***This Earth Is Mine* is very much a soap opera. A happier experience?**

Oh, yes. We had the most wonderful cast.

Rock Hudson plays John Rambeau, and in one scene we had together, he grabs me and kisses me. I, as Elizabeth, am shocked and horrified—at least I was supposed to be. His line is, and he said it in a Southern accent, "You've been kissed befoah, and you lahked it, too." He had me giggling. For each take, he did a different accent. I don't know how we got through the scene. Our director, Henry King, was so patient with us. We really behaved disgracefully. I think we drove poor Henry mad with our giggling. But he didn't get angry with us. He probably threw something at the dog when he got home.

When I'd see Rock at some event, a premiere or whatever, we'd look at each other, and that was it: we'd go into giggles immediately and for no reason. He was such a delightful person, just the most divine man. Everybody loved him. He was just a hell of a guy.

And Claude Rains. That voice! I would sit on the set, not even looking at him, just to hear his voice. One scene I had with him was an exterior, and he has a long speech. I kept hoping he'd make an error and would have to do it again. He never did. I'm sure he must have been told throughout his career what a beautiful voice he had. He didn't seem to be aware of it, though.

As for Dorothy McGuire: she was absolutely, totally truthful in everything she did, a most underrated actress. There were no phony tricks in any performance. I loved working with her. I remember her in *The Enchanted Cottage*. She didn't do the ugly version of her character with makeup. It was the way she stood and walked.

We were on location for the film at several Napa Valley, California, wineries. It was always fun being on location because I got to go to places I never would have visited. The only trouble was that I never had time to do any sightseeing. We were up at 6 a.m., and by the time I'd get to bed at ten or eleven o'clock at night, I was exhausted.

I'd heard through the Hollywood rumor mill that before I was cast, I was replacing Natalie Wood, but I was never told if it was true or not.

***Footsteps in the Fog* was one of four films in which you appeared with Stewart Granger.[3]**

I had met Jimmy on *Caesar and Cleopatra*, and I fell in love with him; at least I thought it was love. But we didn't have scenes together until Harold French directed us in *Adam and Evalyn* where I play an orphan whom he adopts, but I "grow up" in the film. By the time we did *Young Bess*, directed by George Sidney, we were married.

In *Footsteps*, I play Lily Watkins, another wonderful villain, a blackmailer in the employ of Jimmy, who supposedly is heartbroken over the death of his wife, but I know better. What I remember most about that film is Peter Bull; we called him "Bully." Sweet, wonderful man. He wasn't a very good actor, but everybody loved him, so they wanted him to be part of their film. He had such a wonderful face. He collected teddy bears, hundreds of them. He had a whole shelf of them over the fireplace in his home. Oh, God, he was a dear.

***The Big Country* was a difficult shoot because the star and the director were at odds with each other. How did that affect the production?**

I love Westerns, but this was a difficult shoot because the director, William Wyler, and the star, Gregory Peck, who was also producing with Wyler, didn't get along and finally stopped speaking to each other. The whole situation was a bit awkward for the players. We were all caught in the middle of this terrible atmosphere. We could just feel the friction. The script was constantly being rewritten. We'd stay up all night to learn the lines that had been revised, and then when we got on the set the next morning, we'd have to learn new lines that had been written the night before.

After a take, Wyler would often say, "Do it again."

One of us would ask, "What do you want changed?"

He'd say, "Just do it again." That's not what an actor wants to hear. We want direction. Despite the hostility, it is a good picture. Burl Ives and Charles Bickford were wonderful. You don't get that quality of so-called supporting actors anymore.

How surprised were you with the excellent reviews you received in the comedic role in *The Grass Is Greener*?

I was gratified, but I wasn't comfortable on that picture, which we shot at Osterley Park and Shepperton. It was directed by Stanley Donen. I knew Cary Grant socially and was a good friend of his wife at the time, Betsy Drake. Jimmy and I and Cary and Betsy would go out together and joke around. It was fine on a social level, but working with him [Simmons pauses to think about the feeling], I felt terribly uncomfortable. I can't explain it. I felt the same way with Cary that I did with Richard Chamberlain in *The Thorn Birds*, and I admired him tremendously, too.

It was as if Cary were in a glass bubble, and I had to knock to get in. He was such an enormous star, and he had this magical thing about him—the elegance and the good looks. I felt a bit intimidated. It was one of those rare times that I felt as if I were a fan, and that doesn't work when you're working with someone. It's odd that I would feel that way because Cary was best man at my wedding to Jimmy in Tucson, Arizona, December 20, 1950.

Working with Bob Mitchum again was easy and comfortable and no slapping!

What was your experience working on *The Egyptian*, an epic production, directed by Michael Curtiz?

I can't help laughing when I think of that picture; for the time, it was a big-budget film: four million dollars. The less said about the director, the better. When I heard that he had directed Bogie and Bergman in *Casablanca*, I couldn't believe it. Maybe they directed themselves. Curtiz spent a lot of time working with Bella Darvi, and he rehearsed with stand-ins, telling them, "You move over there on that line, and move over here on that line."

Then when the principals were on the set, he told us, "You have to move on that line."

We'd say that we didn't want to.

"You have to because the stand-in did it that way," he'd insist.

It was literally like that. I did not enjoy working with Mr. Curtiz. Fortunately, I spent most of my time with Peter Ustinov, which was heaven. He was a dear, funny, brilliant man. I'd stay near him throughout the production so life wouldn't be so bad.

There's a scene where I've been shot by an arrow, and Edmund Purdom as the hero has to carry me. He was huffing and puffing, and I got the giggles. My brother saw the film and asked, "Were you giggling?" I asked him how he could tell. He said it was the way my body was moving up and down. Nobody else picked up on it. Edmund was a dear man and, oh, so handsome and a good actor, but unfortunately he was in *The Egyptian*.

This was supposed to be another film with Marlon. But after looking at the script, he said no and that he would play Napoleon instead in *Désirée*. He was, of course, right!

Another of your "toga roles" was in the epic *Spartacus* with Kirk Douglas. Great cast; great director. Your thoughts?

Damn good movie. One doesn't usually say that about an epic. Anthony Mann was taken off as director and replaced by Stanley Kubrick, who came in as a favor to Kirk Douglas, who had been in Stanley's 1950s film, *Paths of Glory*. I had been told that Stanley was a demanding director. I never saw any of those disagreeable aspects about him that other people told me about. He was very quiet, and I found him a dear man. I don't think the film was his cup of tea, though. I replaced Sabine Bethmann, who had been cast as Varinia, but they realized she couldn't speak English well enough.

I had a scene with Peter Ustinov—again—and Charles Laughton. Peter would take me aside and say, "When I'm talking, just concentrate on me."

"Yes, of course," I said.

Then Charles would take me aside and say, "I want you just to concentrate on me when I'm talking."

"Yes, of course," I said.

It was literally like watching a tennis match as I looked between the two of them. Left. Right. Back and forth, with little to do except listen.

How did your personal and professional association with Richard Brooks affect your performance during the production as Sister Sharon Falconer in *Elmer Gantry*?

Richard adored actors, and his enthusiasm was very catching. But if he didn't like a take, he would say, "You've done that all wrong," right in front of everybody. Most directors might take an actor aside; not Richard. He didn't worry about anybody listening. If it was something *really* serious, he would take the actor into a corner to speak with them. At one point, though, he said to me—in front of everyone—"You sound like you're talking to your father. You're talking to God, *not* your father!"

I remember my first entrance into the tent. I charged down the aisle to the front. Richard stopped me and asked, "What are you hurrying for?"

I told him, "You've been having me walk fast in other scenes." My thought had been that I couldn't wait to get to the pulpit!

Richard had other ideas. "Here, you've got to stop and talk to someone and then move on," he explained. For the first couple of weeks, I took his comments seriously, but then I saw the twinkle in his eye. From that point on, it was wonderful. When I first started working with him, I thought, "Who is this nut?" I realized later that he'd say things to inspire us.

After *Hamlet*, I never went to rushes. But one day, Richard said, "I want you to come and see rushes." I told him, "I don't think it's a good idea." He insisted. I did, and for the next three days, I couldn't walk, talk, or think about what I was supposed to be doing. I was going over and over the scenes I'd seen. He finally understood, and conceded, shaking his finger at me, and yelling, "Don't you ever see rushes again." He'd learned his lesson.

As a writer, Richard was neurotic about his scripts getting out. We would read the script in his office and then only get the pages for the day. We'd ask him, "What's going to happen to the character?"

He'd say, "Why would you want to know?"

Why, indeed. Because the most difficult aspect of acting in film is not shooting in continuity. You don't necessarily know how your character has progressed, and you really have to be terribly aware of what's *going* to happen or what *has* happened to the character. On stage, you go straight through to the end, in continuity, not in film.

After your marriage to Richard Brooks, he wrote *The Happy Ending* for you with the thought that it would help you face your demons. What was the result?

When I married Richard in November 1960, I "retired," and in my head I thought it would be forever. I played Mrs. Housewife and did the cooking.

Richard said, "It might be interesting for you to go back to work doing what you do best . . . and we'll hire a cook."

Richard was very sweet and patient, and he was right. I did several films: *All the Way Home*, directed by Alex Segal; *Mr. Budwing*, directed by Delbert Mann, a film I never did figure out what it was about; *Divorce, American Style*, directed by Bud Yorkin; and others.

I began having problems, and Richard, who was absolutely sensitive to my feelings and thoughts, realized it. He wrote *The Happy Ending* for me. Mary Wilson, the lead character, is an alcoholic, very much like I was at the time. Yes, it's true. Richard wrote it for me because he thought it would help me to be open and honest about my problem, and that through that role, I would get a lot of garbage out of my system . . . getting rid of all this, which on a personal basis, I didn't really want to *talk* about. It did work. By being the character instead of myself, I *could* get it out. It was very helpful, not only in the film but in our personal relationship. And I received an Actress Oscar nomination.[4]

I knew I had the inner strength to stop, but I didn't know how. He helped me overcome some of my problems with the role. But, in the end, I'm afraid it didn't work. He was so marvelous, very understanding. He was quite remarkable, my old man. At the end of that production, I did start to drink again but not as seriously as before. Maybe a drink, but not *drinking*.

To what do you attribute the end of your marriage to Richard Brooks?

I had divorced Jimmy[5] to marry Richard. In the end, I recognized Richard was a workaholic, and I was an alcoholic. That was just not a good match. We were together for seventeen years and had a daughter, Kate, named after Katharine Hepburn. My other daughter, by Jimmy, is Tracy, named after Spencer Tracy, a hero of mine. Richard and I divorced in 1977.

You made an early and a successful transition into television in the mid-sixties with a role in *The Thorn Birds*, directed by Daryl Duke. Your recollections of that production?

I had read the book by Colleen McCullough, which I didn't want to end. I wanted it to go on and on. I really did. I wanted to play Fiona Cleary, and I lobbied for it—for two years.

Barbara Stanwyck, as Mary, was extraordinary in her manner, attitude, and in her work. And a fun lady and such a giving actor. By that I mean as the character listening to other actors, which is not as easy as everyone thinks. Being with another actor and responding is a talent itself.

I remember we all had a bad time because of the smoke that was poured into the set to give it a period look.

You returned to the stage in a two-hander, *Love Letters* by A. R. Gurney, with Charlton Heston.

I adored doing that two-person play at a little theatre in Beverly Hills, the Canon. It was just a short run, just a week or two in 2000. It was weird doing it because we were looking at the audience reading the letters rather than playing to one another, which we were both used to doing. When we were rehearsing it, we had a tendency to turn toward one another and the director would say, "No. No. You must look out at the audience."

During the course of your career, you worked at several studios, both in the UK and the States. What were the differences?

I was not as aware of the pressure as much in England as I felt in America. We stopped for tea twice a day in those early days in England. There was pressure on *Shadows in the Sun*, directed by David Rocksavage, because of the lack of money and time. Even so, it was a very happy experience.

When I first came to the US, it was pretty much the same, except no teatime. We used to have more time between setups because of the length of time for the lighting, and the camera crew didn't get any rest. They were working while the actors were resting, and they were still working while we were shooting.

Everybody's favorite UK studio was Pinewood because in the restaurant, there was a bar, but not at Denham. You could get a ginger beer. It was wonderful at lunch, and then after lunch . . . well . . . ! Great lunches at Pinewood. Crews in both places were very professional, very good at what they did.

What was your most forgettable work, not that it was a disappointment, but that as good as it was, no one really took notice of it?

[There's a long, thoughtful silence.]

I think it was *The Actress*, an MGM film, but not one of their *big* films, just a little black-and-white production about a little girl who wanted to be an actress. How could I have asked for more: working with George Cukor all those weeks?

And, of course, working with Spencer Tracy was wonderful. He had the most wonderful face; the older he got, the craggier he got and the better looking he became to me. We had a wonderful time on that picture. It's a shame it sort of slid by.

Ha! I just remembered that at the time we made the picture, I had a poodle named Young Bess. The dog wouldn't let the wardrobe woman near my clothes. When I was finished with them, I'd leave them on the floor of my dressing room, and when the wardrobe woman came to get them, Bessie would sit on them and growl.

Looking back, which role do you most identify with?

Definitely Mary Wilson in *The Happy Ending* and, secondly, Ruth Gordon Jones in *The Actress*.

Were all the heartbreaks and the accolades worth it?

My goodness, yes. I've had more experiences, met more fabulous people over the years. Who would have thought somebody like me from Cricklewood would have traveled to Fiji and gone to Switzerland and come to America? It's been a wonderful life. Yes, it's had its ups and downs. A lot of sadness, but that's life.

Meeting Her Majesty Queen Elizabeth II who awarded you an OBE must have been a bewildering experience.

It was thrilling just to be notified of the honor, this kid from Cricklewood. I was initially called, and the voice on the other end of the phone said, "Are you sitting down?" I was informed that I had been selected for the honor, but I was told, "You mustn't tell anyone." I was cool about it and kept my mouth shut. I'd never been to Buckingham Palace. Going to the palace and walking through the halls and seeing all that history I'd studied at school was extraordinary.

I took Tracy with me. She said, "Mummy, I hope you don't mind if I get the giggles." Like mother, like daughter.

My knees are bad, and since I didn't want to curtsy as I shook the hand of my Queen and drag her down with me, I had a page help me. Elizabeth is quite extraordinary. She has an aura about her, that magnificent smile and those blue eyes. I don't remember what she said to me, and I don't remember what I said. I do remember that I was stuttering because she had been my Princess and my Queen all of my life. All I could think was, "My goodness, we're now wearing the same eyeglasses."

I had met Her Majesty once before at a Royal Premiere Performance, but she just walked by. But to actually walk up to her—I can't explain it. I was thrilled with the whole experience.

Jean Simmons died at her home on January 22, 2010, at age eighty. On June 29, 2010, a service celebrating her life was held in London. Among those who participated were Joss Ackland, CBE; Sir Richard Rodney Bennett, CBE; Claire Bloom, CBE; Dame Judi Dench, OBE; Edward Fox, OBE; Stephen Frears; and Hayley Mills.

Selected Credits

Theatre
The Power of Darkness, Manchester Opera House; Lyric Theatre (1949; Peter Glenville); *A Little Night Music*, Forrest Theatre, Pennsylvania; Adelphi

(1974–1975; Harold Prince); *Love Letters*, 2000, Canon, Beverly Hills (2000; Ted Weiant)

Film
Sports Day (1944); *Give Us This Moon* (1944); *Mr. Emmanuel* (1944); *Caesar and Cleopatra* (1945); *Great Expectations* (1946); *Uncle Silas* [a.k.a. *The Inheritance*] (1947); *The Woman in the Hall* (1947); *Hamlet* (1948); *Blue Lagoon* (1948); *Adam and Evalyn* [a.k.a. *Adam and Evelyne*] (1949); *So Long at the Fair* (1950); *Cage of Gold* (1950); *Young Bess* (1953); *The Robe* (1953); *She Couldn't Say No* (1954); *The Egyptian* (1954); *Désirée* (1954); *Guys and Dolls* (1955); *Footsteps in the Fog* (1955); *Hilda Crane* (1956); *This Could Be the Night* (1957); *The Big Country* (1958); *The Grass Is Greener* (1960); *All the Way Home* (1963); *Life at the Top* (1965); *Spartacus* (1967); *Until They Sail* (1967); *The Happy Ending* (1969); *How to Make an American Quilt* (1995); *Howl's Moving Castle* (voice) (2004); *Shadows in the Sun* (2009)

Television
Bob Hope Presents the Chrysler Theatre, "The Lady Is My Wife" (1967); *Heidi* (1968); *Jacqueline Susann's Valley of the Dolls* (1981); *The Thorn Birds*, three episodes (1983); *North and South, Book II*, six episodes (1985); *Great Performances*, "December Flower" (1987); *Murder, She Wrote*, "Mirror, Mirror on the Wall," Parts 1 and 2 (1989); *Great Expectations*, six episodes (1989); *Star Trek: The Next Generation*, "The Drumhead" (1991); *They Do It with Mirrors* (1991); *Dark Shadows*, twelve episodes (1991); *Daisies in December* (1995)

Awards and Nominations

Hamlet, 1948, Academy Award, Supporting Actress, nominee; also, Volpi Cup, Venice Film Festival, *Premio Internazionalie per la migliore attrice* (International Award for the Best Actress), winner; 1950, *Daily Mail* National Film Award, Actress of the Year, winner; *Guys and Dolls*, 1956, Golden Globe, Best Performance by an Actress in a Leading Role, Musical/Comedy, winner; *This Could Be the Night*, 1958, Golden Globe, Best Actress in a Leading Role, Musical/Comedy, nominee; *Home before Dark*, 1959, Golden Globe, Best Performance by Actress in a Motion Picture, Drama, nominee; *Elmer Gantry*, 1961, Golden Globe, Best Performance by an Actress in a Motion Picture, Drama, nominee; *The Happy Ending*, 1969, Academy Award, Actress, nominee; *The Thorn Birds*, 1983, Emmy, Outstanding Supporting Actress—Series/Special, winner; also, 1984, Golden Globe, Best Supporting

Actress—Miniseries, nominee; *Murder, She Wrote*, "Mirror, Mirror on the Wall," Part I, 1989, Emmy, nominee

Honors

OBE, 2003; BFI Fellowship, 1994

Notes

1. Claire Trevor won for *Key Largo*. If Simmons had won, Deborah Kerr would have accepted it on her behalf. *Hamlet* won the Oscar for Best Motion Picture. Olivier won the Acting Oscar and received a director nomination. John Huston won directing honors for *The Treasure of the Sierra Madre*.

2. In her acceptance speech on behalf of Alec Guinness, March 26, 1958, Simmons said, "To accept the award for Alec Guinness tonight gives me a particular delight because thirteen years ago I worked with Alec in . . . *Great Expectations*, and we were lucky enough to have the director David Lean who directed *Bridge on the River Kwai*. Since then, I've watched him give wonderful, wonderful performances and so tonight, to Alec Guinness, a truly great artist, many, many congratulations."

3. Granger's birth name was James Stewart, but he changed it because another actor already had that name.

4. Maggie Smith won for *The Prime of Miss Jean Brodie*. Other nominees: Geneviève Bujold, *Anne of the Thousand Days*; Jane Fonda, *They Shoot Horses, Don't They?*; Liza Minnelli, *The Sterile Cuckoo*.

5. Simmons and Granger divorced August 12, 1960. He died in 1993 at age eighty.

~

CHAPTER TWENTY

David Suchet, CBE

I became an actor because I want to serve writers.

The walk from the station to St. Katharine Docks from the Tower Bridge Underground station was just five minutes. The clock on the tower of Ivory House, still ticking away after more than 130 years, read 9:45 a.m., just fifteen minutes prior to the interview time with actor David Suchet. The actor lives in the historic building, which, during the nineteenth century, housed several thousand elephant tusks, and is the only warehouse on the London docks not demolished by German bombs during World War II. This building, along with the entire area, has since been rebuilt and gentrified. Boats of all sizes and shapes are moored in the nearby marina.

Precisely at the appointed time, Suchet[1] strides across the foyer very unlike the mincing steps he takes as Hercule Poirot. His hand is outstretched in greeting.

~

In the beginning?

I was born in 1946 in London, the middle of three sons. In those early days, I thought I would follow in my father's footsteps as a doctor; he was an eminent Harley Street gynecologist. But, at school, I found out my maths were not good enough.

What about your school experiences?

My brothers and I attended Grenham House School in Kent. I wasn't terribly happy there. Then I attended the Wellington School in Somerset from

Photo courtesy of the author

1960 to 1964, a much happier experience.[2] It was there that I appeared as the lead in a production of *Macbeth*. I also appeared in such plays as *Cockpit* and *Richard of Bordeaux*.[3]

My teacher there, Joe Storr, suggested that I might be interested in the National Youth Theatre. I auditioned and was accepted. Michael Croft headed up the company, and I had a wonderful time. I sadly have lost touch with the organization because I've been so busy. On one level I'm very grateful for my career, but it's prevented me from actually being a part of that group that gave me so much.

I went on to LAMDA. I deliberately—and this is very telling—didn't audition for RADA. I don't know why. Maybe it was fear of failure at what was considered the top drama school at the time. I tried Central School, which turned me down. I only applied to one other, London Academy, where I was accepted. I was very fortunate that the principal, Norman Ayrton, said when I'd finished my audition, "Come and speak to me. You *will* be offered a place."

What were your audition pieces?

There was a speech from Bill Naughton's play, *Alfie*, and my Shakespearean speech was "Oh, pardon me, thou bleeding piece of earth . . . ," from *Julius Caesar* [Act III, scene i].

328   Chapter Twenty

From LAMDA?

I moved to the RSC in 1973, where I appeared in the Shakespearean classics such as *Richard II, Cymbeline, Love's Labour's Lost*, and more, some of which transferred to the Aldwych in London, which, for a time, was the London home of the Company.

What was your initial motivation to become an actor?

I became an actor originally because I wanted to serve writers. I was fascinated at the thought that people were writing to give their work away to others to interpret instead of, say, writing a novel. I felt a huge responsibility that if I were to become an actor, I would want to represent the authors, the playwrights. I still feel that way today.

Besides the classic characters, your roles have encompassed portrayal of real people. Who are some of those characters?

One of the first was as Sigmund Freud in the television series, directed by Moira Armstrong. I really looked like Freud in every aspect of the six hours of that television drama. It was, I believe, the longest single role written for British television up to that time.

There was also Gustave Klimt in *Schiele in Prison*, Edward Teller in *Oppenheimer*, both in 1980; William Shirer in *Morrow* in '86; Robert Maxwell in *Maxwell* in 2007; and even Louis B. Mayer in *RKO 281* in '99, and, of course, Salieri and Benelli. I feel a great responsibility to those people when I choose to portray them.

Your most recent project involving a nonfictional character is *The Last Confession*. What is the process of developing such a project with its historical—and religious—context and the character of Cardinal Benelli who was involved in the events?

The play by Roger Crane is about Pope John Paul I, his election and mysterious death just thirty-three days after he was elected in 1978. He was going to be a very liberal pope. His friend, Giovanni Cardinal Benelli, sets out to investigate his death: Was it by natural causes? Was it murder? So it's a mystery of sorts.

Since I had played real people before, the task of entering into the life of someone who really lived was not new. The fact that I didn't look that dissimilar was lucky, but that was not the exercise of the piece. The main thing about the play is the story.

Crane, an American attorney, was a first-time playwright, and several years before, I had been asked to do this play at the Clwyd Theatr Cymru in Wales. Roger had sent the play to the former RSC director, Terry Hands [now artistic director at that theatre], who rang me and asked if he could send me the play. When I first read it, I didn't think it was ready for performance.

Terry said we would have time, but I said, "Not in rehearsal." Rehearsal time is always limited, and I knew from recent experience that if we tried to rework a new play *in* rehearsal, there would be problems. The 2009 Old Vic production of *Complicit*, which I was in, is a good example.

I never heard about the play again until a dear friend of mine, Amanda Mackey, a top casting director in New York, rang me, saying that Roger had given her a new play to read. He had gone to her to ask advice about who she thought could play the role. Once she'd read it, she told him, "As a casting director, I feel that there is only one person to play the part of Benelli: David Suchet."

Roger told her that he'd already sent it to me, and I'd rejected it. She contacted me and asked me to have another go. I agreed. This second read was a great improvement. It was much clearer. I read it and read it and read it. Something struck me from a different angle this time.

I had read books about the subject and knew the mystery surrounding the death of the pope. I recalled the headlines in the *Evening Standard* at the time and thought, "How strange! The play is a sort of 'whodunit.'" I questioned my role in the project at the time because I didn't want to appear as a detective in the theatre. I'd done too much of that in television up to that time and didn't want to be allied with that type of role in a theatre project. I wanted to stay away from that. But then I thought, "No, this is not just about the question-and-answer aspect and the trial that goes on." This, I realized, is a question of a man and his faith and where his faith takes him and how he makes that final decision to burn his document. That's what interested and fascinated me because I have a very strong faith myself. I'm always interested in writers and where *their* faith takes them, how they deal with things in life that knock them sideways.

With the drama presumptive, I thought that made it a very good piece of theatre.

What was the next step?

I said to Roger, "Before I commit, I'd like to come to New York and work on it again with you."

I had made notes in the script and worked at it myself. When we met, he was very generous, very open to all my suggestions. He wrote another draft and then another. He sent each of those to me, and I came to America again to work with him one more time. As a bit of a perfectionist, I felt I really wanted to get it right. I finally was so excited by the play's potential, I told him, "Yes, I will commit to it. And I will try to set it up."

What did "set it up" mean?

It meant that *I* was going to find a producer. I'd never done that before in my life, but I believed in the piece. The first producer I rang was Duncan C. Weldon, who knew about the play because of Terry Hands all those years ago. Duncan agreed to read it again. After he read it, he told me, "I think it's quite a good piece, and I'd like to work with you again." We had worked together when I played Salieri in *Amadeus*. I joined the production team but not in any official way but as sort of an associate, I suppose.

Once that was in place, what about finding the cast and director?

Roger came to London, and we had a read-through to see how the play *sounded*. This wasn't a public reading. We got some actors who were generous enough to come in. Various directors were invited to listen without any offer being given. I have to say the read-through was not a happy occasion, and at the meeting afterwards we had to make a decision whether to go ahead or not.

It became a difficult process, perhaps more than expected?

Yes, but I made my decision: "I think we should go ahead. I'm not going to let it go now." I thought if we could get a good director on board, he would be able to look at the play again. I can give it over to him, and he can work with Roger.

And you found someone?

As fortune or faith would have it—there was a hand over this play—there was a telephone call to Duncan from director David Hugh Jones. I'd worked with him at the RSC on *Love's Labour's Lost*, *Summerfolk*, and others, asking if Duncan had any plays he was considering. Duncan rang me and said, "Guess who's rung asking for a play? Your friend and mine from the RSC days, David Jones."[4]

It was immediate [Suchet smacks his hands together for emphasis]. I said, "He's going to be the director. I'd love to work with David again—if he would like to work with me."

After he read the play, he agreed that it still needed work and said he would work with Roger and "see how we go."

Working together, they increased some of the roles so that we could get some fine actors to play them. One of the problems at the very beginning was that all the roles were sort of equal, except mine and the pope's. Additional drafts were sent to me, and Roger and I met again to discuss casting.

When did everything finally come together?

I had read the play at Christmas, 2006. By March 2007, the weekend before Easter, the play was fully cast. Because Roger had written up some of the roles, we got some of the really great elder statesmen, some splendid classical actors, which would give the production a certain gravitas. They understood how to think through the lines and to present the roles. I think we worked it out that each person on stage had been in the theatre for more than forty-five years! Michael Jayston as the Confessor gave a most magnificent performance, as did Richard O'Callaghan as the pope and Charles Kay. We got the green light, and rehearsals began the week before Easter.

What were the challenges to this particular role compared to other real-life characters?

That's a very interesting question. As I normally do, I cogitate and work in my study and continue working and thinking and pondering, refreshing my lines and my journey through the play. I found it a very difficult rehearsal period, very hard, indeed. I was starting to use rehearsal to find out how to grapple with the scenes. The great trap, I realized, was that every time I opened my mouth, irrespective of how hard I tried, this piety came through, which I knew was incorrect. But I couldn't help it. It was only about two or three weeks in when I realized where I was making my mistake.

The mistake? I was playing a cardinal in this story, a man of the Church. The fact that he's a cardinal was getting in the way. I knew I had to play him as a *man* who *happens* to be a cardinal. It's a huge difference. I suddenly understood why I was struggling.

I came in to rehearsal one day and said to David, "If you hear a note of piety, stop the rehearsal, and tell me to start again. I don't want to be pious in any way. I want to be as vulnerable as anybody else. Maybe by doing that, it will touch the audience in a way they're not expecting."

If the audience sees a man grappling with faith, they can think, "My goodness, he's a cardinal, so maybe it's all right if I do." Even if there is an agnostic in the audience, it doesn't make it "holier than thou" for them because they're watching a drama. Interestingly, unlike my role as Freud, where I had to age for the series, as Benelli, I already had a similar aspect and didn't have to age, and, of course, the time period was much shorter in the play than in *Freud*.

How much did the wearing of the religious costumes shape the characters?

Since the entire play takes place in the secret chambers of the Vatican, I asked David and the designers whether we really needed to wear anything appropriate to our roles in the Church. It was decided that if we did it in modern dress, everybody would be in black suits, and that's not very attractive on stage. Very few people realize there is a subtle thing happening on stage with the gold crosses. We were told that the cross can be worn in two distinct ways: one means the wearer is conservative; the other means the wearer is more liberal. Those with the loop are the arch-conservatives. Those from the Church who saw the play would know, so we had to do it right.

Had you come to a conclusion about the "whodunit" side of the story, your opinion about what really happened?

Yes, I have an opinion, but I'll never say. It didn't impact my performance because I felt that I knew what Benelli felt. Roger never makes it clear, so I decided to find out *in* the moment, *at* the moment I'm praying to God. God guides me in what to do. That's why I, as Benelli, break down at the end. Everything he's striving for ultimately he knows is against God's will.

Once everything was in place, the play toured the UK prior to coming into the West End. Why not just open in the West End?

Duncan had said we'd open in Chichester and then come into London.

I said, "No, I want to tour first." I wanted to do it for two reasons: first, I didn't want to open in London and flop; second, I fully, *fully* believe that as a person with a high theatre and television profile, it's my duty to go out to the people rather than expect them to come to me.

There are people who write to me who could never come and see me in the theatre in London. I wanted to go out with the play. I've always done that since *Amadeus*. Of course, even with a tour, there's no guarantee the production will be a success.

What was the result of the tour?

We had a great success, and when we came into London, we had wonderful reviews. Although, we had a very good advance at the Theatre Royal Haymarket, in the first week of previews, there was a car bombing right near the theatre. That put audiences off. Then there was the London Marathon; then there were the preliminaries to the Tour de France. It seemed that every single weekend that we depended on for our income, there was a problem.

Then I lost my voice.

We were only scheduled for a ten-week run because of my other commitments. We were just hanging on by our fingertips. I don't know what happened, whether it was because of increased publicity—I just don't know—but suddenly, people knew we were going to close in four weeks' time. From being in the red, we ended up well in the black.

I've been asked to do it again, but am loath to repeat performances. I've got as much out of that role as I need to.

The Last Confession was not the first play you turned down but ultimately accepted and received great acclaim. What were the circumstances with the other production?

When I was at the Royal Court doing *Oleanna*, and Stephen Daldry, the artistic director, offered me Terence Rattigan's *Man and Boy*. I read it and turned it down—four times—because I knew I wouldn't have the courage to be as vile as the leading character, Gregor Antonescu. I finally accepted because, when I read Rattigan's biography by Geoffrey Wansell, I realized how brokenhearted he was that it failed. It had a terrible run here and on Broadway when it was first performed in 1963 [with Charles Boyer as Antonescu] and directed by Michael Benthall. The kitchen sink dramas made Rattigan's plays passé. He wrote this as a comeback.

Rattigan thought it was his greatest play. I don't believe it is, but it is a very good play. It is very distasteful, but it was from his heart.

I wanted to resurrect it, get the play well reviewed—which it was—and I wanted the play to be reprinted. We achieved all those goals in 2005.[5]

You mentioned that you felt Complicit was not ready for performance. Can you explain the circumstances?

That's true; I didn't believe it was, and we knew it wasn't. I took the role at the very last minute. Kevin Spacey, then artistic director of the Old Vic,[6] rang me and said that the original actor who was going to play the role of Roger Cowan dropped out at the last minute. They were due to start rehearsal on the Monday, and Kevin called on the previous Thursday. I read the play and thought it was interesting. I wanted to work with Kevin as a director, and I loved the idea of working with Richard Dreyfuss. I had just worked with Elizabeth McGovern,[7] a wonderful actress, in one of the Poirots, "Appointment with Death."

I told Kevin I wouldn't make up my mind until I came in to read with the cast. This was going to be on the Friday. I came in and read and thought, "Yes, but it needs work." Some of the speeches were not right, but I liked the idea of a journalist, the Richard Dreyfuss character, fighting for what he thinks is right. I've often played roles of characters fighting for their rights going way back to Caliban in *The Tempest* some decades previously.

It interested me from the point of view that I was the lawyer actually playing a double game: keeping the law and trying to manipulate my client. A rather interesting way to go. I really enjoyed performing it. I loved the character I was playing, a lawyer. I loved the power he had as a character. I don't usually play that type of character, and I enjoyed the experience.

Sadly, we didn't have enough rehearsal time. I put the problems down to that. I don't believe playwright Joe Sutton ever got his play to talk properly. There were so many cuts. The first night was put off, and then put on again. Critics don't like that. We struggled. Having said that, I had a wonderful time.

For this play, the Old Vic was reshaped into an "in-the-round" venue. How does that impact performance?

It was a "round" season, just to see how it would work. I found it fascinating having played Salieri on that same stage. I discovered in performance that it wasn't really "theatre in the round." It was "theatre in the pear" because the auditorium was larger in front of me than the auditorium behind me. In fact, it spread out and went 'round in front of me. It was a pear audience and a round stage. It's very interesting to play on a round stage surrounded by the audience. There's nowhere to hide. There are those who see every single gesture, every single grimace. If you need to wipe sweat from your face, you can't. With the exits and entrances, we went right through the audience, through the *voms*.[8]

In that previous role as Salieri, you played yet another historical character. How did you build that character's personality?

Amadeus was a play that I always knew in my heart that I wanted to be in. I also knew I wanted to play Salieri.[9] Interesting, isn't it? Here again is a man, like Benelli, who has a relationship with God and whose voice he hears through this creature called Mozart. He doesn't think this person is worthy to be the voice of God through his music, and he can't understand that even though he's lived a very righteous life, a perfect life, a good life and has so much faith in God, that God would allow this wretch, this bestial, uncouth, horrible person to be God's mouth, and that his music is so much better than his own.

I did a terrific amount of research into Salieri's life, including going to Vienna to see his grave. It's ignominious compared to Mozart's. Salieri's grave is just up against a wall in the *Zentralfriedhof* with other *Kappelmeisters*. When I was there, someone had put a rose on his grave, which I thought was a nice touch. I got every single recording of every piece of his music that I could find. I went to a concert of his music here in London. He was a church organist and composer, so being a *Kappelmeister* obviously restricted him to a certain extent because he wrote for the court church. Then in comes Mozart with his scatological language and his scatological mind and having that very fine line between someone being a genius or mentally deranged. And the music that came out of him was rebellious and populirist.

I had meetings with the playwright, Peter Shaffer, before we started rehearsals. I asked him, "What do you want the audience to go away with thinking about Salieri?"

He thought for a long moment and then replied, "I want them to go away feeling sympathy for him."

"Is that what's on the page?" I asked.

"No," he said. He thought what was on the page was a little melodramatic what with the masks and characters standing over the body saying, "Die. Die. Die."

"With the greatest respect," I said, "shall we revisit the play?"

Peter had the grace and humility to revisit *Amadeus*, this great play. Remember, he had done the original production with Paul Scofield. He embraced the new ending where I try to portray the character who is regretting doing what he feels compelled to do. He rewrote the last third for the Los Angeles production.

What insight can you offer about Peter Hall, the director of that production, one the doyens of British theatre?

Peter is an amazing man of the theatre. He's not a *good* director. He's a *great* director. Undeniably.

The real meaning of *direct* is to point in the right direction, and that is what he does. He leaves the actor with full creativity. He's very open, very honest, very sincere. He may try to get us to do something, but if we disagree, it's fine. In rehearsal, he seems to do nothing. He doesn't say how to play a role. His notes are mainly about positions on the stage and ideas about tone.

This work is, in its own way, also a "whodunit."

Yes, that's true. There were theories at the time that Salieri *did* murder Mozart, so one can't just ignore that. In fact, Salieri went mad towards the end and confessed to killing him. Was that madness or not? We will never fully know, except for the fact that the autopsy on Mozart was very clear that he died of organ failure; he wasn't poisoned.

It's quite astonishing how many detectives you have played since 1973.[10] One of the more interesting was Inspector Japp in a television movie. What is the story behind that character and what it eventually led to?

Inspector Japp in *Thirteen at Dinner*, directed by Lou Antonio, was the worst performance I've ever given. I didn't know what to do with the character. I hated being a policeman. I wanted to be in the film because I wanted to work with Peter Ustinov, who was playing Hercule Poirot. I didn't do any research on Japp at all. I didn't know how to approach the role, so I ended up trying to eat in every scene to hide my performance. I was so bad that, although Peter appeared in other films as Poirot, no one ever asked *me* to return as Japp.

To this day, I say, "Thank you" on my knees that I was that bad. If people had got used to me as Japp, I would never have been asked to play Poirot.

We often say, looking back, how one thing led to another. I've always said that it's like a spider spinning a web from behind; he goes forward but the silk comes out from behind. It's only when he turns 'round that he can assess and see what joins to what. As human beings, we don't know what we're making as we go through life. We turn 'round at an older age and look back. I see certain things that happened, and if those things hadn't happened, I wouldn't be where I am today.

That has nothing to do with me, nothing at all. As a man of faith, I say there is no such thing as luck. It's a matter of a certain way we're meant to go.

For a quarter of a century, Hercule Poirot has been your alter ego. How do you accept this character as someone who, in fact, changed your life?

I make no apology in discussing him. I have many reasons to thank him. He's been part of my life since 1989.

I knew of Albie Finney's role as the detective in *Murder on the Orient Express* in '74, and those other lovely films that Peter Ustinov did as Poirot in *Death on the Nile*, *Evil under the Sun*, and *Appointment with Death*. They were great entertainment, but I never really took them seriously. Then, when I was offered the role, I started reading the books. I read about a little man who I'd never, ever seen. Never! I read nearly every book Agatha Christie wrote, but not *every* book! I found there wasn't a portrayal of Poirot in films or television that was a representation of the character that Christie wrote. It wasn't an easy thing to persuade people to let me play him the way I wanted him to be.

Going back to the reason I'm an actor—to serve my writer—all I did was transform myself into another person to produce the character. I was fortunate enough to be short, five foot five inches tall. I was fortunate enough to have a head like an egg; it's a complete oval. All as described by Christie.

How did you begin the process of developing that iconic character?

I made files about the nature of the character, ninety-three items. We did a screen test, and, yes, Poirot was there, except for one thing: I was moving as myself, so I had to find a movement for this little man. Then I remembered somewhere in the back of my mind, that there was a description of his walk. Since I don't believe in luck, but I do believe in the powers that be—there it was, in the fourth book I opened. Skimming through it, I found the description "Poirot crossed the lawn in his usual, rapid mincing gait, with his feet tightly and painfully enclosed in his patent leather shoes."

Just before we started Poirot, I was filming *When the Whales Came* on Bryher, one of the Isles of Scilly. I practiced walking around the island in that "mincing gait." That made all the difference.

What were Agatha Christie's family's thoughts about your interpretation?

Christie's daughter, Rosalind, and son-in-law, Anthony Hicks, took me out to a meal to discuss that very thing. They told me, "With your Poirot—and the program—we should be smiling *with* him but never laughing *at* him."

And we've always kept that tone. The character had to be true to Agatha Christie. I work very closely with her grandson, Mathew Prichard, to be sure that happens.

By 2003, I became an associate producer on the show, which gave me added responsibility. It was a voluntary, creative position generated for me. I was allowed a voice in script and casting, and, most importantly, I could say, to any director, whether Edward Bennett, Ross Devinish, Brian Farmham, Hettie Macdonald, or others, "No, that's not right."

I do think that a lot of directors find me, as Poirot, a bit intimidating because I'm *him* all day. I can't just switch off and on.[11]

Many actors have played the same character for years and found themselves typecast. That hasn't happened to you.

Poirot has never, ever typecast me. I can't tell you how grateful I am because that role has allowed me to do Salieri, Benelli, Freud, and the others. It's given me a theatre profile that I wouldn't have had without the series. It's allowed me to play all these different characters who bear no relationship to Poirot whatsoever. Audiences accept me in the other roles, totally. How many characters actors have been given that opportunity?

In one episode as Poirot, you say something to the effect, "See the truth from within." Is this something that you, as an actor, subscribe to?

Agatha Christie actually wrote that about Poirot. I do everything from within, but in rehearsal, especially in the theatre, I have to be free enough to just free-fall. Whatever happens in the moment, happens. I don't block any instinct.

The danger in acting is that you can prepare at home, take all that preparation into the rehearsal room, do your thing, and in the course of doing that, cut off the other actors. I do all my preparation at home and carry that within me. But it's all on me like a knapsack, which I can just leave at the door. Yes, it will influence me, but I must stay as free and as malleable as possible to react absolutely in the moment with another person, whether I think it's right or not.

Your mantra is "to serve the writers." Where do those writers come from today?

Theatre has to have houses to foster new writers. The Royal Court has been cutting edge for new writers since the sixties and is still very much in the forefront. We have a wonderful theatre, the Tricycle in Kilburn, doing groundbreaking work. Writers have to be allowed to push the barriers of life and art and faith in order to keep moving forward in order to make the plays relevant to our times.

We have to live in the present. The past is golden, and we have classical theatres that do all the great classical plays, the National and the RSC. They both have modern houses now because they are aware they cannot live in aspic and just do dead playwrights. Shakespeare was, in his day, a new writer. To have no cutting-edge drama, no incentive for young writers to come forward would be a travesty for the arts. The old is terrific and necessary, but we can't just rely on that.

What about the concept of subsidized theatre versus the West End, which is far more commercial?

There's a place for both. The West End does support the classics. But it has to play it safer than the subsidized theatre does. The West End depends on bums in the seats for every penny. That's not the case in subsidized theatre. Consequently, the West End—and Broadway—tend to put on popularist plays for their very survival. Subsidized theatre has the privilege of being able to take more risks. If producers on Broadway, for example, are brave enough to take a play from subsidized theatre and give it an airing—when they know there is no subsidy—then God bless 'em.

How much does your faith affect your personal and professional life?

Very much. Just because I go to church doesn't make me religious. A man or woman of faith doesn't need to go to church. I do go because it's one of the rocks in this mad world in which we live where you can spend a small time and worship. I do have a very strong faith; I became a Christian twenty years ago from nothing, from a sort of Jewish background. It's now the rock of my life. I'm sure that faith helps me be a better actor, to be a more honest actor.

～

Selected Credits

Theatre
Wellington School (1960s): *Macbeth, Cockpit, Richard of Bordeaux I, Bartholomew Fair*, National Youth Theatre, Royal Court (c. 1963; Michael Croft. **Gateway Theatre, Chester:** *Under Milk Wood* (1969–1972), *Merchant of Venice* (1969–1972; Peter McEnery); *The Crucible* (1969); *Waiting for Godot* (1972); *Lady Windemere's Fan* (1972). **Other:** *Sherlock Holmes*, Birmingham Rep (1972; Peter Farago); *The Taming of the Shrew*, RST (1973; Clifford Williams); *As You Like It*, RST (1973; Buzz Goodbody); *Toad of Toad Hall*, RST (1973; Euan Smith); *Richard II*, RSC (1973; John Barton); *King John*, RSC (1974–1975; John Barton, Barry Kyle); *Cymbeline*, RST, also Aldwych (1974–1975; John Barton, Barry Kyle, Clifford Williams); *Summerfolk*, RSC at the Aldwych (1974; David Hugh Jones); *Sherlock Holmes*, Birmingham Rep (1976; Peter Farago); *Iniquity*, Birmingham Rep (1976; Peter Farago); *The Devil Is an Ass*, NT, Lyttelton; European tour (1977; Stuart Burge); *The Kreutzer Sonata*, Royal Court (1977–1978; Peter Farago); *The Tempest*, RSC, Stratford (1978; Clifford Williams); *Antony and Cleopatra*, RSC at the Aldwych (1979; Peter Brook); *Laughter*, Royal Court (1978; Peter Barnes); Aldwych (1978–1979; John Barton); *Taming of the Shrew*, RSC at the Aldwych (1979; Michael Bogdanov); *Measure for Measure*, RSC at the Aldwych (1979; Barry Kyle); *Once in a Lifetime*, RSC at the Aldwych, Piccadilly (1979–1980; Gillian Lynne, Trevor Nunn); *The Merchant of Venice*, RSC, Stratford (1980; John Barton); *Richard III*, RSC (1980; Terry Hands); *Troilus and Cressida*, RSC at the Aldwych (1981; Terry Hands); *Merchant of Venice*, RSC at the Aldwych (1981; John Barton); *Every Good Boy Deserves Favour*, RSC at the Barbican (1982; Trevor Nunn); *The Swan Down Gloves*, RST, RSC at the Barbican (1982; Terry Hands); *Othello*, RST, RSC at the Barbican (1986; Terry Hands); *Separation*, Hampstead Theatre Club; Comedy (1987; Michael Attenborough); *Timon of Athens*, Young Vic (1991; Trevor Nunn); *Oleanna*, Royal Court, Duke of York's (1993; Harold Pinter); *What a Performance*, Theatre Royal Bath, then Queen's Theatre (1994; Roger Redfarn); *Who's Afraid of Virginia Woolf?* Aldwych (1996; Howard Davies); *Saturday, Sunday, Monday*, CFT (1998; Jude Kelly); *Amadeus*, Richmond, Theatres Royal Bath and Norwich, and others; Old Vic; Music Box, New York; Ahmanson, Los Angeles (1998–2000; Peter Hall); *Man and Boy*, Yvonne Arnaud, Guildford; Theatres Royal Bath, Brighton, and Plymouth; Duchess (2004–2005; Maria Aitkin); *Once in a Lifetime*, NT, Olivier (2005; Edward Hall); *The Last Confession*, CFT, UK tour, Theatre Royal Haymarket (2007; David Hugh Jones); also Royal Alexandra, Toronto, Canada; Melbourne Comedy, Australia; Ahmanson Theatre, Los

Angeles (2014; Jonathan Church); *Complicit*, Old Vic (2009; Kevin Spacey); *All My Sons*, Apollo (2010; Howard Davies); *A Long Day's Journey into Night*, Apollo (2012; Anthony Page); *The Importance of Being Earnest*, Theatre Royal Newcastle-upon-Tyne, Vaudeville (2015; Adrian Noble)

Film
Schiele in Prison (1980); *World Apart* (1987); *Trenchcoat* (1983); *Greystoke: The Legend of Tarzan, Lord of the Apes* (1984); *Little Drummer Girl* (1984); *When the Whales Came* (1989); *The Bank Job* (2008); *Effie Gray* (2014)

Television
The Protectors, "Fighting Fund" (1973); *The Professionals*, "Where the Jungle Ends" (1978); *A Tale of Two Cities* (1980); *Oppenheimer*, six episodes (1980); *Play for Today*, "The Cause" (1981); *BBC2 Playhouse*, "Being Normal" (1983); *Red Monarch* (1983); *Reilly, Ace of Spies*, "Prelude to War" (1983); *Freud*, six episodes (1984); *Blott on the Landscape*, six episodes (1985); *Thirteen at Dinner* (1985); *Murrow* (1986); *Cause Célèbre* (1987); *Agatha Christie's Poirot*, seventy episodes (1988–2013); *RKO281* (1999); *Victoria and Albert* (2001); *The Way We Live Now*, four episodes (2001); *Get Carman: The Trials of George Carman, QC* (2002); *Dracula* (2006); *Maxwell* (2007); *Going Postal* (2010); *Hidden*, three episodes (2011); *The Hollow Crown*, "Richard II" (2012); *Encounter: Performers on Performance*, Lyric London (January 24, 2014)

Awards and Nominations

The Merchant of Venice, 1981, Society of West End Theatre Awards, Actor of the Year in a Revival, nominee; *A World Apart*, 1989, BAFTA, Best Actor in a Supporting Role, nominee; *Oleanna*, 1994, Olivier, Best Actor, nominee; *Who's Afraid of Virginia Woolf?* 1996, London Critics' Circle Theatre Award, winner; 1996, Olivier, Best Actor, nominee; *Amadeus*, 2000, Tony, Best Performance by a Leading Actor in a Play, nominee; *The Way We Live Now*, 2002, BAFTA-TV, Best Actor, nominee; *Maxwell*, 2008, International Emmy, Best Performance by an Actor, winner; *All My Sons*, 2010, Critics' Circle Theatre Award, Best Actor, winner; 2011, Olivier, Best Actor, nominee

Honors

OBE, 2002; CBE, 2011

Notes

1. The actor's last name, he points out, is accented on the first syllable: Su´chet, possibly derived from his paternal grandfather's name Suchedowitz when he moved to South Africa from the Pale of Settlement in Russia.

2. According to the school's alumni office, young Suchet was "a keen sportsman, gaining full colours in Tennis [and] was a Bugle Major in the Corps of Drums."

3. Written by Josephine Tey under the pseudonym Gordon Daviot, first produced in the early thirties with John Gielgud at the Albery.

4. Jones died in 2008.

5. The *Guardian* theatre critic Michael Billington wrote in February 8, 2005, "The role gives David Suchet a chance to display his hypnotic technical finesse."

6. Matthew Warchus succeeded Spacey as artistic director in 2015.

7. Elizabeth McGovern is best known for her role as Cora, Countess of Grantham, in the television series *Downton Abbey*.

8. In Roman amphitheatres, the *vomitoria* were accesses below or behind seats where the audience entered or left or for the actors to make their entrances or exits.

9. The original production in 1979, directed by Peter Hall at the National's Olivier, featured Paul Scofield as Salieri and Simon Callow as Mozart.

10. *The Protectors*, "Goodbye, George" (1973; Jeremy Summers); *Trenchcoat* (1983, Michael Tuchner); *Reilly: Ace of Spies* (1984; Martin Campbell); *NCS: Manhunt* (2001; Michael Whyte).

11. Suchet completed the last of the seventy episodes in June 2013.

CHAPTER TWENTY-ONE

~

Richard Todd, OBE, MC

I'm a theatre actor, not a film actor at all.

"Richard fell earlier this week and bruised himself badly," Richard Todd's personal assistant, Judith Devereux, wrote in an e-mail. "He may not be able to meet you as planned." But she rang up a day later to say, "He will be honoring his commitment and will arrive as scheduled at the Ramada Grantham Hotel in Lincolnshire."

Todd was already ensconced in a straight-backed chair facing the hotel entrance waiting to greet his visitor. He stood, albeit a bit wobbly, and extended his hand in a surprisingly strong handshake. The results of the fall were evident in the bruises on the bridge of his nose.

Dressed immaculately in tweed sport coat, olive trousers, tan vest, and checked shirt, and proudly sporting his paratrooper battalion tie with the logo of wings in a green triangle on a burgundy background, Todd maintains a gentlemanly and elegant demeanor as well as a military bearing and courtly manner. He had driven the eight miles from his home in Little Humby in his twenty-year-old Audi, which, after four Rolls Royces and three Bentleys, "will see me out."

Although compact in stature, Todd stands tall in his "reel" roles, which include real-life heroes Major John Howard in The Longest Day; Sir Walter Raleigh in The Virgin Queen; the Reverend Peter Marshall in A Man Called Peter; and Wing Commander Guy Gibson in The Dam Busters.

Todd suggests a sitting area up a flight of stairs, although he has difficulty climbing the twenty stairs—not just from his recent fall but as a result of his parachute jumps during World War II.

"Not good on the knees," laughs the eighty-nine-year-old actor, rubbing the of-fending joints as the waiter takes the order for tea. After pouring the tea, he plops in several sugar cubes. "Oh, dear," he exclaims, peering into the empty bowl, "I've taken all the sugar."

∼

In the beginning?

I was born in Dublin in 1919, but we went out to India with my father, an army physician, when I was about six months old. I was two and a half when my father retired from the army, and on our return, my father didn't know what he wanted to do. I don't think he wanted to do anything much because Granny Todd, his mother, took care of everything. Eventually, he decided to go back to doctoring. We moved to a home called Moneymore, which we called Penniless. We moved about to various places, and I was about six when we went to Holsworthy, West Devon, which I remember as my first real home. I attended several schools as a youngster, including Queen Elizabeth's Grammar School, Dorset; then at about twelve, I enrolled in Shrewsbury School, Shropshire, as a boarder.

Whilst at school I became ill. I was diagnosed with rheumatic fever and pericarditis. I was in bed and not allowed to do anything . . . except read. Finally, I was allowed to learn to walk again, then allowed downstairs, into the garden. Maneuvering about in my wheelchair, I was able to develop my upper body.

Photo courtesy of the author

A miserable existence was forecast for me when doctors told me I was going to be a semi-invalid all my life because of the illness. I would never be able to ride a bike or run, so as part of the recuperation process, my mother and I took a long holiday to my mother's family home in Ireland, Brecart, County Antrim. Grandpa Hunter, really my step-grandfather, had a terrific influence on my life then. I can say he saved my life. He knew about the dire forecast and said, "Nonsense."

He took me rowing on the River Bann. Most days, he pulled the oars. One day he said, "Here. You row. I'll fish."

"I can't do that, Grandpa." But I did.

From then on, I said, "To hell with what the doctors say. I can do anything."

Within just a few years, I was in a parachute regiment. If I wanted to do something, I decided I'd just get on with it.

Before you jumped out of a plane, you leapt into your acting career. How far did your interest in theatre go before the war?

At the school in Wimbourne, I played in John Galsworthy's *Escape*. I had a dual role: first as a lady surprised by the villain in her boudoir—for which I wore a negligee—and then as a vicar. I became more interested in playwriting than acting, and when our school was taken to see a production of *The Tempest*, I became a devoted theatregoer.

I confided my interest to Granny Todd, whose great friend was Italia Conti, the legendary actress-teacher, who had a home in Bournemouth near my grandmother's. She ran a school, which at the time was located in Bloomsbury. Granny organized an interview for me with her.

This formidable lady asked me, "What would you like to do, young man?"

"I'd like to write plays," I told her, which was silly of me because I didn't know anything about the theatre.

"In order to write plays, you ought to know something about the theatre," and she suggested, "You'd better come to my school."

Granny won my parents' grudging approval for me to attend drama school. My father expected me to go to university for a law or medical degree; my mother thought of something in the diplomatic corps. My parents and I rarely seemed to understand each other.[1]

I spent about eighteen months at the school, between about 1936 and 1937 but had the opportunity to play two leading parts, the Witch and the Slacker, in the famous panto *Where the Rainbow Ends* by Clifford Miles and John Ramsey. The school was also a talent agency; through their efforts, I played a season at the Regent's Park Open Air Theatre, and in the 1936 production of *Henry VIII*, I understudied Gyles Isham as the Duke of Buckingham. But he never missed a performance. During one performance, I got Vivien Leigh, who was playing Anne Boleyn, to giggle when, as the Bishop of London, I dropped the crown I was carrying. A highlight for me!

You also appeared in a film called *The Gap*.

[Todd lets out a whoop when the title is mentioned.] Good Lord, that was about 1937, before I even started professionally. It was a government film, sort of a documentary about the defenses of London in the event of war, about what might happen if there was an aerial attack and what "the gap" was in our defenses. It was mainly a recruiting film for the Territorial Army. It was the first time I had ever been on-screen, and I was absolutely dreadful.

About that time, I appeared in two Will Hay films at Gainsborough: *Good Morning, Boys*, 1937; *Old Bones of the River*, 1938; both directed by Marcel Varnel.

What was the next rung on your career ladder?

From the Conti School, I started working in rep, which hardly exists today. A great shame because it was a wonderful learning ground for actors who were serious about wanting to be proper actors. Nowadays, all the young people want to get on to the telly. That's where the money is.

I was never in the technical side of the theatre, such as being an ASM. I was only ever an "actore"! I did venture into producing and directing later.

I tried to warn my oldest son, Peter, who died by his own hand in 2005—I lost two sons that way in the last few years[2] [Todd can barely get the words out and has to pause before continuing]—but he joined a theatre company and couldn't wait to get on stage. He was really keen about it.

When I was running Triumph Theatre Productions, my producing partner, Duncan Weldon, went to watch one of our productions. He told me that Peter had a tiny part at the end of the play as a policeman. He had one line: "What's all this?"

Before he came on, Duncan saw him in the corner running the book and in full makeup. He asked, "Don't you just come on at the end? Why the makeup?"

"Well," replied Peter, "there'll be a curtain call." [Todd smiles at the recollection.]

What was your experience with those repertory companies?

While I was still at the Conti School, Robert Thornely, a small-time impresario, came around looking for youngsters with whom he hoped to form a rep company. He selected me along with several others, and we became the Welsh Players. None of us were Welsh, but no matter. An association called the Miners' Welfare Trust was our sponsor. We were told this was a great opportunity. Off we went for our first production, *On the Spot* by Edgar Wallace, at the Workmen's Hall, Ebbw Vale, South Wales.

Our claim to fame was our director, Charlotte Francis, who had been in the West End production of that play with Charles Laughton that had been directed by Wallace himself [1930]. Her mantra to us youngsters was "Darlings, bring it from the genitals." All emotions, she believed, came from that region.

Another hall we played in was the depressed mining town of Merthyr Tydfil. We were scheduled to be there for two weeks, but there were so few in the audience that, in the end, we knew the Trust wouldn't be able to pay us, and we'd have to go back to London. Word got around that we were closing down. One night, a group of miners came to the stage door in their Sunday best, all spruced up. One of them stepped forward and said to Thornely, "We hear you're having trouble. We hope you'll be able to stay with us for another week. To help, we have something for you."

These were, for the most part, out-of-work miners, yet they'd taken up a collection. It was one of the sweetest things. Of course, we stayed. But by early 1939, the company broke up, and we returned to London.

Thornely again contacted me about organizing another company. But where? As we sat in the tea shop, we pondered where we could launch the company. With a pen in hand, he stabbed an advert page in *The Stage* and hit Dundee. So was born what became the Dundee Repertory Theatre, which continues as a major source of theatre here. It's always been a great source of pride to say I am a founding member of the company.

When I returned to the company after the war, I was in a play that would be the most important play of my early career: *The Hasty Heart* by John Patrick. In the Dundee production, I played Yank.

World War II dramatically changed your life for the next several years. What are some of the details of your military service?

Whilst I was with the Dundee Rep, war was declared. Just twenty-four hours later, I signed up for army service in the King's Own Yorkshire Light Infantry. I eventually reported to the Royal Military Academy at Sandhurst. Few know that the famous training facility was bombed in January 1940. It was kept very quiet. The present commander didn't know about it until I wrote to him a short time ago.

I was there when it was bombed. I'd just had a bath. I'd come out of the bathroom wearing only a towel and was headed down the long corridor to my room. I heard a boom close by. I thought, "That's a bit close."

The next thing I remember—it was like a freeze-frame—I saw a bomb come through the ceiling in front of me and go down through the floor. I remember a flying sensation. I landed thirty yards away on the grass. I was unconscious for a bit, and when I woke up and realized what had happened and saw the rubble all around me, I remembered I was on Passive Air Defence duty, which included fire watching, giving aid to anyone who had been injured.

I thought, "I'd better see if anybody needs help."

I saw cadets coming towards me with a torch. I felt very wet—from the shower, I thought. A cadet came up to me, shined his torch on me, and threw up. I was covered in blood. Looking back, I must have looked like a character in a Hammer horror film. They helped me to the hospital; I was given morphia, a cup of tea, and a cigarette. The next day I was moved to the adjutant's house where I spent the next three weeks recovering from puncture wounds. It was jolly painful. Most of the cadets in my group of buildings were dining out that night, but I think seven were killed.

The evening of my passing out ceremony was in the spring of '41. My lot were going to the Café de Paris, but it was too crowded, and we went to another club, Hatchett's, where we heard Stephane Grappelli, the jazz violinist. The café was bombed, and a lot of the chaps I was with at Sandhurst were killed, as was the leader of the house band, "Snakehips" Johnson.

After graduating from Sandhurst, I reported back to Strensall, thence on to Didlington Camp, Thetford, thence to Hythe on the coast of Kent. I was then posted to, of all places, Iceland, then again, posted back to the UK.

To make a long story short, I was assigned to the newly formed Seventh Light Infantry Parachute Battalion, part of the British Sixth Airborne. A dream! I had been in the service for three years and had been wounded—in the shower! After training and receiving my wings, I met with the battalion commander, Lt. Col. Geoffrey Pine-Coffin. Isn't that a lovely name for a CO!

Training became intense. We learned to "fly" a parachute. We learned to hold the rigging lines: if we were going too fast forward, we'd pull on the back lines, which countered our progress; equally if we were going backwards too fast, we'd pull on the front. How we landed depended very much on the weather conditions and individual abilities.

In May '44, General Bernard "Monty" Montgomery inspected the division. Then came a visit from the King and Queen and the young Princess Elizabeth. There was certainly something big afoot. I was taken aside and told I would be "in the party" as assistant adjutant, so I attended the briefings for our role in Operation Overlord: the invasion of Normandy. The Seventh Paras would come in after the six gliders under the command of Major John Howard.

Then the day: In the landing, which was re-created in *The Longest Day*, I was the first out of the first aircraft. Not that I chose that. We sat on the floor of the Stirling because there were no seats. We straddled the exit. When the signal came to jump, we pulled our legs together and went out, sitting on the slipstream. We had a nice comfortable exit.

Looking back, I still feel that only an airborne force could have achieved what the Sixth Airborne Division succeeded doing that first day. Yes, losses were substantial, but we accomplished our task. Then, after a respite back home, there were other postings: Belgium, Germany, Palestine.

I was demobbed in 1946 and returned to the Dundee Rep at the suggestion of Robert Lennard, who had been my agent and was now casting director at Associated British Pictures Corporation. I met a young actress, Catherine Grant-Bogle, who had also just rejoined the company. We appeared in Rose Franken's *Claudia* together. When I finally had enough resources from my film career, and just after the release of my first major film, *For Them That Trespass*, I asked her family for her hand. On August 13, 1949, we were married at St. Columba's Church of Scotland on Pont Street, London, which still showed the ravages of the war. Our marriage ended in divorce after more than twenty years and two children.

What are your recollections of that first major film role?

Before all this happened, I remember having tea at the Dorchester one day, and I noticed a middle-aged lady staring at me, which was a bit disconcerting. Eventually, she got up and came over and sat beside me.

She said, "I know about you. Do you mind if I tell you what I know?"

Intrigued, I said, "No."

"You've just made a journey from Scotland?"

"Yes."

"You're going to meet prominent men who are going to be important to you and will have a great influence on your life."

As it happened, I had an appointment about a role in *For Them That Trespass* with director Alberto Cavalcanti and Victor Skutezky, the producer at ABPC [originally BIP, British International Pictures], which was going to be made under its aegis at Welwyn Studios in Hertfordshire.

She continued, "I know you're a farmer at heart, but what else do you do? Write?"

"No, I'm an actor." I had a script on the table.

"Is that *the* script?"

"Yes," I said.

"You're going to play a major role in that."

She smiled and left. I never did find out who she was. But her prediction was correct.

The outcome of the meeting was that I was put under a seven-year contract to ABPC. By 1948, Robert Lennard arranged my first year's salary: £25 per week, and over the next years, it would rise to £200 per week.

What about your remembrances of Cav, who was Brazilian, not British?

I remember Cav very well. He was a terrific help to me when I needed to learn how to act for film. What he did to start with was to calm me down. I was *very* theatrical, very much of the *theatah*, where everything is bigger. In film, he explained, "You don't need to throw your arms around or pull faces. Just play it quietly." I learned the difference in playing long shots, medium, and close-ups.

Cav also pointed out a bad habit I had. "When you look from one side to the other, you blink on the way," he told me. "On-screen, that is annoying. Practice looking at yourself in a mirror and not blinking, not moving your eyes at all."

He was particularly helpful with my physical disadvantage. I am about five foot eight inches and was often not at eye level with my colleagues. Cav showed me that camera angles would make up for my lack of height. He also had the carpenters build ramps of varying heights, so I could walk into a shot and be taller!

The film was not outstanding, but it got me started.

Your next film could hardly be called "workaday." Where did your role as Lachie McLachlan in *The Hasty Heart* begin?

After the final day of shooting *Trespass*, I was asked to attend a party at the studio in Elstree. One of the honorees was director Vincent Sherman. He was preparing a production of *The Hasty Heart*, a coproduction of Associated British and Warner Bros. Robert Clark, an Associated board member, introduced us. I told him I was familiar with the play as I had recently played Yank in a Dundee Rep production. Much later, when I had my own production company, I toured in the play as Lachie. I was in my fifties then, but [chuckling at the thought], I could play forty with the help of Mr. Max Factor!

When I was introduced, Vince said, "You're not a Scot; you have dark hair; not right for the role."

I told him, "There are a lot of dark-haired Scots," and that I'd worked at Dundee before the war and for eighteen months after the war, and if I couldn't sound like a Scotsman when I wanted, I wasn't much good as an actor! And I lapsed into my Scottish accent!

I thought I'd scotched that opportunity, but Vincent said, "I want you to test for the role." [Todd laughs at his unintended word choice.]

Bob phoned. "Could you drop into the office?" he asked. When I arrived, he began, "I'm sorry . . ."

Before he finished the sentence, I interrupted and said, "Don't have to tell me. I didn't get on with him, and it didn't work out."

Bob finished his sentence: "I'm sorry to have to tell you. You've got the part."

I took bagpipe lessons from a real pipe major. It must have been excruciating to listen to me practice. I didn't know what the hell I was doing. I'm not a musician of any sort. I also continued working on the Scottish accent.

As far as possible, I've always done films with stories and characters I believe in. Of course, being very military minded, Lachie suited me down to the ground. I'd seen people like him and understood them.

The other leads were Hollywood A-listers.

Definitely. Ronald Reagan, who became a friend, and Patricia Neal, who was very sweet and lovely to work with. I had been concerned about how these two Hollywood royals would accept me, a fledgling film actor. I needn't have worried. They were kind and generous.

The film was shot at Elstree, all on one soundstage where they built a "basher hut," the type of shelter the characters lived in during their stay in an army hospital in Burma during World War II. Surrounding it was an area with sand and a few palm trees. All interiors. We never had to worry about changes in weather or light or noise, which we would have had to contend with on location.

Elstree was about twenty miles from London, and even in those days there was a lot of traffic. Production continued during winter when the roads were icy. I was driving my Railton sports car every day from my flat in Belgravia to the studio. One day, Ronnie, who was staying at the Savoy, said to me, "I'm worried about you driving." So he had his chauffeur-driven car collect me. I secretly thought it was probably because he wanted to make sure I knew my lines. Each day we had two hours together. I got to know him well—his politics, his personal life, generally what made him tick. I do think there was a great sadness about him, especially having to do with the breakup of his marriage to Jane Wyman.

On the set, he was always good-humored and had amusing Hollywood stories to tell. He was a dear chap, and he was a great friend of the British. He was devastated at what London looked like. Even in 1948, London was still a shattered city. He'd never been out of America until he made *The Hasty Heart* even though he was in the Army Air Force. But from that time onward, he had a great respect and admiration for the British. As soon as he became governor of California in 1967, I knew he'd become president. We continued our friendship over the years. Gosh, for nearly forty years, I unfailingly got a birthday card and a Christmas card every year and the odd letter now and then. The last time I saw him was when he was in London to collect his Honorary Knight Grand Cross of the Most Honourable Order of the Bath from Her Majesty Queen Elizabeth II on June 15, 1989.

Prime Minister Margaret Thatcher gave a dinner party at Number 10, and my second wife, Virginia, and I were included, along with several top politicians. I was looking forward to seeing him after all those years. Mrs. Thatcher met us as we arrived and directed us into the drawing room for a drink.

When the Reagans arrived, Mrs. Thatcher took him around the room to meet everybody. When she got to me, she said, "And you remember Richard Todd."

He said, "How do you do?" I thought it strange that there wasn't a more personal greeting.

Later, from across the room, I saw Mrs. Thatcher tug at his arm and point to me. He came over and said, "Lachie," and gave me a hug.

Although we spent time reminiscing that evening, as I look back now, I think, "Could that have been the beginning of his problem?"[3]

What do you recall about Vincent Sherman?

There were quite a few moving scenes in the film, and quite often I'd see tears streaming down his face as he called, "Cut." It was lovely to work with somebody like that. I cried a lot, too, when I was making the film. I'm a soppy date.

Vince told me, "You're going to get an Oscar for this."

He was partly right.

I was on location in America in the Mojave Desert on loan out from AB to Warners on my first American film, *Lightning Strikes Twice*. Jack Warner called to tell me about my Oscar nomination for Actor as Lachie. I didn't win.[4] In those days, awards were important to me. I've now gone off the whole awards business, right from the moment of the choice of nominees and how and why it's done and the ridiculous, ludicrous publicity that follows. I don't want to have anything to do with them.

Did you have an acceptance speech prepared just in case you won?

No! [Todd growls the word.] If I had, it would have been a simple, "Thank you."

That's all that would have been necessary. But all this dreadful gushing that goes on now . . . [his voice trails off]. I did have a speech when I won the *Daily Mail* National Film Award for the role later that year. That night at the Dorchester, in white tie and tails, I accepted the statuette and said, "Above all, I want to thank a lot of people who are not here tonight: the public. I owe them the greatest debt of all. I'm very conscious of that debt."

Jean Simmons won Best Actress for her role as Ophelia in *Hamlet*, and there are photos of us holding the statuettes and beaming.

The years 1948 and 1949 were busy years for you.

Before *Hasty Heart* was released late in '49, I was loaned out by ABPC to play opposite the beautiful Valerie Hobson, who was then married to producer Anthony Havelock-Allan; she later married John Profumo, a high-ranking member [parliamentary secretary to the Ministry of Transport beginning in 1952] in Churchill's government who was involved in a national security scandal, but she stood by him for the rest of her life. That film, *Interrupted Journey*, was a happy production. The promotion people at AB who looked after me, Leslie Frewin and John Parsons, made sure I was seen in all the right places, restaurants, charity events, and with the right people.

Alfred Hitchcock was your next mentor on *Stage Fright*.

I was terrified when I found out I was going to be working with him. I was still really green. Fortunately, when I met with him and his wife, Alma, at the Savoy, we got on terribly well. I think he appreciated the fact that I wasn't in any way demanding, wanting this, wanting that. I was a disciplined person and wouldn't make any demands, unlike my costar Marlene Dietrich. She was meticulous about how she wanted to be lit. She always tried to get a shadow under her nose, a "butterfly" she called it.

When Hitch made a film about "The Making of *Stage Fright*," he asked me to direct it. Imagine: I directed Hitchcock!

What acting technique did you learn from Hitchcock?

Hitch manufactured a device, which was helpful when we were doing very close shots. He told us, "Every time I've got you in a close shot, I'm going to clip a little screen to the side of the camera by the lens. The screen has three dots: one, two, three; two eyes and a mouth. Whenever you're talking to somebody, your eyes are always moving and alive. You look from eye to eye and down to the mouth when they're talking." That was fascinating. It was another lesson.

You began a three-picture association with Disney in the early 1950s. What are your recollections of those Disney years and your costar Glynis Johns?

I ordinarily didn't socialize a lot with my acting colleagues. I did with Glynis Johns. She was so pretty. Those China-blue eyes and that husky voice.

She was a darling. We were very close for two years. Even then, she always seemed to need somebody's help, someone to stand by her. I took that position for a short period.

Our two Disney pictures together were *The Sword and the Rose*, shot at Pinewood, directed by Ken Annakin; and *Rob Roy: The Highland Rogue*, shot on location in Scotland, directed by Harold French.[5]

Walt Disney was my greatest friend during and after those years. Sweet, sweet man. I know a lot of people didn't like him, and I've heard some pretty unpleasant things about him. As far as I was concerned, he was lovely. I remember that he had a barn in his garden, which he had brought out from his family home in Kansas and rebuilt it in Holmby Hills. He also had his miniature railway.

Your third Disney film, *The Story of Robin Hood and His Merrie Men*, was your first portrayal of a real-life character.

I tried to give a sense of reality to that character. I wanted to believe in the character I was playing. A lot of people have told me that it was the only Robin Hood they believed in. The other portrayals were all fantasy.

We had a very good cast: James Hayter as Friar Tuck, who I had to carry, and James Robertson Justice, who I had a choreographed fight scene with on the bridge. It's a good thing it wasn't the other way round in casting!

For each of the Disney live-action films I did, I had a month or so at the studio with a trainer. I never had a stunt double. The front office was worried, but I insisted on doing my own stunts. One of the trickier ones was in *Robin Hood*, the one where I'm up a tree hanging from a branch and the horse canters along, riderless, under the tree. I had to drop onto the saddle, a medieval style, with a high wooden pommel. If I didn't get it right, it would be very painful.

I missed the bloody horse on my first drop. On the second try, the horse knew what was going to happen, and he pulled up, and I landed on his head. The third attempt, he saw me and rushed ahead, and I bounced off his backside. But we finally got it. And, yes, there was some pain associated with that stunt.

As a participant in World War II, you brought a depth to your roles because you had both a real association and a "reel" association with that conflict that other actors who had not been in the service couldn't bring to their roles. What are your recollections of those films and how the stories reflected the war?

When I played Wing Commander Guy Gibson in *The Dam Busters*, directed by Michael Anderson, I was a decade older than he was at the time of the bombing raid in May 1943. During the war, the paras, my lot, had a particular pub in Shepherd's Market; next to it was the RAF place. We used to mix it up occasionally. For all I know, I may have met Gibson then, but I don't remember.

I had to soften his character a bit, unwillingly. He was pretty autocratic and not altogether beloved. He was terribly admired—absolutely revered—by his crews. He was, if I may say, a bit of a shit in many ways. But that portrayal would not have done well with the legend of this very brave VC holder.

I'm still very close to 617 Squadron. I'm an honorary member of the 617 Aircrew Association. During those years, they flew Avro Lancasters. I attend the reunion dinners of the 1939 squadron. I go every year to the dam where they practiced and see the remaining Lancaster bomber come over the dam. I find that very moving. We all do. It's always on May 17 on the anniversary of the raid in 1943.

In the film, we realized we couldn't get away with Gibson's dog's real name in America, so I renamed the dog to Trigger from Nigger for the American version.

After the raid, in a very emotional part of the story knowing that fifty-six of his men were lost, my character, Gibson, is asked by Barnes Wallis, played by Michael Redgrave, "Aren't you going to turn in?"

Richard Todd as Wing Commander Guy Gibson in the Michael Anderson–directed film *The Dam Busters* (1955). *Warner Bros. Pictures/Photofest © Warner Bros. Pictures*

"I have some letters to write," I reply in the last line of the picture, which would have been typical of the man himself.

In *The Longest Day*, Richard Burton, as RAF Flight Officer David Campbell, has the same line when he learns that one of his team is "at the bottom of the Channel." Not having been an ex-serviceman, he overdid it, laid it on a bit thick. It was hell. I know. I was there. The RAF chaps who were there don't make a big song and dance about what a hell of a time they had.

Those actors who had been in the service—army, navy, air force—that made *Dam Busters*, the film, fell into their parts naturally; they knew how to salute; they knew how to march and stand; they knew how service men got on together, mucking about and drinking together.

My favorite line, but not one of mine, was said by a nose gunner during the training flights. They are flying at sixty feet. Gibson is keeping close to the ground; the gunner is up front, sitting in a little caboose, saying, "Up a bit. Down a bit. Up. Up. Trees."

We see the plane take off a treetop. All he says is, "This is bloody dangerous." It's the epitome of understatement. The difference between an American war film and an English one: ours are understated and underplayed.

Years later, I ran *Dam Busters* at a screening room at Fox when I was working in Hollywood. After it finished, there was silence. Then a raspy voice said, "That's a hell of a film!"

It was Darryl F. Zanuck.

In *The Longest Day*, you relived your own wartime experiences. How gut-wrenching was it to go through those events again?

It was all a bit strange reliving what had been real. I was asked to do it because I'd been there. On the day, I was Captain Todd of the Seventh Battalion, Light Infantry Parachute Brigade, Sixth Airborne Division. In the film, I play Major John Howard, D Company, Second Battalion, Oxfordshire and Buckinghamshire Light Infantry. The film is historically accurate in that the gliders went in before us, the paras. What I didn't approve of is the fact that all the kudos were given to the gliders. They did a marvelous job, especially the pilots. Major John Howard, my character, led them very well; they had been trained well; they captured the bridges. The Germans were taken by surprise; there was no resistance.

In the film, I did just the opposite of what I had actually done; where I, as John Howard, talk briefly to a para officer, who is *me*, an actor is playing me. There I was standing beside myself talking to myself!

Lord Lovat, commander of the First Special Service Brigade, landed on Sword Beach and then moved his commandos to Pegasus Bridge. Shimi,

Lovat's nickname, was terribly good-looking and a proper soldier. In the film, Lovat himself was on location and was upset with the way Peter Lawford was playing him. I'm afraid Lawford was completely the opposite. Lovat's personal piper Bill Millin [played in the film by piper Leslie de Laspee] had been with him at the Sword Beach landing and on Pegasus Bridge. Both scenes are in the film.

An old friend from *The Sword and the Rose* and *Robin Hood*, Ken Annakin, shot the British exteriors and was one of four directors on this epic. The film had a lot of reality to it. A bit overdone in places, though.[6]

I was known as "Sweeney" Todd during my six years in the army. There was another officer in John Howard's glider group. His name was Sweeney. He was called Todd Sweeney. There was a mix-up at one stage with a signal that went back from the front to HQ in London saying, "Sweeney's there. He's taken the bridge." They didn't know which Sweeney.

I hardly ever go to see American war films. I just can't believe them. I haven't been to a cinema for twenty-five years. I'm still interested in theatre, but not film.

Then there was *The Long and the Short and the Tall*.

The play originated at the Royal Court and starred Peter O'Toole, but the film people wanted a "name" for the lead, and the role of Private Bamforth went to Laurence Harvey. We had a lot of trouble with Larry. I couldn't stand him. He led Richard Harris astray. They'd go out drinking at lunchtime. The director, Leslie Norman, had his patience ravaged by the behavior of these two.

I was sort of the senior member on the set, and I said to Richard one day, "Would you mind coming up to my dressing room?"

He came in. I said, "Do you realize you're being a bloody nuisance, behaving badly, and upsetting everybody on the film?" I gave him a real tongue-lashing. He burst into tears. He behaved after that.

It was a most unpleasant experience, considering that *The Hasty Heart*, also adapted from a stage play and filmed on a studio stage, and had been a very pleasant experience. It was all shot on a soundstage at Elstree, and it looks like it. It should have been shot in a real jungle.

Another nonfiction character was the Reverend Peter Marshall in *A Man Called Peter*.

I felt a tremendous responsibility playing that character. Marshall's wife, Catherine, had written his biography and sold the screen rights to Fox. She was worried about how her late husband—who, by the way, was a Scot—would be depicted in the film. I had been sent the book, which had a large religious content. I initially didn't think I could do the part. Producer Sam Engel had the bright idea of sending me some audio copies of Marshall's sermons. I listened to them and was enthralled. They are wonderful. I still have them.

I met with Marshall's wife and talked to her and got on with her quite well. She approved of me, but I still wasn't sure I could do the man justice. I'm probably the only actor in the world who insisted on being tested. "I'll do it," I said, "only if *I'm* satisfied that I can do it."

I was making *The Dam Busters* in England at the time. One evening after filming, I asked for an empty soundstage, a cameraman, and a soundman. No set. I just wanted a lectern to lay my papers on. I said to the cameraman, "Just shoot it in a very straightforward manner. No gimmicks. No special lighting."

Several people turned up to watch. I started the sermon, and after a minute or so I saw the cameraman and one or other two people with tears running down their faces. I simply said, "Stop. Don't shoot anymore. Don't bother to print it."

I phoned 20th Century Fox the next morning and said, "I've just done the test myself, and I know I can do it."

For one sermon, which Marshall made to the Naval Academy cadets at Annapolis on December 7, 1941, I spoke for more than three minutes with the camera running. Director Henry Koster never called, "Cut." Had I not had the theatre training—especially those days in rep—I would never have been able to do it.

There is an interesting side note. Actress Marjorie Rambeau, who plays Laura Fowler, was in a wheelchair, having been in a motor accident, and her legs were badly injured. She was told she'd never walk again. Sam told her she could play the part in the chair. Then, he had an idea: he sent her a copy of Peter Marshall's published sermons. She came to the studio and watched while I filmed one of the sermons. The story is that she turned to Sam and said, "I'm going to play that part, but I won't be in a wheelchair. I'll be walking." She told me later that watching me film that sermon, "I had the faith that I could do anything." She started from the wheelchair with two sticks and finished with just one.

I remember when we were on a soundstage at the studio, Marilyn Monroe, who was working on the lot on Billy Wilder's *Seven Year Itch*, used to come in and watch us, and we'd see *her* crying.

The picture was a success in Australia, South Africa, and the States, many places all over the world—but not in England. Why? In this country, it opened on the first day of a national press strike, which lasted a month. In those days, there was little radio advertising, less television—and no newspapers. The film opened cold in London and died. Nobody heard about it. It got off to a pretty bad start having no coverage at all. Just shows what the power of the press can be.

You returned to the theatre in the 1950s with a variety of productions, including those with your own company, Triumph Theatre Productions. With a successful film career, why the move back to the theatre?

I've always considered myself a theatre actor, not a film actor at all. I'd had seventeen years in films. During that time, I had never been on stage, and I was missing it and getting a little dissatisfied with my film work. I felt I was beginning to fade away. But I was sure that if I went back into the theatre, people would say, "That bloody little screen actor. What does he think he's doing coming back?" I knew if I was going to do anything, it had better be done well.

I was on holiday in Ibiza reading Oscar Wilde's *An Ideal Husband*, sent to me by producer Peter Bridge. He had seen me on stage for a charity event and was impressed with the reception I'd received. People on the beach that day must have thought I was daft. I was laughing my head off. So funny. So wonderful. With the offer to play Lord Goring—and what a role for an actor—I began my second theatrical journey.

At the time, what was happening in the UK was that provincial theatre was dying. Leading actors, in fact most actors, didn't want to go on tour, and many still don't. As a result, only rubbish was going out. Every time there was a successful play in London, if it ran six months, there would be a cast change. If it ran a year, another change of cast. By the time it got to the provinces, it was with a fourth-rate cast and tatty, worn-out sets. This is what the provincial public was getting. It was turning them off. They didn't bother with theatre anymore; they could stay home and watch the telly.

I was determined—in fact, it became my fixation—to do something toward revitalizing provincial theatre in England. I thought we could do that with the revival of the Wilde play.

Peter had assembled a brilliant cast: two husband-and-wife teams—Michael Denison and Dulcie Gray and Roger Livesey and Ursula Jeans—along with Margaret Lockwood. Our director was the meticulous James Roose-Evans.

Peter not only chose some of the most popular theatres in the provinces but also the biggest. We opened in 1965 at the Manchester Opera House, one of the largest theatres in England: just under two thousand seats. We sold every seat for every performance. The problem was that on a matinee day, the place was full, and to get that many people out and another audience in was difficult. On the first Saturday, there were an additional four hundred standing. Ten weeks later, in December, we opened to marvelous reviews at the Strand in the West End, and, later, we transferred to the Piccadilly Theatre and then moved on to the Garrick after yet another tour! It tallied up to fifteen months.

This happened in all the theatres we played. We could do it with leading names and get bums in seats. On tour, the local authorities woke up to the fact that running a theatre could be a paying proposition.

After Peter died, I thought I should continue what he was doing in the provincial theatre. But I didn't know anything about the business side, all the ramifications of putting on productions. I began to search for those who knew what I didn't. I found them in Paul Elliott and Duncan Weldon. They organized a tour beginning with a twenty-one-week tour of Lesley Storm's *Roar Like a Dove* at the New Theatre in Oxford.

Triumph Theatre Productions was something that I was part of for some time. In the end, I finished up pretty nearly bloody penniless. Today there are a lot of theatres in this country, which, because of our tours, are now totally revitalized, all due to my company. We brought theatre, *good* theatre [he punches the air with his fist] to areas that hadn't seen good theatre for years. I felt we were carrying on the great actor-manager tradition.

Several of the plays in which you appeared had "murder" in the title. Your recollections about those productions?

Terence Feely's *Murder in Mind* was a Triumph production. My costar was Joan Collins. The plan was to open in Guildford, go on a brief tour, and then move on to the West End. During a hiatus, Joan was approached by the people in Hollywood for a role in *Dynasty*. That was that. Nyree Dawn Porter replaced her. I didn't take the play into the West End.

Instead, I received a play, *The Business of Murder*, which had been playing successfully at the Duchess. A trio of actors would be replacing those whose contracts had come to an end. I played the role of Mr. Stone, which I took over from Francis Matthews; we moved to the Mayfair Theatre . . . for eight years and 2,500 consecutive performances. Certainly some sort of record. I can tell you those years helped the bank account.

As the interview comes to a close, Todd makes a poignant comment: "I'm coming to the end now. I'm going to be ninety in six months' time. That has its drawbacks and advantages. I'm quite cozy living by myself, and I have lots of friends who look after me." Richard Todd died December 3, 2009, at age ninety.

Selected Credits

Theatre

Henry VIII, Queen Mary's Garden, Regent's Park Open Air Theatre (1936; Robert Atkins); *Where the Rainbow Ends*, Holborn Empire (1937; an Italia Conti production); *Tony Draws a Horse*, Forester's Hall, Dundee Rep (1940; n/a); *Claudia*, Dundee Rep (1946; n/a); *The Hasty Heart*, Dundee Rep (1947; producer, A. R. Whitmore); *An Ideal Husband*, Strand, (1965; James Roose-Evans); *Dear Octopus*, Piccadilly, Strand, (1967–1968; Frith Banbury); *The*

Grass Is Greener, RSC; (1970; David Scase); *The Winslow Boy*, Theatre Royal Bath; Grand, Wolverhampton (1971; Hugh Goldie); *The Marquise*, Bristol Hippodrome; Royal Alexandra, Toronto; Eisenhower Theatre, Kennedy Center, Washington, DC; Shubert, Boston; US tour (1972; Roger Redfarn); *Death on Demand*, Ashcroft, Croydon (1973; Warren Jenkins); *Sleuth*, Richmond; Theatre Royal Bath (1975–1976; Jan Butlin); *Quadrille*, Richmond (1977; Charles Hickman); *This Happy Breed*, Theatre Royal Bath (1979; Val May); *Murder in Mind*, Yvonne Arnaud, Guildford (1981; Anthony Sharp); *The Business of Murder*, Duchess; Mayfair, (1981; Hugh Goldie); *A Murder Is Announced*, Theatre Royal Bath (1990; Tony Clayton); *Beyond Reasonable Doubt*, Thorndike, Leatherhead (1992; Roger Clissold); *Sweet Revenge*, Thorndike, Leatherhead (1993; Val May); *Brideshead Revisited*, Theatre Royal Bath (1994–1995; Charles Vance); *An Ideal Husband*, UK tour, Albery [now the Noël Coward] (1998; Peter Hall)

Film
A Yank at Oxford, uncredited role (1938); *For Them That Trespass* (1949); *The Interrupted Journey* (1949); *Stage Fright* (1950); *Lightning Strikes Twice* (1951); *Flesh and Blood* (1951); *The Assassin* [a.k.a. *The Venetian Bird*] (1952); *24 Hours of a Woman's Life* [a.k.a. *Affair in Monte Carlo*] (1952); *The Sword and the Rose*, [US title: *When Knighthood Was in Flower*] (1953); *Rob Roy: The Highland Rogue* (1953); *The Dam Busters* (1955); *D-Day, the Sixth of June* (1956); *Saint Joan* (1957); *Intent to Kill* (1958); *Chase a Crooked Shadow* (1958); *The Hellions* (1961); *The Long and the Short and the Tall* (1961); *The Longest Day* (1962); *Operation Crossbow* (1965); *The Big Sleep* (1978)

Television
Wuthering Heights (1953); *ITV Television Playhouse*, "The Man Who Could Find Things" (1960); *The Danny Thomas Hour*, "The Last Hunters" (1968); *Doctor Who*, four episodes (1982); *Murder, She Wrote*, "Appointment in Athens" (1989); *Incident at Victoria Falls* (1992); *Midsomer Murders*, "Birds of Prey" (2003); *Holby City*, "We'll Meet Again" (2004); *Heartbeat*, "Seeds of Destruction" (2007)

Awards and Nominations

The Hasty Heart, 1950, Academy Award, Actor, nominee; also, Golden Globe, Best Newcomer—Male; Golden Globe, Best Motion Picture Actor, nominee; May 29, 1950, *Daily Mail* National Film Award, Actor of the Year

Honors

OBE, 1993; Disney Legend, 2002

Publications

Caught in the Act (1986); *In Camera: An Autobiography Continued* (1989)

Notes

1. Todd's mother committed suicide in 1938.
2. Todd's other son, Seamus, committed suicide in 1997.
3. Reagan died in 2004 from complications of Alzheimer's.
4. Broderick Crawford won for *All the King's Men*. Other nominees: Kirk Douglas, *Champion*; Gregory Peck, *Twelve O'Clock High*; John Wayne, *The Sands of Iwo Jima*.
5. Todd and Johns also appeared together at the Bristol Hippodrome in a 1972 production of Noël Coward's *The Marquise*, directed by Roger Redfarn.
6. Todd attended a sixtieth anniversary event celebrating the end of World War II at the Lincolnshire Aviation Heritage Centre, East Kirkby, August 19, 2005.

~

CHAPTER TWENTY-TWO

Michael York, OBE

Occasionally, as an actor, I'm involved in a project where I actually change the way people see the world, and that's very exciting.

Michael York's home in the Hollywood Hills is up a long drive at the end of a cul-de-sac, an oasis of calm high above the frenetic Sunset Strip. The actor shares his home with his wife, Pat, a highly regarded photographer. Sitting in his drive is his car; the license plate reads ExIsle, which says it all about this peripatetic actor.

From the den, there is a spectacular view of Los Angeles. There is also an eclectic mix of mementoes from the actor's career and world travels: a Chippendale mirror with a chinoiserie theme, rugs of various design, cabinets holding a collection of Staffordshire and Crown Derby porcelains. One figurine is of Shakespeare leaning on a clock, which, at 2:15 is "stuck in time," observes York. Other figures in the collection include Edmund Kean as Shylock and Ellen Terry and Henry Irving in a scene from Henry VIII. Under glass domes are two museum-quality wax busts: Sarah Siddons and John Philip Kemble as Volumnia and Coriolanus.

Enter the actor, stage left, dressed in California casual: open-collared blue shirt and khaki trousers. The only item of apparel that gives away his British heritage is his footwear: classic brown suede wing tips. He immediately apologizes for the dust in the cabinets; he has been away on location, and his wife has recently returned from an exhibition of her photography.

As with most interviews with Brits, he proffers tea and biscuits preceded by a discussion of the pros and cons of brands during the preparation of the warming brew.

Los Angeles Herald-Examiner/*Los Angeles Public Library Collection*

⁓

You were born in March 1942 in Fulmer, Buckinghamshire, during World War II. What do you remember about that time?

When my father came back from the war, everything changed. I had been living in a matriarchal society, with my mother and two sisters. I remember rationing. And I remember when sugar became available. There was no candy, and what we never had, we never missed. We all had wonderful teeth then, but when candy became accessible, our teeth, within two years, became wretched and rotted. The thought of being able to go into a candy store and get anything we wanted was inconceivable. At the age of three, I made an attempt to fly. I jumped from the roof of the coalhouse and broke my nose, which, to this day, is askew. [He taps his slightly off-kilter nose to illustrate.]

I have a feeling for those gray, postwar years and the exhaustion of the country. Perhaps that's being wise after the fact, as I was just a youngster at the time. There was a lack of glamour in those years as well as a feeling that it was the last gasp of the empire. That's why the sixties were such a tremendous contrast. Everything became psychedelic and colorful.

I also remember that when I was young and the King or Queen gave their Christmas speech, it was sacrosanct. We almost stood and saluted. But today cynicism has taken over. I think manners, real manners, not artificial ones, are very important. They keep us civilized. When I was eighteen or nineteen, I won a New Year's resolution contest that a newspaper ran. I used George Bernard Shaw's words for my entry: "Without good manners, human society becomes intolerable." I still believe that. It's a different world. Respect has fallen away.

What led to acting?

As we moved to accommodate my father's rise at Marks & Spencer, I was enrolled in various schools: Hurstpierpoint College as a day boy in the Junior House from September 1951 to July 1953, then Bromley Grammar School for Boys, where I first found my acting wings in 1956 as Moy Fah Loy in *The Yellow Jacket*. Then there was my first starring role as Bassanio in *Merchant of Venice*, my first association with Shakespeare. A performance as the villain of *My Three Angels* was deemed, if I recall correctly, "up to professional standards" by a local paper.

Then I went on to the National Youth Theatre, an important component of my theatrical upbringing under the guiding hand of Michael Croft, one of the founders. I auditioned—the first of many—and won the role as Voltemand in *Hamlet* with one line, "In that all things will I show my duty." The company, for the most part, maintained the Shakespearean tradition of males in all roles. It was here that I learned by doing.

At one time, I was associated with the California Youth Theatre. We wanted to pass on the British tradition. Although the students might never have become actors themselves—although many of them had so much potential—they were the recipients of the passing along of culture and possibly producing not only better citizens but also better audiences. They were learning what to do as an audience and also what *not* to do as an audience member. But there were problems and, sadly, it no longer exists. It was a winning opportunity for youngsters.

You chose University College, Oxford, where you read English. Why Oxford?

I chose it because it was an acting college. I attended when it was still a medieval monastic time there: no women. One of my contemporaries was Stephen Hawking, the theoretical physicist, who seemed to spend his whole time coxing the College Eight.[1] I joined the Oxford University Dramatic Society, where I had my first starring role in *Prometheus Bound*, directed by John Duncan, which Elizabeth Taylor and Richard Burton came down to see. Who would have thought that just a few years later, I would be working with this reigning cinematic couple!

I had my filmmaking initiation when the university was used as a location for *The Mind Benders* in 1963, directed by Basil Dearden. Students were asked to play "student" roles. Again, who would have thought that Dirk Bogarde, the star of the film, would become one of my future mentors! I was to learn that things go around in circles in my chosen career.

In my final year, I appeared in *Twelfth Night*. By then I was convinced that what I wanted was not acting *school* but acting. I invited some agents up to Oxford. They always came up to see our productions because the universities were a great breeding ground for theatre people. From those who saw the production and were kind enough to respond, I chose Philip Pearman as my first representative. I eventually had an agent in England, the US, and a French agent for all the French movies I made.

What was your next theatrical career move?

I had to change my birth name because there was already a Michael Johnson, an actor with that name on the Equity rolls. My choice? There were two cigarette brands that had just come on the market, Richmond and York. A friend took Richmond; that left York for me. Thus, I was born anew.

Philip suggested that I audition for the Birmingham Rep and the RSC. My college friend, Adrian Brine, recommended auditioning for the Dundee

Rep, and it was there I was accepted at £15 a week! Dundee was a repertory company in the finest sense, with such disparate productions as *Much Ado*, *The Hostage* and *Salad Days*, and more. Later, on a visit to London, director Michael Anderson said I should again audition for the RSC as well as the National, Laurence Olivier's company, which I did in front of the great man himself.

When both companies offered me a place, I chose [York pauses dramatically] . . . the National. I joined the company on January 4, 1965, the same day that Ian McKellen and Albert Finney joined, and where I was initially relegated to a small role in *Much Ado*. I was just twenty-two.

The National, then, became your drama school. What was the curricula?

There were classes in movement—especially fencing, which came in handily in later theatrical and film productions—voice, and breathing. Anything I lacked in my previous technique, I gained at the National.

That production of *Much Ado about Nothing* led to your association with Franco Zeffirelli.

Yes, I first came into contact with Franco at the National at the Old Vic. The company had not yet transferred to the South Bank complex. Here we did his famous Sicilian production of *Much Ado*. I played a Sicilian gentleman— and I understudied Derek Jacobi as Don John. That cast included Albert Finney, Ian McKellen, Maggie Smith, and Lynn Redgrave! I also understudied Derek in *Black Comedy*, directed by John Dexter.

Franco asked me if I'd ever done films. I said I hadn't, and that was that. Then a year later, I got this call to go to Rome for a screen test for *Taming of the Shrew*.

I was reminiscing about *Taming of the Shrew* some time ago with Christopher Wilding, whose father was Michael Wilding, Elizabeth Taylor's second husband, about the production. He'd been on the set when he was a kid. I told him, "I owe your mother a great deal."

He asked, "How do you mean?"

"She was not only the star in the film; she was also an uncredited producer," I told him. "She had approval of my casting. It was my entrée into the world of movies. She was very kind."

What elements of Zeffirelli's cinematic visual sense were you aware of during the production?

His visual sense was extraordinary; he arranged his tableaux like an Old Master. He took photographs of every extra, arranged them on the wall, and selected faces for placement in the shot. It was never a casual arrangement, although it may give that impression when watching the film. Zeffirelli even asked the wardrobe mistress her thoughts, which most directors wouldn't do.

Two years later, you continued your association with Zeffirelli in another Shakespearean role in *Romeo and Juliet*.

Filming it was *very* different from *Shrew*, which was a big studio picture made at Dino De Laurentiis's Cinematographica Studios in Rome, a brand-new studio then. *Romeo and Juliet* was shot on location in those glorious Tuscan hill towns, which was fantastic.

The ball scene in which Romeo and Juliet first meet actually shimmered with gold. It looked glorious, but then it should have. Franco had gold dust sprinkled from up above. Pat, who was a stills photographer on the production, was appalled because the dust got in her camera, not to mention our noses. But it *was* gorgeous.

Franco was great working with us young actors. He had a real affinity for us.

You have said you preferred playing Tybalt rather than Romeo because Romeo was "a wimp."

Compared with Juliet, who has all the guts and glory, he *is* a wimp. And she has all the sexuality. My God, those lines which Shakespeare gives her: "I long to die" [Act IV, scene i], which is Elizabethan for orgasm.

Hadn't you played "the wimp" several years earlier?

Yes, I hasten to say, I did in 1963. I played Romeo with the Oxford Players at the Minack in Penzance, where the stage is set against the Atlantic. On a moonlit night, there isn't a more romantic theatrical setting. It's now hugely popular, and companies from Britain and all over the world come to perform. I later was associated with the theatre as honorary president of their Theatre Society.

Sheridan Morley, who became the noted critic and biographer, played Capulet. Our costumes were rented from Franco's Old Vic production. Unbeknownst to me at the time, I would soon be employed by Franco.

Shakespeare has been part of your professional life for decades.

I keep hearing myself referred to as a "Shakespearean actor." I can't get rid of it. I guess people like labels. Ian McKellen, Derek Jacobi, Patrick Stewart . . . *they're* Shakespearean actors. Stewart made such a smart move to take on those roles in *Othello*, *The Tempest*, and *Macbeth*. It's been years since I've performed in Shakespeare. But because Shakespeare's so clever, the words stay in the mind in sort of an unyielding way. I do lectures, which keeps the association current. One lecture is entitled "Will and I," in which I use the

Shakespeare that I've been involved with . . . because where do you start with Shakespeare? I performed this twice at the Lyndon B. Johnson Library in Austin, Texas, with Lady Bird Johnson in the audience both times. Despite its running time of an hour and twenty minutes, the audience wanted more, but I am a believer in leaving audiences wanting more.

You made a literary leap from Shakespearean words to Harold Pinter dialogue in *Accident*. What are the memories of that film?

What a contrast between Shakespeare's extravagant use of words and writer Harold Pinter's spare script! I certainly wanted the part of William, and my American agent, Ed Limato—who remained my friend and agent for decades—supported my interest.

I was thinking of the film today. It has quite a fine pedigree, a Pinter script, and a really good cast, including Stanley Baker and Vivien Merchant, who was married to Pinter at the time. Harold even gave himself a small role in one scene as a television producer. The role of William was mine, and the day I finished *Shrew*—and it was touch and go to finish in time—I flew to back to London and began *Accident* that same afternoon.

I remember that our director, Joseph Losey, gave a lot of freedom to the actors on that film. I was just so thrilled to be working with Dirk Bogarde, who was a sort of my hero, not just from the early films, but also from Basil Dearden's *Victim* in the early sixties onwards. By then, he wasn't just someone from the Rank Charm School. He had real acting chops. He was very generous with his advice to me. Our relationship was similar to our on-screen relationship: professor and pupil. He taught me about technique, and he advised me about screen business and how to watch which lenses were being used and how to adjust my performance to the lenses. But there is only so much advice one can receive and use. I believe in the Aristotelian method: learn by doing.

It was a terrible summer during the production, no sun, and it was so damn cold. Gerry Fisher, the director of photography, created sun with his brilliant work. There's a shot of me through a window. Oddly, I'm wearing a turtleneck sweater, and everyone else is in summer clothes.

I'm the kind who ordinarily makes copious notes on scripts. But on this one, nothing. There was a scene in the film that takes place in a tutorial, and I remember writing sort of a false essay, years away from doing the real thing at school. I wish I had it. But the script, everything's gone. I really should have kept a diary of those things.

Have you kept your scripts?

Unfortunately, no. It's a folie de grandeur. They're in Oxford's Bodleian Library, alongside the First Folio of Shakespeare! I gave my scripts to them years ago.

I knew one of the librarians, who said, "We are a bit weak on twentieth-century literature, such as film scripts. Would you ever consider loaning us your scripts?"

"Loaning them?" I asked. "You can have them." I sent them, together with production notes, call sheets, and photographs. Somewhere in that august building, I hope, is my archive, unless they've thrown them all away. I'll have to make a note and contact them.

You moved to Broadway, but your debut was in the short-lived Tennessee Williams play. What happened?

Ah, yes, the play that never was: *Out Cry*. David Merrick had the rights to *Red Devil Battery Sign*, which was the play that was to follow *Out Cry*. But apparently Tennessee insisted that if Merrick wanted *Red Devil*, he would have to present a production of *Out Cry*, which he did without putting much commercial wind behind our sails. It ran for about a dozen performances at the Lyceum Theatre on Broadway in early 1973.[2] But it was worth doing because the playwright became a great friend. I really should get *that* script back because I received daily sheets from Williams in his handwriting.

But if it had run longer, though, I would never have done *Musketeers*.

Speaking of *Musketeers*, your role as D'Artagnan in that trio of films is among your best-known roles. Those films began in triumph and ended in tragedy. What are your recollections?

Costumes were a problem, especially in the heat of a Spanish summer. I remember the scene we shot in a white marble castle at the height of the heat, with all the lights on the set. We were wearing costumes of leather and wool—and wigs. It was excruciating. A wonderful mental picture I still retain is the actresses playing the ladies of the court sitting with these enormous skirts pulled up above their knees trying to keep cool between takes!

The sword fight scenes were very physical. While we shot one fight scene, we were rehearsing the next. If we weren't fit at the beginning, we were at the end.

The tragedy occurred in the midst of production on the third, *The Return of the Musketeer*, in 1989 on location in Toledo, Spain. It had been sixteen years since the cast had made the other two. I was reunited with Oliver Reed, among others, who I had just worked with earlier that year in *The Lady and the Highwayman*.

Looking back, I remember two slight mishaps early in the production: Richard Chamberlain had a relatively harmless fall from his horse. I had a more painful fall when a stuntman pulled me off my horse, and my back hit the steel pommel of my sword. But we carried on.

Acting is *not* a nine-to-five career. If you're sick, you just get on with it. Touch wood, I haven't been sick often. I remember there was one scene in the first film when I was so ill, I'd have to lie down between takes. And we were filming a great, physical fight.

But those were just precursors to the tragedy: Roy Kinnear, who played Planchet in the two previous films, fell from his horse galloping across a bridge. He was rushed to hospital where he was diagnosed with a broken pelvis. He died later of shock and a massive hemorrhage.

If there is a tragedy that occurs while in the midst of production, it is a true horror. The decision was made to carry on. The consensus was that there was so much that Roy had done that was worth preserving. We finished the film. I don't think people realize there was a substitute for his role. [York's voice cracks with emotion as he recalls the events.]

After all the detours, the accidents—when you end a film, there is a great sense of relief that you've made it. Disappointment, too, that it's finished. And, in this case, a sense of loss.

The cast didn't know they were actually making two films during the production of The Three Musketeers in 1973. What was the contractual dispute that followed?

The film was made into two movies. The original *Musketeers* contract read "project." Now in contracts, there is a phrase, now called "the Salkind clause," that states "film" or "films." It can't just say "project."[3]

In a way, it was a courageous position by the producers to make two films out of one. If the first one hadn't worked, they would have had a turkey on their hands. But we already had the lead into the second because the first one was so successful. It may well have been the beginning of the whole sequel mania. Originally it was just one big, road show picture.

In a trio of 1970s films, you played characters who were morally naive or morally decadent.

I played Konrad in *Something for Everyone*, from Harry Kressing's novel *The Cook*. This was the only film Harold Prince, the famed Broadway director, had directed to that point.[4] Konrad was, as I've written, "greedy, opportunistic, materialist and downright immoral," and, I might add, manipulative. The film is listed as "musical/comedy," but, in reality, it was a black comedy.

One of our main locations was one of Mad King Ludwig's castles, Neuschwanstein, a folie de grandeur. It was a wonderful Bavarian summer. We would often go into Munich. I didn't think I would ever be there again, but I spent weeks there again for *Cabaret*.

I had to audition for the role of Brian in *Cabaret*, and I remember reading the full script and found the role a cipher. I should have listened to Ed

Limato, who cautioned against the part. But, happily, director Bob Fosse and screenwriter Hugh Wheeler agreed that the part needed revisions.[5]

Fosse was obviously a director under the gun because his 1969 film, *Sweet Charity*, had not been financially successful. Like every great director, he had a vision for this project. Being a director is not a journeyman thing. To be a great director, you have ideas above your station. Every spare moment he had while the next shot was being set up, he would rehearse us. He would try a scene this way. He would try it that way. He must have driven the producers crazy. But he pulled off his vision.

My character, Anthony Ferrant, in *England Made Me*, directed by Peter Duffell, is a ne'er-do-well, a failure, but in a way he's not a failure. That's what's so great. He has a streak of decency that eventually kills him. I almost didn't take the role because I'd just played what I thought was a similar role in *Cabaret*, especially since the story had been reset in Nazi Germany rather than Stockholm, a very good choice, actually. I hemmed and hawed. I read the book by Graham Greene, and I then decided to do it. I'm glad I did.

There was another film, *Logan's Run*, you initially didn't want to do. What changed your mind?

When I was in Los Angeles doing *Ring Round the Moon*, I was in a car accident and was badly shaken, so the producer said, "We'll have someone to take you to rehearsals." I had the script of *Logan's Run*, which was going to be directed by Michael Anderson, and my driver asked if he could read it. He told me that I should do it, that it was perfect for me, and I thought, "Maybe he's right."

Especially in America, the film really became a huge hit with kids. I don't know what it was: possibly the whole idea of a parentless society; a hedonist society; a society with tremendous Freudian implications that really struck home with the young audiences at the time.

Peter Ustinov played the Old Man; he inhabited that role and made a character out of it, improvising, pulling dialogue out of the air. It was magic.

Working with Marty Feldman as the director of *The Last Remake of Beau Geste* must have been an interesting experience.

It was funnier before it was hacked to pieces by some executive who shall remain nameless, who probably saw it at ten o'clock in the morning . . . alone in a screening room. That's one film where I'd love to see the director's cut made available.

The script was so funny. I remember that it, too, was after that car crash, and Pat and I were recovering. Like a fool, I gave her the script to read, and she laughed so hard she broke some stitches.

Marty really had a tough time during the shoot. All the odds were against him, including that he got chicken pox, and it didn't stop raining in Spain. He had such responsibility and was in such dire circumstances, but he was always charming and lovely, always concentrating. Those eyes and that face, and we played twin brothers! [He laughs at the recollection.] And those weren't wigs. They curled my hair every day. And it was dyed, too. It was painful, and I have an abiding memory of getting poisoned from the dye. I guess they overdid it.

In 2008, the BBC4 did a tribute to him: *Marty Feldman: Six Degrees of Separation.* He was sweet and zany, and he was cut off far too soon at forty-eight.

Wasn't there a previous "hair-raising" experience?

My poor, battered hair. For my walk-on in Zeffirelli's *Much Ado*, I wore the first of my wigs; that one was jet black. But as Tybalt, Juliet's cousin in *Romeo and Juliet*, my blond hair was dyed black so that I would look like Olivia Hussey's relative. Then permed. That was my real hair.

You mentioned "zany" in reference to *Beau Geste*. What about the zaniness of the Austin Powers films?

That first script came to me from Ed Limato. He asked, "What do you think?" and raised a verbal eyebrow. There was something about it . . . again instinct. I'd seen what Mike Myers had done, what he was capable of. I love Austin Powers. Little did I realize what would happen with those films. You often don't know what you have.

I'd lived through swinging London and made a movie about it, *Smashing Time* with Lynn Redgrave and Rita Tushingham, in which I played a swinging London photographer; that was *the* coveted role at the time. They were the kings of London, like David Hemmings's character in Antonioni's *Blowup* in '66.

Since he was going to play a photographer, I said, "It's all very well to re-create swinging London, but you've got to see this movie, which is like a documentary, but it's not," and I showed it to him. I also mentioned to him that "those people wearing the red uniforms are the real pensioners from Royal Chelsea Hospital. Not extras."

A more serious project was *Conduct Unbecoming,* an example of a small-budget film that turned out quite well. What was the challenge?

At one point it was going to be shot on location in India, and that might have been one way of getting foreign color. A second unit did go out to Pakistan, but the film was shot at Shepperton, so local color was minimal. But the story had a lot going for it.

The challenge was how to make a good film from Barry England's play on a small budget. Basically, we were working quickly, in a very short period of time—I'd never done this before where the scene would be lit in one direction and then shoot a whole sequence of scenes in that direction. It was made with a great deal of resourcefulness by Michael Anderson. Sometimes when there is a problem, how you get around it is much more interesting.

Can you believe I got top billing over Richard Attenborough and Trevor Howard!

Among the greats of film and theatre, you also worked with Sir John Gielgud . . . twice.

We became lifelong friends from the time we appeared in the musical version of *Lost Horizon*.[6] Although the general consensus about that film was that it missed the mark, I receive letters from people who love it. Coming away from it with the friendship of the great Gielgud made it worth doing.

The second time I worked with him was in *Murder on the Orient Express*. Everyone in the *Murder* company was starstruck with each other . . . Lauren Bacall, Sean Connery, Ingrid Bergman, Albert Finney, Vanessa Redgrave. It was a happy time. It was directed by Sidney Lumet. I wish we could have done something together again.

Sir John was the youngest old person I've known; he was unstoppable. He'd read all the books, had seen all the movies. And looking at theatre heritage and his lineage with the Terry family of actors, he *was* British theatre. In speaking about acting, he told me, "This is a business with no cutoff time. You never have to retire." He was a living example of that.

What advice do you give yourself when you begin a role?

Obviously, I'm not the only one who comes to the table with suggestions. I value the talents [he emphasizes the plural] that go into the production. I'm very instinctive—about a role, about a line of dialogue, the physical appearance of the character. I'm open to everything. I don't know where it comes from.

I do believe that any contribution from the actor has to be in sync with everything—and everyone—else. Everyone has to have the confidence that everyone is on the same page, doing the same thing. Often what happens after I get into a role, it starts playing me. That's always a great moment to look for when I realize that *all* the theory and preparation, the words and the discussion—all that is thrown out the window because something else is taking over.

How intimidating is it to take on a new role?

I think to be challenged, to be scared a bit, gets me going. It's easier to say no than yes. Taking challenges keeps me mentally aware. It's good for me. It builds dendrites.

You toured in *Camelot* for six months, with eight performances a week. Challenging?

It was tough. It really was. I had no idea. I didn't read the small print. The whole six months I was touring, I was working on voice and learning how to use it properly. I took lessons and then had to put them into practice eight times a week. We crisscrossed America: Florida, then Minnesota, then Texas. No logic to the booking. We had no royal progress around the country. It was a great travel experience.

The performances during tours are heavily loaded toward the weekend. Monday, which, ironically, is supposed to be a day of rest, is, in fact, a travel day to the next city, sometimes coast to coast. It's a matter of endlessly trying to catch up. One reason I wanted to tour was I was curious to see America. Unfortunately, the ambition to see the great views, the museums was thwarted because I had to take a nap!

I take my hat off to those performers, the gypsies who do it all the time.

Your film projects have taken you around the world: Austria, Israel, South Africa, Czech Republic, Spain, France, India, Hungary, Hong Kong, Croatia, and Australia being just a few of your stops. Do you still enjoy traveling?

I credit my parents for my interest in foreign travel, but I don't know my native England as well as some of the foreign locations where my films have been shot. I've become a tourist there. I am discovering all the places I missed out on when I was a kid. We only have one home now, which means we have the luxury of staying in hotels. One year, I slept in ninety-seven different beds! One proviso Pat and I have made is that we go together whenever possible.

With decades of acting in various media, what thoughts do you have about your profession?

Acting is an art *and* a craft. Not everything is going to be of great significance. It's all basically entertaining . . . I hope. Occasionally, as actors, we're involved in a project where we can actually change the way people see the world, and that's very exciting, but it doesn't always happen.

I have tended to *do* things rather than *not* because one never knows. We regret the sins of omission rather than of commission. I take a variety of roles, some of which work famously, others not so well. I realized the industry is very much about bottom line. It's about bankability, which I respect. It's a business, a viable business, and they don't get state handouts.

Is there a difference between the training of American and British actors?

The virtue to the British actors is that they just get on with it. There used to be the repertory companies where we'd get experience. Everyone in my day did rep all over the country where we learned by doing. All kinds of experience: Shakespeare one week, modern the next, and a pantomime at the end of the season. We didn't talk so much about the work; we just got on with it. I don't mean to cast aspersions on the American system, but maybe there's a lot of theory taking precedence over practice. I'm all for that. I have this sort of heresy as to whether you *can* teach technique, but, in the end, it's that individual spark.

What have you learned about your profession over the years?

Life has a rhythm, a wave pattern, up and down. Sometimes you're in favor; sometimes not. An actor, like a surfer on a wave, has to get into the rhythm of the business; not even a surfer rides the crest of the wave all the time. I never know what my schedule is going to be, unlike opera singers who know where they'll be performing three years from now. It's very challenging. The only one thing I can say about this business is that if I had formulated a rule, I'd have to have changed it. This business is organic; it's changing all the time. They keep moving the goal.

What are some of your interests outside your work?

I am an opera fan and mad about Richard Wagner. I've seen three *Rings* at Bayreuth. At the end of the last performance I saw, there was an hour and a half of applause and curtain calls. I love Puccini, and one of the great thrills was seeing Maria Callas in *Tosca* at Covent Garden. But I'm certainly not a connoisseur. I'm still filling in the gaps.

Writing is another medium for expression. How did those projects begin?

When I was asked to write my autobiography, I thought it was way too early. But now that it's done, I realize it was rather cathartic, and the slate, to this point, has been wiped clean. Interestingly, the publisher and I couldn't agree on a title for the work for both England and America. In England, it was published as *Traveling Player*, which the American publisher felt sounded a bit like a minstrel show. In America, the title is *Accidentally on Purpose*.

I enjoy the writing experience, and once, on a nine-hour flight from Brussels, I wrote straight through. I've written at airports, on flights, on film sets, but never at a desk. It actually gives the work a dynamic that it might otherwise not have. It became an obsession.

There is also a children's book, which came about when I was in Jamaica years ago with my son and his children. Alexandra, my granddaughter, would not eat her papaya, called pawpaw there. I made up the most elaborate story to convince her to eat it. It worked. The rest is publishing history. Now parents can read about *The Magic Paw-Paw* to convince children to eat this exotic fruit.

Your two granddaughters must have been appropriately impressed when you lent your voice to a character in a *The Simpsons* episode.

I earned—for the first time—respect from them, now grown up, that I finally did something worthwhile as the voice of Mason Fairbanks. Now my granddaughter Olivia is the one who has inherited the film gene. She went to film school, and now she's actually on location in Prague on a movie [*Wanted*] as production assistant. She's doing what her dad, producer Rick McCallum, did. My other granddaughter, Alexandra, is a student.

What about recent projects?

Over the last few years, I've done a lot of work with orchestras. I've really enjoyed it. I've done two things with the Fort Worth Symphony, with James Conlon. The Long Beach Opera piece—*Enoch Arden*—is the Strauss version of Tennyson's poem, which I've actually recorded with a piano. They've now upgraded the score, so it's something new again.

I've performed at La Fenice, the opera house in Venice. Roger Rees, Kate Burton, pianist Bryan Louiselle, and I gave a show called *Grand Tour* for the Save Venice group about the great literary pieces written about Venice, and there are lots of them . . . from both British and American perspectives. It was so successful that we were asked to do it in New York.

I also played Salieri in 2006 in a new version—with full orchestra—of Peter Shaffer's *Amadeus*. That was quite thrilling and terribly intense. You know that great speech when he hears the *Grand Partita* and thinks he's hearing the voice of God? When the real orchestra started up in the night air, I could feel the hairs stand up on my neck.

I'd like to do something in some capacity where I can make a difference. It may involve my work as an actor, maybe not.[7]

Where did you receive your OBE?

I could have received it here in Los Angeles, but I wanted to go back to my roots. Fortunately, I didn't have to dress in a cutaway and top hat. I've spent too much of my life in costumes, so I just wore a suit when I received the award from Prince Charles.

⌣

Selected Credits

Theatre
School/University Productions: *My Three Angels*, Bromley (1960; Grace Collett-Franklin); *Hamlet*, National Youth Theatre, Queen's Theatre (1960;

Michael Croft); *Julius Caesar, The Devil's Disciple, Serjeant Musgrave's Dance, A Man for All Seasons*, Trinity College, Dublin; *Hang Down Your Head and Die, Twelfth Night* (n/d; Michael Rudman); *Romeo and Juliet*, Oxford Players at Minack (1963). **Dundee Repertory Company, 1964:** *Arms and the Man* (Adrian Brine); *All in Good Time* (Derrick Goodwin); *Salad Days* (Adrian Brine); *The Hostage* (Adrian Brine); *Antigone* (Derrick Goodwin, Donald Sartain, Adrian Brine); *The Interview* (Daniel Morgan). **Other:** *Royal Hunt of the Sun*, NT at CFT; NT at the Old Vic (1964–1965; John Dexter); *Armstrong's Last Goodnight*, NT at CFT (1966), NT at the Old Vic (1965; John Dexter, Hugh Gaskill); *Much Ado about Nothing*, NT at Old Vic (1965; Franco Zeffirelli); *Trelawny of the "Wells,"* NT at CFT; Old Vic (1965; Desmond O'Donovan); *Any Just Cause*, Adeline Genee Theatre, East Grinstead (1967; Philip Grout); *Hamlet*, Thorndike, Leatherhead (1970; Joseph O'Conor); *Out Cry*, Lyceum, New York (1973; Peter Glenville); *Ring Round the Moon*, Ahmanson, Los Angeles (1975; Joseph Hardy); *Bent*, New Apollo, New York (1980; Robert Allan Ackerman); *The Little Prince and the Aviator*, Alvin, New York (1980–1981; Jerry Adler); *Cyrano de Bergerac*, Santa Fe Festival Theatre, Santa Fe, New Mexico (1981; Travis Preston); *The Crucible*, Belasco, New York (1990–1991; Yossi Yzraely); *Someone Who'll Watch over Me*, Booth, New York (1993; Robin Lefevre); *Amadeus*, Hollywood Bowl, Los Angeles (July 20, 2006); Wall Street Theatre, Philadelphia; staged concert performances (2011; conductor: Leonard Slatkin); *A Grand Tour*, recital, Teatro la Fenice, Venice, Italy; New York (2006); *Camelot*, US tour, including 5th Avenue Theatre, Seattle, Washington; Broward Center for the Performing Arts, Ft. Lauderdale, Florida; La Salle Bank Theatre, Chicago (2007; Glen Casale); *Abduction from the Seraglio*, Chicago Symphony Orchestra, Merida, Spain (2008; conductor: James Conlon); *David Lean Film Tribute*, Chicago Symphony (2009; conductor: John Williams); *Strauss Meets Frankenstein*, Long Beach [CA] Opera (2008; Andreas Mitisek); "The flow of your kisses . . ." Part 2 of *Lion in Love: Exploring the World of Leoš Janáček*, Long Beach [CA] Opera (2009; Sonja Berggren); *Lisztian Loves*, with pianist Andre Watts, Ravinia Festival, Chicago (2011); *My Fair Lady in Concert*, Kennedy Center (2013; Marcia Milgrom Dodge); *King Lear*, rehearsed reading, Old Vic, St. James's (2013; Jonathan Miller)

Film
The Mind Benders (uncredited) (1963); *Accident* (1967); *Smashing Time* (1967); *Romeo and Juliet* (1968); *Justine* (1969); *Alfred the Great* (1969); *Something for Everyone* [a.k.a. *Black Flowers for the Bride*] (1970); *La poudre d'escampette*, [a.k.a. *Touch and Go*] (1971); *Cabaret* (1972); *England Made Me* (1973); *Lost Horizon* (1973); *The Three Musketeers* (1974); *The Four Musketeers: Milady's*

Revenge (1974); *Murder on the Orient Express* (1974); *Conduct Unbecoming* (1975); *Logan's Run* (1976); *The Last Remake of Beau Geste* (1977); *Fedora* (1978); *Return of the Musketeers* (1989); *The Long Shadow* (1992); *Austin Powers: International Man of Mystery* (1997); *Austin Powers: The Spy Who Shagged Me* (1999); *Austin Powers in Goldmember* (2002); *The Mill and the Cross* (2011); *Flatland* (2011); *Flatland 2: Sphereland* (2012); *Quantum Investigations: The Quantum Heist* (2015)

Television
The Forsyte Saga, "The Challenge," "In the Web" (1967); *The Secret of the Sahara*, miniseries (1988); *The Far Country* (1988); *The Lady and the Highwayman* (1989); *Night of the Fox* (1990); *SeaQuest 2032* (1995–1996); *Law & Order: Criminal Intent*, "Slither" (2006); *The Simpsons*, "Homer's Paternity Coot" (voice) (2006); *How I Met Your Mother*, "Robots vs. Wrestlers" (2010)

Honors

Chevalier de l'Ordre des Arts et Lettres, 1995; OBE, 1996; Hollywood Walk of Fame, 2002, 6385 Hollywood Blvd., Hollywood

Publications

Accidentally on Purpose: An Autobiography [UK: *Traveling Player*] (1992); *Are My Blinders Showing? Filmmaking in the New Russia* (1993); *Dispatches from Armageddon: Making the Movie* Megiddo . . . *a Devilish Diary!* (2001)

Notes

1. A coxswain is in charge of steering the boat and giving commands to the eight rowers.
2. The play had opened at the Kennedy Center prior to its Broadway run.
3. The result is that the SAG contracts now include specific wording as to the nature of the type or types of films being produced. The producers, Ilya and Alexander Salkind, settled out of court, indicating the cast would be given a percentage of the profits.
4. Prince has directed only one other film, *A Little Night Music*, in 1977.
5. Christopher Isherwood, the author of *Goodbye to Berlin*, on which *Cabaret* was based, said that of all the actors who played the role, York looked most like him in the film; they both had broken noses, and York grew his hair so it had the same swath over one eye as Isherwood's.

6. In an interview in 2009 with the author, director Charles Jarrott recalled, "The thing about the score is that no one could remember a single note of it after they left the cinema, not one note. . . . It's a damn good film, until we get to Shangri-la."

7. Unbeknownst to York at the time of the interview, this comment was prescient. In 2011, he was diagnosed with amyloidosis, a rare and often fatal disease, and underwent a stem cell transplant at the Mayo Clinic in 2012. He is now "making a difference" as a spokesperson, raising awareness of the disease.

~

Afterword

Before paper and even parchment, history had to be passed on by word of mouth. Molded to listeners' prejudices, dramatic incidents grew to legend or shrank to gossip. Even when monks had written it all in manuscript form, ordinary people still relied upon storytellers, for few could read: even fewer could read Latin. But storytellers enhanced history to capture attention. They improved what people said—or made it up.

Phonograph recordings offered the ideal answer, but it was complicated and interviews recorded on disc were usually read from carefully prepared scripts.

The arrival of tape recorders was thus greeted as a miracle. They were developed in Nazi Germany, one of the few valuable things that the Third Reich bequeathed us. The first machines available to the public after the war were built like tanks, but you forgot that when you heard the tapes—their fidelity in capturing tone of voice as well as all that was said was astonishing. But even then, human fallibility could affect history.

I remember in the sixties when I sent a tape to the BBC, where a secretary typed it out for an educational program. When I saw the typescript, I was startled to see an unfamiliar name. Who was Jack Hughes? Was he really a seminal figure in the cinema of World War I? It turned out the typist had misunderstood the title of an early war film—J'accuse (1919).

As a young film historian, devouring books and magazines, I was puzzled as to why articles on early films should be so strong on opinion but so feeble in terms of fact. And such facts as were used were often wrong. It was as though information from the silent era had been cut off—as though everyone who had lived through the twenties had been wiped out. Yet a surprising number of veterans were still alive in the sixties, some still working.

This was the thought that took me to America in 1964, to track down their equivalents from early cinema. However much you admire someone, you do not usually pick up a telephone and start arranging an interview. It requires a certain amount of gall and a measure of courage to do that. My wife remembers that I often looked white and drawn when trying to organize face-to-face encounters, and some of the veterans, sensing my shyness, were reluctant to get involved. When I contacted the notoriously difficult director Josef von Sternberg in California, he asked how long I was staying. I advanced the day of my return so he would see me quickly. "Why," he asked, "do you leave me until last?"

To my relief, most were glad to be remembered, and I was astonished by the sharpness of their recall. However, I could never have kept an accurate account of what they said without a tape recorder, and the fact that, fifty years later, I'm still referring to both tapes and transcripts demonstrates the value of those remarkable machines.

Barbara Roisman Cooper wore out four tape recorders in recording all her interviews, perhaps a record in itself. She has done a superb job on behalf of British artists and performers of our era. Being an intelligent interviewer, she found out as much as she could before she met her subjects. She asked enlightened questions and, knowing that silence could sometimes be more effective than speech, she sensed when *not* to ask a question.

The interviews fill me with envy. Once you have summoned up the courage and have actually met these people, you realize what a marvelous time an oral historian can have! These enthralling encounters support the theory that art is the concealment of effort. And they serve as a cultural history of our time. And you will learn how astonishingly hard the work of a creative artist can be.

I am convinced that for those concerned with and interested in the arts, *Great Britons of Stage and Screen: In Conversation* will prove one of the most valuable books they could own.

—Kevin Brownlow
Film Historian/Filmmaker

~

Bibliography

Barrow, Kenneth. *On Q: Jack & Beatie de Leon at the Q Theatre*. Richmond, UK: Heritage, 1992.

Blair, Isla. "Three Cheers for the High Range Tiger." *Finlays*, vol. 46, no. 1 (Spring/Summer 2010): 16–17.

———. *A Tiger's Wedding: My Childhood in Exile*. London: Julian Calder, 2011.

Blakemore, Michael. *Stage Blood: Five Tempestuous Years in the Early Life of the National Theatre*. London: Faber and Faber, 2013.

Brown, Shirley. *Bristol Old Vic Theatre School: The First 50 Years, 1946–1996*. Bristol, UK: BOVTS Productions, 1996.

Brownlow, Kevin. *David Lean: A Biography*. New York: A Wyatt Book for St. Martin's Press, 1997.

Callow, Simon. *Being an Actor*. New York: St. Martin's Press, 1984.

———. *Charles Laughton: A Difficult Actor*. New York: Fromm International Publishing, 1997.

———. *My Life in Pieces: An Alternative Autobiography*. London: Nick Hern Books, 2010.

———. *Orson Welles*. Vol. 1, *The Road to Xanadu*. New York: Vintage, 1996.

———. *Orson Welles*. Vol. 2, *Hello Americans*. London: Jonathan Cape, 2006.

Cochrane, Claire. *The Birmingham Rep: A City's Theatre 1962–2002*. Birmingham, UK: Sir Barry Jackson Trust, 2003.

Collins, Joan. *Past Imperfect: An Autobiography*. New York: Simon and Schuster, 1984.

Courier and Advertiser. Dundee, Scotland, July 30, 1940, n.p.

Fleischer, Richard. *Just Tell Me When to Cry: A Memoir*. New York: Carroll & Graf, 1993.

Fry, Stephen. *Moab Is My Washpot*. New York: Random House, 1997.

Gottfried, Martin. *Balancing Act*. New York: Little, Brown, 1999.

Granger, Stewart. *Sparks Fly Upward*. London: Granada, 1981.

Jacobi, Derek. *As Luck Would Have It*. New York: HarperCollins, 2013.

Kendal, Felicity. *White Cargo*. London: Michael Joseph, 1998.

Lee, Anna, and Barbara Roisman Cooper. *Anna Lee: Memoir of a Career on* General Hospital *and in Film*. Jefferson, NC: McFarland, 2007.

MacQuitty, William. *A Life to Remember*. London: Quartet Books, 1991.

Mills, John. *Up in the Clouds, Gentlemen, Please*. New York: Ticknor and Fields, 1981.

Neame, Ronald, with Barbara Roisman Cooper. *Straight from the Horse's Mouth*. Lanham, MD: Scarecrow Press, 2003.

Osborne, Robert. *80 Years of the Oscar: The Official History of the Academy Awards*. New York: Abbeville Press, 2008.

Parker, John, ed. *Who's Who in the Theatre*. 10th edition. London: Pitman & Sons, 1947.

Rusinko, Susan. *The Plays of Benn Levy: Between Shaw and Coward*. Rutherford, NJ: Fairleigh Dickinson University Press, 1994.

Smith, Gary A. *Forever Amber: From Novel to Screen*. Duncan, OK: BearManor Media, 2010.

Straits Times. February 7, 1927, 11.

Todd, Richard. *Caught in the Act*. London: Hutchinson, 1986.

———. *In Camera: An Autobiography Continued*. London: Hutchinson, 1989.

Waklin, Michael. *J. Arthur Rank: The Man behind the Gong*. Oxford, UK: Lion Publishing, 1997.

York, Michael. *Accidentally on Purpose: An Autobiography*. New York: Simon & Schuster, 1991.

———. *Are My Blinkers Showing? Adventures of Filmmaking in the New Russia*. Cambridge, MA: Da Capo Press, 2005.

~

Index

Note: Page numbers in italic denote photographs. Page numbers in bold denote interviews.

~

About the Author

Barbara Roisman Cooper is a freelance author who writes on a variety of topics, with an emphasis on British film. Among the publications she has written for are *British Heritage*, *The Baker Street Journal*, *Sherlock*, *Soap Opera Weekly*, *Biblio*, *Modern Maturity*, and *Evergreen*. She has had two books published, *Straight from the Horse's Mouth* (2003), the autobiography of director-cinematographer Ronald Neame, which she wrote with him; and *Anna Lee: A Memoir of a Life on* General Hospital *and in Film* (2008), which she wrote with the actress. She taught film studies in the Los Angeles Unified School District for more than three decades. She is a member of the British Academy of Film and Television Arts (BAFTA), Society of Authors, and the Royal Society of Literature and is an invested member of the Baker Street Irregulars. After graduating from UCLA, where she was an editor of the *Daily Bruin*, she studied at Brasenose College, Oxford, and the Royal Academy of Art, London. She lives in Encino, California.